Glamorgan Churches in 1837

+ Dowlais

+ Merthyr Tydfil
St Tydfil

+ Aberpergwm

+ Blaengwrach

+ Aberdare
St John the Baptist

+ Glyncorrwg

Gelligaer
+

Ystradyfodwg +

+ Llanfabon
St Mabon

+ Llanwonno

Eglwysilan
+

+ Llangynwyd

+ Llangeinor

+ Llandyfodwg

+ Rudry

+ Bettws

+ Llantwit
Vardre

+ Lisvane

+ St Brides Minor

+ Llantrisant

+ Llanishen

Pentyrch
+

+ Coity

+ Llanilid

Radyr +

+ Whitchurch

Pyle

+ Llanharry

Llanilterne +

Laleston +

Bridgend
St Illtyd

+ Coychurch

+ St Mary Hill

Ystradowen

St Brides-
s-Ely

St Fagans

Tythegston +

Llangan +

Llansannor +

Pendoylan +

St George-super-Ely

r Mawr +

+ Ewenny (Priory)

+ Penllyn

Welsh
St Donats +

Peterston-
s-Ely

Michaelston
-s-Ely

Caerau +

See Inset
Cardiff

+ Newton Nottage

Colwinston +

Llanfrynach +

Bonvilston

Leckwith +

+ Llandough-juxta-Penarth

+ St Brides Major

Llysworney +

+ Cowbridge

+ St Nicholas

Wenvoe +

Michaelston
-le-Pit

+ Penarth
St Augustine

Llandow +

Llanblethan +

+ St Hilary

+ Llantrithyd

St Lythans +

St Andrews
Major

+ Old Cogan

Wick +

Llandough +

Llanmihangel +

+ St Mary Church

+ Llancarfan

Merthyr
Dyfan +

Cadoxton-j- Barry +

Lavernock +

+ Monknash

Llanmaes +

+ Flemingston

Penmark +

+ Sully

Marcross +

+ Eglwys Brewis

Porthkerry +

Barry
St Nichlas

St Donats +

Llantwit Major +

+ St Athan

+ Gileston

wansea

one-super-Avon

CHURCH BUILDING AND RESTORATION IN VICTORIAN GLAMORGAN

CHURCH BUILDING AND RESTORATION IN VICTORIAN GLAMORGAN

AN ARCHITECTURAL AND DOCUMENTARY STUDY

GEOFFREY R. ORRIN

UNIVERSITY OF WALES PRESS
CARDIFF
2004

British Library Cataloguing-in-Publication Data.
A catalogue record for this book is available from the British Library.

ISBN 0–7083–1837–1

Printed in Great Britain by Cromwell Press Limited, Trowbridge, Wiltshire

To the memory of
The Venerable Archdeacon of Brecon,
William David George Wilkinson, MA (Oxon) (1897–1990),
Vicar of Oystermouth 1939–1954,
who instilled in me the love of my parish church

CONTENTS

ILLUSTRATIONS

FOREWORD

The Victorian era in the county of Glamorgan, which today includes most of the diocese of Llandaff and parts of the diocese of Swansea and Brecon, witnessed a remarkable period of church building and restoration closely linked to the growth of population arising from the industrial development which dominated much of this age. However, the two need not necessarily have gone together. Whilst it is fair to say that some buildings were put up as a tribute to the local industrialists, it is equally true to state that there was an enormous commitment from the Church, its clergy and laity, to provide places of worship for these developing communities, and to establish churches at the heart of their everyday life. The Church of the day had a real vision of how best to meet the spiritual needs of the people of Glamorgan and was brave enough to make this vision a reality either by building new churches or by restoring and adapting existing ones. By so doing, it made its own distinctive contribution whilst also valuing that of previous generations.

Obviously, this was an enormous undertaking in terms of finance and clerical numbers. As you read through Geoffrey Orrin's work, you quickly see that the quality of the building work varied enormously and also that in places too many churches were built. It is interesting to note, for example, the number of churches that were built to meet perceived needs but that have now been demolished – either because of their condition or because they were no longer needed. At the same time, there are many buildings that stand as fine examples of churches – both as living, active, witnessing communities and as architecturally inspirational. In every generation, the Church needs to be humble enough to realize that it does not have all the answers, honest enough to admit failure and celebrate success, and brave enough to accept change.

This is certainly true for the Church of 2004. Our communities are constantly changing, and more than ever we need a clear vision of how to meet the spiritual needs of people. We have more buildings than we need, which have to be maintained at enormous cost. Sometimes churches are in the wrong place, or their design fails to accommodate modern advances in liturgy. We need the same confidence that inspired the people responsible for the buildings discussed in this book, so that we too can be brave enough to do what is necessary to equip today's Church for it to be able to pass on to those who follow a vibrant and strong community of believers.

This is a book that is alive with Geoffrey Orrin's love for his subject and his attention to detail. It is enormously valuable as a celebration of church architecture and will be essential reading for anyone with a love for church buildings in this area of Wales. It is also a thought-provoking read for all of us involved in the mission and ministry of the Church of God, and for that Dr Orrin has put us in his debt. I commend his work wholeheartedly. It is a remarkable achievement.

+Barry Cambrensis
Archbishop of Wales

PREFACE

The idea of writing this book on church building and restoration in Victorian Glamorgan was first suggested to me at my viva in 1999 by my principal examiner, the late Professor Chris Brooks, Department of Victorian Culture, Exeter University and Chairman of the Victorian Society. He thought that by revising and enlarging the architectural and documentary gazetteer which formed Appendix II of my doctoral thesis, it would become an important work of reference on the subject.

With this end in view I approached Susan Jenkins, director of the University of Wales Press, who subsequently approved the subject of my proposed book, once sufficient funding had been obtained from grant-making trusts. I am indeed grateful to her for her indefatigable efforts in guiding my manuscript through the various pre-publication hurdles to its final publication. My thanks go also to Ceinwen Jones, editorial manager, Liz Powell and Nicola Roper for the design and production of this fine book. I am deeply indebted also to Professor Emeritus Sir Glanmor Williams, the Revd Chancellor Dr David Walker and Miss Julie A. Jones, librarian of Rhondda-Cynon-Taff Borough Council who kindly acted as referees in my applications for grant-aid from the Church in Wales and other grant-making bodies in England and Wales. The Rt Reverend Roy Davies, former Bishop of Llandaff and the Rt. Reverend Dewi Bridges, former Bishop of Swansea and Brecon, kindly gave me letters of introduction to the clergy of both dioceses to visit over two hundred churches in Glamorgan. I am indebted to Guy Lewis, former senior cartographer, Department of Geography, University of Wales Swansea, for drawing the fine maps of Glamorgan churches dated 1837 and 1901. Over my long period of research and writing beginning in 1989 many people have generously given me their kind advice and invaluable information, both published and unpublished. I wish to thank the following: Mark Child, Dr F.G. Cowley, Peter Howell, John Vivian Hughes, Olwen Jenkins, Robert Lucas, John Newman, Julian Orbach, Dr David Painting, Reverend Canon D. T. W. Price, Father Anthony Symondson, Howard Thomas, Clive Towse, Anne Warren and Huw Williams. The Most Reverend Dr Barry Morgan, Archbishop of Wales and Bishop of Llandaff, has done me the honour of contributing the foreword for which I thank him warmly.

I acknowledge with thanks grants which have assisted me to publish this book from the following bodies: Diocese of Swansea and Brecon; Diocese of St Davids; The Marc Fitch Fund, Oxford; The Isla Johnston Fund of the Church in Wales; The Gower Society; The Mr and Mrs J. T. Morgan Trust in Swansea; The Welsh Church Acts Fund of the Rhondda Cynon Taff Borough Council; and The Welsh Church Acts Fund of the Vale of Glamorgan Borough Council.

I have received so much kindness and assistance from archivists and librarians throughout Glamorgan and England and Wales, that it would be invidious not to mention everyone who has been of help, but I must single out the following for my special thanks: Melanie Barker, deputy librarian, Dr Colin Gale and Clare Brown, assistant archivists at Lambeth Palace Library, London; Adrian James, assistant librarian, Society of Antiquaries of London; Dr Michael Pearson, assistant archivist, Department of Manuscripts and Records, and Anwen Pierce, assistant librarian, Department of Printed Books, National Library of Wales, Aberystwyth; Richard Morgan, assistant archivist, Glamorgan Record Office, Cardiff, Dr Ian Glen, Arts subject librarian, University of Wales Swansea; J. Brynmor Jones, senior local studies librarian, Cardiff Central Library, Cardiff; Evan John Davies, former reference librarian, Mid Glamorgan

Library, Robert Nicholas, former reference librarian, Bridgend Library and John Woods, librarian Bridgend Library and his reference staff for their kind and ready assistance; Geraint James, librarian and Carolyn Jacob, local studies librarian, Merthyr Tydfil Borough Council Libraries, Merthyr Tydfil; Mrs Kay Warren-Morgan, reference librarian, Rhondda Cynon Taff Libraries, Treorchy; Marilyn Jones, local studies librarian and Richard Brighton, supervisor, Cambrian Indexing Project, Swansea City and County Library, Swansea.

SURVEY OF THE LITERATURE OF CHURCH BUILDING AND RESTORATION IN VICTORIAN GLAMORGAN

In Wales a considerable amount of pioneering work on church building has already been carried out by Emeritus Professor Ieuan Gwynedd Jones of Aberystwyth, but his field of research was mainly concerned with north and mid Wales, although he did write an article, 'The building of St Elvan's Church, Aberdare' in the *Glamorgan Historian* (1975). However, his paper entitled 'Ecclesiastical economy: aspects of church building in Victorian Wales', in *Welsh Society and Nationhood: Essays presented to Glanmor Williams* (1984), is an outstanding contribution to the study of Victorian church building in Wales during the nineteenth century. The late Archdeacon Owain Jones also addressed the work of church building in the nineteenth century in the area covered by the Diocese of Swansea and Brecon with particular reference to Radnorshire in cooperation with R. W. D. Fenn, in *Links with the Past: Swansea and Brecon Historical Essays* (1974). Owain Jones's other article, 'Church building in the nineteenth century', in *Merthyr Historian* (1980), traces the development of Victorian church building in the Merthyr Tydfil area in the High Victorian period with reference to the erection of several new churches at Cyfarthfa, Merthyr Tydfil, Penydarren and Troedyrhiw.

John Hilling, a retired architect and a former member of the staff of CADW, has done more than most people to publicize the historical architecture of nineteenth-century buildings in Glamorgan including churches in his various articles in the Glamorgan Historian. These articles formed the basis of his book *Cardiff and the Valleys: Architecture and Townscape* (1973). His *Plans and Prospects: Architecture in Wales, 1780–1914* (1975) is a catalogue of the Welsh Arts Council's first major exhibition of architectural drawings for Glamorgan buildings of the nineteenth century. His article 'Architecture in Glamorgan' in *Glamorgan County History*, Vol. VI (1989), Chapter XIX, summarizes ecclesiastical as well as secular building in modern times, but is restricted in length and comprehensiveness by lack of space. John Newman's long-awaited *Buildings of Wales: Glamorgan* (1995) is the third volume in the series and fills a void in the literature of architectural history in Glamorgan. Apart from Olwen Jenkins's excellent thesis for the Diploma in Building Conservation on the restoration work of John Prichard and John Pollard Seddon as exemplified in seven Glamorgan churches, and the present writer's *The Gower Churches* (1979), *Medieval Churches of the Vale of Glamorgan* (1982) and a *History of All Saints' Church, Oystermouth* (1990) in cooperation with Dr F. G. Cowley, little has been done on church restoration in nineteenth-century Glamorgan. However, a monograph by the late Dr D. R. L. Jones, entitled *The Restoration of Llangynwyd Church, 1891–93* (1993), is a competent study of church restoration in Victorian Glamorgan. Also Dr Cowley's book, *Llanmadoc and Cheriton: Two North Gower Churches and their Parishes* (1993), contains excellent sections on the Victorian restorations of these two churches by John Prichard of Llandaff. Canon John C. Read's *A History of St. John's Cardiff and the Churches of the Parish* (1995), completed before his death in 1996, is an excellent supplement to his book *The Church in Our City*, published in 1954 but which is still in demand. It is a fine work of scholarship of the oldest church in Cardiff and is now the standard work of reference on the Parish of St John's, Cardiff. Roger Brown's book, *Reclaiming the Wilderness: Some Aspects of Parochial Life and Achievements of the Diocese of Llandaff during the Nineteenth Century* (2001), is essentially a historical account of church extension in the Diocese of Llandaff during the nineteenth century. Roger Brown relates the great difficulties encountered by the Anglican Church in Llandaff in restoring and enlarging existing churches, building new churches and parsonage houses, and providing and paying curates to assist the clergy in their official and pastoral duties. This survey of the literature concludes with an article in *Morgannwg*, Vol. XLVI (2002), entitled 'The role of the Talbot family in church building and restoration in Victorian Glamorgan, 1837–1901' by the present author.

THE SCOPE OF THIS BOOK

My aim was to present the first comprehensive study of the building work that took place in all Anglican churches in Glamorgan that existed in 1837 and those that were built, rebuilt, restored and enlarged before 1901. However, the lack of documentary material for ten churches which have since been demolished, especially those 'mission' churches in the industrial areas of the county which were of little architectural merit but important nevertheless for those parishes, compelled me to limit my study to 255 churches out of a possible total of 265 churches which existed in 1901. However, several other fine church buildings, now demolished, are included in this study. The original gazetteer which formed Appendix II of my doctorate thesis has been thoroughly revised and enlarged.

The term 'Glamorgan' needs some explanation. It refers to the old county of Glamorgan as it existed in the nineteenth century prior to the reorganization of local government in 1974. The old county was then divided into West, Mid and South Glamorgan and has subsequently been further subdivided into local government districts in 1996.

This study contains a few omissions which require further explanation. These are monuments and stained glass. Both monuments and stained glass are specialized subjects, especially the latter and need to be treated as separate studies.

DOCUMENTARY SOURCES

As far as Glamorgan is concerned basic documentary sources such as faculties, churchwardens' accounts, architects' drawings and specifications and builders' contracts, are completely lacking for many churches throughout the county. In fact, the individual church files relating to over thirty churches (eleven in Glamorgan) built through grants made by the Church Building Commission between 1818 and 1856 which were transferred to Wales from the Church Commissioners' Archives in Bermondsey, London, shortly after the Disestablishment of the Church in Wales in 1921, have completely disappeared. However, the Ecclesiastical Commissioners' files which were transferred from London at the same time are deposited in the Representative Body of the Church in Wales Archives at Cathedral Road, Cardiff. The sources that do exist are widely scattered between the National Library of Wales, Aberystwyth, the National Museum of Wales, Cardiff, the two County Record Offices at Cardiff and Swansea, the public libraries of principal cities and towns throughout the county and in the archives of individual parishes, which have failed to deposit their documents in the National Library of

Wales or in the Record Offices as recommended by the Bishops of the Dioceses of Llandaff, St David's, and Swansea and Brecon.

My research for this book has taken me to London where I have consulted the archives of the Incorporated Church Building Society at Lambeth Palace Library and scanned the rare issues of copies of nineteenth-century Glamorgan newspapers at the British Newspaper Library Colindale, as well as the archives of the Society for the Protection of Ancient Buildings. Basil Clarke's manuscript notes were consulted at the Council for the Care of Churches, as were architectural journals at the British Architectural Library in Portland Place, London. At the Bodleian Library at Oxford I examined the rare sets of *The Ecclesiologist* and the *Church Builder*. The full details of the documentary sources consulted in Glamorgan in other parts of the country are listed in the bibliography, but the primary sources consulted were faculty and consecration records of the Church in Wales, Aberystwyth, the files of the Incorporated Church Building Society in Lambeth Palace Library, nineteenth-century newspapers in Glamorgan and London, church and parish histories written by incumbents and local histories of parishes, as well as architectural periodicals such as *The Builder* and *The Building News* and learned journals.

Any errors or omissions that remain are entirely the author's own responsibility. Finally, I owe a special debt of gratitude to my wife Julia for her forbearance and tolerance in accepting the presence of hundreds of dusty files in our home for many years and for accompanying me on many journeys to scores of churches throughout Glamorgan.

Pitminster, March 2004

INTRODUCTION

Although church building and restoration in England and Wales in the Victorian era was principally related to the growth of the population in large urban areas, the demographic changes produced by the rapid development of industry in the upland areas of Glamorgan were unparalleled elsewhere in the country except in Monmouthshire. This was due to the vast expansion of the coal industry in the south Wales coalfield, especially from 1860 into the twentieth century. The population of Glamorgan grew from 70,879 in 1801 to 231,849 in 1851, and by 1901 it had reached 859,931.[1] In 1837 there were 127 Anglican churches in Glamorgan. By 1891 that number had increased to 229 and by 1901 this figure had risen to 265. This tremendous increase in the number of churches, some 138 new structures – more than double the number that existed in 1837 – was accounted for firstly by the dramatic increase in the population and secondly by the Anglican Church Revival. Most of the new churches were erected in the diocese of Llandaff as a result of the intense and rapid development of industry there. Not only were many new churches built, but the existing medieval parish churches which were in a dilapidated condition as a result of centuries of neglect were almost all restored, enlarged or in some cases completely rebuilt. Even Llandaff Cathedral which had stood in a partly ruined state for many long years was completely restored and rebuilt by 1869.

The building of new churches and the restoration of old parish churches took place later in Glamorgan than in many other counties of England and Wales; in fact not until after 1850. Llandaff and St David's were the poorest dioceses in the Church of England since tithe income had been small compared with rich English dioceses and, as a result, the commuted tithe rent-charge was low. Also the widespread alienation of tithes and lands at the Reformation had permanently impoverished the Church in these two dioceses.[2] To augment their income some bishops of St David's served as prebendaries or deans of Durham, while their colleagues at Llandaff were appointed deans of St Paul's. This state of affairs had serious consequences, especially for the diocese of Llandaff when it was confronted with the problem of building new churches in the developing industrial areas. The 1830s had seen a marked revival of the Established Church. Parliamentary reforms and the establishment of the Ecclesiastical Commissioners in 1835 to administer its estates allowed the Church to make a more equitable distribution of its income, which removed long-standing abuses and causes of discontent. Nevertheless, it was only on the appointment of Bishop Ollivant, who came to reside permanently in the diocese of Llandaff in 1849, that the Church in Llandaff was able to free itself from the torpor of the eighteenth century and early nineteenth century.

The Religious Census of 1851 clearly showed the continuing weakness of the Established Church in Glamorgan, particularly in the mountain parishes of the north of the diocese of Llandaff.[3] The rigid structure of the Established Church before Church reforms took place meant that it could not easily adapt its old parochial system to the new centres of population. Whereas the building of a new church previously required an Act of Parliament before it could be erected, the Nonconformists could open a meeting-house in a barn without the least impediment. Therefore Nonconformity largely benefited from the failure of the Established Church to make adequate provision for a rapidly increasing and shifting population. Although tremendous efforts were made by the Church of England in church extension it was part of a wider movement for church and chapel provision in Wales as a whole. Remarkable exertions were also made by the Nonconformists during this period, and much of the building by Anglicans and Nonconformists alike was inspired by competition between them.[4]

Bishop Ollivant's inauguration of the Llandaff Diocesan Church Extension Society in 1850 was an attempt to provide licensed places of worship in National Schools, to erect temporary corrugated iron churches and to build permanent stone churches, as well as providing additional curates to carry out the evangelization of the south Wales coalfield.[5] This Society made a significant contribution to church extension in the diocese, but it failed to achieve all its objectives due to lack of support from the middle class and tradesmen. Its support came largely in the form of annual subscriptions, mostly from the landowning gentry. After Ollivant's death in 1882 Bishop Richard Lewis's foundation of the Bishop of Llandaff's Fund was successful in supplementing the existing diocesan church extension societies as a means of providing substantial sums of money to assist in building new churches. In some cases these grants were as much as £400, representing a third of the cost of the cheap churches erected in the coalfield area.[6] It was only by providing plain and comfortable utilitarian churches that the Anglican Church in Glamorgan was able to provide additional church accommodation in the south Wales coalfield. One of the aims of Bishops Ollivant and Lewis was to provide separate church accommodation for the Welsh-speaking church people, but during their episcopates they failed to build as many churches as they would have wished.

The Gothic Revival was the major movement to influence the style in which churches were built during the Victorian era. By that time the influence of the Oxford Movement, the Cambridge Camden Society (later known as the Ecclesiological Society) and the writings of A. W. N. Pugin had changed the whole character of church building and altered the appearance and arrangement of new and restored churches alike. According to Pugin and the Ecclesiologists, Gothic was the only style suitable for churches and Middle Pointed or Decorated Gothic was regarded as the ideal style for church architecture. The Ecclesiologists stressed the sacramental elements of worship centred on the celebration of the Holy Eucharist, which turned the focus of attention away from the pulpit of the eighteenth-century and early nineteenth-century auditory church to the altar, sanctuary and chancel. In fact they urged a return to the formal setting of worship that existed in the parish church of the fourteenth century.[7]

Although the building of new churches was the most spectacular aspect of church extension in the Victorian era, restoration and reconstruction of the old parish churches and the enlargement of the existing buildings were also important parts of the process of providing much-needed additional accommodation. As a result of centuries of neglect and piecemeal 'churchwardenized' repairs the old parish churches were in a dilapidated state by the mid-century; they had to be either partially or completely rebuilt from the foundations as otherwise they would have become ruins. In the 1850s there was more concern with the need to provide additional accommodation than to reorder old churches to suit the new ideas in the Anglican liturgy. This was usually achieved by the addition of a nave aisle or, in some cases, by 'destructive' restoration which demolished the church and rebuilt it on a larger scale as at Newcastle, Bridgend.[8] Almost all the medieval parish churches in Glamorgan were restored at least once during the Victorian era. Some were restored once in the early Victorian period and again in the late Victorian period. The early restoration was primarily to make the church wind and watertight to prevent further dilapidation, and in many cases to rebuild and restore a dilapidated building after years of neglect. The later restoration in the 1890s was to carry out a thorough Victorian restoration, which rearranged the interior and provided the church with standardized church fittings and furnishings in keeping with the new liturgical ideas.

Church restoration was slow compared with other counties such as Leicestershire where more than two hundred churches were restored in the High Victorian period.[9] In Glamorgan the priority in church extension was the building of new churches, particularly in areas affected by the Industrial Revolution, such as the immediate vicinity of Swansea, Neath and Merthyr Tydfil and, to a lesser extent, Cardiff, on which industry made a marked impact at a relatively early date. Consequently, the ancient parish churches in the rural Vale of Glamorgan remained unrestored until the final decades of the nineteenth century. Moreover, church restoration was dominated by the work on Llandaff Cathedral, which was given priority over church building and restoration elsewhere in the county, much to the disapprobation of the clergy in Aberdare.[10] However, it was necessary to restore the building to its cathedral status not only as a symbol of the revival of the Established Church in the diocese of Llandaff but also to prevent its further decay. The late Victorian period in Glamorgan was characterized by an intense programme of church restoration in the Vale of Glamorgan and Gower, areas untouched by industrial development. This was in complete contrast to the pattern of church restoration in other counties of England and Wales where church restoration, both urban and rural, reached a peak in the middle decades of the century. Church restoration during the late Victorian period was greatly influenced by the Society for the Protection of Ancient Buildings founded by William Morris in 1877 as a protest against the widespread practice of drastic 'destructive' restoration.[11] The influence of this Society caused a change from destructive to more sensitive restoration or 'reparation' in Glamorgan in several important churches. Eglwys Brewis Church, for example, was restored under the auspices of the Society for the Protection of Ancient Buildings by its architect, William Weir, in 1900. In general, church restoration in the period 1877–1901 was much more sensitive, and conservation and reparation replaced the 'destructive' Victorian restoration of the early part of the century. It is a well-known fact that many twentieth-century architectural historians did not entirely approve of the early Victorian practice of building, and especially of restoring ancient Anglican churches in the 'Gothic' styles that tended to ignore the style indigenous to Welsh counties in earlier centuries.

Churches were built and restored by a combination of grants from the two national funding bodies, the Church Building Commission (1818–56) and the Incorporated Church Building Society, diocesan building societies and building boards, the Llandaff Church Building Society (1845), the Llandaff Diocesan Church Extension Society (1850), the Bishop of Llandaff's Fund (1883), the St David's Diocesan Church Building Board and the Swansea (1883) and East Gower Church Extension Fund (1885). The Glamorgan aristocracy and the landowning gentry and laymen, as well as industrialists to a lesser extent, erected fine churches at their own expense throughout the county on land that they owned. Some forty churches were built by them in Glamorgan at considerable personal cost. They also made generous donations to church building schemes and restoration funds. The Talbot family of Margam Abbey, for example, played an outstanding role in church extension throughout the county, as did Mrs Madelina G. Llewellyn of Baglan House in the Rhondda. Building sites for new churches were almost always donated by the landowners in the county. Not only did the Glamorgan gentry finance the building and restoration of parish churches, but their substantial contributions helped to restore Llandaff Cathedral.[12] Church rates, before their abolition in 1868, were used to a very limited extent in church extension in Glamorgan, mostly to restore medieval country churches. However, the main source of money for church extension in the county came from public subscriptions given by all members of the community, by rich and poor alike. At the beginning of the nineteenth century it was apparent that the building and restoring of churches were supported by the state, but by the end of the century a gradual transformation had taken place, and church extension was then supported by public subscription.

In the early part of the Victorian era churches were built either in Classical or Gothic style. Gothic church architecture was dominated by the Perpendicular style from 1820 to c.1847, and

St John's, Clydach (1846–7) was built in this style. However, the 1840s brought a significant change in the style of Gothic architecture as a result of Pugin's writings and the formation of the Cambridge Camden Society. Consequently, after 1845 very few churches were erected which were not built in the Gothic style of architecture as advocated by the Ecclesiologists. In Glamorgan a true Puginesque church was erected at Merthyr Mawr, which exemplified many of the principles of the Ecclesiologists in both its structure and fittings and furnishings. It showed medieval authenticity of plan, symbolism and archaeological correctness of architectural detail, which now became of supreme importance.[13] However, at mid-century, two events occurred which were of architectural significance. In 1849 John Ruskin published his book *The Seven Lamps of Architecture* and William Butterfield was commissioned to build All Saints', Margaret Street, in a constructional polychromatic style, which influenced church design for the next two decades. The building of All Saints' Church marked a turning point from an ecclesiological as well as an architectural point of view.[14] In Glamorgan, Butterfield built St Augustine's, Penarth, the finest expression of constructional polychromy to be found locally. By 1860 there was enthusiasm for French Gothic as a reaction against the excesses of Ruskinian-influenced constructional polychromy. It was characterized by boldness, breadth, strength and massiveness. French Gothic was seldom used in a pure style; it merely formed the basis of a style mixed with English and Italian precedents. This is exemplified in Norton's church, St David's, Neath, which is the best example in Glamorgan of the broad eclecticism of Victorian Gothic architecture. Although many churches were built in this eclectic style, some, such as St Peter's, Pontardawe, by Baylis, were erected in a truly Middle Pointed idiom. The year 1870 was regarded as a turning point in the development of Gothic and there was a relaxation in strict correctness of style. The Gothic Revival returned to late Gothic forms and St German's, Roath, designed by Bodley & Garner in a late Decorated style, is influenced by their church at Pendlebury with its vast scale and simplicity of detail.[15] St German's showed the shift towards the Perpendicular Gothic style which became a popular idiom in the late Victorian period. Nicholson's church of St Gabriel's, Swansea, was the first to be built in a late Gothic style, early Perpendicular, as a conscious effort of the architect. Halliday, who favoured the Perpendicular style, designed St George's, Cwmparc, in this idiom, with Arts and Crafts influence. Carter, of Seddon & Carter, built two churches, at St Paul's, Grangetown and All Saints', Penarth, with tall and spacious interiors suited to accommodate large congregations. The development of the Gothic style in Glamorgan paralleled that in the rest of England and Wales.

Glamorgan was fortunate in that eminent Victorian architects such as Ferrey, Norton, Street, Scott, Bodley & Garner, and Pearson, as well as local architects such as John Prichard, George Halliday and Bruce Vaughan, all built or restored churches in the county. Prichard was outstanding amongst these, and he designed and restored many fine churches in the county. His greatest work was the restoration of Llandaff Cathedral. The majority of churches built in Glamorgan were erected in the Early English style, advocated for its cheapness, especially during the late Victorian period by Bruce Vaughan in the Rhondda.

By 1901 the Anglican Church in Glamorgan had to a great extent solved the problem of church accommodation in the industrialized areas. Also it had gone some way towards tackling the problem posed by the existence of English- and Welsh-speaking communities. As a result, the Church was far better equipped materially and spiritually to meet the coming crisis of Disestablishment. The movement for church extension did not come to an end in 1901 but went confidently ahead until the outbreak of the First World War in 1914. For example, approximately forty new churches were built and many more enlarged and completed rather than restored in the years up to 1914. However, with the threat and subsequent outbreak of hostilities in 1914 church building ceased altogether. Work on new churches did not resume until the 1920s.

NOTES TO THE INTRODUCTION

1 Moelwyn Williams, 'Observations on the population changes in Glamorgan,1800–1900', *Glamorgan Historian*, 1 (1963), 109–20.

2 E. T. Davies, *Religion and Society in the Nineteenth Century* (Llandybïe, 1981), p. 52.

3 Ibid., pp. 27–30.

4 Chris Brooks, introduction, *The Victorian Church: Architecture and Society* (Manchester, 1995), p. 10.

5 Wilton D. Wills, 'Ecclesiastical reorganisation and church extension in the Diocese of Llandaff, 1830–1870' (unpublished MA thesis, University College of Swansea, 1965), pp. 153–5.

6 Thomas J. Prichard, *Representative Bodies* (Llandysul, 1988), pp. 147–8.

7 James White, *The Cambridge Movement: The Ecclesiologists and the Gothic Revival* (Cambridge, 1962), pp. 10–14.

8 ICBS file no. 4224 (1850), Newcastle, Bridgend.

9 Geoffrey K. Brandwood, 'Church building and restoration in Leicestershire, 1800–1914' (unpublished Ph.D. thesis, University of Leicester, 1984), pp. 139ff.

10 *Monmouthshire Merlin*, 9 September 1848 (letter from John Griffith, vicar of Aberdare).

11 Linda Parry (ed.), *William Morris* (London, 1996), pp. 80–7.

12 Wills, 'Ecclesiastical reorganisation', pp. 293–8.

13 Brian M. Lodwick, 'The Oxford Movement and the Diocese of Llandaff during the nineteenth century' (unpublished M.Phil. thesis, University of Leeds, 1976), pp. 225–6.

14 David Brownlee, 'The first High Victorians: British architectural theory in the 1840s', *Architectura*, 15, 1 (1985), 33–46.

15 John Newman, *The Buildings of Wales: Glamorgan* (Cardiff, 1995), p. 96.

NOTES TO THE GAZETTEER

This gazetteer summarizes the documentary evidence and personal architectural observations of the fabric of the churches made by the writer during his fieldwork for work on Glamorgan churches in the dioceses of Llandaff and St David's between 1837 and 1901 in strict alphabetical order of place name, with brief accounts of work carried out on these churches after the Victorian period. This study includes 255 churches which were in existence before 1837 and restored, enlarged or rebuilt before 1901 and new churches which were built and enlarged between 1837 and 1901 in both dioceses in Glamorgan. The churches are listed in the form and spelling that existed in the period under study. Reference is also made in brief to important work carried out before 1837 and after 1901 in annotated form when the structure of some churches was completed in the early part of the twentieth century, mostly during the Edwardian period. The major part of each entry refers to the Victorian period, 1837–1901.

Documentary sources

Most statements are based mainly on documentary evidence. The references are recorded throughout the text in parentheses. The references include primary sources such as church records, contemporary newspaper accounts and reports from architectural journals which tend to take precedence over secondary sources such as modern publications in the form of church guides and histories of parishes.

ABBREVIATIONS

Arch. Ass.	Architectural Association, London
Arch. Camb.	*Archaeologia Cambrensis*
B. Chr.	*Bridgend Chronicle*
Bldr	*Builder*
BN	*Building News*
BNC	*Bridgend and Neath Chronicle*
CDL	*Cambria Daily Leader*
CGG	*Central Glamorgan Gazette*
CMG	*Cardiff and Merthyr Guardian*
Ch. Bldr	*Church Builder*
D. Graphic	*Daily Graphic*
Eccl.	*Ecclesiologist*
Eccl. Comm.	Ecclesiastical Commissioners
GCM	*Gower Church Magazine*
GG	*Glamorgan Gazette*
Glam. Free Pr.	*Glamorgan Free Press*
GLRO	Gloucestershire Record Office
GRO	Glamorgan Record Office, Cardiff
HOW	*Herald of Wales*
ICBS	Incorporated Church Building Society
LCBS	Llandaff Church Building Society
LDCES	Llandaff Diocesan Church Extension Society
LDM	*Llandaff Diocesan Magazine*
LL/C	Llandaff Diocesan Consecration Manuscript at National Library of Wales, Aberystwyth
LL/F	Llandaff Diocesan Faculty Manuscript at National Library of Wales, Aberystwyth.
MCVG	Geoffrey R. Orrin, *Medieval Churches of the Vale of Glamorgan* (Cowbridge, 1988)
Newman	John Newman, *The Buildings of Wales: Glamorgan* (Cardiff, 1995)
NLW	National Library of Wales, Aberystwyth
OCM	*Oystermouth Church Magazine*
Penarth Chr.	*Penarth Chronicle*
Pontypridd Chr.	*Pontypridd Chronicle*
RBCW	Representative Body of the Church in Wales, Cardiff
SD/C	St David's Diocesan Consecration Manuscript at the National Library of Wales, Aberystwyth
SD/F	St David's Diocesan Faculty Manuscript at the National Library of Wales, Aberystwyth
SGH	*Swansea and Glamorgan Herald*
SPAB	Society for the Protection of Ancient Buildings
SWDN	*South Wales Daily News*
SWDP	*South Wales Daily Post*
W. Mail	*Western Mail*

GAZETTEER OF CHURCH BUILDING AND RESTORATION

ST MARGARET'S CHURCH, ABERAMAN

1883: New church built on new site by Sir George Elliot, Bt, MP, for his employees in the Powell Dyffryn mines and as a memorial to his wife, Lady Margaret, and his daughter Elizabeth, at his own personal cost. Designed by E. H. Lingen Barker of Hereford in the early Decorated style and cruciform in plan, consisting of chancel with semicircular apsidal end (35ftx22ft), north and south transepts (each 14ft 6ins sq.), nave (63ftx28ft) with north porch (9ft sq.) and bellcote over chancel arch. Sloping character of site utilized so as to provide three useful rooms beneath chancel and transepts, the floors being supported on iron girders and white brick arches. Pitch-pine nave and transept roofs open to ridge and plastered between rafters, and chancel with boarded wagon ceiling. Although main walling of church is built of local rock-faced Pennant sandstone from the Aberaman quarries, the copings, quoins and other dressed stone came from 'Mr Pictor's' Westwood Quarry. Carving, in imitation of natural foliage and fruit, executed by George Frederick Herridge, sculptor of Cardiff. Chancel and sanctuary paved with Maw's encaustic tiles. Wrought-iron and brasswork, including gas-fittings, from Brawn's of Birmingham. Heating by means of hot-water piping carried along walls and passages. Seating accommodation for 400 worshippers. Contractor: Charles Shepherd, Cardiff. (*Bldr*, 27 October 1883, 573) Consecrated on 29 September 1883. Cost £5,500. (*Aberdare Times*, 6 October 1883)

Comments: Although Newman regarded the building 'as an unexceptionable cruciform church' (Newman, 129) it contains fittings and furnishings of a high standard of Victorian workmanship carried out by well-known firms. These were not ordinary fittings such as one would expect to find in a church built in a small mining community. An unusual feature of the church is the polychromatic effect of the hood moulds of the windows, executed in contrasting Bath stone and Pennant sandstone as used by John Prichard at St Mary's Church, Aberavon in 1859.

ST MARY'S CHURCH, ABERAVON

1858–9: As a result of its dilapidated state the old parish church of Aberavon was demolished in 1857 and a new and larger church was built on same site. (*CMG*, 28 March 1857) Foundation stone laid on 7 June 1858 by Mrs Madelina Llewellyn of Baglan Hall. (*The Cambrian*, 11 June 1858) Built by John Prichard in the Decorated Gothic style with some constructional polychromy in hoods of windows. It consists of chancel, nave, south aisle and south porch (ICBS file no. 5290 (1858)), and is constructed of Welsh Pennant sandstone in thin courses with Bath stone dressings. Furniture of pitch-pine, stained and varnished. Seating accommodation for 414 worshippers. Contractor: Thomas Williams, Cardiff. Cost £2,300. ICBS grant £250; LDCES grant £100; LCBS grant £40; Griffith Llewellyn £100; C. R. M. Talbot £500. Consecrated on 19 October 1859. (*CMG*, 20 October 1859)

1870: Embattled upper part of tower added. (Newman, 352)

1890: Chancel refurbished. Alabaster and marble reredos erected as a memorial to Griffith Llewellyn (d.1888) of Baglan Hall. Centre of reredos containing therein five arches: the centre represents the Good Shepherd, while the other four are filled in with figures of the four Evangelists. Marble and alabaster work prepared by William Clarke and figures by Henry Hugh Armstead. Complete new fittings for chancel designed by Kempson & Fowler. Floor paved with encaustic tiles. Cost £1,200, defrayed by Mrs Madelina Llewellyn. (*Bldr*, 23 August 1890, 149)

1899: Enlarged by addition of north aisle providing 200 additional seats. Base of tower strengthened and western porch built to nave. Cost £3,200. Architect: George E. Halliday, Llandaff. Contractors: Messrs J. Shepton, Cardiff and Messrs Jenkins & Sons, Swansea. (*W. Mail*, 16 June 1899)

Comments: It is surprising that Prichard designed the church in the more expensive Decorated Gothic style rather than Early English. This is even more astonishing when it is noted that architectural ornamentation was to be sacrificed for additional accommodation. The new church provided for approximately 414 worshippers, double that of the old parish church, but lack of funds prevented the building of a new north aisle. The fact that the north aisle was built so plainly, with its arcade just a series of simple Decorated-style clustered columns with moulded caps, shows that economies were introduced when the north aisle was added by Halliday in 1899. The striking feature of the interior of the church is the use of anachronistic French late twelfth-century-style foliage capitals, while the exterior is noteworthy for the constructional polychromy around the external window heads. Although this device certainly had a parallel in Victorian secular architecture of the period it did not in any way imitate any feature of fourteenth-century church building around the windows either in construction or decoration. St Mary's Church clearly demonstrates, as John Newman states, a lack of commitment on the part of Prichard in his design of the building. (Newman, 532) We can only assume that he was restricted by the apparent lack of funds and mindful of the need to limit the cost to £2,300. As a result, a considerable amount of money had to be spent on the church in the 1890s to beautify it as well as to increase the seating accommodation.

ST TEILO'S CHURCH, ABERAVON

(Demolished 1980s)

1895: New church built on new site donated by Mrs Madelina Llewellyn, as daughter church to St Mary's Church, Aberavon for services in the Welsh language. Designed in Early English style by the architects, Messrs Thomas & James, Port Talbot and Bridgend, it consisted simply of chancel, nave, vestry and bell turret over chancel arch. Constructed of local Pennant sandstone with Bath stone dressings. Nave lighted by lancet-headed lights, and at west end was a five-light window with traceried heads, the whole being filled with tinted Cathedral glass. Furniture and fittings of pitch-pine provided by Wippell's of Exeter. Accommodation for 200 worshippers. Contractors: Messrs J. & S. Rees, Aberavon. Cost £1,030. (*Bldr*, 14 December 1895, 447) Dedicated on 5 December 1895. (*W. Mail*, 6 December 1895)

Comments: When St Mary's Church, Aberavon was taken down and rebuilt in 1859 there was an outcry against the demolition of the old parish church. The Welsh-speaking population of the town felt that English-language worshippers should have erected a church elsewhere in the town. Thus for nearly thirty years the Welsh churchgoers at Aberavon were forced to worship in English, and it was not until 1885, during the incumbency of Revd H. Morris, that Welsh services were revived and held in a room adjacent to the parish church. The first service was conducted by Revd Thomas Harris and attended by twenty-one persons. By 1895 numbers had increased considerably to 200 worshippers with a roll of communicants numbering 110 and eighty Sunday school scholars with eight teachers. The mayor of Aberavon, Councillor Williams, who together with the vicar of Aberavon was actively involved in the establishment of Welsh services in the parish, approached Mrs Madelina Llewellyn for support. She offered magnanimously to build a church for Welsh services in Aberavon, and St Teilo's was built that same year. (*W. Mail*, 6 December 1895)

ST DONAT'S CHURCH, ABERCYNON

1898: New church built on new site donated by Dr John Stradling-Carne of St Donat's Castle. The correspondent in the *Church Builder* reported that: 'This district containing a population of upwards of 6,000 is practically destitute of church accommodation. Services for some years past have been conducted in a large room attached to a hotel with seating accommodation for 250 persons which is quite inadequate for the needs of the district. The need for the new church is considered to be one of the most pressing works in the diocese. The total population of the parish of Llanwonno is 20,000. It is a very poor one and rapidly increasing; when the coal-pits are fully developed as they will be in a year or so the population of this district will reach 7,000 or 8,000. The parish church is five miles from this district.' (*Ch. Bldr* (1898), 69) Built in Early English Gothic style by George E. Halliday, consisting of chancel, nave, south aisle and western gallery (ICBS file no. 9928 (1898)), with latter supported by a brick arcade of three pointed arches. Saddleback tower at south-west corner supported by two-stage clasping buttresses. Constructed of Welsh Pennant sandstone with external dressings of red Cattybrook brick, apart from east and west windows and buttress weatherings which are of hard Doulting stone. Lined internally with red Cattybrook bricks. Both chancel and nave have open timber hammerbeam roofs of pitch-pine left free from stain or varnish. East window of three grouped lancets springing from slender shafts, with west end of nave lighted by a large Rose window above six rounded single lights divided in the centre by a slender two-stage buttress. Roof of south aisle constructed of transverse gables. Aisle, which is separated from nave by three pointed moulded arches, lighted by three two-light windows with intervening slender buttresses. (Personal observation) Seating accommodation for 500 persons. Church designed by George E. Halliday. Contractor: William Games, Abercynon. Cost £3,000. (*BN*, 23 September 1898, 425) Opened for divine service on 16 September 1898. (*W. Mail*, 17 September 1898) However, the church fulfilled the strict requirements demanded by the Ecclesiastical Commissioners and the church was consecrated eventually in April 1907 after long-drawn-out legal disputes. (*Bldr*, 9 March 1907, 301)

Comments: The red-brick interior has now been painted out. The west gallery, supported by an arcade of three pointed brick arches, is an unusual feature for a church built in the late Victorian period. Halliday's brief was probably worded so that he was required to design a church which would accommodate 500 worshippers, and without the funds to erect a north aisle he was forced to build a gallery, much against his wishes. Although constructed in an outwardly plain manner the interior has a substantial hammerbeam roof, an unusual feature for a church in a small mining community. The building cost £6 per sitting, which was a reasonable amount to pay at the end of the nineteenth century. Although St Donat's external appearance is compromised by the use of red Cattybrook brickwork the traditional-style Glamorgan saddleback roof, the Rose window in the west wall and the transverse gabled roofs of the south aisle enhance the architectural design of the church far above the cheap utilitarian structures erected by Halliday's contemporary Bruce Vaughan in the south Wales coalfield.

ST ELVAN'S CHURCH, ABERDARE

1851–2: New church built on new site donated by marchioness of Bute in her late husband's name as chapel of ease to St John the Baptist's Church, Aberdare. Foundation stone laid in 1851. Built in Geometrical Decorated Gothic style by Andrew

1. St Elvan's Church, Aberdare. Photo: Rock & Co., London (Source: Aberdare Library: Rhondda Cynon Taff Council)

Moseley of London. The ICBS accepted the design, although they made recommendations which increased the cost. The contractor's tender came to £4,685 and the Society's architects had difficulty in reducing the cost. Thus, the thickness of the walls was reduced by six inches all round, the south door and south transept omitted, the height of the nave reduced and the amount of Bath stone and ornamental work severely restricted. (ICBS file no. 4219 (1850)) Church consists of a chancel (30ftx20ft), nave (82ftx23ft) with north and south aisles (82ftx13ft9ins), north transept and north-east vestry, with organ-loft over (18ftx16ft), north porch and western tower with spire rising to a height of 180ft. (*Bldr*, 9 October 1852, 640) Constructed of uncoursed Dyffryn sandstone pointed with blue mortar and rusticated quoins of Bath stone. Aisles divided from nave by four alternating round and octagonal Bath stone columns, all with octagonal capitals. Roofs of Baltic fir of open timber construction, stained and varnished in imitation of oak. Total length of church including chancel, nave and tower is 140ft. Four-stage tower crowned by parapet pierced with trefoils and large corner pinnacles and spire with double-gabled spirelets on cardinal sides. Seating accommodation for 710 persons. Heated on hot-water principle. Opened for divine worship on 30 September 1852, but not consecrated until 25 September 1854. Contractor: J. N. Strawbridge, Bristol. Cost £3,995. Trustee of the Bute Estate £500; Church Commissioners' grant £250; ICBS grant £400; LDCES grant £50. (*CMG*, 2 October 1852)

1869: Fabric found to be in need of 'very considerable repair' and the vicar, Revd Henry Edwards (1876–84), considered the church as 'large and pretentious . . . ill financed . . . and in parts very slightly built'. Cost of repairs was £700.

1884: Further work required in 1884 when the architect Thomas Nicholson reported that 'the building was wet through and through' as the result of 'want of proper construction and defective workmanship'. Entire building completely reroofed by a local builder, John Morgan. At the same time chancel given a north chapel. Cost £2,000.

1890: New Perpendicular chancel screen designed by William Tate of London and painted by Dykes-

Bower erected in the church. (Geoffrey Evans, *St Elvan's Church, Aberdare* (2nd edn, 1989), 7–10)

Comments: The building of St Elvan's Church in the years 1851–2 was an important milestone in church building at mid-century in the diocese of Llandaff. St Elvan's was the first church to benefit from a grant from the newly formed Llandaff Diocesan Church Extension Society and it was one of the eleven Commissioners' churches built in Glamorgan. As a result of the amendments made to the original plans, it turned out to be a much plainer church than Moseley had originally intended. Nevertheless, a Puginesque building, with its tall tower and spire, St Elvan's is a notable landmark in the area. The church itself is rather a modest structure, and its appeal as an architectural feature lies in its four-stage tower and spire. The belfry stage of the tower, pierced by two double bell openings on each side, adds to the comparative richness at the top. The three-light west window is well proportioned with its intersecting arches which form elongated trefoils and dagger shapes in the heads. Inside, the Decorated period is represented by the lofty chancel and tower arches, the tall columns of the nave arcade and the alternative octagonal and circular pillars with all their octagonal capitals. When Moseley's original drawing of the church is examined and compared with the actual building there does not appear to be much evidence of too many economies, although later reroofing and repairs to the church showed obvious deficiences in its original construction. Moseley was a lecturer in the Arts of Construction of the Department of Applied Sciences at King's College, London.

In the years 1910–12 the church was enlarged by the addition of an outer south aisle designed by George E. Halliday. Known as the 'Green aisle' after the Revd C. A. H. Green, vicar at the time and later archbishop of Wales. Other work included parochial and priest's vestries, the enlargement of the chancel and Lady chapel, new oak seating throughout, a complete system of heating and lighting, reflooring throughout with wood blocks, and considerable enlargement of the organ. Cost £7,000. (LL/F/25. Enlargement of church. Faculty dated 3 September 1910) Work completed March 1912. (*Bldr*, 5 April 1912, 403)

2. The view of St Fagan's, Aberdare (Source: Gareth Thomas, Aberdare. Collection of Prints) (By kind permission of Gareth Thomas, Aberdare)

ST FAGAN'S CHURCH, ABERDARE

1853–4: New church built on new site through generosity of Hon. Robert H. Clive of St Fagans. Built in Early English Gothic style by Thomas Talbot Bury of London. (ICBS file no. 4393 (1851)), it consisted of chancel (29ftx19ft), nave, with west gallery (68ftx22ft), north and south aisles (29ftx11ft), south porch and western bellcote. Chapel at east end of south aisle accommodated sixty children and west gallery seated fifty parishioners. Constructed of squared Dyffryn sandstone, with windows, doorways, buttresses, copings and bellcote of Bath stone. (*Bldr*, 20 November 1852, 737) Chancel paved with Haywood's black and red tiles. Roof, which was 47ft to ridge, constructed of best Memel timber stained and varnished, with the open seats of same material. Roof covered with Delabole slates from Cornwall. Seating accommodation for 700 worshippers, as laid down by the ICBS. Contractors: Messrs James & Price, Cardiff. Cost £1,800. ICBS grant £400. Consecrated on 31 July 1854. (*CMG*, 4 August 1854)
1856: Church destroyed by fire on 12 January 1856 and rebuilt more or less to original design by Talbot

Bury and by original contractors. West gallery not restored, but skilful arrangement of seats ensured same accommodation. New chancel east window an improvement on former one, and chancel paved with Minton's tiles. Cost £5,000, defrayed by Baroness Windsor of St Fagans. Reopened on 26 August 1856. (*CMG*, 30 August 1856)

Comments: In designing the original church Talbot Bury took great care to select a style of architecture which would suit the locality and be in keeping with the surrounding landscape. Therefore he used the Early English style, which proved highly suitable. Although the church was simple and solid in its construction, Talbot Bury did not overlook the importance of sound proportions and comfortable arrangement. The gallery at the west end of the nave was erected against the wishes of the architect, but it was insisted upon by the Church Building Committee, since it provided additional accommodation for fifty worshippers, a high priority at the time. The rebuilding of the church in 1856 followed the original design, but with a few improvements which were considered desirable at the time. The west gallery was not replaced because the architect regarded it as an anomaly in the arrangement of the interior, as well as being anathema to the Ecclesiologists. Moreover, this gallery had the effect of excluding light from the west window; its omission from the restored church much improved the light of the interior and effected a saving of £103. The re-arrangement of the fenestration improved the appearance of the building, especially the three-light east window which replaced the former two-light one. After the rebuilding and restoration of the church the parishioners considered themselves as being in the old church. (*CMG*, 30 August 1856)

In the years 1909–10 the nave was extended and the south-west tower built to replace the belfry. Architect: George E. Halliday. (LL/F/33. Repair of church and erection of belfry. Faculty dated 26 May 1909)

ST JAMES' CHURCH, LLWYDCOED, ABERDARE

1895: New church built on new site as chapel of ease to St Fagan's Church, Aberdare. There had long been a need for a church in the area, which was within reach of a population of some 1,500 inhabitants scattered over a wide hill district remote from existing churches and consisting of the mining and labouring classes. Piece of land upon which church stands donated by James Lewis of Plasdraw. Built in Early English Gothic style by George E. Halliday, consisting of chancel, nave, south porch and western bellcote. Constructed entirely of red brick with brick chancel arch and window dressings. Pulpit and seats of pitch-pine and church warmed by Porritt's patent heating apparatus. All windows of Cathedral glass. Seating accommodation for 210 worshippers. (*Bldr*, 7 December 1895, 426) East window of three grouped lancets, and west window of two single lancets between slender brick-built buttresses. Chancel and nave have arch-braced open timber roofs of pitch-pine. Western bellcote of open timberwork structure and half-timbered south porch as at Garth. (Personal observation) Contractors: Thomas & Williams, Cardiff. Dedicated on 2 December 1895. Cost £1,465. LDCES grant £50. (*W. Mail*, 3 December 1895)

Comments: It is difficult to overestimate the role of individual church people in the church extension movement of the late Victorian period. This is exemplified by the building of St James' Church, Llwydcoed in 1895 as a direct result of a generous donation of a site for the new church, as well as a donation of £50 to inaugurate the building fund by James Lewis, JP, of Plasdraw. George E. Halliday, who designed the church, was regarded as one of the most forward-looking architects in Glamorgan during the late Victorian period, and his use of red brick was an innovative material for the external walling of churches in Glamorgan and in complete contrast to the ubiquitous Pennant sandstone. His openwork timbered western bellcote and half-timbered porch at Llwydcoed made it an unusual structure for Glamorgan and is reminiscent of churches in the counties of Breconshire and Herefordshire.

ST JOHN THE BAPTIST'S CHURCH, ABERDARE

1857–9: Chancel, described by Revd John Griffith in 1847 as 'a damp and dingy place', repaired in 1857 at a cost of £26 which included removal of an unsightly 18ft-high brick chimney stack from corner of north wall where chancel joins nave. In 1859 the building was virtually in ruins and there was a movement afoot for its demolition and the erection of a new church for the Welsh-speaking population on the site, but wiser counsels prevailed. (Geoffrey Evans, *An Account of the History of the Ancient Chapelry of St John Baptist and Parish Church of Aberdare and its Memorials* (1982), 48)

1871–6: £500 spent on church at this time failed to arrest decay of structure. By 1871 the church was in a dilapidated state: the windows had fallen in and the roof was in danger of collapsing so that no services, not even the necessary funeral and marriage services, could be held there. Fortunately by 1876 the Revd J. D. Jenkins, vicar of the parish, had raised a sum of £900 with the intention of restoring the church to its original Gothic design. Sir George Elliot was the principal benefactor, contributing £300 to the fund. (*Aberdare Times*, 26 February 1876) Restoration included replacement of several windows in nave with eight pairs of ogee-foliated lancets said to be exact pattern of original windows. Chancel enlarged and old round-headed east window, recorded by the Ecclesiastical Commissioners in 1857, replaced by a three-light ogee-foliated one and a new single lancet placed in north wall of chancel. Entire roof rebuilt and old-fashioned high-backed pews replaced by open benches of deal. Church seating increased from 176 to 200 sittings. Reopened on 24 June 1876. (*Aberdare Times*, 1 July 1876)

Comments: George E. Halliday, the then diocesan surveyor, who carried out a considerable amount of church restoration and reconstruction during the early years of the twentieth century, stated in a report entitled *The Parish of Aberdare* prepared for the vicar and churchwardens and dated 9 April 1915 that 'the church was most ruthlessly dealt with at that time'. There is no doubt that the building of new churches in the parish of Aberdare during the period 1851–65 drained the parish coffers and that the small ancient parish church was completely neglected as a result of the need to provide additional church accommodation for the ever-increasing population of the parish. This demand led to the building of St Elvan's (1852), St Fagan's (1854) and St Mary's (1864). During these years of church extension there were proposals to enlarge, rebuild and even demolish St John's, so that a new church could be built on the site. Despite Halliday's comments St John's retains its basic medieval appearance with its barn-like west front. After the building of St Elvan's Church in 1852 the parish church became the Welsh church. Despite the increase in accommodation achieved in 1876 it was soon found to be insufficient for the congregation who wished to attend the old parish church of St John.

In 1915 further repairs were carried out at a cost of more than £500. The vestry was partially rebuilt and completely reroofed and a new heating apparatus was installed. Architect: George E. Halliday. (William Edwards, *Notes on the Ancient Parish Church of St John the Baptist* (2nd edn, Aberdare, 1946), 17–19)

ST JOSEPH'S CHURCH, CWMAMAN, ABERDARE

1869–70: New church built on new site donated by John Bruce Pryce of Dyffryn, St Nicholas. Constructed of corrugated iron lined with wood. Seating accommodation for 200 people. Cost £300, of which £100 was given by John Bruce Pryce. Church opened for divine worship on 28 April 1870. (*Cardiff Times*, 7 May,1870)

1882: New chancel built to existing iron structure, during incumbency of Revd A. E. H. Hyslop. Cost £400 (*Kelly's Directory of South Wales*, 1926, 49)

1890: New nave built to existing chancel, replacing old iron nave. (*Ch. Bldr* (1890), 34) Nave built in Early English Gothic style by E. M. Bruce Vaughan. Constructed of local Pennant sandstone with Bath stone dressings. It measures 58ft by 25ft and has a bellcote 48ft above west end of nave. West window of four trefoiled lights with Geometrical tracery above. Font of Bath stone stands at west end. Pulpit well-designed and a fine specimen of carved yellow pine. Roof and seats also of yellow pine, the main rafters from roof resting on projecting stone corbels. Seating accommodation for 350 worshippers. Contractor: John Haines, Canton, Cardiff. Consecrated on 19 May 1890. Cost £1,000. (*Aberdare Times*, 24 May 1890)

Comments: St Joseph's Church, Cwmaman had a protracted building history and illustrates the difficulty of the Anglican Church in the late Victorian period in trying to provide additional church accommodation in the industrial areas of Glamorgan, especially in the diocese of Llandaff. The church, which was an iron, corrugated structure in 1870, had to wait until 1882 until a stone chancel could be built and another seven years until a stone-built nave could replace the iron nave. Another twenty-seven years were to pass before the church was enlarged to cope with increasing demand for additional church accommodation after 1901.

In 1917 the aisles with transverse-gabled bays were added to nave and extended westwards to cope with demand from area's increasing population. Additional accommodation provided for

276 worshippers at cost of £2,000. ICBS grant £50. Architect: James J. Jenkins, Porth. (*Ch. Bldr* (1915), 24) New additions consecrated on 2 August 1917. (LL/C/100. Sentence of consecration dated 2 August 1917)

ST LUKE'S CHURCH, CWMDARE, ABERDARE

1886–7: New church built on new site as chapel of ease to St Fagan's Church by E. M. Bruce Vaughan. As early as 1880 William Jones had begun work as a lay reader in Cwmdare, and the first services were held in the long room of The Castle. Then on 17 June 1883 a licensed Mission Room was opened in Bwllfa Road at a cost of £35. In May 1886 Revd R. B. Jenkins, vicar of Aberdare, launched an appeal for funds to build a permanent church. Sum of £600 raised, including donation of £100 from Colonel C. K. Kemeys-Tynte. Piece of land donated by J. P. W. Gwynne Holford of Buckland. Foundation stone laid on 18 October 1886 by Lady Aberdare. Built in Early English Gothic style consisting of chancel and nave. (*W. Mail*, 20 October 1886) Constructed of buff-coloured brick with Bath stone dressings. Contractor: Edward Lumley of Merthyr Tydfil. (*Bldr*, 9 July 1887, 80) Roof covering of green slates and finished off with ornamental ridge-tiles and three crosses of neat design. Cost £672. Opened for divine worship on 28 June 1887. (*W. Mail*, 29 June 1887) East window of three grouped trefoiled lancets. Nave walls pierced by single lancets and west end of nave lighted by a group of pointed lancets, the centre light being much taller than the two flanking windows. The nave has an arch-braced roof with scissors-beam trusses. Seating accommodation for 190 worshippers. (Personal observation)

Comments: St Luke's Church, Cwmdare was a very simple building consisting of chancel and nave only, without the ubiquitous western bellcote. It was churches of this kind, built in a very simple 'lancet' style at a cost of less than £1,000 and constructed of cheap materials, which enabled the Anglican Church to provide church accommodation in the parish of Aberdare in the 1880s.

ST MARY'S CHURCH, MAESYDREF, ABERDARE
(Church demolished 1966)

1863–4: New church built on new site donated by the Ecclesiastical Commissioners for the Welsh-speaking population of Aberdare. Foundation stone laid on 2 July 1863 by Mrs Thomas Wayne of Glandare. (*The Civil Engineer and Architect's Journal*, 1 April 1864, 85) Built in Decorated Gothic style with French Gothic influence consisting of chancel with chancel aisles, nave, north and south aisles, vestry on south side of chancel beneath the tower with saddleback roof. Extreme internal dimensions were length 97ft and width 51ft 8ins, providing seating accommodation for 680 adult sittings. Twin columns of nave arcades of iron. Architect, Arthur W. Blomfield of London, and contractor, Philip Rees of Aberdare. (*Bldr*, 11 July 1863, 501) Constructed of Newbridge stone (taken from local quarries) with Bath stone dressings. Exterior had a marked appearance, derived from the peculiar colour of the Newbridge stone and the profuse Bath stone dressings, as well as the number of gables (six) thrown up on the north and south sides of building and relieving it from the monotonous appearance of the slated roof. Some of the windows placed in gables. The 90-ft-high tower sprang from south side of building and was topped with ornamental ironwork. Shafts on responds and in chancel of green Bridgend stone with carved Bath stone capitals. Roof, which was of open timber construction, sprang nearly from centre of arches. At west end of nave under the floor was a baptistery for total immersion. All carving executed by George Whittington of Newport, Salop. Cost £3,800. (*Bldr*, 19 November 1864, 845)

Comments: St Mary's Church, Maesydref, Aberdare (also known in Welsh as Eglwys y Fair Forwyn) was designed by Blomfield with a view to the greatest economy possible, together with strength, durability and a sufficient amount of ecclesiastical character. An unusual feature of the interior was the use of twin iron columns for the pillars of the nave arcade. The use of ironwork for the structure of churches was advocated by Viollet-le-Duc, the

French architectural writer, during this period and its use for arcade pillars at Maesydref was rare for Victorian churches in Glamorgan. Whilst the French Gothic influence in St Mary's was evident, it was subdued and derived mostly from the use of round windows in the gables and its horizontal bands of decorative foils. The church did not have an apsidal chancel or peripheral chapels, which would have added to the French Gothic design. For reasons of economy no clerestory was built, but the church was sufficiently lighted by the additional height gained for some of the windows by throwing up the gables in the aisles. The saddleback tower, so much a feature in northern France, was built to achieve two purposes, firstly to maintain the French Gothic influence, and secondly in keeping with an established tradition in this area of Glamorgan. At St Mary's the saddleback tower was transversely gabled to the axis of the church. Blomfield probably did this to create an illusion of width. By offsetting his tower and placing it asymmetrically at the south-east side of the church he took the opportunity to mirror the gables over the south aisle and by so doing increased the apparent width of the church. It is unfortunate that the church was demolished in 1966.

ST GABRIEL'S CHURCH, ABERGWYNFI

(Church in ruins)

1893–4: New church built on new site donated by earl of Dunraven. Foundation stone laid on 11 September 1893 by Mrs Annie Jackson on behalf of Miss Olive Talbot. Built in Early English Gothic style from designs by George E. Halliday, consisting of chancel, nave with west gallery, north porch and western bellcote. Constructed of local Pennant sandstone with external dressings of hard Doulting stone, and with interior fittings of pitchpine. (*Bldr*, 13 October 1894, 264) Owing to nature of site it was found impracticable to build an aisle; hence a gallery supported on three stone arches was erected, surmounted by a Rose window some 12x 15ft in circumference. Seating accommodation for 400 worshippers. Contractor: Philip Gaylard of Bridgend. Cost £2,600, exclusive of £500 for excavation of site. Consecrated on 1 October 1894. (*W. Mail*, 2 October 1894) The terms of the Ecclesiastical Commissioners' grant of £110 stipulated that the church should accommodate 400 worshippers. However, because of the restricted nature of the site, Halliday found it impossible to comply with this precondition without erecting a gallery, which neither he nor the Commissioners favoured. As a result, several amendments had to be made to Halliday's design. Stone steps had to be substituted for wooden ones of gallery stairs, additional windows were required on north side of church and wider steps in chancel. In addition, a mining engineer was required to confirm that colliery workings beneath the site would not affect the stability of the new building. Further problems ensued when it was discovered that, for some obscure reason, the contractor built the church facing west instead of east. However, it was found impossible to remedy this defect without demolishing the total amount of work already constructed. Plans were hastily amended to allow the porch to be built on the more accessible north side of the road. (Roger L. Brown, *Through Cloud and Sunshine: A History of the Church in the Upper Afan Valley* (1982), 130–8)

Comments: St Gabriel's Church was hemmed in on one side by the main road and on the other by the mountain side. The church with its massive buttresses and overall solidity conveyed the idea of a mountain church which indeed it was. The high costs of building this church were caused by the additional expense of £500 needed to excavate a site from the solid rock of the mountain side. Furthermore, the construction of a west gallery was a rather novel feature for a church built in the late Victorian period. Halliday was also forced to build a gallery at St Donat's, Abercynon to comply with the brief to accommodate sufficient worshippers. The outstanding architectural feature of the building, especially for a mountain church, was the Rose window of large circumference which was obviously erected by Halliday to ensure that enough light was projected into the church despite the gallery's position at the west end of the nave.

ST CATTWG'S CHURCH, ABERPERGWM

1840–1: Enlargement and restoration of church. Length of church increased to double its width. Chancel provided with baptismal font and a Communion table approached by several steps. Family seat, or 'Cathedral' benches placed near the Communion table for the Williams family of Aberpergwm, and one for their servants opposite. Accommodation provided for a congregation of approximately 200 parishioners. A Gothic doorway with steps led from churchyard at north-west corner into family seat. Porch constructed at west end for men and a small door for women. Windows placed so that nobody in the church could see people outside. Vestry room constructed at north-west corner and an organ loft and gallery built for school children and women over west entrance. Stove provided to heat church. Church constructed of the 'best Combe Down (Bath) stone' and floor paved with black and white tiles. Reopened after enlargement and restoration by the Williams family of Aberpergwm on 19 May 1841. (Elizabeth F. Belcham, *About Aberpergwm: The Home of the Williams Family in the Vale of Glamorgan* (1992), 81–3)

1884: Restoration by John Bacon Fowler, Brecon. Work consisted of rearrangement of interior. Old-fashioned box pews, which had become dilapidated, replaced by open benches of pitch-pine seating 180 parishioners. Contractors: Messrs Bowers & Co., Hereford. Reopened after restoration on 25 September 1884. (*CGG*, 3 October 1884)

Comments: Despite the rearrangement of the interior of the church in 1884, when the church was closed for six months for internal repairs, St Cattwg's retains its appearance as an estate church of the 1840s, especially the chancel with its enclosed altar rails and the 'Cathedral' benches. Each seat-back with its crocketed triangular top is still *in situ*. Although Newman states that the 'big three-light Perp windows of red sandstone must be of 1883' (Newman, 360), the report of the restoration in the *Central Glamorgan Gazette* for 3 October 1884 makes no mention of this fact and the work was only a reordering of the interior without any work being done to the structure of the church.

ST JOHN THE BAPTIST'S CHURCH, ALLTWEN

1886–7: New church built on new site donated by Howel Gwyn of Dyffryn. Foundation stone laid on 24 June 1886 by Howel Gwyn. Built in Early English Gothic style consisting of chancel (26ftx 20ft), nave (46ftx24ft), vestry (14ftx12ft), and north porch. Constructed of local Pennant sandstone with Ruabon red brick dressings and corresponding gable stones. Chancel arch also built of Ruabon red brick and chancel and sanctuary steps of red Forest of Dean stone. East and west windows have three-light windows, and chancel's side windows are enriched with figured devices with monograms and coloured borders. The roof is an open one of pitch-pine, stained and varnished, the chancel roof being boarded panels. Centre floor of the nave, chancel and sanctuary laid out with encaustic tiles supplied by Messrs Maw & Co., Worcester. Reredos and font of Caen stone, the former divided with eight panels supported by Devonshire marble columns, the centre of the reredos being filled with raised monograms IHC and IHS with the letters alpha and omega carved in the stone. Chancel and the sanctuary steps, as well as base of font, are of red Forest of Dean stone. Church heated with Porritt's slow combustion stoves. Carved sedilia and chairs of ancient Welsh oak, 300 years old and presented by Herbert Lloyd, Cilybebyll. There is a fine bellcote over the chancel arch and finial crosses. Opened for divine worship on 14 April 1887. Contractor: John Griffiths, Pontardawe. Cost £1,300. (*The Cambrian*, 15 April 1887) Font and credence table both carved by William Dodd, Pontardawe. (*W. Mail*, 15 April 1887)

Comments: No architect is recorded for this church and John Newman has omitted it entirely from his book *The Buildings of Wales: Glamorgan*. It is conceivable that Howel Gwyn, who was involved with so much church building in Glamorgan, especially in and around Neath, drew up the plans himself in cooperation with the builder. It was built on Gwyn's property on the side of Alltwen Hill in the centre of the most populous part of the parish of Cilybebyll, whose population numbered nearly 2,000 in 1881. Erected nearly three miles from the parish church, its erection in 1887 satisfied a long-felt need for a church in that part of the parish. Although it was built of cheap brick and Pennant sandstone it also contained much Forest of Dean and Caen stone. The material for the main walling of the church was probably supplied from Gwyn's own quarries in the area.

TRINITY CHURCH, ALLTYGRUG (GODRE'R-GRAIG)
(Church demolished in 1987)

1844–5: New church built on new site given by Richard Douglas Gough of Yniscedwyn House as chapel of ease to Llangiwg (Llanguicke) parish church from a design by William Whittington, county surveyor of Neath. J. H. Good, consulting architect to the ICBS, made criticisms relating to the construction of the gallery, the position of the font and the wording of the specification and returned the plans for amendments. (ICBS file no. 3094 (1842–60). Foundation stone laid on 1 October 1844. (*The Cambrian*, 4 October 1844) Built in simplified Early English Gothic style consisting of chancel, nave and western bell-cote. Constructed of Welsh Pennant sandstone with Bath stone dressings. East window of three grouped lancets and the chancel and nave lighted with simple lancet windows. Roofs of open timber construction. Vault constructed under sanctuary as a burial chamber for the Budd family but never used. Accommodation for 140 worshippers. Contractor: William Rayner, Swansea. Opened for divine worship on 27 May 1845. Cost £850. ICBS grant £200. (*The Cambrian*, 31 May 1845)
1864: Enlarged by addition of north and south transepts and an expanded chancel forming a cruciform building of graceful proportions. North transept housed organ with choir vestry at rear, while choir stalls occupied south transept. Floor of chancel covered with encaustic tiles of an appropriate ecclesiastical design. New hot-water heating system installed. Enlargement almost doubled the seating accommodation for worshippers to 250 sittings. Reopened for divine worship after enlargement and restoration on 26 July 1864. Enlargement of church designed and supervised

by Mr Newton, manager of Yniscedwyn Iron Works. Cost £759. (*The Cambrian*, 29 July 1864)

Comments: The architect, William Whittington, also designed St John's Church, Clydach in the years 1846–7. These were the only churches that he designed in the county. At the time of Trinity's enlargement in 1864 no application was made to the ICBS, which would have required plans submitted by a professional architect. Mr Newton, although not a professional architect, drew up the plans and superintended the building work. Trinity Church was a simple structure built in the 'lancet' style, which did not require much architectural expertise. Subsidence due to coal-mining in the area was responsible for its demolition in 1987.

ST CATHARINE'S CHURCH, BAGLAN

1875–82: New church built on new site adjacent to old church. It was a growing awareness of the need for a larger church which inspired Griffith Llewellyn

3. St Catharine's Church, Baglan (Source: Photograph by kind permission of Jeffrey Evans, Yeovil)

to build this new church in 1875. Foundation stone laid on 26 June 1875 by Mrs Madelina Llewellyn of Baglan Hall. (Eben Jones, *Baglan and the Llewellyns of Baglan Hall* (Port Talbot, 1987), 130) Built in early Decorated Gothic style by John Prichard. Cruciform in plan consisting of chancel, nave, transepts, central tower with spire and south porch. Masonry of church built of alternate thin and thick courses of local sandstone with dressings of red Forest of Dean stone. West window an unusually fine specimen of the Geometrical style, and tower and spire of wrought ashlar of same stone. Internal walls of green Bridgend stone banded with red Forest of Dean stone and Penarth alabaster. All woodwork including roofs, choir stalls and open benches, seating 240 worshippers, of Baglan oak. Passage aisle on north side of nave. Reredos consists of arcade of alabaster, gabled and crocketed and covering whole width of chancel. Central panels designed by Henry Hugh Armstead. Whole pavement of church including chancel floor of glass mosaic. Chancel enclosed by two low brass gates which serve as altar rails. Walls of chancel almost entirely of pink Penarth alabaster with a few bands of red and green stone. Tower arches spring from corbelled shafts which rest on heads of the four Evangelists with their insignia. Above roof, tower assumes an octagonal form, the angles being filled with bold pinnacles. Eight steps of Devonshire marble lead up to the altar. Roof panelled with ribs springing from angels holding emblems of the Passion. Octagonal pulpit with moulded and tracery panels in red sandstone. Wood and stone carving by William Wormleighton, architectural sculptor of Cardiff. (*Bldr*, 25 March 1882, 370–1) Consecrated on 7 March 1882. Cost £17,000. (*W. Mail*, 8 March 1882)

Comments: St Catharine's Church, Baglan is an outstanding example of a church in the Geometrical Gothic style, that is the early fourteenth-century style regarded by Pugin and the Ecclesiologists as the purest style of Gothic architecture. This church was probably Prichard's masterpiece and was an appropriate monument to his skill and architectural ability, which gave him a reputation as the finest ecclesiastical architect in south-east Wales during the greater part of the nineteenth century. Nothing

was spared in its construction, which took seven years to complete. It has often been referred to as the 'Alabaster Church' on account of its dominant material: pink Penarth alabaster. The internal arrangement of the church is most effective, and it is this which makes the church such a fine Victorian building. Prichard achieved this by making the crossing under the tower a quasi-chancel and then developed the sanctuary more than is usually the case in small churches. Inside there is polychromatic opulence. However, the black and marble reredos was considered as a mistake, since Prichard in an unguarded moment accepted Armstead's suggestion that 'black and white' was the most orthodox treatment for a reredos, forgetting that all the surroundings glowed with colour. The church is remarkable for its complete ensemble of Victorian fittings.

ST GWLADYS' CHURCH, BARGOED

1876–7: New church built on new site given by E. R. Wingfield of Barrington Park and Miss Richards of Plas Newydd. Great growth in population of parish and distance from parish church at Gelligaer made additional church accommodation absolutely necessary. Foundation stone of church laid on 18 April 1876 by Miss Richards of Plas Newydd. Chancel only built in Early English Gothic style by John Prichard. Constructed of Pennant sandstone with Bath stone dressings. East window is triplet of grouped lancets. Barrel-shaped roof. Small corrugated-iron nave built onto chancel. Contractor: W. T. Morgan, Bargoed. Cost £1,666. Consecrated April 1877. (*W. Mail*, 19 April 1876)

1893–4: By 1893 the temporary iron nave was in a dilapidated condition and beyond repair and it was replaced by a stone one by E. M. Bruce Vaughan. (*Ch. Bldr* (1891), 72–3) During the term that Revd J. L. Meredith was rector of Gelligaer, he collected funds towards the building of the nave and this work was carried out by the Revd T. J. Jones, rector. Foundation stone of new nave laid on 29 June 1893 by Miss Harries, eldest daughter of Revd Canon Gilbert Harries, then rector of Gelligaer. (*W. Mail*, 30 June 1893) Church now consists of chancel, nave, south porch and bellcote over chancel arch containing a sanctus bell. West window of three lancets and interior of church lighted by single lancet windows between single buttresses. Nave has open arch-braced roof, with woodwork of nave constructed of pitch-pine. Seating accommodation for 342 persons. Contractors: Messrs W. Williams & Son, Bargoed. Cost £1,850. ICBS grant £50; LDCES grant £25; Bishop of Llandaff's Fund £350. (*W. Mail*, 16 January 1894) **1919:** White stone reredos depicting the Last Supper erected as memorial for those fallen in the First World War. (LL/F/53. St Gwladys', Bargoed: Reredos and roll of honour. Faculty dated 12 June 1919)

Comments: When the chancel, with its side aisles for organ chamber and vestry, was nearing completion, it was discovered that the erection of such a structure would exceed the sum estimated, namely £1,500, for the building of the whole church. Consequently the nave was a small iron corrugated structure which remained *in situ* until 1893. This was not the first time that Prichard had designed an over-elaborate, expensive structure which exceeded the sum estimated for the whole church (cf. St Andrew's, Cardiff). Although he built the chancel with two fully formed bays either side in the less expensive Early English Gothic style, his ornate treatment of the features of the building – its heavy double-chamfered chancel arch with drop corbels and the east window of three separate trefoil-headed lights with heavy internal arch mouldings and centre light flanked by Early English-style columns – was undoubtedly the reason for his exceeding estimate. This church, built partly by Prichard and partly by Bruce Vaughan, gives us an opportunity to compare the contrasting styles in which the two architects used the local Pennant sandstone. Prichard's masonry is laid in thin uniform courses while Bruce Vaughan's masonry takes on a more random form. Kathleen Lewis, in her booklet entitled *In the Steps of St Gwladys: A History of the Parish of Bargoed with Brithdir* (Merthyr, 1959), states erroneously on page 7 that the church was consecrated on Tuesday in Easter week, 1876. This was, in fact, the date of the laying of the foundation stone and the church was not consecrated until its completion in April 1877.

ST NICHOLAS' CHURCH, BARRY
(Church became redundant in 1955)

1866: Sir Stephen R. Glynne visited the church on 9 September 1866 and described it thus: 'A very small mean church, externally whitewashed, roof and all. It has a chancel and nave and over the west end a bell-cot for two bells in open arches. The chancel arch is flat, plain and diminutive. There is a south porch . . .' (Sir Stephen R. Glynne, 'Notes on the older churches in the four Welsh dioceses', *Arch. Camb.* (1901), 245–6)

1874–6: By 1873 the medieval parish church of St Nicholas, Barry had become so decayed by the ravages of time that the rector, Revd Canon E. E. Allen, requested a faculty for its demolition and the building of a new church on the same site. Petition for taking down old church stated 'that the said church of Barry is in a state of decay, the fabric thereof of rough and poor construction, the interior arrangements ill ordered & designed that the said church does not afford necessary and convenient accommodation for the inhabitants of this parish and requires to be pulled down and rebuilt on an enlarged site, and altered and reseated so as to afford the required accommodation for such inhabitants'. (LL/60/F. Demolition of old parish church and erection of new church. Faculty dated 26 February 1873) New church built on same site. Work commenced 1874. Rebuilt in Early English Gothic style and 'altered and reseated so as to afford required accommodation for such inhabitants'. (Ibid.) Church designed by Romilly Allen of Barry, a noted antiquarian, at a cost of £2,700, consisting of chancel with north vestry, south porch and western bellcote. Constructed of lias limestone with Bath stone dressings. (Brian C. Luxton, 'Barry' in Stewart Williams (ed.), *South Glamorgan: A County History* (Barry, 1975), 145) Inner walls of dressed lias limestone. East window of three plain lancets. Chancel and nave lighted by plain lancets, including west window. Double bellcote corbelled out over western gable. Double-chamfered, pointed chancel arch of Bath stone of two orders; the inner arch springing from semi-circular columns with faceted abaci. Solid Early English buttresses support corners of chancel and nave walls. Plain interior with open timber roofs.

Floor lined with seventeenth- and eighteenth-century ledger stones from old church. Accommodation for 120 persons. Built by direct labour under supervision of Canon Allen. Consecrated on 22 June 1876. (Personal information from Howard J. Thomas, Barry, formerly of RCAHM (Wales))

Comments: St Nicholas' Church was a plain structure and devoid of any ornamentation reflecting the Low Church persuasion of Canon Allen and his patrons, the Romilly family of Barry. This was evident from the large metal panels on the wall behind the Communion table on which were inscribed the Ten Commandments, the Apostles' Creed and Lord's Prayer. Soon after its erection it proved to be too small for the dramatic increase in population which followed the construction of the Barry docks in the 1880s. As a result the first stage of All Saints' Church, Barry, designed in 1902 by E. M. Bruce Vaughan, was built in the years 1907–8 and the second stage was completed in 1915. All Saints' was designated as parish church of Barry in 1919.

ST PAUL'S CHURCH, BARRY

1892–3: New church built on new site given by Mrs Jenner of Wenvoe Castle. Foundation stone laid on 29 November 1892 by Miss Ida Evans, Morgannwg, Brecon. Built in Early English Gothic style from a design by Messrs Kempson & Fowler, Llandaff. (*Barry Dock News*, 2 December 1892) New church built to replace temporary iron church of St Paul's which accommodated only 320 persons and had cost £433 to erect. (*St Paul's Appeal Letter of 1890*) First portion built consisted of chancel (32ftx20ft), nave (70ftx25ft), south aisle (70ftx10ft) and heating chamber under south transept (18ftx13ft). Constructed of Cattybrook brick both inside and out, the exterior of red brick and the interior of buff relieved by bands of Bath stone and red brick. Wagon-shaped roof with tie beams across in nave, and chancel roof barrel-shaped with moulded ribs of Glamorgan type. Both roofs covered with Belgian slates. Arcade of pitch-pine with solid, upright octagonal shafts carried up in one piece to the wallplates. Arches

also of pitch-pine filled up in the spandrels with tracery. Height from floor to ridge 41ft, and dimensions of church approximately 129ftx53ft including tower. Sanctuary paved with Godwin's tiles with steps leading to it of wilderness stone. Open benches of pitch-pine. Accommodation for 470 worshippers. Contractor: William Richards of Barry. Cost £2,340. Consecrated on 6 September 1893. (*Barry Dock News*, 8 September 1893)

Comments: St Paul's Church, Barry is as Newman says 'a cheap church of red Cattybrook brick with sparing Bath stone dressings'. (Newman, 147) Despite the cheapness of local Pennant sandstone, which was readily available in the area, and although the architects had intended using stone the matter of cost had to be taken into consideration and they decided to use cheap Cattybrook brick. So restricted was the funding that the nave arcade was built of cheap pitch-pine with octagonal pillars of the same material. The roof was supposed to have been covered with Welsh Bangor slates, but the architects chose to use cheap Belgian slates. Financial restrictions also made it necessary for the church to be built on plain but strong lines without any ornamentation. The original design of the church was never fulfilled and the north aisle was not built until 1906 when more funds were available. The proposed south-east tower was never built. The new north aisle accommodated an additional 236 persons, making the total seating capacity over 700. Organ chamber also erected by Frederick R. Kempson, Cardiff. Cost £4,775. (*Ch. Bldr* (1906), 4)

ST DAVID'S CHURCH, BETTWS

1886: New vestry constructed from a design by E. W. Burnett, architect, of Tondu. (LL/F/72. Bettws. (Glam.): New vestry. Faculty dated 6 May 1886)
1892–3: Restoration of church and addition of new aisle. Petition for faculty stated 'that in consequence of the unsafe and dilapidated condition of the roof of the above named church it is thought a convenient time to restore, enlarge and partly rebuild the fabric from plans and specifications prepared by George E. Halliday of Cardiff'. Halliday restored the church in the Perpendicular style. Work comprised

restoring and renewing parts of dilapidated nave roof and removing west gallery; replacing south-east and south-west windows with stone of more suitable design; replacing dilapidated flooring; and providing new seating where necessary. Chancel arch completely rebuilt and floor of chancel restored. New stonework put to the east and south windows. Porch reroofed and walls repaired. Vestry erected in 1886 taken down and new north aisle and vestry constructed, with arcade to nave having four pointed arches. New pulpit erected. Church fitted with Porritt's hot-air heating system. Accommodation in church increased from 121 to 223 seats by 102 additional sittings. Sculpture and carving executed by William Clarke, Llandaff. (LL/F/73. Restoration and enlargement of church. Bettws. (Glam.) Faculty dated 3 November 1891) Contractor: John W. Rodger, Cardiff. Cost £2,000 partly defrayed by Miss Olive Talbot. Reopened after restoration on 4 August 1893. (*W. Mail*, 5 August 1893)

Comments: Halliday restored the church in the Perpendicular style, which he favoured in the late Victorian period. Although he rebuilt the chancel arch he was not responsible for pulling it down, as the petition for a faculty stated that the present arch had been demolished before Halliday started the work of restoration. We can only assume that it had become dangerous or that the parishioners had it demolished because of its narrowness. Halliday rebuilt the chancel arch with a large pointed arch with double chamfers in the fifteenth-century style in keeping with the rest of the church. By constructing a larger arch he was in fact remodelling the church to suit the new liturgical arrangements of the Victorian Church. Halliday was careful to preserve the surviving ancient features of the church such as the piscina, numerous important mural monuments on the south wall of the chancel and the rood-loft window on the south side as well as the medieval tub-shaped font. His main brief was to enlarge the church for the increasing population of the parish and he achieved this admirably. The work of restoration was due entirely to the generosity of Miss Olive Talbot who spent thousands of pounds restoring and enlarging many churches in Glamorgan at this period.

ST JOHN'S CHURCH, BIRCHGROVE

1890–1: New church built on new site as chapel of ease to St Samlet's Church, Llansamlet. One acre of land given to church by Thomas Jones, Llanfair Grange, Llandovery as executor of the late Captain William Jones of Glanbrane, Llansamlet on behalf of representatives of the late Captain Jones. John Birch Paddon, a local steel magnate and generous churchman decided in 1890 to build a church in Birchgrove because of his concern for the church-going people of the village who had to walk once a month to the parish church of Llansamlet for the communion service. (Ken Pritchard, *St John's Church, Birchgrove, 1891–1991* (Swansea, 1991)) Built in Perpendicular Gothic style consisting of nave, vestry and west tower and west porch, with ample room for eastward extension at some future date. Constructed of local grey Pennant sandstone with Bath stone dressings. External walls of nave strengthened by solid buttresses. No separate chancel built, but space railed off at east end as substitute for chancel. Floored with encaustic tiles and furnished with Communion table. Total length of church 46ft 6ins by 18ft 11ins in width. Nave 34ft 5ins in length and aisle in front of communion rails more than 7ft wide. Height of building 15ft to top of wallplate. Tower 10ft square. Church seated with open benches of pitch-pine. Seating capacity for 200 worshippers. Nave has arch-braced roof of pitch-pine, with principal rafters supported on solid Bath stone corbels. Main entrance to church through west doorway in tower. Plans drawn up by John Birch Paddon, The Drymma, Neath, who paid for the erection of the church. Contractor: Rhys Llewellyn, Birchgrove. Cost £1,700. Consecrated on 27 August 1891. (*The Cambrian*, 28 August 1891)

Comments: St John's Church, Birchgrove is an unpretentious building, but substantial and well built. Paddon did not employ a professional architect but engaged a builder, Rhys Llewellyn of Birchgrove, to construct the church according to Paddon's own design. It is interesting to note that he chose the Perpendicular style, a style which had again become fashionable now that strict correctness of style had been relaxed. It clearly showed that

Paddon was *au fait* with the architectural development of the Gothic style in the late Victorian period. Although he was a senior member of the Royal Institution of Engineers Paddon would have benefited from the advice of a professional ecclesiastical architect. An architect would have advised him to build a chancel and nave first and complete the tower at a later date as was the case at St John the Baptist's Church, Nelson, a mining community in the parish of Llanfabon.

In 1930 the church was extended to the east by two bays. (Ken Pritchard, op. cit., 9)

ST TEILO'S CHURCH, BISHOPSTON

4. Bishopston Church, Gower, Swansea (Source: Geoffrey R. Orrin: Postcard Collection of Glamorgan Churches)

1846: Church roof repaired at a cost of £39 1s 8d raised by a church rate. ICBS grant £25. (ICBS file no. 4419 (1851))

1851–2: Restoration and rearrangement of seating. Restored during incumbency of Revd David Jones, rector of Bishopston (1831–91). Work comprised underpinning church walls and insertion of five new windows of Bath stone in the nave, which were glazed with lead quarries. New wooden floors laid down under seats in nave. Old-fashioned square box pews removed and replaced with open benches of pitch-pine, stained and varnished. Rearrangement of interior seating increased accommodation to 274 seats, of which 144 were reserved for the use of the poorer inhabitants, thirty of whom were seated in

the west gallery, erected in 1831 at a cost of £40. Parapets of tower repaired and new coping stones provided. Roofs of tower and nave repaired and covered with 'Countess Caernarvon slates'. New pulpit erected. Date of restoration recorded on stone plaque above south porch. Architect: William Richards, Swansea. Cost £250. ICBS grant £70. (Geoffrey R. Orrin, 'Church restoration at St Teilo's Church, Bishopston during the nineteenth and early twentieth centuries', *Gower*, 52 (2001), 3–14)

1896: Renovation of church and general repair of interior. Cost defrayed by Thomas Penrice of Kilvrough. (*The Cambrian*, 14 August 1896)

Comments: Unlike many of the other Gower churches, St Teilo's did not undergo any drastic restoration in the Victorian era which changed the character and appearance of the church. In 1851 Bishopston was a poor agricultural parish with no resident gentry. The population at that time had reached its first peak of the nineteenth century when the inhabitants numbered 513. The rector, Revd David Jones, had already increased the number of sittings in the church in 1831, when he was appointed to the living, by the erection of a small west gallery seating thirty worshippers. The restoration work carried out in 1851 was a re-arrangement of the seating to provide more accommodation in the church at a time when the population appeared to be on the increase. The aim was to prevent the drift of parishioners away from the Established Church to dissenting chapels at Murton. The rector was obliged to rearrange the seating in the church since a small and poor community could ill afford to build a north aisle, as at Newcastle, Bridgend. In no way did the restoration work on St Teilo's reflect the influence of the Ecclesiological Society, since the rector was of Low Church persuasion and, unlike many other churches in Glamorgan, Bishopston remained typical of the Georgian period of ugliness and barrenness. The services were of the usual order of extreme Evangelicalism during the long period of sixty years in which the Revd David Jones held the living.

In the years 1926–7 the church was again restored. This comprised the taking down of the low plaster ceiling which revealed a fifteenth-century arch-braced roof of oak. Two old windows of the thirteenth and fifteenth centuries were un-blocked and the interior of the church refurbished. Architect: William Douglas Caröe (1857–1938). Contractors: Cornish & Gaymer, North Walsham. Cost £2,600. Reopened for divine service on 28 July 1927. (*SWDP*, 29 July 1928)

ST JAMES' CHURCH, BLAENGARW

1890: New church built on new site donated by earl of Dunraven. The correspondent in the *Church Builder* wrote, 'It has been decided to build a church at Blaengarw in the Garw Valley. This Valley has developed wonderfully of late and it is essentially necessary that the church should make immediate and adequate provision for the rapidly increasing population. The room now used for Divine Services is only lent temporarily, the accommodation it affords is very inadequate and the building al-together is very uninviting. The proposed church will accommodate 450 persons; all seats are free . . .' (*Ch. Bldr* (1890), 30). Foundation stone laid on 7 July 1890. (*W. Mail*, 8 July 1890) Built in Early English Gothic style by Bruton & Williams, architects of Cardiff. Cruciform in plan consisting of chancel (22ftx19ft), with north vestry and organ chamber on south side giving the appearance of short transepts, nave (61ftx28ft) and western bell-cote. Design of the church criticized by Committee of Architects of ICBS in various respects such as arrangement of seating etc., but also considered unsatisfactory from architectural point of view. The architects replied that it was an unfair condemnation without giving reasons in support and 'as the cost is very limited it would be impossible to introduce much architectural design without exceeding the limit of expenditure'. (ICBS file no. 9398 (1889)) Constructed of local Pennant sandstone with Bath stone dressings. Roof of open timberwork, of red deal, stained and varnished and covered with Portmadoc slates and tile cresting. Ground wood-work all pitch-pine including the open benches; there are also choir stalls. Seating accommodation for 300 worshippers. Windows on north and south sides are plain lancets between solid Early English-style buttresses and east and west windows are of three grouped lancets. Church heated by Porritt's

hot-air system. Contractor: John Rees, Ynysybwl. Cost £1,400. ICBS grant £100. Consecrated on 8 December 1890. (*CGG*, 12 December 1890)

Comments: St James' Church, Blaengarw is a very simple and plain structure, typical of many churches built in the south Wales coalfield area during the final decades of the nineteenth century. In many respects it was superior to some of Bruce Vaughan's utilitarian churches such as St Matthew's, Treorchy erected in 1884. It can only be assumed from the comments of the Committee of Architects of the ICBS that they were too far away in London to appreciate the difficulties encountered by the Anglican Church in raising funds for building permanent stone churches in the industrial areas of Glamorgan, particularly in the diocese of Llandaff at that period. The original contract price of £1,085 was exceeded by extras to £1,400, which was a reasonable price for a plain church at that time accommodating 300 worshippers.

In 1924 a new organ was installed and the organ chamber was rebuilt and raised altering the appear-ance of the building. (M. M. Davies, *The Young Valley: A History of the Church in the Garw Valley* (Blaengarw, 1969), 14)

ST MARY'S CHURCH, BLAENGWRACH

According to the *Western Mail* report on the restora-tion of St Mary's in 1879, the original structure was founded and built in the reign of Queen Elizabeth I and that according to some old documents 'a very low wretched edifice' standing on the same site was restored in 1783. (*W. Mail*, 3 September 1879)
1853: A contemporary newspaper reported that 'the ancient chapel of Blaengwrach having through lapse of time become rather dilapidated it was proposed at a meeting of the parishioners by the incumbent and churchwardens to restore it and render it more meet for the worship of the Most High.' Consequently the fabric of the church was substantially repaired and a west porch added. Restoration initiated by Revd Walter Griffiths, vicar of Glyncorrwg. Reopened after restoration on 13 October 1853. (*CMG*, 15 October 1853)

1879: Restoration and enlargement of church. Work included building new chancel and vestry, lined with black and white glazed bricks. Old-fashioned square box pews removed and replaced by open benches of pitch-pine seating 100 parishioners. Old portion of church reroofed with Caernarfon slates underlined with boards, and new bellcote, constructed of Forest of Dean stone, placed over west gable. Whole of interior refurbished with pulpit, reading desk and seats, all of pitch-pine. Cost £560. Reopened after restoration on 2 September 1879. (*W. Mail*, 3 September 1879)

Comments: In contrast to the account given in the *Western Mail* for 3 September 1879 John Newman states that St Mary's is a rebuilding in 1830 of a chapel of 1704. (Newman, 156) This also contradicts the account given by the eminent local historian, D. Rhys Phillips, in *The History of the Vale of Neath*, published in Swansea in 1925, where he states that 'there is authority for stating that the church was built between 1595 and 1600, for in the latter year George Williams died . . . and was buried therein' (p. 124). The original building erected in 1853, which had no claim to architectural merit and consisting only of a nave and porch, was transformed in 1879 into a typical Victorian church with newly built chancel, vestry and western bellcote and all the appurtenances necessary for the celebration of divine worship according to the new liturgical interpretations of the Anglican Church.

ST MARY THE VIRGIN'S CHURCH, BONVILSTON

1862–3: Restoration and rebuilding. Repairs carried out in 1824 at cost of £120, raised by local subscription, were inadequate to arrest decay of structure which had long been neglected. Consequently, by 1862 the medieval church was in such a dilapidated state that it was virtually rebuilt, only the tower, the fifteenth-century chancel arch and part of the north wall remaining of the original medieval building. (ICBS file no. 5660 (1860)) Rebuilt in Early English Gothic style by John Prichard, with reconstruction following plan of original building. Seating rearranged so as to provide

extra accommodation for sixty-nine parishioners on open benches. Woodwork including seats, choir stalls, altar, pulpit and lectern of pitch-pine. Chancel has an arch-braced roof with diagonal braces, with arches supported on plain stone corbels and decorated wallplates. In addition, vestry and organ chamber, fitted with custom-made organ built by V. G. Vowles of Bristol, constructed on north side of chancel. New porch with high-pitched roof and trefoil arch added on south side of nave. Windows and dressings of church of mustard coloured Bath stone. Seating capacity for 117 worshippers. Cost £1,600. IBCS grant £40. (*MCVG*, 109–113)

1895: In 1895 tower restored on account of its dangerous condition. In addition, peal of bells rehung. Architect: Charles Busteed Fowler, Llandaff. Contractor: W. A. James, Cowbridge. (*Bldr*, 14 September 1895, 191)

Comments: St Mary the Virgin's Church, as it stands today, is an example of Early English Gothic architecture of the nineteenth century and it appears that the reconstruction followed very closely the plan of the old church. Evidence for this can be found in the alignment of the nave and chancel, as the latter had a definite inclination to the north, the east window being out of line with the chancel arch – the phenomenon of the so-called 'weeping chancel'. The windows of the church are well conceived; the window surrounds being of dressed Bath stone. They comprise single and double trefoil-headed lancets with hood moulds, the latter with plate tracery in the head typical of the thirteenth century. The rebuilt south porch with its high-gabled roof is typically Victorian with cusping on the inner arch of the doorway. The mouldings, caps and little shafts with stiff-leaf foliage simply mirror the severe Early English style restoration work within.

In 1908 new choir stalls, altar rails, pulpit and lectern of carved oak, designed by Messrs J. Wippell of Exeter, were erected in the church as a memorial to Joseph Benjamin Brain (d. 1907) and his wife, Ellen Allwood Brain (d. 1908) by their sons and daughters. The pulpit and choir stalls are a matching set and of unusual design, a mixture of classical motifs in the eighteenth-century style executed in Edwardian times. These replaced the pitch-pine furniture erected when the church was restored in 1863. (LL/F/80. New pulpit, lectern, choir-stalls, altar-rails. Faculty dated 27 August 1908)

ST ILLTYD'S CHURCH, NEWCASTLE, BRIDGEND

1850: Due to small size of parish church, which could accommodate only 106 adults and eighty children, and because there were no free sittings for poor of parish, parishioners decided at vestry meeting held on 21 May 1849 to take down nave and rebuild it on a larger scale. (ICBS file no. 4224 (1850)) Consequently, in 1850, St Illtyd's considerably enlarged by new nave and by addition of north aisle, sacristy on north side of chancel and south porch. With exception of chancel, most of church entirely rebuilt and remodelled in Geometrical Gothic style by John Prichard. Seating accommodation in church more than doubled by addition of 115 new sittings. In new church there were 107 appropriated seats, 212 free seats and also 80 seats for children. Nave divided from north aisle by an arcade of three bays constructed of dressed Bath stone. Nave pillars of early fourteenth-century type with flatter and better proportioned bell caps. Roofs all of open Memel timber construction with moulded braces supported on carved stone corbels. Just as on the outside Prichard has taken the opportunity to add little heads wherever possible; at base of each roof corbel, as terminations to arch mouldings, on drop corbels of inner chancel arch and heavily moulded arch into the organ loft. Carving executed by Edward Clarke of Llandaff. Contractors: Herbert and Edward Powell, Neath. Cost £2,400. ICBS grant £120; William Llewellyn; Court Colman £100; C. R. M. Talbot £50; Revd William Lewis £50; Revd Lynche-Blosse £50; Bishop Ollivant £35. Reopened after restoration on 23 December 1850. (*CMG*, 4 January 1851)

1893–4: In 1892 a faculty for proposed new chancel, organ chamber and vestry stated 'that by reason of the chancel of the above church being too small and inconvenient for the due performance of divine worship it is proposed to reconstruct and enlarge the same and to extend the north aisle so as to secure space for an organ chamber and vestry'. (LL/F/587. Restoration and enlargement of church. Faculty dated 24 May 1892) Chancel thus pulled down and rebuilt to larger dimensions and north chancel aisle erected to form organ chamber and choir vestry. Architect: E. M. Bruce Vaughan. Old chancel was 20ft long by 16ft wide and 19ft to apex of roof. New chancel is 28ft 6ins long, 29ft to apex of roof, and 20ft 6ins wide. Foundation stone laid by Miss Emily Talbot, Margam Abbey on 26 April 1893. Light-brown local sandstone used for external work, Bridgend Quarella stone for arches and mullions of windows, Bath stone for ashlar lining, oak for barrel roof of chancel, with bosses decorated with gold and vermillion, teak for north chancel screen, choir stalls and vestry fittings. Chancel floored by Webb & Sons with dark, red, buff and brown tiles. Reredos of Bridgend stone with panels of Halesowen, with the central canopies left unfilled for treatment with sculpture or mosaics at some future date, erected to extend over east end of church. Contractor: Edmund Rees, Pencoed. Cost £3,000. Reopened after restoration on 21 June 1894. (*CGG*, 22 June 1894)

Comments: Prichard restored and rebuilt St Illtyd's in the Geometrical Gothic or early Decorated style which became his favourite idiom. With regard to his design the ICBS suggested that it would be better to lower somewhat the position of the east window of the north aisle, as they felt that internally as well as externally it would improve the composition. On studying the plan of the church it is evident that Prichard positioned the east window of the north aisle at that height so as not to interfere with the north wall of the sacristy. Bruce Vaughan's rebuilding of the chancel of St Illtyd's Church in 1894 was described by Newman as executed in a 'Prichardesque idiom'. (Newman, 159) This was because he reused Prichard's chancel arch, copied Prichard's masonry technique of building walls in thin-coursed Pennant sandstone walling externally and used Prichard's method of using ashlar lining internally. It is interesting to note that Bruce Vaughan decided to use his own personal masonry style at Bargoed Church in 1894 by building external walls of random rock-faced courses when the position was reversed and he added a nave to Prichard's chancel, built in 1877. Probably Bruce Vaughan felt that a twelfth-century church such as St Illtyd's should have narrow-coursed walling in imitation of the medieval style.

In 1915 the panels and niches of the reredos were filled with sculpture. The panels depict the Crucifixion, the Ascension and the Adoration of the Magi, with St David and St Patrick in the niches. Erected as a memorial to the late Richard Knight Prichard of Bryntirion by his family and parishioners. Design by E. M. Bruce Vaughan; sculpture by William Clarke. (*LDM*, Vol. 9, no. 4 (1916), 98)

ST MARY'S CHURCH, NOLTON, BRIDGEND

1834–6: Nolton chapel erected on site of ancient chapel of ease to St Mary's Church, Coity. Foundation stone laid on 21 August 1834 by Revd John Harding, rector of Coity. Chapel cruciform in shape with short chancel, nave with north and south transepts containing high-backed pews, west gallery for organ and choir and west entrance with lobby surmounted by bell turret. Seating accommodation for 280 worshippers. Chapel opened on 5 July 1835. (*The Cambrian*, 8 July 1835) Architect and contractor: William Roberts, Chepstow. Cost £1,190. ICBS grant £325. Consecrated on 9 November 1836. (ICBS file no. 1411 (1834))

1848: Repairs to fabric of church. Cost £40. Llandaff Church Building Society £5. (*CMG*, 18 March 1848, 4)

1885–7: New church built on new site adjacent to Nolton Chapel donated by earl of Dunraven. Built as chapel of ease to St Mary's Church, Coity since old Nolton chapel erected in 1835 could no longer accommodate increasing population of district, which had trebled since 1835 to 4,000 persons by the 1880s. (*Ch. Bldr* (1884), 76) Foundation stone laid on 9 September 1885 by countess of Dunraven. (*W. Mail*, 23 November 1887) Built in Early English Gothic style by John Prichard with assistance of Frederick R. Kempson. Church consists of chancel with aisles, north transept, nave and clerestory and tower (partly built to the height of the north aisle) at north-west corner. External walls

5. Exterior of St Mary's Church, Nolton, Bridgend (Source: Geoffrey R. Orrin: Postcard Collection of Glamorgan Churches)

constructed of Quarella stone with dressings of Box Ground stone, and grey Forest of Dean columns. Steps throughout church of red Forest of Dean stone. Whole pavement of church laid with encaustic tiles by Godwin's of Lugwardine, Herefordshire. Wagon roofs of church of red pine. Open benches of pitch-pine. Pulpit executed in green Quarella stone with Dumfries and green Connemara marble columns. Heating apparatus supplied and fitted by Messrs J. Grundy, London and Tilsey, Manchester. Accommodation for 570 parishioners. Baptistery under tower. Contractor: John Pearce, Minehead, then William Williams, Roath, later William McGaul, Bridgend. Sculpture by William Clarke. Cost £5,260. ICBS grant £60. Consecrated on 23 November 1887. (*CGG*, 25 November 1887)

1898: Tower completed and spire erected measuring 143ft in height. Architect: Frederick R.

Kempson, Llandaff. Contractor: Messrs E. Turner & Sons, Cardiff. (*Bldr*, 14 May 1898, 474)

Comments: The building of St Mary's was beset by numerous difficulties. The contract to build the church was awarded in 1885 to John Pearce of Minehead for £4,415 exclusive of tower and spire. But after a short time Pearce gave up the contract and the Building Committee decided to proceed without a general contract but under the supervision of William Williams of Roath, the clerk of works. Then a new contract for the stonework was taken out with William McGaul of Bridgend at a higher price than that quoted by Pearce. Another complication arose from the death of John Prichard in October 1886. His chief assistant, Frederick R. Kempson, thus supervised the completion of the church. Another temporary setback occurred in December 1886 when a storm damaged most of the stonework of the great west window. The main part of the church was completed in September 1887. However, the original cost of £4,415 had risen to £5,620 as a result of the various setbacks which had occurred during the course of its construction. Kempson completed the church by adhering faithfully to Prichard's design and conception of the building. The aisled nave and chancel were constructed as a harmonious whole, and the general impression of the completed church is one of spaciousness and verticality created by its lofty clerestory, wagon roofs and east and west windows set high in their respective walls. This was in keeping with the style adopted by many architects in the late Victorian period but using later Gothic forms. Kempson completed the tower and spire in a style based on Prichard's church of St Catharine's, Baglan.

ALL SAINTS' CHURCH, PEN-Y-FAI, BRIDGEND

1901–3: New church built on new site as an estate church by Robert William Llewellyn, Court Colman, at the gates of his house. Church designed by Llewellyn but plans redrawn by John Christopher Jones, assisted by his father, John Jones, clerk of works on the Baglan estate, who was involved in building of Prichard's church at Baglan. Built in a Transitional style between Early English Gothic and early Decorated Gothic, as far as can be ascertained with any certainty. First sod on site cut on 22 November 1900, and contract with Messrs Thomas, Watkins & Co. signed in March 1901. Foundation stone laid on 2 May 1901 by Mrs R. W. Llewellyn. (Transcript of a MS made by Colonel Robert Llewellyn, the son of the builder of the church. Deposited with church deeds at the vicarage, Pen-y-fai) Cruciform in plan consisting of chancel, nave, transepts and central tower. External walls built of thin-coursed local Pennant sandstone and ashlar linings of interior and arches, etc. are constructed of green Bridgend stone and buff stone from Ham Hill, Dorset. Reredos carved of alabaster inlaid with green Connemara marble pillars, executed by William Clarke. Three central panels depicting white marble groups of Nativity, Crucifixion and Descent from the Cross are by Goscombe John. Mosaic floor of chancel is green glass laid on cement, with aisles similarly paved. East window of three broad lancets, which are deeply recessed and separated internally by three continuous pointed arches springing from four Silverleigh marble pillars. Trefoil-headed sedilia on south side of chancel exhibit similar marble pillars, but pillars of piscina and credence table of white marble. Lacquered brass communion rails are work of Messrs Benham & Froud, London. Barrel roof of oak to chancel. Choir stalls also constructed of oak and carved by William Clarke, who also executed pulpit of green Quarella stone and Penarth alabaster with red Ogwell marble pillars. Oak used throughout for woodwork of roofs, which are covered with Pembrokeshire slates. Open benches of oak seat 244 worshippers. Heating carried out by Grundy. Font of Carrara marble on a grey marble base is a copy of Thorvaldsen's Angel of Baptism in the Church of Our Lady in Copenhagen. Contractors: Messrs Thomas, Watkins & Co., Swansea. Cost £7,000. Consecrated on 23 November 1903. (*GG*, 27 November 1903)

Comments: William Llewellyn conceived the idea of building All Saints' over a considerable number of years, and when he started work he spared no trouble or expense in making it one of the most elaborately appointed and furnished smaller churches in Glamorgan. It is apparent that the best materials and workmanship were obtained and that artistic taste and skill were liberally lavished upon the sculpture, carvings and adornment that make this church a Victorian period piece. Llewellyn had hoped to emulate Prichard's church of St Catharine's, Baglan, but All Saints' demonstrates both in its structure and fittings the absence of Prichard's genius and architectural skill, both of which are conspicuously lacking in this building. Peter Howell, the architectural historian, regarded it 'more or less a paraphrase of the far superior church at Baglan'. (Peter Howell and Elizabeth Beazley, *The Companion Guide to South Wales* (London, 1977), 282)

ST CLEMENT'S CHURCH, BRITON FERRY

1866: New church built on new site donated by dowager countess of Jersey to provide additional church accommodation in Briton Ferry since the parish church of St Mary's was too small to meet the spiritual needs of the increasing population. Cruciform in plan consisting of polygonal apsidal chancel (36ft 6insx18ft), which has on its north side a sacristy and chapels for organ and choristers on either side, nave (62ft 9insx38ft), including the north and south aisles, which are 9ft wide, south porch and north and south transepts, 17ft 3ins by 13ft. Built in Early English Gothic style with hint of Early French Gothic influence from a design by John Prichard. (ICBS file no. 7139 (1865)) Constructed of local Welsh Pennant sandstone with Combe Down Bath stone dressings. Double bellcote over chancel arch. Nave has arch-braced collar beam roof with carved pendant posts forming canopied niches, some of which are occupied by painted statues. In contrast, aisle roofs are moulded kingpost construction, also arch-braced, with pierced wooden arcade running all around the church above the wallplate. Pillars supporting arch-braced roof have octagonal bases with set-offs and square capitals decorated with stiff-leaf foliage and are constructed entirely of timber. (Personal observation) Accommodation for 468 worshippers; all sittings are free and unappropriated. Contractor: Rees Roderick, Margam. Cost £3,250. ICBS grant

£200; LDCES grant £100; LCBS grant £25; countess of Jersey £1,300; C. R. M. Talbot £100; Richard Hall £100. Opened for divine worship on 7 October 1866. Consecrated on 15 January 1867. (*The Cambrian*, 18 January 1867)

1889: Reredos erected by parishioners and friends of Revd David Lewis (1863–1902) in commemoration of his vicariate of twenty-five years. Designed by Messrs Seddon & Carter, costing £130 and unveiled on Christmas Day, 1889.

1893: Pulpit of Caen stone designed by Jones & Willis, Birmingham dedicated on 28 February 1893. Donated by Revd J. Ll. Thomas, curate.

1900: Church renovated, new vestries added, brass altar-rail erected and new heating apparatus installed. Cost £550. Heating apparatus supplied by Messrs Saunders & Taylor at cost of £96. Tiles supplied by Godwins of Lugwardine. Carving by William Clarke. Reopened and vestries dedicated on 29 October 1900. (*St Clement's Church, Briton Ferry Centenary Souvenir Book* (1967), 7–10)

Comments: Prichard built St Clement's in the Early English Gothic style with Early French Gothic influence. This is suggested by the polygonal apse *per se* and the Early French Gothic-style square capitals with foliage. In comparison with the outside, the interior of the church is very ornate and something of a surprise. The roof is rather complicated because it was conceived of a single design together with the arcading which is constructed entirely of timber. Wooden pillars are unusual and a wooden arcade even more so. Did Prichard use timber as a result of economic restrictions or was it purely an idiosyncratic whim? In 1850, he had used a timber arcade in the restoration of St Michael's Church, Michaelstone-super-Avon, where he incurred the displeasure of the ICBS's Committee of Architects. He repeated this feature to some extent at St Catherine's, Canton (1883–6) when he used wooden springers to carry the vaulted roof of the nave, but in this instance they were supported on clustered shafts of Bath stone. It appears that the wooden pillars and arcade at Briton Ferry were built as an original concept, particularly in the light of the fact that there was only a small deficit on the church when it was completed. Although Prichard's church at Briton Ferry cannot be counted among his most successful churches it was nevertheless remarkable for its original timber arcade and unique roof construction.

ST MARY'S CHURCH, LLANSAWEL, BRITON FERRY

1870–1: Church refloored and reseated to accommodate 108 parishioners. General repairs to fabric of church also carried out. Architect: Henry Francis Clarke, Briton Ferry. (ICBS file no. 7139 (1870))
1891–2: Old chancel and nave of church, described as of a nondescript style and built *c.*1740, demolished and new church rebuilt on same site but on a larger scale. Last service in old church took place on 2 June 1891. The correspondent in the *Church Builder* wrote: 'It is used as a Welsh church and is not endowed. The inhabitants are composed of manufacturers, miners and seafarers and the approximate number of poor inhabitants is 5,700. Estimated cost £1,890.' (*Ch. Bldr* (1891), 28) Medieval square tower of old church retained. Built as separate place of worship for Welsh-speaking population of Briton Ferry. (*BN*, 26 June 1891, 874) Foundation stone laid on 30 July 1891 by Lady Caroline Jenkins, sister of earl of Jersey. Architect: John Coates Carter of Seddon & Carter, but work carried out under superintendence of Henry Francis Clarke, Briton Ferry. Contractor: Walter Dowland, Abergavenny. (*Briton Ferry Parish Magazine*, June 1891, 3–4) Church consists of chancel, nave, south porch and embattled western tower. Constructed of local Pennant sandstone plastered internally with red brick dressings. A very simple – almost barn-like – arcade has been used in the nave. Chancel a continuation of nave and distinguished from latter by three-tiered barrel roof. Open benches of pitch-pine. Seating accommodation increased from 108 to 346 seats. Norman font from old church placed in body of nave near south door. Cost £1,775. IBCS grant £200; Bishop of Llandaff's Fund £300. Consecrated on 27 May 1892. (*Briton Ferry Parish Magazine*, March 1892, 2–4)

Comments: St Mary's was built as cheaply as possible and, with this object in mind, a simple, barn-like arcade constructed entirely of timber was used in the nave, similar to Carter's church at Melincryddan, Neath which was erected about the same time. The continuous roof construction is characteristic of Carter's work at that date in Glamorgan. Although the nave and chancel of St Mary's were demolished because they were devoid of any architectural merit and too small to accommodate the Welsh-speaking parishioners, the new structure was just as bereft of architectural character as the old church with its barn-like nave. The old Norman tower stood incongruously attached to this modern church building. Nevertheless the rebuilding of the church did achieve its main purpose which was to provide sufficient church accommodation for the Welsh-speaking parishioners of Briton Ferry.

ST THEODORE'S CHURCH, BRYNCETHIN
(Demolished *c.*1995)

1895–6: New church built on new site as chapel of ease to St Bride's Church, St Bride's Minor. The correspondent in the *Church Builder* reported that 'The proposed church has been sadly needed for many years. The district is two miles from the parish church and the population is growing rapidly. The Parish church which was in a very dilapidated condition has been restored and the schools enlarged in order to avoid a Board school. The parish is a very poor one, great strain has been put upon the inhabitants for years for church needs and they have subscribed most liberally but are quite unable to provide all the necessary funds.' (*Ch. Bldr* (1896), 27) Built in Decorated Gothic style from designs by Edward Jenkin Williams of Bruton & Williams, Cardiff. Plans sent back for amendment several times regarding thickness of walls, design of roof and space between benches. Plans finally approved in February 1893. (ICBS file no. 9693 (1891)) Church consisted of chancel, nave with west doorway, north aisle, vestry and organ chamber on north side of chancel, south porch and western bellcote. Constructed of Welsh Pennant sandstone with Bath stone dressings. East window of three cinquefoiled lights with tracery in form of two cinquefoils and one quatrefoil in apex. West window of four cinquefoiled lights with three large trefoils in head.

6. Old Church, Cadoxton (Source: Geoffrey R. Orrin: Postcard Collection of Glamorgan Churches)

Floors of deal under seats, aisles of marble mosaic with steps to chancel and vestry and at Communion rail and altar of marble. Hard stone steps fitted to all doorways. Chancel divided from nave by chancel arch springing from plain imposts and by railed oak screen with crosses surmounting low stone wall. Chancel, nave and north aisle have arch-braced roofs whose principals are supported on stone corbels. Pulpit of panelled oak on moulded stone base with stone steps. Open benches of pitch-pine, stained and varnished in imitation of oak. Seating accommodation for 240 worshippers. Heated by Porritt's patent heating apparatus with a pilot stove in vestry. Contractor: A. J. Howell, Cardiff. (*Bldr*, 4 July 1896, 15) Cost £1,560. ICBS grant £100; Bishop of Llandaff's Fund £300. Consecrated on 18 June 1896. (*W. Mail*, 19 June 1896).

Comments: Although built in the Decorated Gothic style, St Theodore's lacked any of the ornamentation expected of this style of architecture. It was a typical Victorian church, built in a plain but solid fashion in the tradition of the Anglican Church in Glamorgan to provide additional church accommodation in an industrialized parish where the popu-

lation had increased dramatically in a district some miles from the ancient parish church.

ST CADOC'S CHURCH, CADOXTON-JUXTA-BARRY

1870: Sir Stephen Glynne visited the church in September 1865 and his account is the only description that exists before the extensive restoration twenty years later. He described the east window, inserted in 1828 as 'modern and poor'. (Sir Stephen R. Glynne, 'Notes on the older churches in the four Welsh dioceses', *Arch. Camb.* (1901), 246–7)

1885: Restoration carried out during incumbency of Revd Ebenezer Morris, rector of Cadoxton from 1871 to 1902. In a letter dated 15 January 1885, Morris explained his reasons for restoring the church as follows: 'As for our present Church at all meeting the future requirements of the parish it is simply absurd. One can't put an imp. gal. into an imp. ½ pint mug. If I had my way, it wd. be a wholly new Church in a New Situation.' Restoration commenced in March 1885 shortly after the granting of a faculty. Work limited to rebuilding of nave and renovation of lower part of tower under supervision of architect, John Price Jones of Cardiff. It was 'to be done in the Best Manner using only the very best materials of the different kinds required, wrot and fixed and fitted in the Best style and all left perfect at Completion'. Contractors further instructed that 'the works are simply works of restoration and care must be taken to keep every feature of the church as it is of present'. (LL/F/90. Restoration of church. Faculty dated 19 March 1885) New rafters of nave roof overlaid with red match boarding and felt and covered with 'best Blue Duchess Palmerston Quarries slates'. 'Best Combedown' Bath stone used for roof ridges and gable copings with cross at east end. Floor of nave excavated to depth of six inches and filled with fine concrete and old paving carefully replaced in aisle to carry new open benches of pitch-pine which replaced the old-fashioned, dilapidated box pews, which could only accommodate 100 worshippers. Windows fitted with 'fixed sash windows' and glazed with coloured pattern 'tinted Cathedral glass of approved quality'. New doors of red deal fitted to tower and new belfry put in. New pulpit erected. Rood staircase, walled up since the Reformation, exposed and masonry cleaned. Inside was discovered a fine octagonal holy-water stoup which was newly faced before being replaced in its traditional position on right side of south door. Font, cleaned of whitewash, moved to its traditional position near south door and fitted with new ornamental metal cover. Contractors: Jones Bros, Cardiff. Cost £600. (Brian C. Luxton, *St Cadoc's Church: A History of the Village Church, Cadoxton-juxta-Barry* (Barry, 1980), 46–56)

Comments: David Jones of Wallington, a severe critic of Victorian restoration, made no disparaging remarks when he visited the church on 20 September 1888. (David Jones of Wallington, *Notes on Some Glamorgan Churches, 1881–1888* (Cardiff Central Library, MS.1.187)) This thorough Victorian restoration of St Cadoc's in 1885 achieved two purposes: firstly it restored the dilapidated fabric of parts of the church and secondly it stressed by its ecclesiological reordering the change of liturgical emphasis away from the

pulpit and onto the sanctuary and altar where the Holy Eucharist was celebrated. The rector, Revd Ebenezer Morris, was one of the few influential clergy in Glamorgan. He was educated at Trinity College, Cambridge in the late 1850s and no doubt had come under the influence of the Ecclesiological Society, which advocated such changes.

ST CADOC'S CHURCH, CADOXTON-JUXTA-NEATH

1843–4: Petition for faculty for rebuilding stated that 'the church is so greatly out of repair and the walls have become so dangerous that it is thought impracticable to repair the sacred edifice'. (LL/F/99. Faculty dated 30 June 1843) However, chancel and nave partly rebuilt and church enlarged by addition of north aisle with tiered seats facing south into nave. Architect: William Richards, Swansea. Contractor: John Harris, Neath. Cost £1,500. Reopened after rebuilding on 18 December 1844. (*CMG*, 28 December 1844)

1872: Restoration of church. Work consisted of reseating with open benches, relevelling and re-flooring nave and north aisle. Removal of west gallery and stairs. Apex of chancel arch raised six feet above sanctuary steps. New wider arch placed under tower. Pulpit removed from its position against centre of south wall and placed on north side of chancel arch. Open benches in north aisle placed to face east instead of south towards the old position of pulpit. Arcade along north aisle raised. West doors to north aisle closed up and replaced by three-light window. Seating capacity increased by an additional thirty-two sittings to accommodate 432 worshippers. Contractor: John Harris, Neath. Cost £980. Benefactor: Nash Edwards Vaughan, Rheola (north aisle). (LL/F/101. Reflooring and reseating. Faculty dated 22 February 1872) Reopened after restoration on 10 October 1872. (*The Cambrian*, 18 October 1872)

1883: Construction of organ chamber from space gained by 1872 restoration. Organ renovated at cost of £506. In 1883 organ rebuilt and enlarged by Vowles of Bristol. Architect: E. H. Lingen Barker, Hereford. (LL/F/102. Alteration of organ chamber. Faculty dated 18 September 1882)

1897: Restoration of tower. Parapets lowered and tower repointed. Architect: Charles B. Fowler of Kempson & Fowler, Llandaff. Contractor: William Clarke, Llandaff. Cost £300. (*Bldr*, 10 July 1897, 32)

Comments: The decision taken to enlarge St Cadoc's by the addition of a north aisle in 1843 was a compromise solution between two influential families in the parish, one of whom wished to rebuild the church, while the other felt that the dilapidation of the structure had been overstated and was in favour of restoration. (D. Rhys Phillips, *The History of the Vale of Neath* (Swansea, 1925), 73) As at St Cadoc's, Cadoxton-juxta-Barry, the typical Victorian restoration and reordering of the church in 1872 changed the whole focus of the congregation away from the pulpit and onto the chancel and altar, thus bringing the church into line with the new liturgical arrangements demanded by the Anglican Church revival in the second half of the nineteenth century.

In 1909 an alabaster font on marble pillars was erected in the church by parishioners as a memorial to Lewis Jones, vicar of the parish (1875–99). (Keith Tucker, *A History of St Catwg's Church* (1990), 25–6)

ST MARY THE VIRGIN'S CHURCH, CAERAU

(Deconsecrated 1973 – in ruins)

1885–6: Petition for faculty to repair and rebuild parish church, dated 1 January 1885, stated 'that the church was in such bad repair as to render it unfit for usual parochial services'. Thus a faculty was issued according to John Prichard's specification which is still extant. Work included taking down four corners of nave and south-west corner of porch and rebuilding them using old and new quoins. New roof of red pine raised on nave and covered externally by green Pembrokeshire slates crowned with ridge cresting of Bath stone. Chancel roof treated correspondingly. New steps constructed of red Forest of Dean stone and movable chairs placed on ventilated boarded floors which rested on brick piers set in concrete. Centre aisle of nave, chancel, and porch as well as tower floor and west end of nave paved with encaustic tiles. New window of two trefoil-headed lights inserted into north wall of nave. New furniture, doors and ironwork provided. All new doorways built of Box Ground stone and relieving arches constructed of Pennant sandstone. Chancel arch renewed in Bath stone, remains of ancient rood-loft taken down and tower arch replaced by one of larger span. Cost £760. (LL/F/105. Repair of church and belfry tower. Faculty dated 19 March 1885)

Comments: St Mary the Virgin's Church, Caerau, like many other parishes in Glamorgan, suffered from non-resident incumbents and pluralism. Consequently the fabric of the church had been neglected during the eighteenth and nineteenth centuries, so that by 1885 it was in need of a thorough restoration and rebuilding. The restoration, carried out by John Prichard, could certainly be described as 'destructive' and many features of the medieval church were lost forever, including the chancel and tower arches and the remains of the rood-loft arrangement.

ST DAVID'S CHURCH, CAERAU-WITH-ELY

1871: New church built on new site given by Baroness Windsor of St Fagans. Foundation stone laid on 7 March by bishop of Llandaff. (*CMG*, 11 March 1871) Built in Early English Gothic style by John Prichard, consisting only of nave (54ftx28ft) and north porch. Nave lighted by simple window in west end consisting of five trefoil-headed lights under an arch with hood mould. From this the west gable is surmounted by well-proportioned bellcote. Nave further lighted by trefoil-headed couplet windows dividing bay by substantial pier enriched on inside by isolated shaft. There are three of these windows on the south and two on north side separated externally by two-stage buttresses. Constructed of local Welsh Pennant sandstone with Bath stone dressings. Interior of nave fitted with open benches which seat 232 parishioners. At east end of nave were three arches, which were bricked up – the central and larger one would open into the future chancel and the smaller ones to chancel aisles. Seating for 200 worshippers. Consecrated on 23 November 1871. Contractor: J. Williams, Canton,

Cardiff. Cost £900. ICBS grant £80; LDCES grant £100. (*W. Mail*, 24 November 1871)

1881–2: New chancel added to church with twenty-two additional seats by Prichard. East window of three trefoil-headed lights. Opened for divine worship on 10 May 1882. Cost £400. ICBS grant £15. (*W. Mail*, 12 May 1882)

Comments: Prichard's original plan was for a chapel and vestry to flank the chancel, but these were never built, as the present building clearly shows. The striking features of Prichard's design of the nave are the trefoil-headed couplet windows, three on the south, and two on the north, shafted internally. The composition of the west facade of the church is particularly good. It exhibits a great breadth of wall surface and an expression of strength combined with fine detailing. Although Prichard was restricted by lack of funds the design of the church shows his skill and thought.

ST MARTIN'S CHURCH, CAERPHILLY

1874–9: Old parish church, known as St Martin's Chapel, erected in 1821 by Edward Haycock of Shrewsbury, had become too dilapidated for use and too small for crowds that flocked there to worship. Thus new church built on piece of land adjoining old churchyard. Original design prepared in 1870 by Charles Buckeridge (d. 1873) and, after his death, work transferred to John Loughborough Pearson. (ICBS file nos 272 (1821) and 7647 (1874)) Built in Early English Gothic style consisting of chancel, nave, north and south aisles, vestry, organ chamber, clerestory and north porch. Constructed of Pwllypant Pennant sandstone and Bath stone, latter used for interior, with Bath stone dressings. East and west windows of five trefoiled lights with Geometrical-style tracery in head. Owing to peculiarity of site, chancel is of some considerable height externally as ground falls from west to east, so that east wall is supported by massive buttresses. Roof of chancel barrel-shaped and of three bays. Chancel laid with encaustic tiles and containing oak choir stalls. Altar, pulpit and altar-desks are work of William John of St Fagans.

Nave divided from chancel by low screen wall with fine chancel arch above it, springing from bell-shaped capitals on clustered shafts. Roof of nave, which is composed of open timber, arched. Nave separated from aisles by arcades of four bays with pointed arches springing from moulded circular capitals on round pillars. Aisles lighted by three-light windows with plate tracery above between solid buttresses. The open benches, free and un-appropriated, are constructed of American pitch-pine and seat about 300 worshippers. Font is that removed from old church. Contractor: Messrs Wall & Hook, Brinscombe, Gloucestershire. Cost £5,500. ICBS grant £100; LDCES grant £100. (*BN*, 26 December 1879, 814) Consecrated on 17 December 1879. (*W. Mail*, 18 December 1879)

Comments: Although the general style of St Martin's is Early English, as depicted in the double-chamfered nave arches on short round pillars with modestly moulded mid-period-style capitals, the arches into the transepts are quite different; the columns are more slender and the capitals deeper and more bell-shaped, of a style consistent with the early part of the fourteenth century. Its verticality and spaciousness show a certain shift towards late Victorian forms of church architecture.

In the years 1904–5 the church was extended to the west by two additional bays, providing an additional 293 seats, making in all 575 sittings. Cost £3,300. Architect: George E. Halliday, Cardiff. (*Ch. Bldr* (1904), 42) In the years 1907–10 the north tower was erected by Halliday. Contractors: Messrs E. Turner & Sons, Cardiff. Cost £1,500. (*W. Mail*, 15 March 1911)

ALL SAINTS' CHURCH, CARDIFF
(Church made redundant in 1901 and demolished in 1980)

1854–6: New church built on new site as Welsh church for Cardiff at sole expense of marchioness of Bute. Foundation stone laid on 5 July 1854 by 9-year-old marquess of Bute. (*CMG*, 9 July 1854) Built in Transitional Neo-Norman or Anglo-Norman style by Alexander Roos, architect to Bute estate. It consisted of apsidal chancel with vestry,

7. All Saints' Church, Tyndall Street, Cardiff (Source: Stewart Williams, *Cardiff Yesterday*, Vol. 10 (Barry, 1980), pl. 145) (By kind permission of Stewart Williams, Barry)

nave with west gallery and tower with spire at south-west corner. Constructed of Newbridge sandstone with Bath stone dressings. Principal entrance to nave and west gallery was through base of tower which formed porch. Tower square and Norman in style up to belfry and surmounted by octagonal spire in Early English style – height of both tower and steeple 105ft. Nave 80ftx34ft with semicircular apse (25ft wide and 16ft deep) at east end. Windows in side walls plain Norman, arched and filled with diagonal cross-lined glass instead of lead frames. Three windows in apse glazed in same style with coloured glass. Gallery, pulpit, reading desk and pews stained and varnished in dark oak. Roof of open timber framed of deal stained in imitation of oak. Octagonal pedestal font of Bath stone just within entrance to tower. Pillars supporting arch of apse finished with carved capitals in white stone. Communion rails bronzed and Norman in style. Church accommodated about 500 worshippers. (*Bldr*, 26 April 1856, 232) Contractor: W. Griffiths, Cardiff. Cost £4,000. LDCES grant: £200. Opened for divine worship on 10 April 1856. (*CMG*, 12 April 1856) Consecrated on 13 December 1866. (John C. Read, *The Church in Our City* (Cardiff, 1954), 25)

Comments: The church was entirely Neo-Norman in concept apart from the Early English-style broach spire, ribbed and with small gabled lights. The spire was not part of the original design, but the marchioness of Bute subsequently determined on its erection as a memorial to Tyndall Bruce, one of the young marquess's trustees. Apart from the spire, the shallow clasping buttresses, the corbel table all round the nave and the apsidal chancel were all in the Norman style. So too were the round-headed windows which would have originally come from the twelfth century. Though intended for Welsh services the church served that purpose for only a few years; it was badly situated in the midst of a non-Welsh-speaking population composed chiefly of Irish immigrants.

ST AGNES' CHURCH, ROATH, CARDIFF
(Demolished in 1980s)

1886: New church built on new site, which had its origins in small mission chapel opened in Bertram Street, Cardiff on 21 January 1884. Built in 1886 by a 'Mr Taylor' as daughter church to St Margaret's Church, Roath to provide additional church accommodation for rapidly increasing population of parish. Small and architecturally insignificant building, but interior provided a marked contrast to rather drab exterior. Dominant feature of church was the high altar with its panelled reredos rising from the altar almost to the roof. Organ stood on south side of chancel. Chancel divided from nave by single step, and in nave were two altars against south and north walls. (Revd John R. Guy, 'Churches of Cardiff', *South Wales Echo*, 8 May 1964) Church accommodated 120 worshippers. Opened for divine worship on 31 August 1886. (John C. Read, *The Church in Our City* (Cardiff, 1954), 53)

Comments: St Agnes' was prominent among the churches in Cardiff associated with the Anglo-Catholic movement towards the end of the nineteenth century.

ST ANDREW'S CHURCH, CARDIFF
(Now Eglwys Dewi Sant)

1860–3: New church built on new site given by third marquess of Bute as chapel of ease to St John the Baptist's Church, Cardiff in response to increased demand for church accommodation in town. Foundation stone laid on 21 June 1860 by John Boyle, one of trustees of Bute estate. (*CMG*, 23 June 1860) Shortly after the foundation stone was laid work progressed rapidly until it was found that the erection of such a building would exceed the sum intended, and work was stopped for lack of adequate funds. There was a considerable gap before Alexander Roos, architect to Lord Bute, received instructions to complete the building by constructing the chancel and roof of the church and by reducing the cost. Church designed originally by John Prichard. Built in Early English Gothic style consisting of nave with narrow aisles on either side, which are merely passages to pews, west porch and chancel with vestries. Constructed of Newbridge stone with bands of Bath stone. Walls divided into compartments which were filled with multicoloured popple stone. Nave is 80ft long by 63ft wide. Carving of capitals of pillars done by Mr Grierson of Cardiff. Internal surface of walls as carried out

in nave to height of clerestory consist of yellow brick facework with bands of Bath stone. Rest of building plastered in the ordinary way. East window of three lights with Geometrical-style tracery. Nave lighted by two-light clerestory windows above aisle roofs. (*Bldr*, 21 March 1863, 210) Church accommodates 583 persons. Contractor: Thomas Williams, Cardiff. Cost £2,254. ICBS grant £300. Consecrated on 3 March 1863. (*CMG*, 7 March 1863)

1885: New transepts added and church restored by William Butterfield. (LL/F/193. Restoration and enlargement. Faculty dated 25 March 1885)

Comments: St Andrew's bears the work of two different hands, Prichard's and Roos's. Thus, the chancel instead of being the most ornamental, as laid down by the tenets of the Ecclesiological Society, is the plainest, whereas the nave, with arcades reaching as high as the clerestory, is the most ornate. The nave had narrow aisles three to four feet wide on either side which act merely as passages to the pews. Prichard's design of the nave was original in that the introduction of these 'passage aisles' had the advantage of having no columns to obstruct the view of the chancel for the congregation. St Andrew's was Prichard's first attempt at constructional polychromy, with his use of compartments of popple stone used as a type of random treatment in keeping with the High Victorian period. These had been influenced for example by thirteenth-century flint and stone churches in areas where there was a dearth of good building materials.

ST ANNE'S CHURCH, ROATH, CARDIFF

1886–7: New church built on new site. Foundation stone laid on 26 June 1886. (John C. Read, *The Church in Our City* (Cardiff, 1954), 52) Built in early Decorated Gothic style by Joseph Arthur Reeve of Cardiff. Church consists of chancel and nave, with north aisle. Constructed of brick with Newbridge stone facings with external dressings of Box Ground Bath stone. Internally, dressings of Corsham Down stone with remainder of wall surfaces plastered. East window of three trefoiled

8. St Anne's Church, Roath, Cardiff. Archt. Mr J. Arthur Reeve (Source: *The Builder*, 5 November 1887, p. 632)

lights with moulded mullions and clustered column jambs surmounted by richly decorated tracery. Chancel lighted on each side two single-light windows with pointed heads and moulded jambs. North and south of chancel are moulded transept arches at present blocked up. Roof of chancel has panelled wooden ceiling with moulded ribs. Chancel arch carved with richly moulded arches of wood and surmounted by a bell flèche. Intermediate arches between chancel and east end also of wood. Chancel floor laid with four-inch red tiles, and steps of Robin Hood stone with wood platform on either side of choir stalls. Roof of nave is an open timber structure with tie-beams. Nave added in 1893, but to a radically modified design. Accommodation for 250 parishioners on individual chairs. (*Bldr*, 5 November 1887, 632) Contractor: Messrs S. Shepton & Sons, Cardiff. Cost £2,500. Bishop of Llandaff's Fund £100. (*Cardiff Times*, 1 October 1887)

Comments: The unusual feature of St Anne's is the chancel arch carved of wood, which is almost unique in Glamorgan churches. The original design of the nave was never carried out due to financial restraints and consequently the nave dates from 1893. This accounts for the unusual shape of the church with its lofty three-bay chancel, which is in sharp contrast to the much plainer, lower nave with its temporary west end. Consequently, the whole of the church is dominated by the chancel.

The south aisle was not added until 1937 by Caröe & Passmore. (Revd John R. Guy, 'Churches of Cardiff', *South Wales Echo*, 29 May 1964)

ST CATHERINE'S CHURCH, CANTON, CARDIFF

1883–6: New church built on new site purchased from grant made by the Ecclesiastical Commissioners. Cardiff's westward growth in latter part of nineteenth century caused creation of new parishes, such as Canton, out of medieval parish of Llandaff. Continued increase in population of Canton soon rendered one parish of St John the Evangelist too small, and in 1883 St Catherine's was built to meet demand for additional accommodation. (Revd John R. Guy, 'Churches of Cardiff', *South Wales Echo*, 28 August 1964) Corner stone laid on 14 November 1883 by Mrs Catherine Vaughan, wife of dean of Llandaff. (*W. Mail*, 15 November 1883) Built in early Decorated Gothic style by John Prichard, consisting of nave, north and south aisles each of three bays and south porch. Exterior walls constructed of Pennant sandstone and interior walls of yellow brick with bands and patterns in red and black brick. Arcade, constructed of wood instead of stone, forms part of roof construction which is supported on clustered shafts of Bath stone. Roof boarded and panelled and covered with Broseley tiles. Open benches of red pine. Accommodation for 422 worshippers. Heating apparatus by Robert Renton Gibbs, Liverpool. (*BN*, 23 November 1883, 823) Contractor: Joseph Shepton, Cardiff. Cost £2,420. ICBS grant £200; LDCES grant £100; Dean Vaughan £1,000. Opened for divine worship on 7 January 1885. Consecrated on 18 August 1886. (John C. Read, *The Church in Our City* (Cardiff, 1954), 29–30)

1892–3: Completion of church in early Decorated Gothic style by addition of chancel with vestries and south chancel aisle with organ chamber and bellcote over chancel arch. Architect: Frederick R. Kempson, Cardiff. Foundation stone of chancel laid on 9 March 1892 by Mrs Vaughan. (*W. Mail*, 10 March 1892) Chancel rectangular in form with three-light traceried east window and two-light traceried window in east end of chancel aisle. Outer walls constructed of Treforest sandstone with Bath stone dressings. Floor laid with encaustic tiles. (*Bldr*, 14 October 1893, 287) Seating accommodation for 836 worshippers. Contractor: W. Symonds, Cardiff. Cost £2,450. Consecrated on 27 September 1893. (*W. Mail*, 28 September 1893)

1899: Completion of church by addition of two bays at west end. Architect: George E. Halliday, Cardiff. Cost £2,800. (*Evening Express*, 7 May 1901. Round the Churches: No.10. St Catherine's, Canton, Cardiff)

Comments: The building of St Catherine's resembled closely that of St John the Evangelist's Church, Canton, which was also designed by John Prichard. In both instances the bishop of Llandaff insisted on the nave being constructed first so that more church accommodation would be provided for this densely populated parish. Realizing that funds were limited, Prichard built the arcade of the nave of St Catherine's Church of wood, a technique that he had used on previous occasions, for example, St Michael's Church, Michaelstone-super-Avon (1851) and St Clement's Church, Briton Ferry (1866). The cruciform plan which Prichard intended for St Catherine's Church proved over-ambitious and was never fulfilled.

ST DYFRIG'S CHURCH, CARDIFF
(Church demolished 1969)

1888–9: New church built on new site as a new district church in the parish of St Mary's, Cardiff. Church intended to seat 936 persons, mostly of the working class – railwaymen, clerks, artisans and labourers. (*Ch. Bldr* (1888), 25) Replaced St Dyfrig's Mission opened on 26 April 1876. Foundation stone laid in 1888 by Lady Hill of Llandaff. (John C. Read, *The Church in Our City* (Cardiff, 1954), 33–4) First stage of church built according to designs by John Dando Sedding in Early English Gothic style. Constructed of Doulting stone outside and Bath stone inside. It consisted of chancel and two bays of the nave, with north and south aisles, accommodating 400 worshippers. East window of three two-light windows with plate tracery in heads. Open timber roof of chancel with kingpost. Cost £6,000. ICBS grant £450; Bishop of Llandaff's Fund £400. Consecrated on 14 November 1893 and on 11 May 1895 an Order in Council assigned it as a district chapelry. (*Cardiff Times*, 18 November 1893)

Comments: The style of St Dyfrig's was simple and effective and was a free adaptation of the Early English Gothic style, which Sedding chose to use in this instance instead of the late Gothic forms that were fashionable at the time. The Victorian fittings to the church, which have now been transferred to the Cardiff churches of St Mary, St Dyfrig and St Samson, were made in the best Sedding tradition.

In 1904 a reredos was erected in the chancel from a design by Henry Wilson of Kent as a memorial to the parents of Hector Allan Coe. (LL/F/201: Reredos. Faculty dated 15 September 1904) In 1907 the church was enlarged by the addition of three bays which accommodated an additional 400 worshippers. Architect: Arthur Grove of London. Contractor: Messrs James Allan & Co., Cardiff. Cost: £3,689. (*Bldr*, 23 March 1907, 372) Consecrated on 8 October 1907. (*W. Mail*, 8 October 1907)

EGLWYS DEWI SANT, CARDIFF
(Destroyed in Cardiff blitz, January 1941)

1890–1: New church built on new site given by Lord Tredegar. Built to replace Capel Dewi Sant Mission Church erected in the years 1888–9 on the same site. (*Ch. Bldr* (1890), 30) Foundation stone laid on 2 July 1890 by Lord Tredegar. (*W. Mail*, 3 July 1890) Built in Perpendicular Gothic style by E. M. Bruce Vaughan, consisting of chancel (38ft 6insx22ft 3ins), vestry, organ chamber, nave (67ftx24ft 3ins), north and south aisles (67ftx11ft 6ins), and a north-eastern tower (68ft high, with a 34ft spire). (*BN*, 11 July 1890, 61) Principal entrance to church through a stone porch on north side, but west entrance also provided. Constructed of Maesycymmer sandstone laid in thin courses with dressings of windows and doors of Box Ground stone. Roof covered with small green Bangor slates. Chancel roof barrel-shaped, divided into three bays and constructed of unpolished pitch-pine. Roofs of nave and aisles similar but divided into five bays with hammerbeam principals. East window of five lights with moulded jambs and mullions with traceried arch. West window was similar in design. Nave divided from aisles by arcades of pointed arches carried on octagonal columns with moulded caps and bases. These arches were surmounted by a clerestory pierced with two-light windows; the aisles being lighted with traceried windows of different designs between two-stage buttresses. Sanctuary, chancel

and passages in nave paved with encaustic tiles of a beautiful pattern, rich in colour, from Carter's works in Poole, Dorset. Pulpit of a very rich design in Riga oak made by Jones & Willis of Birmingham. Open benches of unpolished oak. Reredos of Caen stone. Accommodation for 500 worshippers. Heating apparatus installed by Robert Renton Gibbs of Liverpool. Contractor: Samuel Shepton, Cardiff. Cost £5,500. ICBS grant £200;. Bishop of Llandaff's Fund £400. (*W. Mail*, 22 October 1891)

Comments: Bruce Vaughan built the church in a late Gothic form, Perpendicular Gothic, a style that was to become fashionable in the latter part of the nineteenth century. He concentrated the enriched work in the chancel with its reredos of Caen stone. Its outstanding feature was the east window of five lofty lights with two orders of mouldings to the jambs and mullions and with the arch filled with rectilinear tracery. It was, to date, Bruce Vaughan's finest ecclesiastical building in Glamorgan.

ST GERMAN'S CHURCH, ROATH, CARDIFF

1882–4: New church built on new site given by Lord Tredegar. A circular issued by the vicar and churchwardens of the parish appealing for subscriptions for the new church said that the increase in the population had been so great in the last ten years, rising from 8,000 to 25,000, that it had been impossible to meet the demands for church accommodation. (*Ch. Bldr* (1882), 37) Foundation stone laid on 18 April 1882 by Lord Tredegar. (*W. Mail*, 19 April 1882) Built in late Decorated Gothic style according to designs by Bodley & Garner, London. It consists of chancel with aisles and nave with aisles. A flèche 50ft high above the ridge of the roof over the chancel arch contains a sanctus bell. Church's internal dimensions are 120ft in length by 62ft in width. The chancel arch, from floor level to apex, is 55ft high. Constructed of local Swelldon stone with Bath stone dressings and roof covered with blue Welsh slates. East window of six lights with rich flowing tracery in head carried on Forest of Dean mullions and transoms. Clerestoried chancel. Chancel roof

9. New Church of St German's, Cardiff. G. F. Bodley & T. Garner, 14 South Square, Gray's Inn (Source: *The Building News*, 23 December 1881)

carried by three moulded Bath stone arches, supported by three-quarter Bath stone columns resting on moulded corbels. Main altar approached by six steps of slate filled with Hopton Wood stone and slates, the pattern giving the appearance of black and white marble. Behind the altar is a super-altar surmounted by silver cross and reredos. From chancel is suspended a richly carved rood resting on a massive moulded beam supported on two carved corbels supplied by Messrs Farmer & Brindley, London. Roofs of nave and north and south aisles divided by Bath stone arches springing from eight moulded columns. Nave has no clerestory, but tall aisles. Principal entrance to church through west and south-west doors. Flying buttresses spring from dividing walls of aisles. Floors of nave and aisles laid with wood blocks. In aisle of south chancel is organ-loft approached by winding stone stairs. Brass fittings supplied by Messrs Watt & Co., Baker Street, London. (*Bldr*, 15 November 1884, 675) Church accommodates 1,000 worshippers on separate chairs. Contractor: Messrs S. Shepton & Sons, Cardiff. Cost £12,000. ICBS grant £500; Bishop of Llandaff's Fund £300. Opened for divine worship on 1 October 1884. Consecrated on 9 March 1886. (*W. Mail*, 2 October 1884)

1887: Pulpit by Cecil Hare of Bodley & Hare erected. Also organ case. (Newman, 301)

1898: Font dedicated on 18 May 1898. Designed by G. F. Bodley and executed by Messrs R. Rattee & Kett, Cambridge in memory of Harry North (d. 1894). (Marmaduke Warner and A. C. Hooper (eds), *The History of Roath St German's* (Cardiff, 1934), 47)

Comments: The interior of St German's Church, Roath shows the new shift towards the Perpendicular Gothic style which was to become increasingly common in the late Victorian period. The church has the character of a cathedral, but this is attained to a greater degree by height and the use of certain architectural features rather than overall dimensions. Bodley used clustered columns as slender as possible with fillets and angle shafts so that the eye sees a forest of vertical lines increasing the perception of height. The clerestoried chancel is also employed to give an impression of height. The full-width east window, which is a principal feature of the church, is built right up to the ceiling. This was only done in important buildings and thus enhances the perception of status. St German's is the most important church in Glamorgan in the late Victorian period.

In the years 1921–2 the reredos over the high altar by Hare was erected in memory of Father Ives (d. 1920). Executed by Thompson's of Peterborough. Dedicated 24 May 1922. Doors added 1926–7. (Marmaduke Warner and A. C. Hooper (eds), *The History of Roath St German's* (Cardiff, 1934), *passim*)

ST JAMES THE GREAT'S CHURCH, CARDIFF

1891–4: New church built on new site given by Lord Tredegar as chapel of ease to St John the Baptist's Church, Cardiff. Church services previously held in an iron church, but growth of population of mainly working-class people necessitated building of new permanent church in parish. (*Ch. Bldr* (1892), 78) Foundation stone laid on 25 July 1891 by Lord Tredegar. (*W. Mail*, 27 July 1891) Built in Early English Gothic style by E. M. Bruce Vaughan, consisting of apsidal chancel, ambulatory communicating with sacristy and vestry on each side of chancel, nave with clerestory, and aisles, tower with spire on north side of chancel and stone porch with timber gable at north-west end. (ICBS file no. 9508 (1891)) Constructed of rose-coloured Swelldon stone and for all jambs, facings and mouldings selected Box Ground stone from the Bath quarries. Height of tower 92ft, height to finial of spire 161ft. In length building measures 144ft from east to west. Its width is 65ft and height of roof

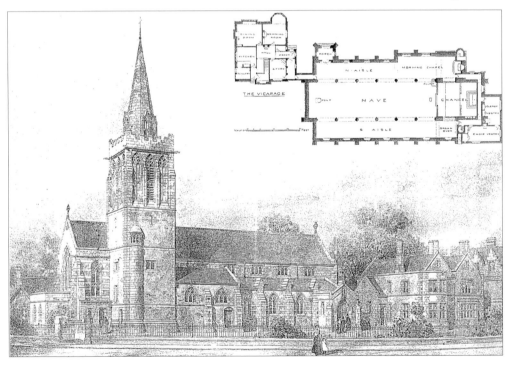

10. St James' Church and Vicarage, Cardiff. E. M. Bruce Vaughan, Archt. Photo-tint by James Akerman, London (Source: *The Building News*, 4 September 1903)

is 58ft. Nave roof raftered and chancel roof panelled geometrically. Carved work within and without church from studio of William Clarke, Llandaff. Inner wall of chancel pierced with five arches. Choir stalls of richly carved oak. Font, an exact copy of old font at Llantrisant Church, of Forest of Dean stone, and pulpit built of three different kinds of stone, namely Camden, green Bridgend and red Forest of Dean stone. Floor of wooden blocks and aisles laid down with encaustic tiles. Organ chamber, built by Gill of Cardiff, raised above south side of chancel, immediately above choir vestry. Open benches of pitch-pine. Accommodation for 800 worshippers. (*Bldr*, 23 June 1894, 485) Building of church severely delayed by a long and bitter strike in building trade, which lasted a year, and all efforts to raise funds during that period were paralysed. (*Ch. Bldr* (1894), 103) Contractor: Messrs Burton & Co., Cardiff. Cost £10,000. ICBS grant £250;. Bishop of Llandaff's Fund £400. Church consecrated on 15 June 1894. (*W. Mail*, 16 June 1894).

Comments: Bruce Vaughan's original plan of the church was in a later Gothic style, but the Building Committee insisted on the Early English style. His conception of the church is a reproduction of a type very commonly found in Normandy and the north of France, but executed in the Early English style. St James's is unique among the Cardiff churches in possessing an apsidal east end and also an ambulatory or processional way behind the altar. The finest feature of the nave is the sumptuously carved pulpit. It has slender columns of coloured marble upon the face, and the recesses are filled with figures of famous preachers. St James's Church is Bruce Vaughan's *opus magnum* and remains one of the most imposing churches in Cardiff with its lofty spire towering over the surrounding streets and the beauty and simplicity of its Early English-style Gothic architecture.

ST JOHN THE BAPTIST'S CHURCH, CARDIFF

1851: Restoration of church comprising enlargement of organ loft and placing of carved oak screen over the principal entrance. Pulpit and reading desk renewed and moved from west end, where they were originally, to east end. High pews replaced by low open benches of coarse American oak. New roof placed over chancel, the gift of Revd John Montgomery Traherne. No architect employed during this restoration. (*Bldr*, 3 January 1852, 67) Contractors: Messrs Thomas & Norris, Cardiff. Cost £1,400. Reopened after restora-tion on 23 December 1851. (*CMG*, 27 December 1851)

1887: Enlargement of church by construction of new chancel and vestry. Low chancel roof removed and chancel walls considerably heightened to incorporate a clerestory of eight Perpendicular-style windows. A fine east window of five cinquefoiled lights with Perpendicular-style tracery in head inserted in the east wall. Noteworthy ribbed barrel roof raised over chancel. Corbels of shafts supporting roof carved with heads representing prominent and national churchmen, including Bishop Richard Lewis, Revd Charles J. Thompson, vicar, and the High Churchmen John Keble and Edward Pusey. Organ removed from west gallery to an aisle south of chancel called 'the Alderman's aisle'. Chancel paved with tiles by W. Godwin & Sons, Lugwardine. (*BN*, 25 March 1887, 454) Church enlarged according to designs by John Prichard (d. 1886) and completed under supervision of Frederick R. Kempson, Hereford. Cost £3,000. Reopened after restoration on 16 March 1887. (*W. Mail*, 17 March 1887)

1889: Enlargement of church by addition of outer north and south aisles, constructed of Swelldon stone, to inner aisles of nave to accommodate an additional 500 persons, and general restoration. Windows of old north and south walls reset in the new aisles. Galleries on north and south sides of nave, erected in 1813 and 1824 respectively to provide additional accommodation at that time, removed and whole of seating remodelled. South aisle, the larger of the two, seated 440 persons and intended to supply accommodation for all who had been dispossessed by removal of galleries. Great attention paid to the roofs, both of old building and new. New slating carried by panelled, boarded and felted roof in place of simple battens which supported the huge old slates. North and south arched doorways of tower restored. Architects: Kempson & Fowler, Cardiff. (*Bldr*, 5 October

1889, 30) Contractors: Messrs Samuel Shepton & Sons, Cardiff. Cost £13,000. Bishop of Llandaff's Fund £100. Reopened after restoration on 24 September 1889. (*W. Mail*, 26 September 1889)

1897: Restoration of tower. In January 1896 the architect, Charles B. Fowler, reported on dangerous condition of tower and recommended measures for its restoration. (*Bldr*, 1 February 1896, 98) Work included taking down about half the embattled parapets and rebuilding the same and taking down some 25ft of decayed stonework from top of the north-west and south-west buttresses, which had broken away from the walls entirely. Buttresses rebuilt. Windows all restored and whole of tower repointed. West window also restored and reglazed. Architect: Charles B. Fowler, Cardiff. Wrought-iron gates and railings by Leathern's, Cheltenham. Carving by William Clarke, Llandaff. Contractor: George Shepton, Cardiff. Cost £3,000. Reopened after restoration on 15 December 1897. (*BN*, 24 December 1897, 903)

Comments: St John the Baptist's Church, Cardiff, like many other churches in Glamorgan, had retained its out-of-date arrangement of the church well into the late Victorian period simply because the Church in Cardiff lacked the financial resources to make improvements earlier in the century. By the late 1880s Cardiff had become a prosperous Victorian town as a result of its port and the wealth of its hinterland. Consequently, it was able to raise the large sums of money required to restore and reorder the church at this time. The reconstruction of the chancel by the removal of the galleries and the enlargement of the church by the addition of the outer nave aisles transformed the former structure, which the correspondent in the *Western Mail* of 26 September 1889 described as 'mean and shabby in the extreme', into a building with which 'the mind is pleasureably impressed with the massive dignity of the structure and with the variety of form and outline possessed by its rich irregularity of treatment . . . in a word, all parts of the building group together into perfection'. The chancel, with its display of carved heads of prominent churchmen, was intended to illustrate the catholicity of spirit which now inspired the churchmanship of St John's Church.

ST JOHN THE EVANGELIST'S CHURCH, CANTON, CARDIFF

1854–5: New church built on new site given by John Homfray of Penlline Castle. Bishop Alfred Ollivant was far-sighted, and he foresaw that the expansion of Cardiff was bound to go westward and engulf the small hamlet of Canton, then within the extensive parish of Llandaff. Consequently, the decision to build a large church in Canton was taken in January 1852. Ollivant directed that the nave should be built first so that services could be held even though the building was not completed. Foundation stone laid on 17 April 1854 by bishop of Llandaff. (*CMG*, 22 April 1854) Built in early Decorated Gothic style by John Prichard consisting of nave only. Arcades temporarily filled with brickwork and west facade was tolerably complete. Constructed of Newbridge stone faced with granite with Combe Down Bath stone dressings. Four-light west window has Geometrical-style tracery in head

11. St John's Church, Canton, Cardiff, 1854 (By kind permission of National Museums & Galleries of Wales, Cardiff)

and columns which support outer arch mouldings of polished serpentine marble from Cornwall. Nave divided on either side by arcade of four bays, with clerestory above lighted with cinquefoil lights. Roof of Memel timber, stained and covered with Bangor slates. Passages between seats paved with Godwin's tiles. Open benches with sloping backs of pitch-pine. Accommodation for 250 worshippers. (*Bldr*, 6 May 1854, 237) Contractors: James & Price, Cardiff. Cost £1,400. ICBS grant £200; LDCES grant £100. Church consecrated on 6 March 1855. (*CMG*, 10 March 1855)

1858–9: North and south aisles added to church. (Revd John R. Guy, 'Churches of Cardiff', *South Wales Echo*, 17 July 1964)

1870: Central tower built, 90ft high, surmounted by broach spire, 84ft with corner spirelets. (Ibid.)

1871: Chancel completed in accordance with general style of church and lighted by five-light east window with Geometrical-style tracery. Additions made with Newbridge stone and Bath stone dressings in harmony with rest of design. Chapels in chancel occupied with seats for school children. Choir stalls carved with rests similar to those in Llandaff Cathedral. New gas pendants of tasteful design introduced in nave. Total seating capacity of church increased to 540 seats. (*CMG*, 22 July 1871)

Comments: The correspondent in *The Ecclesiologist* stated 'that this is a church of some rather marked dignity of outline'. (*Eccl.*, 17 (1856), 310) John Hilling, the architectural historian, quite rightly states that 'the most successful of Prichard's Cardiff churches is St John the Evangelist at Canton'. Incidentally, he says that 'it was originally known as Christchurch'. (John Hilling, *Cardiff and the Valleys: Architecture and Townscape* (London, 1973), 118) John Newman states erroneously that 'the steeple (was) a new design by W. P. James'. (Newman, 275) However, the original plans for the spire were submitted by W. P. James, but these plans were not approved and they were modified by Prichard into the broach spire with corner spirelets. (John Redpath, *The Church of St John the Evangelist, Canton, Cardiff, 1854–1979* (Cardiff, 1979), 2) Despite the fact that St John the Evangelist's Church was built in stages over a

period of seventeen years the original conception of the design has been maintained throughout and every part of the building is in harmony with the other, which reflects great credit on the architect, John Prichard, and his contractors.

In 1902 the church was enlarged by an additional west bay, seating additional free accommodation for 116 worshippers, and the construction of a larger vestry. Cost £2,847. Architect: George E. Halliday. (LL/F/118. Enlargement of church and new vestry. Faculty dated 21 March 1902)

ST MARGARET'S CHURCH, ROATH, CARDIFF

1869–70: New church built on new site of old church. With expansion of Roath in 1860s, old church of St Margaret's Roath became inadequate for rapidly increasing population. Old church demolished in 1869 and new and larger church built. (Revd John Guy, 'Churches of Cardiff', *South Wales Echo*, 17 April 1964) Foundations laid by Alexander Roos, architect to the Bute estate, but on his coming of age, the third marquess of Bute asserted his newly found independence and dismissed Roos and ordered the work already started to be demolished. He then commissioned John Prichard to build a new church on Roos's foundations. Built in Early English Gothic style with early Geometrical-style tracery. Cruciform in plan consisting of chancel with organ chamber, nave (38ftx24ft), transepts (22ftx 24ft) and south porch. Central tower to be completed at later date. Principal entrance to church on south side, approached by porch and leading into south transept. Constructed of Newbridge sandstone in thin courses with Bath stone dressings. Roof covered with small green Pennants Bangor slates. Each apex of roof surmounted with ornamental carved cross. Church laid with wooden flooring except in aisles of nave and transepts, which are paved with black and red tiles. Interior walls lined with white pressed bricks, relieved in various patterns and bands by Lord Bute's red and Staffordshire blue bricks. Nave and transepts covered by open timbered roof. Chancel arch, composed of five moulded ribs of alabaster, Radyr and Bridgend stone in alternation, supported on double capitals. Chancel divided from nave by panelled screen and paved with ornamented tessellated tiles, supplied by Godwin's of Lugwardine. East window of five lights with early Geometrical-style tracery. Chancel walls partly lined with Penarth alabaster. Reredos, formed of alabaster and inlaid green marble, composed of three arches surmounted by canopies and triple battlements: the centre arch filled with a handsome 'Agnus Dei' in inlaid marble. Font hexagonal in form worked in yellow Mansfield stone. West window of nave of four lights with moulded tracery. Open seats of pitch-pine, stained and varnished. Church heated by apparatus supplied by Messrs Dicks & Green of Bolton. Accommodation for 380 worshippers. Whole of beautiful stone carving executed by Messrs Clarke & Son, Llandaff. (*Bldr*, 16 July 1870, 564.) Contractor: Thomas Williams, Cardiff. Cost £4,938. Church consecrated on 10 July 1870. (*W. Mail*, 11 July 1870)

1883: Marquess of Bute's private mausoleum, formerly a plain plastered chapel on north side of chancel, rebuilt with different richly coloured stones and alabaster and separated from church by metal screens. Architect: John Prichard. Contractor: F. S. Lock, Cardiff. (Diane Walker, 'The Bute Mausoleum at St Margaret's Church, Roath', *Archaeological Journal*, 150 (1993), 482–97)

Comments: The splendour of St Margaret's undoubtedly lies in its interior. The church is full of colour in the form of strident constructional polychromy. Great emphasis has been laid by Prichard on the polychromy of the chancel arch, which is composed of two orders of alternating bands of alabaster, Radyr and Bridgend stone, supported on paired colonnettes. The arch is in effect a single capital composed of integral colonnettes. Indeed, it is the detailing of the architectural features, fittings and fixtures – not the strident polychromy – which makes this a building of quality. The richness of the chancel is exemplified by the fine detailing of the trefoil-headed arcade in the choir, together with the pointed arches which form the sedilia in the sanctuary. The five-light east window is of magnificent proportions and is filled with early Geometrical-style tracery. St Margaret's is a notable example of High Victorian Gothic architecture and is regarded as one of Prichard's finest churches.

In 1926 the tower was completed to a much modified design by John Coates Carter, Cardiff. (LL/F/722. Completion of tower. Faculty dated 29 July 1926)

ST MARK'S CHURCH, GABALFA, CARDIFF
(Demolished in 1968)

1876: New church built on new site. Prior to building of St Mark's, the people who lived in that area were members of parish of Llandaff but separated from it geographically by River Taff. The ferry was only means whereby some parishioners reached their place of worship. For benefit of parishioners who did not wish to cross the Taff, services were held in a schoolroom at Maendu under Revd John Davies. As population increased it was decided to form a new ecclesiastical district, then known as Maendu, and build a permanent church. (Revd John R. Guy, 'Churches of Cardiff', *South Wales Echo*, 25 September 1964) Built in early Decorated Gothic style from designs by local architect, Charles E. Waring. Cruciform in plan consisting of chancel, nave, north and south transepts, south porch and western bellcote. Length, measured externally, was 88ft and width of nave was 33ft, the height being 28ft from floor to ridge. Western bellcote rose to elevation of nearly 60ft above ground surface. Constructed of Newbridge polled stone with Bath stone strings, quoins and copings and western bellcote constructed entirely of Bath stone. Nave covered by open timbered roof with curved ribs to principal rafters and boarded diagonally. Covered with Caernarfon slates, curved and plain and in alternate bands of copper colour and blue. Floor, passages and chancel laid with Minton's encaustic tiles of three different patterns. Nave lighted by seven two-light windows, cusped and with trefoil pierced heads; the transepts with two-light windows and with quatrefoil piercings; the chancel with a three-light cusped window and three trefoil piercings. West window of three grouped lancets divided by piers about three feet wide, the centre light being 30ft above ground. Open benches of pitch-pine framing with red deal panelling, as were choir stalls, pulpit, Communion table and altar rails (which were supported by wrought-iron standards). Font constructed of Caen stone. Building heated by means of Haden's hot-air apparatus. Accommodation for 240 parishioners. Contractor: Charles Shepherd, Roath, Cardiff. Cost £1,000. (*W. Mail*, 27 September 1876)

1893: Renovation of church. Organ erected in north transept and door inserted in east wall of transept. Pulpit removed from its original position on north side outside chancel steps to position in corner of north aisle. Removal of temporary brick screen between south transept and chancel and erection of ornamental wooden screen. Cost £180. ICBS grant £120. Architect: James Wride, Pantbach, Whitchurch. (LL/F/319. New organ, removal of pulpit and screen. Faculty dated 11 September 1893)

Comments: The correspondent's description of the church in the *Western Mail* of 27 September 1876 stated that 'the reveals, arches and mouldings were bold and plain, the object of the architect being to have as little decorative work as is compatible with the ecclesiastical character of the structure; in fact, whether regarded from an exterior or interior point of view, the edifice is entirely free of superfluous embellishments and is remarkable for the neatness of the details'. The cost of building St Mark's amounted to £1,000, a small sum compared with other churches erected at that time in Cardiff, which, according to the description in a contemporary newspaper, clearly shows that Charles Waring was working under severe financial restrictions in designing and building the church in the early Decorated style.

In the years 1927–8, due to the fact that the church was too small for the rapidly increasing population, a new north aisle was added and the nave extended westwards. Seating accommodation was increased by 307 sittings so that the completed church could seat 536 parishioners. Church extensions dedicated on 1 February 1928. Architect: E. M. Bruce Vaughan. Cost £3,030. (LL/F/323. Enlargement of church. Faculty dated 25 March 1927)

ST MARTIN'S CHURCH, CARDIFF
(Church destroyed by blitz in February, 1941)

1899–1901: New church built on new site. Prior to building of St Martin's, iron church opened on its site in Albany Road on 10 November 1886 and served by curate from St Margaret's Church, Roath. Given by the Mackintosh of Mackintosh. By 1899 population of parish of Roath had risen to 29,000 consisting entirely of wage-earning classes, dock labourers and artisans of all descriptions. Population of district of St Martin's totalled 15,000 and iron church accommodated only 500 persons. Consequently, central site acquired for building permanent church to accommodate more than 1,000 worshippers. (*Ch. Bldr* (1899), 37) Foundation stone laid on 16 December 1899 by mayoress of Cardiff, Mrs S. A. Brain. (*W. Mail*, 18 December 1899) Built in late Decorated Gothic style by Frederick R. Kempson. Because of shortness of site, church consisted of broad nave and chancel under continuous roof with wide aisle at south side; on north side was narrow north aisle and slightly wider chancel aisle which formed a side chapel. Lean-to north chapel. Chancel raised above nave by three steps and divided from it by short stone screen on south side and by unusually wide and large pulpit on north side. Constructed of red brick with minimal dressings of Bath stone. (*Bldr*, 5 October 1901, 298) Nave divided from aisles by four moulded, pointed arches springing from clustered columns with octagonal capitals. Continuous roof of church consisted of three-tiered, ribbed sections, with larger central section flanked by two smaller ones. (ICBS file no. 10,093 (1898)) Elaborately decorated interior. East window, set high in east wall of chancel, of five cinquefoiled lights with early Perpendicular tracery in apex, which mirrors tracery of west wall of south chancel aisle. West end of church lighted by two four-light windows. Four-light windows to nave aisles. High altar surmounted by magnificent reredos in which lower panel was a painting of the Last Supper, whilst carved centre panel contained a painting of the Crucifixion. Erected in memory of members of Brockett family who fell in First World War. (John C. Read, *The Church in Our City* (Cardiff, 1954), 55) Accommodation for 750 worshippers on individual chairs. Contractor: George Beames, Cardiff. Cost £9,700. ICBS grant £1,000; Lord Tredegar £500. Church consecrated 20 October 1901. (*W. Mail*, 21 October 1901)

Comments: Frederick R. Kempson designed St Martin's in the late Decorated style, the same style as St German's Church, Roath by Bodley. Kempson was obviously influenced by Bodley's church, as St Martin's shows a shift towards the Perpendicular style, which underwent a revival in the late Victorian period. The church was tall and spacious, and the window tracery, as well as that in the west wall of the north aisle, was early Perpendicular. St Martin's was undoubtedly one of Kempson's finest churches and shows a more mature architectural style than witnessed hitherto.

ST MARY'S CHURCH, BUTETOWN, CARDIFF

1841–3: New church built on new site given by second marquess of Bute. Since old St Mary's Church had been encroached upon by River Taff, causing it to collapse in seventeenth century, there had been no church to serve southern part of Cardiff. By 1840 population of the area had increased to 6,000 as a result of opening of Docks, and new church built largely through generosity of Bute family. (John C. Read, *The Church in Our City* (Cardiff, 1954), 59) Built in Neo-Norman style by Thomas Foster of Bristol. (ICBS file no. 2666 (1841)) It consists of chancel with apse, nave, aisles, clerestory and twin towers, one at east end of each aisle. Constructed of coarse, dark-coloured sandstone with dressings of Bath stone. Roof covered with blue slates. East end of church has two massive towers with pyramidal stone roofs with fish-scale tiles, while between towers is an arcade of sham windows fronting onto small apse which forms small chancel. Three-decker pulpit blocks view of altar. Central gable of east wall has a Rose window and moulded, round-headed doorways on ground level which provide principal entrances to church. Nave divided from aisles by arcades of five semicircular arches supported on massive round columns with scalloped capitals

which in turn support plain, flat ceiling. Clerestory has single round-headed windows and those of aisles below are similar, but larger. West end flanked by square turrets with pinnacles and has two tiers of round-headed windows beneath central circular window. Galleries on north, south and west sides of the nave. Original design included gallery for free seats at back of altar, but surveyor to the Church Building Commission, J. H. Good, in his report dated 30 October 1839 stated that 'this was objectionable' and consequently it was deleted from the final design. (Church Building Commission: Surveyors Reports, Vol. V, 63) Nave originally filled with square high-backed pews which seated 1,800 worshippers. Church funded by a grant of £1,663 from the Church Commissioners. Cost £5,724, largely defrayed by Bute family. ICBS grant £500. Church opened for divine service on 14 December 1843. (*Glamorgan, Monmouth & Brecon Gazette and Merthyr Guardian*, 16 December 1843) Consecrated on 6 November 1845. (*CMG*, 8 November 1845)

1879: Renovation of church. Removal of old three-decker pulpit, and modern pulpit placed at north-east side of nave. Organ removed from west gallery and placed at north-east side of church. Old-fashioned box pews removed from nave and replaced with individual chairs. (LL/F/186. Internal changes for reseating. Faculty dated 11 June 1879)

1884–5: Reordering of church to suit new High Church liturgical arrangements. Old three-decker of pulpit, reading desk and clerk's desk removed from its original position where it obstructed view of altar, organ moved to east end, old square pews discarded and replaced with chairs. New altar and choir stalls erected and whole of sanctuary re-arranged and redecorated. Apse decorated with twelve white life-size figures of the Apostles by Searle of Exeter. Reredos of high altar erected with its painting of the Adoration of the Shepherds, 1884 by Philip Westlake. Most of work carried out under guidance and architectural direction of John Dando Sedding. (*Evening Express*, 22 October 1901)

Comments: The Ecclesiologists were not impressed with the building of St Mary's Church, the only Church Commissioners' church in Cardiff. The reviewer in *The Ecclesiologist* said, 'We readily grant that the church in question is greatly superior to the kindred specimens in Stepney and Bethnal Green, yet we unfortunately cannot speak of it in terms of general approbation. For we disapprove in the first place of the adoption of this style for churches and secondly we find much to condemn in the arrangement . . . We freely acknowledge that many of the details are well executed, but we fear that is pretty all we can conscientiously say in praise.' (*Eccl.*, 8 (1848), 254–5) Its interior in 1843 was typical of the Commissioners' churches which represented a rectangular 'preaching hall' to seat as many worshippers as possible. John Newman is absolutely right in describing Foster's plan as 'a foolish design' as the parishioners had to traverse the whole length of the building to gain access to the church at the west end. (Newman, 265) John Hilling described St Mary's Church, as 'an *avante garde* building for its time'. (John B. Hilling, 'The Buildings of Cardiff', *Glamorgan Historian*, 6 (1969), 45) However, Hilling erroneously attributes the building of St Mary's Church, Butetown, Cardiff in all his writings to the architect, John Foster of Liverpool.

In the years 1904–7 the galleries on the north and south sides of the church were removed and new choir and priest's vestry constructed. (*Bldr*, 14 September 1907, 296)

ST PAUL'S CHURCH, GRANGETOWN, CARDIFF

1889–91: New church consisting of nave only, 75ft long by 26ft 6ins wide, built on new site given by Lord Windsor. Built by Lord Windsor to provide for wants of poor and rapidly growing district of Cardiff. Services in Grangetown first held in loft in North Street in 1860s and then from 1864 to 1879 in the National School. In 1870 Lady Windsor Clive gave £500 to build an iron church and the church people worshipped there until the new church was built. (Revd John R. Guy, 'Churches of Cardiff', *South Wales Echo*, 2 October 1964) Foundation stone laid on 16 March 1889 by Lord Windsor. (*W. Mail*, 18 March 1889) Built in Early English Gothic style by John Coates Carter of Seddon & Carter, and on completion it consisted of nave and aisles with

chancel, side chapel and vestries with organ loft above chapel. Materials used for external wallings are Newbridge stone in narrow layers, ashlar dressings of door and windows of pink Penkridge stone, and quoins and other plainer dressings of Portland cement concrete cast in moulds. Internally, dressings of same materials. Three-tiered panelled roof of red deal covered with red Broseley tiles. No chancel arch in design, but division marked internally by arcade being broken by large pier and by three roof principals grouped together at this point. Externally, one continuous roof over chancel and nave, the junction on which would later be marked by a bell turret. Trefoil wagon roof to nave. Nave arcade of five bays of high pointed arches supported on slender clustered columns. Each bay of the aisles has transverse roof ending in gable over tall two-light window with quatrefoils. Single-light windows at west end of aisles. West front of church with four-light window with Geometrical-style tracery above ornately moulded triple doorway, the two flanked by massive octagonal buttresses with pyramidal caps and rectangular bases. Open benches of pitch-pine. Accommodation for 450 persons. Contractors: Messrs Bowers & Co., Hereford. Nave completed in February 1891, but not consecrated until 5 April 1900. Cost £4,000 donated by Lord Windsor. (*Bldr*, 25 January 1890, 62)

1901–2: Foundation stone of chancel laid by Lord Windsor on 18 June 1901. (*W. Mail*, 19 June 1901) Church consists of three-bay chancel of same height as nave. Panelled oak fittings with choir stalls and pulpit. East window of five lights with Geometrical-style tracery above. Cost £2,500, of which Lord Windsor donated £1,000 with rest raised by parishioners. Contractors: Knox & Wells, Cardiff. Consecrated on 26 April 1902. (*Cardiff Times*, 3 May 1902)

Comments: St Paul's was built by John Coates Carter in a free adaptation of Early English Gothic architecture that shows the influence of Bodley's church at St German's, Roath in its spatial handling. Newman stated that 'it is the finest late Victorian church in the county after Bodley's at Roath'. Furthermore he felt 'it was modelled on St Augustine's Church, Pendlebury, Manchester with its unbroken internal spaces'. (Newman, 96) The chancel, completed nearly eleven years after the nave, exhibits a modified east end showing discrepancies in ornamentation specified in Carter's original design, as well as the absence of its proposed south-east steeple. St Paul's Church is typical of Carter's innovative choice of building materials seen in most of his Glamorgan churches.

ST SAVIOUR'S CHURCH, ROATH, CARDIFF

1888: New church built on new site in Splott Road given by Lord Tredegar as chapel of ease to St German's Church, Roath. At first an iron church stood here, brought from St German's when that church was completed in 1884. Intended to accommodate rapidly increasing population of that part of parish of Roath until permanent church could be built. This iron church was reopened as St Saviour's Mission Church on 3 December 1884. (John C. Read, *The Church in Our City* (Cardiff, 1954), 65) Foundation stone of a new permanent stone-built church finally laid on 28 February 1888 by Lord Tredegar. (*W. Mail*, 30 January 1888) Built in Perpendicular Gothic style by Bodley & Garner of London, consisting of chancel of three bays, nave of five bays, north aisle with chapel and western bellcote. Sacristy provided at back of choir altar by a low stone screen. Principal entrance at west end. Constructed of local Welsh sandstone with Swelldon stone facings and Bath stone dressings. Nave is 66ft long by 24ft wide, and length of church from east to west is 120ft. Nave divided from north aisle by low pointed arches springing from four clustered columns. South aisle not completed, the columns and arcades being solidly blocked up. East window of five lights with rectilinear and flowing tracery in head. West window of three lights with similar early Perpendicular-style tracery. Roofs are panel vaulted and simply decorated with colour and with scrolls inscribed with appropriate legends. When the church was completed to the original plan, it would accommodate 850 worshippers. Contractors: Messrs Stephens & Bastow, Bristol. Cost £6,000. ICBS grant £200; Bishop of Llandaff's Fund £400. Consecrated on 30 October 1888. (*W. Mail*, 31 October 1888)

1894–5: South aisle added. (ICBS file no. 9200 (1887))

Comments: When Bodley & Garner were commissioned to build St Saviour's their brief stipulated that the church should be modelled on the fifteenth-century church of St Mary's, Tenby. St Mary's is a spacious and dignified structure. It is notable for its loftily placed sanctuary, approached by a long flight of steps which is also present in St Saviour's. The conception of St Saviour's, however, is low spreading and dark within compared with the loftiness of St Mary's with its spire placed on top of an 84ft battlemented tower. In contrast, St Saviour's has only a western bellcote of fifteenth-century character. Again following the design of St Mary's, the vestries at St Saviour's are behind and below the High Altar. In Roath there are clustered shafts with bell capitals to the arcades, but at Tenby there are engaged shafts as a central core separated by deep hollows and fillets without capitals, which is far superior to Roath. At St Saviour's there are panelled, vaulted roofs, but at St Mary's there are typical fifteenth-century wagon roofs. The Perpendicular style was one dealing with vertical lines, principally in mullions, and the basic vertical line was employed throughout the church. This verticality is lacking in St Saviour's. Although the design is influenced by that of St Mary's, in no way does it replicate faithfully the medieval features of that church.

ST TEILO'S CHURCH, CARDIFF
(Now known as St Andrew's and St Teilo's Church, Cardiff)

1895–7: New church built as chapel of ease to St Andrew's Church, on new site donated by Mrs Mackintosh of Mackintosh. Foundation stone laid on 13 February 1895 by Mrs Mackintosh of Mackintosh. (*W. Mail*, 14 February 1895) Although additional church accommodation had been provided in Cardiff since 1884 in the several new churches and mission chapels this was totally inadequate to provide for the spiritual needs of the Cathays district. A temporary iron church on a site in Woodville Road, given by Colonel Wood, accommodated 270 worshippers and had been enlarged in 1885 to seat 400. (*Ch. Bldr* (1894), 105) Built in Perpendicular Gothic style by George E. Halliday. Only nave and aisles built. Constructed of Swelldon stone in broken, coarsed work with Box Ground Bath stone dressings. Portion completed at this time provided seating for 750 persons, chairs being used. West window of seven lights with Perpendicular panel tracery. Nave arcades supporting clerestory consisted of five bays of pointed stone arches supported on columns and responds with moulded vertical shafts carried upwards from tops of piers to support springing of roofs. Clerestory lighted by ten three-light windows. Tower foundations laid. Nave of open timber roof with tie-beams. Roof timbers of pitch-pine left free from stain or varnish. Contractors: Messrs S. Shepton & Sons, Cardiff. Cost £7,240, of which Mrs Mackintosh of Mackintosh gave £3,000. ICBS grant £300; Bishop of Llandaff's Fund £400. Church dedicated on 13 July 1897. (*W. Mail*, 14 July 1897)

1901: Chancel, vestries, organ chamber and south porch completed. Total seating accommodation for 812 parishioners. Architect: George E. Halliday. Contractor: William Cadwalladr, Cardiff. Cost £2,000. Consecrated on 11 December 1901. (*W. Mail*, 12 December 1901)

Comments: George E. Halliday, who was one of the more forward-looking architects in Glamorgan in the late Victorian period, designed St Teilo's in a late Gothic form, Perpendicular Gothic, in line with national trends. The most striking feature of St Teilo's is the west front with its richly moulded and recessed double doorway filled in with teak doors and wrought ironwork surmounted by a magnificent seven-light window filled with a network of panel tracery. This window is believed to be the largest of its kind in the diocese of Llandaff.

In 1913 the tower and Lady chapel were built. Consecrated on 12 December 1913. (John C. Read, *The Church in Our City* (Cardiff, 1954), 28)

ST CADOC'S CHURCH, CHERITON

1846–7: During the incumbency of the Revd William Lucas Collins, rector from 1840 to 1867,

repairs were carried out to the church which comprised new roof, and old square pews removed and replaced by new open benches. This increased the seating accommodation by 20 sittings, mainly for the poor of the parish, formerly confined to seating under the tower. (ICBS file no. 3725 (1846))

1861: When Sir Stephen Glynne visited the church on 28 August 1861 he reported that 'the nave has recently been fitted with open benches of plain character and some improvements have been effected in the condition of the church'. (Sir Stephen R. Glynne, 'Notes on the older churches in the four Welsh dioceses', *Arch. Camb.* (1897), 296)

1874–5: The petition for faculty to restore the church in 1873 stated that 'portions of the fabric presented as being in an unsound, dangerous and decayed state'. (SD/F/109. Altering and restoring. Faculty dated 30 August 1873) The work of restoration consisted of thorough repair of the tower, occasioning rebuilding of the upper part of the structure, renewal of lofts and complete re-pointing of all four faces. New roofs of pine raised on chancel and nave, new vestry constructed on the north side of the chancel and new south porch built. New choir-stalls, altar rails, altar and embossed wooden ceiling, all in a light-coloured wood, carved by Revd J. D. Davies, rector of Cheriton and Llanmadoc, a skilled wood-carver. New floors were laid down throughout the church. Architect: John Prichard, Llandaff. Contractors: Messrs Henry & George Rosser, Reynoldston. Cost £1,200, paid for by Davies from money he had inherited from his parents. (F. G. Cowley, *Llanmadoc and Cheriton: Two North Gower Churches and their Parishes* (Llanmadoc and Cheriton, 1993), 20–5)

Comments: The work of restoration of Cheriton Church in 1875 by John Prichard, who had come under the influence of the Oxford Movement early in his career and who was further influenced by the Tractarian practices of Revd J. D. Davies, was reflected in the new Victorian fittings and furnishings of the chancel and sanctuary, which transformed the consolidated rectory into a stronghold of Anglo-Catholicism.

ST JOHN THE EVANGELIST'S CHURCH, CILYBEBYLL

1837: Restoration of church. Work consisted of raising new roof to nave, removal of narrow arch between chancel and nave, putting up new ceiling in part of the tower and putting in benches in tower space, repointing the tower, lowering floor of nave, inserting new window to nave on east side of porch on south side and one on north side. Seating accommodation increased by forty-two places. Reopened after restoration in September 1837. Architect: Philip Thomas, Neath. Cost £179. ICBS grant £30. (ICBS file no. 2168 (1837))

1867–9: Rebuilding of church. Petition for faculty to rebuild church in 1867 stated that 'the parish church is in a state of decay and is much too small to afford proper accommodation to the inhabitants of the said parish'. (LL/F/229P. Demolition and rebuilding of church. Faculty dated 25 November 1867) Consequently, it was decided to pull down body of church and rebuild church on same site. Tower, however, left intact. New building, consisting of nave, chancel and south porch, constructed in Norman style of Welsh sandstone with seating accommodation on open benches of pitch-pine. Rebuilding of main body of church increased seating accommodation from 90 to 130 sittings. Open timber roof with scissors-beam construction supported by double principals resting on stone corbels. (LL/F/229. Demolition and rebuilding of church. Faculty dated 26 November 1868) Reopened after restoration on 20 July 1869. Contractor: John Griffiths, Twyn-y-Morgrug, Alltwen. Cost £735. (LL/C/71. Kilybebyll Church: Sentence of consecration dated 20 July 1869)

Comments: According to a photograph of St John the Evangelist's taken in 1867, the original church was much longer than the one rebuilt in 1869 and the roof appeared to be covered with stone tiles. A pointed chancel arch of large span divided the chancel from the nave in the new building, whereas in the old church the narrow chancel arch was removed in the earlier restoration of the church in 1837. The cost of rebuilding the church was raised by public subscriptions, since church rates levied on the whole of the parish and used as the main source of finance to restore the parish church were abolished in 1868.

ST JOHN'S CHURCH, CLYDACH

1846–7: New church built on new site given by Richard Hill Miers of Ynispenllwch House, Clydach. Foundation stone laid on 13 April 1846 by Mrs Richard Miers. (*The Cambrian*, 17 April 1846) Built near Swansea canal, a short distance from populous district of Ynispenllwch. Construction necessitated by considerable growth in population and distance from parish church situated at Llangyfelach, five miles away. John Henry Good, one of Committee of Architects of ICBS who examined the architect's plans, stated that 'I see no objection to the principles of the proposed construction of the building as far as is shown by the plans submitted by Mr Whittington. Means should be provided for the escape of the water produced by condensation on the inside of the windows to the outside of the building.' (ICBS file no. 2907 (1845)) Built in Perpendicular Gothic style by William Whittington, county surveyor of Neath, consisting of chancel, nave, north transept and vestry. Principal entrance through north transept which is flanked by castellated octagonal turrets and surmounted by bellcote. Facade of building pierced with three elongated lancets and centrally positioned north doorway. Constructed of Welsh Pennant sandstone with Bath stone dressings. Chancel arch is high and acutely pointed and small chancel lighted by triplet of grouped lancets at east end and by single lancets in north and south. West end of nave lighted by two-light window with quatrefoil in apex and nave walls pierced with single lancet windows. Square pews of pitch-pine together with seats in north gallery accommodated 362 worshippers. Contractors: Messrs Lewis & Jones, Clydach. Cost £1,600. ICBS grant £50; Church Commissioners' grant £200. Consecrated on 24 June 1847. (*The Cambrian*, 25 June 1847)

1873: Chancel paved with encaustic tiles. Four square pews removed from east end of nave and replaced by choir stalls. Whole of church reseated and new stone pulpit installed. (SD/F/122. Faculty dated 14 August 1873)

Comments: St John's was one of only two Church Commissioners' churches built in the Glamorgan part of the diocese of St David's, the other being St Peter's, Cockett, erected in 1856. The church was built in the Perpendicular Gothic style, which was popular from 1820 to the mid-1840s, when it came to be regarded as debased by the Ecclesiological Society. The odd feature about the church is its main entrance through the north transept, which is flanked by octagonal castellated turrets. This part of the structure has more affinity to the Non-conformist chapel architecture of the late nineteenth century than to that of the Anglican Church. The chancel is so shallow that it is merely an appendage of the nave. No doubt, Whittington provided more seating in the nave by shortening the chancel. This was a period when churches were being built to accommodate as many people as possible, which was a requirement laid down by the Church Building Commissioners.

ST THOMAS' CHURCH, CLYDACH VALE

1894–6: New church built on new site. Portion on Thomas estate donated, whilst that on Meyrick estate purchased for £101. Foundation stone laid on 9 October 1894 by Miss Clara Thomas, Llwyn-madoc. (*W. Mail*, 10 October 1894) New church required because district of Clydach Vale in parish of Llwynypia near Pontypridd had grown rapidly to population of some 8,000 people on account of new mining operations. Nearest church two miles away. (*Ch. Bldr* (1892), 1–2) Built in Early English Gothic style by E. M. Bruce Vaughan, consisting of chancel with north organ chamber and vestry, nave and north aisle with schoolroom below, and north porch formed below north tower. Constructed of local Pennant sandstone and Bath stone dressings while windows of chancel, nave and north aisle have dressings of red Ruabon brickwork. East window of three trefoil-headed lights, the middle higher than the flanking lights with Geometrical-style tracery in head. Sedilia and credence table in sanctuary. Barrel roof of chancel comprising of square panels with gilded bosses at intersections of purlins and rafters. Wide moulded continuous chancel arch. Nave

divided from north aisle by an Early English-style arcade of five pointed arches springing from circular capitals on round columns. Nave roof has scissors-beam arrangement. Walls of nave lighted by four trefoil-headed lights with three circles enclosing trefoils in head, all under an obtusely pointed arch. Tower of two stages with slit openings on lower stage and two pairs of Early English-style belfry lights below stylized corbel table. Clasping buttresses to lower stage of tower. Open benches of pitch-pine. Seating accommodation for 450 worshippers. Schoolroom constructed below church in large basement. Contractors: Hatherley & Carr, Bristol. Cost £3,350. Miss Clara Thomas £1,050; ICBS grant £125; LDCES grant £25; Bishop of Llandaff's Fund £300; Lord Tredegar £50. Thomas Riches £50. (*W. Mail*, 29 September 1896)

Comments: The construction of St Thomas' in the years 1894–6 showed some idiosyncracy on the part of Bruce Vaughan in his use of red Ruabon brick-work for the dressings of the windows of the chancel, nave, north aisle and schoolroom below. This was in spite of the fact that he was well provided with funds from the national and local diocesan grant-making bodies, together with private subscriptions from individuals such as Miss Clara Thomas, who not only donated a portion of the site from her estate, but also made a handsome donation of £1,050 towards the building fund. Nevertheless, Bruce Vaughan succeeded in building a well-designed and substantially built structure with all the fittings and furnishings of a Victorian Anglican church in a mining community in the Rhondda.

In the years 1911–12 the church was enlarged by the addition of a south transept. Total accommodation increased to 650 persons. Architect: John W. Rodger, Cardiff. Cost £1,200. (LL/F/232. Enlargement of church. Faculty dated 18 November 1911)

HOLY NATIVITY CHURCH, COGAN

1893–4: New church built on new site given by Lord Windsor at South Bank on main road at Cogan Pill. Foundation stone laid on 27 July 1893 by Lord Windsor. (*W. Mail*, 28 July 1893) Due to

12. St Peter's Church, Cogan. R. Thorne, 1984 (Source: Roy Thorne, *A History of St. Peter's Church, Old Cogan* (1984))

vast increase in population of that district of Cogan Pill (numbering 2,422 and still rising), it was necessary to build a new church to seat 300 people, mostly dock workers and their families, since Old Cogan Church was nearly two miles away and accommodated only forty-five parishioners. (*Ch. Bldr* (1893), 64) Built in Perpendicular Gothic style from designs by Charles B. Fowler, of Kempson & Fowler, Llandaff. It consists of chancel (15ftx14ft), nave (59ftx25ft), south transept (15ft sq.), organ chamber, vestry, south porch and western bellcote. (*BN*, 2 February 1894, 169) Constructed of local blue lias limestone in thin courses, lined internally with red and buff Cattybrook bricks, relieved with Bath stone bands. South wall of nave supported by two-stage buttress with gablet. Chancel window of three cinquefoiled lights with panel tracery above, set high above altar. Other windows of similar pattern except west window, which is of two cinquefoiled lights with panel tracery at its apex. Nave floored with wood blocks throughout and choir and sanctuary with encaustic tiles. Church lighted artificially by gas from wrought-iron coronas and brackets and heated with Musgrave's hot-air apparatus. Font is a facsimile of Norman font at Old Cogan Church. Pulpit constructed of alabaster, red Dumfries and green Bridgend stone, the panels being filled with green inlaid marble. Western bellcote carried on arch springing from two-stage buttresses. Built to accommodate 311 worshippers,

all seats free and unappropriated. Contractor: William Richards, Barry. (*Bldr*, 10 February 1894, 121) Cost £2,630. ICBS grant £100; Bishop of Llandaff's Fund £250. Consecrated on 14 November 1894. (*Penarth Chr.*, 17 November 1894)

Comments: Holy Nativity Church, Cogan was built in the Perpendicular Gothic style, an idiom which had become fashionable in the late Victorian period, when Ecclesiological correctness of style had been relaxed. By lining the interior of the building with cheap red and buff Cattybrook bricks, relieved with bands of Bath stone, Fowler gave the inside a slightly polychromatic effect. The unusual feature of the exterior was the western bellcote, which was constructed to spring off the tall, two-stage buttresses, which formed a supporting arch above the west window.

ST PETER'S CHURCH, COGAN

1888–94: Restoration of church. When David Jones of Wallington visited the church on 19 September 1888, he stated 'Dr James Lewis took me to see this old church. Small nave and chancel. There is a good deal of herringbone masonry in both nave and chancel, inside and out. Church has been entirely neglected and cattle used to shelter themselves in it. At the present time it is undergoing restoration at the cost of the marquess of Bute. Much ivy had overgrown it, working its way into the walls and destroying them . . .' (Cardiff Central Library: David Jones of Wallington, Diaries. Vol. VI, 1888) Church underwent careful preservation and reparation under third marquess of Bute's architect, William Frame, who took special care to preserve all the ancient architectural features of church such as the early Norman herringbone masonry, and stone benches on north, south and west walls, which he boarded over with oak panelling. Nave has arch-braced roof, and chancel has collar and tie-beam roof. Low narrow chancel arch, round-headed upon plain imposts preserved. (Personal observation) Tudor arch of porch and stone benches retained, but new tie-beam roof raised over south porch. New early Decorated-style window inserted in south-east wall of nave and single lancets in north and south walls of chancel. Old plaster allowed to remain on all walls except west wall. Contractors: workmen from Bute estate. Cost £250. (*SWDN*, 2 November 1894) Reopened after restoration on 1 November 1894. (*Penarth Chr.*, 3 November 1894)

1898: Italianate bronze reredos erected in chancel in memory of James Andrew Corbett (1890), second son of John Stuart Corbett, and solicitor, to his kinsman, Lord Bute. Designed by A. H. C. Westlake, London and executed by N. H. J. Westlake, London. Dedicated 6 November 1898. (LL/F/238. Reredos. Faculty dated 23 September 1896)

Comments: William Frame carried out a careful and sensitive restoration of St Peter's. He resisted the temptation to strip plaster and the walls show patches of old plaster adhering to the surface. Newman in *The Buildings of Wales: Glamorgan* makes no mention of Frame (1848–1906), who restored the church for the marquess of Bute. Furthermore, the bronze reredos erected in 1898, not 1896, as stated by Newman, was in memory of James Andrew Corbett, second son of John Stuart Corbett, not the latter. Also Newman fails to state that the reredos was designed by A. H. C. Westlake, according to the faculty details.

ST MARY'S CHURCH, COITY

1859: Restoration of church by John Prichard. Work took place in 1859 during incumbency of Revd John Harding, MA, JP (1819–61), and comprised raising new roofs over chancel and transepts, and restoring south windows of chancel and fifteenth-century wagon roof of nave. Architect's plans show that parts of south and west wall and south porch were rebuilt at this time. (ICBS file no. 5440 (1859)) Old-fashioned square box pews replaced by modern benches of pitch-pine, and new baptismal font, reading desk and pulpit erected in nave. Altar raised and steps leading up to it hewn from tombstones which had probably formed part of original chancel floor. Level of sedilia in sanctuary reveal that chancel floor at that point was two feet lower than now. This took place during restoration of church. (Royston Griffiths, *The History of the Church of St Mary, Coity in the Diocese of Llandaf* (Cardiff, 1976), 28) Chancel floor paved with encaustic tiles. Additional seating accommodation for 176 parishioners provided by removal of old pews and installation of open benches, bringing total seating capacity to 270 sittings. Cost £850. (*B. Chr.*, 28 October 1859). Reopened after restoration on 25 October 1859. (*CMG*, 29 October 1859)

Comments: Fortunately Revd John Harding, rector of Coity, who undertook the restoration of the church in 1859, proved to be a conscientious restorer of the fabric of the church. This is confirmed by Newman's statement that the church 'was restored with restraint by Prichard & Seddon in 1860 (*sic*)'. (Newman, 325) The reconstruction of the chancel floor to suit the new interpretations in the Anglican liturgy was the most controversial aspect of the restoration, since the three sedilia have been impaired by this change in the level of the floor and their symmetry has been lost. Apart from the rebuilding of the south and west walls of the nave and the restoration of the windows of the chancel, the main structure of the church remained untouched.

ST MICHAEL'S CHURCH, COLWINSTON

1879: Restoration of church by Henry J. Williams of Bristol. (ICBS file no. 8569 (1881)) Work confined to interior of church. New windows inserted in church. Old stone pulpit replaced by one of oak. New oak Communion table, lectern and chancel furniture installed. Alterations provided more accommodation in church, and renovation of roofs and rebuilding parts of wall added greatly to comfort of congregation. In course of restoration work, a rood-loft was discovered and doors at the entrance and upper opening were replaced and a new door was also placed in the porch. Medieval wall paintings in church, which mural experts say depict consecration of St Thomas à Beckett and martyrdom of St Vitus, left untouched. Contractor: Thomas Thomas, Colwinston. Cost £800 defrayed by Mrs Mary Collins Prichard of Pwllywrach. Reopened after restoration on 22 September 1879. (*CGG*, 26 September 1879)

1881: Reseating of church. Additional accommodation for sixty-four parishioners provided. Architect: John Prichard. Cost £120. ICBS grant £10. (*Ch. Bldr* (1881), 26)

Comments: The restoration of St Michael's in 1879 was prompted by the recent arrival at Colwinston of Mrs Mary Collins Prichard, wife of Charles J. Collins Prichard, who came to reside at Pwllywrach, the big house on the outskirts of the village. As the new patron of the living, she set her mind on restoring the church and to this end she commissioned the Bristol architect, Henry John Williams (1842–1912), to undertake the work of restoration. His brief was to put the church in a good state of repair and to secure thoroughly its walls, roofs and windows and to improve the interior. Williams proved to be a sensitive restorer and did not make any changes to the original structure of the medieval church. When additional accommodation was required in 1881 Prichard simply reseated the church with open benches.

HOLY CROSS CHURCH, COWBRIDGE

1848: Restoration of tracery of old windows in chancel, which had been blocked up for several years as shown in a drawing by J. Garsed (*c.*1840) of south view of church, and partly filled with stained glass. Architect: Edward Haycock, Shrewsbury. Cost defrayed by chancellor of Llandaff Cathedral. (*Bldr*, 1 January 1848, 8)

1849–50: Restoration of fabric of church, levelling of floors and rearrangement of pews. Grant of £150 obtained from ICBS 'on condition that 258 of the 645 seats should be set apart and declared to be free for the use of the poor forever'. Erection of oak chancel screen. New windows inserted in south aisle and west end of nave. Church rate of two shillings in the pound levied and £1,000 raised by public subscription. Architect: John Prichard. Cost £1,800. Cowbridge Corporation grant £50. (ICBS file no. 4170 (1849)) Reopened after restoration on 18 December 1850. (*CMG*, 21 & 28 December 1850)

1893: Restoration of tower, rehanging of bells, repair and replastering of interior walls, removal of old organ and gallery at west end of nave, installation of new three-manual organ, built by Nicholson of Worcester, in south aisle near choir stalls. New stone pulpit. Improved heating apparatus. During this work of restoration, piscina of Sutton stone in remarkably good state of preservation found in blocked-up niche beneath south window of sanctuary. Architects: Bruton & Williams, Cardiff. Contractors: Messrs Hatherley & Carr, Bristol. Cost £800. (LL/F/255. Restoration of church. Faculty dated 11 September 1893) Reopened after restoration on 29 October 1893. (*CGG*, 27 October 1893)

Comments: One of the objects of the restoration of Holy Cross Church, Cowbridge in 1850, which involved the extensive relevelling and repewing of the nave, was to provide more accommodation for the poorer members of the parish, who, because of lack of adequate accommodation set aside for them, were excluded from worshipping in the parish church. As a result they were forced to attend Dissenting chapels. The work of restoration at this

13. Interior of Cowbridge Church looking east. (Photo: W. P. Pring, L.R.P.S.) (By kind permission of D. Brown & Sons Ltd, Cowbridge)

time, therefore, showed a growing concern by the vicar of Cowbridge, Revd Thomas Edmondes, for the loss of potential worshippers to the Nonconformists. The restoration of 1893 was a late reordering of the church to suit the new interpretation of the Anglican liturgy; the old west gallery, which had housed the old organ, was removed and a new organ was installed in the south aisle adjacent to the choir stalls and chancel. The space, vacated by the removal of the west gallery, was used to erect additional seating in the west end of the nave.

In the years 1912–13, the tower was renovated and repairs made to nave roof. Cost £450. Architect: George E. Halliday. (*MCVG*, 138) In the years 1925–6 the roof of the nave was completely renewed and the leaning arcade to the south aisle was taken down and rebuilt stone by stone on sound foundations. Architect: Thomas Guy Clarke, Llandaff. Cost £4,000. (LL/F/258. Repairs to roof of nave. Faculty dated 4 July 1923)

ST CRALLO'S CHURCH, COYCHURCH

1868–70: Restoration by John Prichard. (ICBS file no. 6573 (1866)) Chief features of work were restoration of nave roof with its arched and finely moulded principal and reparation of roofs of porch, chancel, transept and aisles. Interior stonework of church scraped of its coat of whitewash, and exterior stonework thoroughly repaired and reglazed. Aisles and nave repaved and chancel floor covered with tessellated tiles. Old-fashioned box pews removed and replaced with open benches to accommodate 400 parishioners. Pulpit and lectern also replaced anew, and choir placed in chancel in newly erected choir stalls. An old sacristy was preserved and new screens introduced in chancel in keeping with character of building. Tower repointed, but no structural repairs carried out due to lack of funds. Contractor: Rees Roderick, Margam. Cost £2,000. Restoration costs defrayed by dowager countess of Dunraven and other county families; ICBS grant £45; LCBS grant

£25. (*W. Mail*, 15 October, 1870) Reopened after restoration on 4 October 1870. (*CGG*, 7 October 1870)

1877: On 7 February 1877, tower suddenly collapsed crushing south transept and damaging north transept and chancel. (*CGG*, 9 February 1877) After its fall, tower temporarily walled up so that divine worship could still be held in church.

1888: Church remained in this condition for about ten years until its restoration was undertaken and completed in 1888. Architect: Frederick R. Kempson, Llandaff. (*Arch. Camb*, (1888), 401–3. Coychurch or Eglwys Llangrallo)

Comments: John Prichard took particular care with the restoration of St Crallo's as it was considered at that time to be one of the finest proportioned ecclesiastical buildings in Wales. It had attracted the attention of antiquarians and Ecclesiologists and much had been written about its architectural features. The most controversial aspect of the restoration was Prichard's wish to replace the old Perpendicular tower with a high saddleback roof with battlements, which brought him into dispute with the restoration committee. His suggestion was turned down. It was certainly the intention to restore the tower at this time, but this was never carried out, as funds were unavailable. After the tower's fall in 1877 temporary repairs were carried out so that divine worship could continue to take place in the church. Ten years later in 1888 funds were found to effect its restoration by Prichard's successor, Frederick R. Kempson.

ALL SAINTS' CHURCH, CWMAVON

(Church demolished due to subsidence in 1980)

1855–6: New church built on new site as chapel of ease to old parish church of St Michael, Michaelstone-super-Avon. Foundation stone laid on 15 May 1855 by Sir John Dean Paul. (*The Cambrian*, 18 May 1855) Built in Early English Gothic style by John Prichard of Prichard & Seddon, consisting of nave with lean-to aisles on either side with west, north and south porches, chancel with organ chamber on one side and vestry

and heating chamber on other. These, together with chancel eastward of tower and western porch, roofed with freestone on bold moulded stone ribs. Constructed of Pennant sandstone in bands of irregular rangework alternating with river pebbles in random work with quoins and dressings of Combe Down Bath stone. East window consisted of an unequal triplet, the centre light higher than flanking

14. Cwmavon Church – Messrs. Prichard & Seddon, archts (Source: *The Building News*, 24 August 1860, p. 661)

ones. West window of four lights with early Decorated-style tracery above. Chancel arch from nave to tower richly moulded and supported on double-banded serpentine columns from Cornwall. Tower with its broach spire with two tiers of lucarnes rose over western bay of chancel to a height of 180ft. On north side of tower, externally, was staircase leading to ringing loft, and on each side three deeply moulded lancet windows supported on columns with carved capitals and label stops. All carved work executed by Edward Clarke of Llandaff. Ironwork by Mr Skidmore of Coventry. Glazing of windows of green Cathedral glass, with white border next to stonework. Roofs built of Memel timber covered with boarding, felt and

Bangor slates. Doors of oak and seats and other furniture of varnished pitch-pine. Floors laid with Minton's tiles, those in sanctuary being of rich encaustic pattern. Seating accommodation for 740 parishioners. (*Bldr*, 28 June 1856, 356–7) Cost of church, £5,000, paid for by the Governor and Company of Copper Miners in England, Cwmavon. Contractors: Messrs James & Price, Cardiff. Consecrated on 10 June 1856. (*CMG*, 14 June 1856)

Comments: Just three years after his decade-long partnership began at Llandaff with John Pollard Seddon, Prichard designed All Saints. At Cwmavon he reverted to the Early English Gothic style from his customary, early Decorated or Geometrical style. He produced a functional church, well proportioned and impressive and very English despite the fact that Lyn Allen included All Saints' Church, Cwmavon in a list of churches influenced by French Gothic. (Lyn Allen, 'Some notes on the architectural work of John Prichard (1817–86) and John Pollard Seddon (1827–1906)', *The Victorian Society South Wales Group Aberystwyth Weekend*, 9–11 April, 1976, 6) Although the treatment of a light, high up in the west gable, might be indicative of French Gothic, the motif, a little lancet beneath a trefoil on capped columns is quintessentially Early English. This was a church of lancets, singles, doubles and triples. The small gabled lucarnes on the splayed broach spire with their double, slender lancets with a circular trefoil above, were just the final flourish on Prichard's thirteenth-century excursion.

ST MARY MAGDALENE'S CHURCH, CWMBACH

1881–2: New church built on new site. District in which church is situated was centre of a population of about 3,200, chiefly working-class people. There was no other church within two miles and, although a clergyman had been resident in the neighbourhood for twenty years, services held up to that time in a schoolroom which was entirely unsuited to the purpose. Foundation stone laid on 1 November 1881 by Lady Aberdare. (*W. Mail*, 2 November 1881) Built in Early English Gothic

style by E. M. Bruce Vaughan, consisting of apsidal chancel, nave, south porch and western bellcote. Constructed of blue Penrhiwceiber stone with Bath stone dressings. Nave lighted by simple lancet windows between each buttress and large west window and the west end is surmounted by a bellcote containing a single bell. Roof of open timber construction and open benches, which seat 300 worshippers, are of pitch-pine. Rood screen, which separates chancel from nave, was gift of students of Cuddesdon Theological College near Oxford. Heated by a Gurney's patent Gill stove. Pitch-pine altar, the gift of James Lewis, Plasdraw, has carved ornamental work. Contractor: John Morgan, Aberdare. Cost £959, of which Lord Windsor and Lord Aberdare contributed £100 apiece. LDCES £50; Aberdare Coal Company £50; J. C. Browne, Llettysiencyn £50. (*BN*, 25 August 1882, 245) Consecrated on 18 August 1882. (*W. Mail*, 19 August 1882)

Comments: The building committee chose E. M. Bruce Vaughan as their architect to design St Mary Magdalene's Church, Cwmbach. It was the first church built by Bruce Vaughan in Glamorgan, for it was only in 1881 that he commenced independent practice. He built the church as cheaply as possible by designing it in the less expensive Early English Gothic style with an apse at the east end: a cheap method of building a chancel. Despite the fact that the church was a plain and austere structure, costing only £959, the deficit on the building continued to be a problem for the vicar of Aberdare, the Revd J. Wynne Jones, for the next ten years. (Jeffrey Gainer, *A Short History of St Mary Magdalene's Church, Cwmbach* (Aberdare, 1982), 11)

ST GEORGE'S CHURCH, CWMPARC

1895–6: New church built on new site at Parc Isaf given by Mrs Madelina G. Llewellyn, Baglan Hall. Mrs Llewellyn had already provided mission church at Cwmparc in Rhondda Fawr in 1895 as temporary arrangement until church could be built on her land at Parc Isaf. Foundation stone laid on 17 September 1895. (*Bldr*, 21 September 1895, 208)

Built in Perpendicular Gothic style by George E. Halliday, consisting of chancel, nave, south aisle, organ chamber and square tower on south side of chancel. External walls constructed of local Welsh Pennant sandstone with hard Doulting stone used for window tracery as dressings. Internal face of walls of pointed rubble work. Pulpit and font of green Bridgend Quarella stone. Reredos of polished pink alabaster richly carved. Open benches of pitch-pine. Seating accommodation for

15. St George's Church, Cwmparc, Rhondda, built 1896 (Source: Cyril Batstone, *Rhondda Remembered* (Barry, 1983), pl. 150. (By kind permission of Stewart Williams, Barry)

400 worshippers. Hammerbeam roofs of nave and chancel constructed of pitch-pine. Five steps lead down to immersion font placed at north-west corner of nave, white brick-lined and white tiled floor. Contractor: Knox & Wells, Cardiff. Cost £4,500. Consecrated on 22 December 1896. (*W. Mail*, 23 December 1896)

Comments: At Cwmparc, Halliday chose to build the church in the Perpendicular style, a style that became his favourite idiom in the late Victorian period, when Ecclesiological correctness of style

was relaxed, and late Gothic forms were regarded as acceptable. In designing the church, Halliday followed the edicts of the Arts and Crafts movement, who complied with Pugin's rule that the church should be an honest reflection of materials and carefully related to its site. The church is particularly well crafted with its fine hammerbeam roof.

ST JOHN THE EVANGELIST'S CHURCH, MAESYGWYN, CYMMER

1888–9: New church built on land on Bedw estate given by joint owners, Revd Robert Lynche-Blosse and J. G. K. Homfray of Penlline Castle. Anglican services first held by Revd E. Morgan, vicar of Llantrisant, in a schoolroom in the area, which served as place of worship for districts of Ynyshir, Dinas, and Trehafod as well as Cymmer and Porth. (*Ch. Bldr* (1888), 31) Foundation stone laid on 14 June 1888 by Archdeacon John Griffiths of Llandaff. (*W. Mail*, 15 June 1888) Built in Early English Gothic style by E. M. Bruce Vaughan, consisting of chancel, nave, aisles, organ chamber, morning chapel, narthex at west end and flèche over chancel arch. Constructed of local Pennant sandstone with Bath stone dressings. East window of five trefoil-headed lights with Geometrical-style tracery in head. Chancel has wagon roof with flat square bosses at intersections of ribs and with vaulting shafts between arches. Pillars, capitals, arches and trefoil-headed piscina all in thirteenth-century style. Chancel arch is plainly corbelled out on a similar drop arrangement to vaulting shafts. Small deeply splayed trefoil-headed windows with plate tracery between massive two-stage buttresses light nave. Nave separated from aisles by arcade of five high-pointed arches with pierced spandrels and stylized clerestory above, springing from slender octagonal pillars, all constructed of wood. West end of nave lighted by four trefoil lights with Geometrical-style tracery above. Nave has arch-braced roof. Open benches of pitch-pine. (Personal observation) Seating accommodation for 500 worshippers. Contractor: William Rees, Merthyr Vale. Cost £2,500. Consecrated on 5 June 1889. (*Pontypridd Chr.*, 8 June 1889)

Comments: John Newman regarded St John the Evangelist's Church as a good example of Bruce Vaughan's 'cheap and simple buildings for valley communities' with its 'ingeniously economical timber arcade'. (Newman, 95 and 527) The use of timber for the arcade was questioned by the consulting architect in his report on the design of the church to the ICBS. Bruce Vaughan replied that there was a precedent for such a structure in Lower Peover Church, Cheshire. (ICBS file no. 9230 (1888)) In fact, Bruce Vaughan could also have cited Prichard's church at St Clement's, Briton Ferry, erected in 1866 with timber arcade. St John the Evangelist's Church, Cymmer was a typical, cheap Victorian Anglican Church under one large, continuous, steeply gabled roof supported on principals springing from the stone corbels, which were in turn supported by solid buttresses.

ST JOHN'S CHURCH, DOWLAIS

1893–4: First St John's Church, founded by Sir John Guest and consecrated on 27 November 1827, was smaller, square building with tall windows and square tower with windows on each side. There was a flat roof to church and a gallery immediately opposite chancel and pulpit. Its neat classical lines were in many ways more reminiscent of a Nonconformist chapel than an Anglican church. Small additions made to chancel in 1873 and to transept in 1881 to design by William Lintern. Most of expense borne by Lord Wimborne.

During the years 1893–4, church restored and enlarged to accommodate 800 parishioners. Restored church is a fine building of Llancaiach blue Pennant sandstone with dressings of Forest of Dean and Bath stone. Internally, parts of nave and aisle lined with buff pressed bricks pointed in red cement. Church lies along a north–south line. Restored in Early English Gothic style by Edwin Arthur Johnson of Abergavenny, consisting of chancel, nave, aisle, transept, Lady chapel, clerestory and vestry inside, and a western turret and east and west porches. New extended aisle was gift of Edward Pritchard Martin, general manager of the Dowlais Iron Company, in memory of his parents. (Huw Williams, *A History of the Church in Dowlais on the 150th anniversary of St John's Church, Dowlais, 1827–1977* (Mountain Ash, 1977), 9) Flat roof gives way to arch-braced hammerbeam roof with tie-beams supported on stone corbels, and gallery removed. Old high-backed pews replaced by open benches. Joinery, of both roof and seats, of pitch-pine. Tile flooring by Messrs Godwin & Sons, Hereford. Heating apparatus fitted by George Davis, Abergavenny & Newport. (*BN*, 12 October 1894, 510) Contractor: Walter Dowland, Abergavenny. Cost £4,500. Consecrated on 4 October 1894. (*Merthyr Times*, 11 October 1894)

Comments: The rebuilding and enlargement of St John's in the years 1893–4 by Edwin A. Johnson was a total remodelling and reordering of the old square-shaped church built in 1827 and altered in 1873 and 1881. Johnson designed the new church in the Early English Gothic style taking as his precedent the chancel and transept. His high, wide nave is lighted by elongated Early English-style lancets which mirror the tall round-headed windows of the original building. They are mostly in pairs with a quatrefoil in the head, but the west window is a triplet in the same style. The interior of the nave was reordered by the removal of the old high-backed pews and three-decker pulpit characteristic of the early nineteenth-century auditory church with its emphasis on the sermon and the spoken word. At Dowlais, the survival of the church furniture and fittings of the early part of the century could be witnessed late into the last decade of the century.

In 1906 a new vestry was added on north side of the chancel and a new three-manual organ by Norman & Beard was erected in a newly constructed organ chamber. Architect: E. M. Bruce Vaughan, Cardiff. Contractor: Enoch Williams, Dowlais. (*Bldr*, 3 March 1906, 238)

ST BRICE'S CHURCH, EGLWYS BREWIS

1900: Restoration of church. During incumbency of Revd H. C. Davies (1894–1906), church restored under auspices of Society for the Protection

16. St Brice's Church, Eglwys Brewis (Photo: W. P. Pring, L.R.P.S) (By kind permission of D. Brown & Sons Ltd, Cowbridge)

of Ancient Buildings under direction of their architect, William Weir. (*Bldr*, 18 August 1900, 159) Church probably smallest in Glamorgan consisting of nave (24ft 6insx15ft 5ins) and chancel (17ft 9insx12ft 10ins). (*BN*, 24 August 1900, 246–7) Great care taken to retain original character of church and work regarded more as a 'reparation' than a restoration. Work consisted mainly in strengthening walls, especially chancel arch which was of thirteenth-century date. This was in a very poor state due to the fact that it had been built of small stones embedded in clay. Weir rebuilt damaged core by interspersing seams of concrete with coarse bands of flat stones which were inserted through one side of wall leaving other side intact throughout. Parts of east side of chancel arch also repaired including a bulge above apex of arch and the fifteenth-century doorway on north side leading to former rood-loft. East wall of chancel also strengthened and dropped relieving arch above east window raised. On removal of whitewash and plaster, a coffin-shaped niche on

north side of wall was uncovered and restored to its original state. Old oak principals of roof, which were of slight construction, replaced by sturdier ones of oak. Cost £500. (*SWDN*, 9 August 1900) Reopened after restoration in September 1900. (*MCVG*, 143)

Comments: Eglwys Brewis Church was one of Glamorgan churches restored in the late Victorian period in accordance with the principles of the Society for the Protection of Ancient Buildings. As Eglwys Brewis Church was such an important building, with its interior dominated by wall paintings in the form of seventeenth-century biblical texts as well as the Royal Arms of William and Mary, the Society was careful to send its own architect, William Weir, to carry out this important work of reparation. His method of repair, which consisted of interspersing seams of concrete with coarse bands of flat stones through one side of the chancel wall, was known as 'Webb's sandwich', a process evolved by Philip Webb, a founder member of the Society. As it now stands, apart from the work of reparation mentioned above and the remodelling of the nave in the fifteenth century, the structure of Eglwys Brewis Church remains virtually unaltered since the church was built in the thirteenth century.

ST ILAN'S CHURCH, EGLWYSILAN

1873–5: Restoration of church by Charles Buckeridge. A schedule for complete rebuilding of church, dated 1871, exists in ICBS files in Lambeth Palace library. Chancel completely rebuilt at time, but nave restored simply by rebuilding large parts of walls. Pennant sandstone used for reconstruction of church. East window of three trefoiled lights. Apart from three-light window in south of nave, all other windows date from this restoration. Fifteenth-century wagon roof of nave repaired and restored. Interior of nave reseated with open benches of pitch-pine. In north-east corner of nave behind pulpit are remains of staircase that led to the rood-loft. Original twelfth-century Norman font with its large cylindrical bowl remains in its traditional place near stone doorway. (Personal observation) Chancel arch left untouched by Buckeridge and is a plain, pointed one, rather straight-sided, which fits Glynne's accurate description when he visited the church on 17 May 1851. (Sir Stephen R. Glynne, 'Notes on the older churches in the four Welsh dioceses', *Arch. Camb.* (1901), 267) Reseating of interior provided accommodation for 180 worshippers. Cost £1,040. Reopened after restoration in November 1875. (ICBS file no. 7233 (1871))

1888: Unbuttressed west tower of church restored at cost of £446. ICBS grant £50. (*Kelly's Directory of South Wales*, 1926, 431)

Comments: Buckeridge's restoration of St Ilan's destroyed much of the upland church's medieval character, including the ancient stone bench along the south wall of the chancel. Fortunately, the fifteenth-century wagon roof remained intact, apart from some restoration of the timbers. At least the new windows inserted on the north side of the church improved the light in the previously dark nave described by Glynne. The reseating and reordering of the interior improved the comfort of the church for those parishioners who braved the elements to attend St Ilan's Church in its exposed and isolated position above Abertridwr.

ST MARY'S CHURCH, EWENNY PRIORY

17. Ewenny Priory Church – south transept from presbytery (Photo: W. P. Pring, L.R.P.S.) (By kind permission of D. Brown & Sons Ltd, Cowbridge)

1870: Restoration of church. Work of restoration, begun fifty years previously, continued by Lt. Col. Thomas Picton Turbervill on advice of Professor Edward Freeman, the medieval historian and famous Victorian Ecclesiologist. Two of three enormous buttresses on both sides of presbytery were removed leaving one at east end. Interior of presbytery repaired and reglazed and all traces of whitewash removed. Old oak screen repaired and presbytery paved with encaustic tiles. Large tombs, which encumbered presbytery, were removed to south transept and floor of transept repaired and concreted. Walls also repaired. (*MCVG*, 158–9)

1875–7: Restoration of nave. Old-fashioned square box pews were removed and replaced by open benches. Present pulpit erected on north side of nave. Tower restored. (*MCVG*, 159)

1889: Great arch separating nave from choir opened out and separating wall brought down to its original level. (Ibid.)

1895–6: Restoration of church by John Thomas Micklethwaite, London. Construction of new north aisle, narrower than that built in sixteenth century and in keeping with original Norman aisle. Tudor porch pulled down and rebuilt in new position. Masonry blocking up arcade removed. Floor of nave lowered to its original level exposing bases of pillars of arcade. Two large Tudor windows in south wall removed and Norman windows restored. Flat plaster ceiling taken down and plain oak roof raised to its original height. New vestry built on site of ruined north transept. Clerestory windows above north arcade restored. Architect: John Thomas Micklethwaite, London. Contractors: Turbervill estate workforce. Cost £1,000. Reopened after restoration on 29 September 1896. (*SWDN*, 30 September 1896)

Comments: At St Mary's, the traditional Anglican liturgical arrangements with the retention of the three-decker pulpit and old-fashioned high-backed pews had survived well into the second half of the nineteenth century. Therefore the restoration in the years 1875–7 was essentially a reordering of the nave, which included the removal of the three-decker pulpit and square box pews and their replacement with modern furniture. The work carried out in the years 1886–96 was a restoration of the nave of Ewenny Priory Church, which had always formed the parish church, and had always been kept separate from the monastic east end used by the monks. The work was aimed at undoing the damage done to the nave during the sixteenth century and restoring it to its original Norman design. Micklethwaite's painstaking re-construction of the Norman church during the years 1895–6 completed the work of restoration undertaken by the Turbervill family, who had been for centuries past generous benefactors of the Priory Church.

CHRIST CHURCH, FERNDALE
(Church demolished in 1968)

1885–6: New church built on an acre of ground which had been site of St Paul's Church, Ferndale, an iron church erected in 1877 and which necessitated removing the latter to another part of the ground to be the church for Welsh congregation. New church required to meet demand for additional church accommodation resulting from great increase in population of district of Ferndale. (*Ch. Bldr* (1885), 34) Built in Early English Gothic style by E. M. Bruce Vaughan. Cruciform in plan (without central tower) consisting of chancel with north vestry, nave with transepts, north porch and western bellcote. Constructed of Welsh Pennant sandstone with Bath stone dressings. East window of three trefoil-headed lights with three circular apertures punched through plate tracery with internal hood mould. Transepts lighted by pairs of single lancets with oval orifice above and nave by trefoil-headed lancets between Early English-style buttresses. West window similar in design to east window. Sedilia in south wall of sanctuary and credence table on north wall. Chamfered pointed chancel arch sprang from moulded capitals on pillarets. Similar arches to transepts. Chancel had arch-braced roof and nave had open timber arrangement with ceiling plastered between common rafters. Two-stage buttresses supported walls of church. (Personal observation from an old photograph of interior) Transepts provided seating facing east. Seating accommodation for 352 worshippers. Contractor: D. J. Davies, Cardiff. Cost £2,082. (*W. Mail*, 24 July 1886)

Comments: Christ Church was another rather plain church designed by E. M. Bruce Vaughan in the Rhondda, but with the benefit of transepts. It was one of the first churches to benefit from a substantial grant of £350 by the Bishop of Llandaff's newly inaugurated fund. Although plans to enlarge the church were drawn up in 1899 by Bruce Vaughan, the work was never carried out due to the fact that Ferndale was formed into a separate parish in 1902, and the new vicar, Revd John Rees, decided to build another church, St

Dunstan's, erected in 1905. This new church was built to accommodate 509 worshippers in the parish of Ferndale. (ICBS file no. 10, 190 (1899))

ST MICHAEL'S CHURCH, FLEMINGSTON

1858: Restoration of general fabric of church including south chapel carried out at entire expense of Caroline, countess of Dunraven, patron of living. Work included insertion of several modern windows with Portland stone dressings and new east window. Sir Stephen R. Glynne visited the church on 27 September 1848 and described it thus, 'A small church, consisting of a nave with south transept, a porch and chancel. Over the west end of the nave is a gable for two bells in open arches. The porch is set very close to the west end of the nave, and has a wood roof, and a stone seat on the west side only . . . At the west end of the nave is a stone bench . . . The chancel arch is a rude misshapen one, bulging out, and without mouldings . . .There is a rood-door at some height on the south side of the chancel arch . . . The exterior walls of the church are white-washed, according to the practice of the neigh-bourhood.' (Sir Stephen R. Glynne, 'Notes on the older churches in the four Welsh dioceses', *Arch. Camb.* (1901), 252) The restoration, ten years after Glynne's visit, swept away all traces of former rood-loft. Chancel arch replaced with pointed one of larger span with mouldings, and whitewash, which Glynne also noticed on exterior walls, removed, and lancet high in west end of nave blocked up. West end of nave wall strengthened on either side by solid buttresses. Pulpit and open benches of oak erected in nave. (*Bldr*, 14 August 1858, 559) Exterior fabric completely restored and surmounted with double bellcote containing two bells recast by John Warner & Sons, London. Reopened after restoration on 4 August 1858. (*CMG*, 7 August 1858)

Comments: The architect who restored the church is not recorded, but it was probably John Prichard of Llandaff. As John Newman properly states, the architect introduced several 'oversized' Decorated-style windows throughout the chancel and nave, taking the windows on the south and west side of the funerary chapel of the Le Fleming family as the basis for the style of these new insertions. (Newman, 349) The west windows of the nave lack the 'bulbous' appearance of the other windows of the church and are more appropriate to the style of the original fourteenth-century church. The restoration, which was considerable and costly with the use of Portland stone dressings, was carried out by an architect clearly influenced by the new interpretation of the Anglican Church liturgy, which is manifest in the ecclesiological reordering of the interior of the church.

ST MARY THE VIRGIN'S CHURCH, GARTH

1891–2: New church built on new site. Early services in district held in 'upper room' of nearby Garth Inn. Church owed its existence to generosity of two members of landed gentry, Miss Olive Talbot of Margam Abbey and Lt. Col. J. P. Turbervill, principal landowner in the Garth district. Miss Talbot donated cost of building, a sum of £1,600 and the colonel donated land on which church was built. Foundation stone laid on 14 September 1891 by Mrs J. Picton Turbervill of Ewenny Priory. (*CGG*, 18 September 1891) Built in Perpendicular Gothic style from designs by George E. Halliday, consisting of chancel (30ftx24ft), nave (57ftx27ft), south porch framed with oak timbers and a western bellcote. Open timbered roof covered with Broseley tiles. Roof of chancel panelled with moulded ribs, and floral bosses placed at intersections over sanctuary. East window of four cinquefoiled lights with rectilinear tracery in head, and west window consists of a large Rose window. Nave lighted by eight cinquefoiled windows, six of which are massed on south side, four of two lights, one of three lights, and one of four lights with panel tracery above and separated externally by two-stage buttresses. Chancel paved with ornamental encaustic tiles. Open benches of pitch-pine, stained and varnished. (Personal observation) Seating accommo-dation for 208 parishioners. Contractor: William

Cox, Llandaff. Cost £1,600. Church opened for divine service on 30 November 1892. (*W. Mail*, 1 December 1892)

Comments: Miss Olive Talbot chose her favourite architect, George E. Halliday, to design the church. He built the church in the Perpendicular Gothic style, an idiom he used frequently during his career, when late Gothic forms were accepted. His use of half-timbering in the porch at Garth was an innovative feature for Glamorgan churches. Halliday followed the example of the majority of Welsh churches by massing six windows on the south side of the nave in contrast to two on the north.

ST CATWG'S CHURCH, GELLIGAER

1866: Restoration of nave by Charles Buckeridge. By 1862 when Revd Gilbert Harries became rector of Gelligaer, St Catwg's Church had become neglected and in poor state of repair. Collapse of nave roof in September 1866 prompted rector to set about immediate restoration of nave. Work included raising an entirely new arch-braced roof of Memel timber. Walls strengthened by addition of two-stage solid buttresses, two on north side and three on south. Floor lowered to its original level by about 15 ins. During excavation work which was necessary for this purpose and for installing heating apparatus, bones of some 200 people found. Around wrists, some still-perfect wreaths of box discovered. Chancel arch, which was formerly very narrow, entirely rebuilt. Old doorway to rood-loft on north side of chancel discovered and exposed to view. New pulpit installed in nave and built from timber obtained from rector's Llanunwas estate in Pembrokeshire. Baptistery near south doorway, which was used for adult baptism by total immersion, constructed at this time. (*Bldr*, 2 February 1867, 85) Cost £1,200. Reopened after restoration on 20 December 1866. (*CMG*, 4 January 1867)

Comments: Harries commissioned his favourite architect, Charles Buckeridge of Oxford, whom he had employed previously while rural dean of Breconshire. His design of the new chancel arch

included a double-chamfered continuous arch of a well-proportioned lancet shape. During the reconstruction of the chancel arch, a piscina was discovered in the north wall and the architect, a follower of the Ecclesiological Society, was careful to preserve it in the church. Buckeridge renewed the fenestration of the nave, modelling his new insertions on those of the chancel – two windows of three trefoil-headed lights each side of the south porch and a four-light window in the south-east wall of the nave, which was an unusual arrangement for a Glamorgan church. As at St Tyfaelog's Church in Pontlottyn, Buckeridge built an immersion font because Harries was determined that no one should be deterred from the Anglican Church by scruples about total immersion, such as the Baptists in the parish. Only the nave was restored at this time, since funds were not sufficient to restore the chancel as well.

ST GILES' CHURCH, GILESTON

18. St Giles' Church, Gileston (Photo: W. P. Pring, L.R.P.S.) (By kind permission of D. Brown & Sons Ltd, Cowbridge)

1884–5: Restoration of church. When Sir Stephen R. Glynne visited the church on 24 July 1871 he wrote, 'A small church, prettily placed close to the mansion-house and comprising nave and chancel only, with south porch. Over the west end is a small square-topped bell-cot, embattled like that of Eglwys Brewis, and set on corbels. The chancel arch is Pointed, but very rude; within it is a plain wood screen of Perpendicular character. There are no windows on the north . . . The west door is closed. The interior is pewed, but neat.' (Sir Stephen R. Glynne, 'Notes on the older churches in the four Welsh dioceses', *Arch. Camb.* (1901), 254) Church partially restored in 1885 when Revd Montague Welby of Gileston Manor complained to patron of living, Lady Hills-Johnes, that Gileston church was unfit for divine worship. (*MCVG*, 170) Old-fashioned high-backed pews removed and replaced by individual oak chairs, thereby providing additional seating for twenty-five parishioners. Old broken paving stones taken up and wood flooring laid down. Chancel not touched in any way except for removal of high-backed pews, cost of which was borne by Revd Welby. (LL/F/330. Repair and enlargement of church. Faculty dated 29 April 1885)

Comments: The restoration of St Giles' in 1885 was basically a reseating and repair of the nave floor. The more extensive restoration was carried out in 1903, when the dangerous condition of the bell-turret, supported only by a rusty iron band, caused services to be suspended until the church was restored and made safe for divine worship. Some controversy was caused when the rector wrote to Halliday asking him to raise the chancel floor above the nave and alter the arrangement of the altar steps. Halliday immediately referred this matter to the bishop since the architect had given the bishop his word that no structural alteration would be undertaken under his direction, and Halliday felt that this was an 'unnecessary and uncalled for innovation'. (LL/F/331. Corr. Letter from G. E. Halliday to the bishop of Llandaff, dated 26 August 1903) No alteration was permitted in the level of the chancel floor as a result of Halliday's letter. (LL/F/331. Restoration of church. Faculty dated 2 July 1903) Cost £700. Mrs Johnes and Lady Hills-Johnes, principal landowners in the parish, subscribed £88, and the remainder came from public subscriptions and a grant of £20 from the ICBS. (ICBS file no. 10,436 (1903))

ST BARNABAS' CHURCH, GILFACH GOCH

(Church reconstructed in 1950s after bomb damage)

1896–7: New church built on new site by E. M. Bruce Vaughan. The district of Gilfach Goch was most inaccessible from every direction, being shut in by high ranges of mountains from the remainder of the three parishes of Llantrisant, Llandyfodwg and Llwynypia of which Gilfach Goch was constituted. Situated eight miles from parish church of Llantrisant. Prior to building of church, services held since 1867 in iron church near Scotch Row. Also found necessary to build a permanent church because of growing population of district. (*Ch. Bldr* (1896), 64) Foundation stone of new church laid on 24 September 1896 by Mrs Christmas Evans. Original estimate for building was £1,867, but by building only the nave the cost was reduced to £1,489. Built in Early English Gothic style with south porch and west bellcote. Constructed of local Pennant sandstone with Bath stone dressings. Nave lighted by pairs of two-light windows with plate tracery in heads positioned between solid buttresses with set-offs. West window of two single lights and west wall supported by three tall buttresses, connected by stringcourse, necessitated by fact that church was built on sloping site. Seating accommodation for 300 worshippers. (ICBS file no. 9903 (1896)) Church opened and dedicated on 19 August 1897. (*St Barnabas' Church Magazine*, September 1964)

Comments: St Barnabas' was one of many churches built in Glamorgan during the Victorian period which, because of lack of funds, consisted of nave only. It was a very plain structure without any ornamentation and designed by Bruce Vaughan who had a reputation for building cheap churches in poor mining communities. In most cases half-built churches were completed in the early part of the twentieth century, but St Barnabas was not completed until 1933, more than thirty years later.

ST PAUL'S CHURCH, GLAIS

1881: New church built on new site, donated by Mrs Wood of Velindre. Basic plan of new church was to adapt a disused barn as basis of new building. Glais, with some 500 inhabitants (principally colliers), was a remote part of parish of Llansamlet for whom there was neither church nor chapel accommodation; the parish church was three miles off, a range of hills intervening. (*Ch. Bldr* (1881), 32) At east end an apsidal chancel with choir stalls was added to the building and an extension of about 15ft was made at west end, which was later surmounted by a bellcote. Building in its renovated form is 74ftx20ft and Gothic in style with freestone dressings. Accommodation on open benches of pitch-pine for 250 worshippers and floors paved with encaustic tiles. Well furnished with font, reading desk, altar table and altar rails, all modelled after most approved style. Architect: Henry Francis Clarke, Briton Ferry. Contractor: David Rees, Ystalyfera. Cost £450. Church dedicated on 15 September 1881. (*The Cambrian*, 23 September 1881)

Comments: St Paul's is undoubtedly one of the plainest and humblest of churches erected in Glamorgan during the Victorian period. Yet it served its purpose as an Anglican church where the colliers and their families could worship in the latter years of the nineteenth century. It was by erecting such plain places of worship that the Anglican Church in Glamorgan was able to provide church accommodation at this period.

ST JOHN THE BAPTIST'S CHURCH, GLYNCORRWG

1858: At this time roof of church was so badly holed that in wet weather rain fell into seats and onto worshippers, while part of chancel was used by farmers as a store for red markings used on their sheep. Some money raised by public subscription, but insufficient to replace old roof which was taken down in that year. Consequently, church stood without a roof and in ruins until restoration was undertaken in 1863. (Revd Alan

Davies, *St John the Baptist Church, Glyncorrwg: Jubilee Souvenir 1957: Observations on the History of the Church* (1957), 10)

1863–4: Restoration of church. Church had been restored by 1864, but faculty issued for rebuilding church in 1905 was uncomplimentary about restoration work. It stated 'a bad modern roof' had been put on, new windows built into the nave walls, new porch erected, tower walls roofed over by a continuation of nave roof and a badly designed bellcote placed on apex of west wall. West doorway and doorway in south side of chancel bricked up at same time. (LL/F/333. Demolition of old church and erection of new and larger church. Faculty dated 31 July 1905) *Llandaff Diocesan Handbook* for 1874 mentions that church furnishings were donated by Mrs Nash Edwards Vaughan of Rheola and the 'chandeliers' by vicar. Cost £520. Reopened after restoration on 7 July 1864. (*CMG*, 8 July 1864)

Comments: St John the Baptist's Church, demolished in 1905, was clearly of medieval foundation and its thirteenth-century chancel did not survive earlier rebuilding. However, a fifteenth-century east window, a holy-water stoup and an ancient font were all incorporated in the new building, which accommodated 300 worshippers compared with eighty-nine in the old church. The church was situated in a poor mountain parish, and churchwardenized repairs carried out in the early part of the nineteenth century and an ineffective restoration in 1864 were inadequate to arrest the decay of the structure.

In the years 1905–7 the church was rebuilt in the Perpendicular Gothic style, a late Gothic form, which had been generally accepted as a suitable idiom by architects at that period. Seating 300 persons, it was built on a larger scale on the same site by E. M. Bruce Vaughan. Contractor: Philip Gaylard, Bridgend. Cost £3,000. Foundation stone laid on 18 August 1905. (*Bldr*, 2 September 1905, 258; Revd Roger L. Brown, *Through Cloud and Sunshine: A History of the Church in the Upper Afan Valley* (Port Talbot, 1982), 105) Consecrated on 12 March 1907. (*W. Mail*, 13 March 1907)

ST MARY'S CHURCH, GLYNTAFF (NEWBRIDGE)

1837–9: New church built on new site. Built in Neo-Norman style by Thomas Henry Wyatt, of Wyatt & Brandon, London, consisting of apsidal chancel, nave with north and south aisles, west gallery, vestry at south-west corner and north-west tower. (ICBS file no. 2026 (1836)) Constructed of Welsh Pennant sandstone with Doulting stone dressings. Apse lighted by three narrow, round-headed lights. Chancel arch round-headed springing from scalloped capitals and on either side are two round-headed doorways above which are two round-headed lights. Large nave lighted on either side by seven tall round-headed windows between flat slender buttresses, and west end of nave by pair of tall round-headed lights above which is an oculus in west gable. Norman-style doorway has nook shafts with scalloped capitals and is decorated with chevron mouldings. Nave has a flat plaster ceiling and west gallery is approached by staircase in a projection in north-west corner of nave. Pair of high pulpits, one for service, other for sermon, tower over square-box pews which accommodate 800 worshippers; 710 are free and unappropriated. Asymmetrically placed tower at the north-west corner of four stages with low belfry stage of five round-headed lights on its west and east faces beneath which is a slit aperture. Font stands near Communion table. Church opened for divine worship on 22 April 1838. (*Glamorgan, Monmouth & Brecon Gazette and Merthyr Guardian*, 28 April 1838) Church endowed with £400 by the Hon. R. H. Clive and J. Bruce Pryce. Cost £2,500. Church Commissioners' grant £414; ICBS grant £400. Consecrated on 29 October 1839. (*Glamorgan, Monmouth & Brecon Gazette and Merthyr Guardian*, 2 November 1839)

Comments: St Mary's was the first Commissioners' church to be built in Glamorgan. Wyatt built the church in the Neo-Norman style, which was briefly popular in the 1840s. In 1838 the church had an austere, cavernous interior with only a small chancel arch between the shallow chancel and nave with wall-to-wall west gallery, seating altogether 800 worshippers. Its design was obviously intended as a preaching-box, housing as many worshippers as possible, which was typical of the Commissioners' churches at that time. The repair and improvement of the church in 1906 was long overdue to bring it up to date with modern church arrangements.

In 1906 the church was restored and reseated. Individual chairs replaced old benches. Font placed at west end of church. Architect: Arthur Lloyd Thomas, Pontypridd. Cost £800. Additional accommodation of fifty seats in the gallery. (LL/F/339. Repair and improvement of church. Faculty dated 27 June 1906)

HOLY TRINITY CHURCH, GORSEINON

(Church demolished in 1984)

1882–3: New church built on new site given by William Lewis, Melyn Monach, as chapel of ease to parish church of Llandeilo Tal-y-bont. Architect: Edward Bath of Swansea. (ICBS file no. 8792 (1881)) Foundation stone laid on Thursday 29 June 1882 by Mrs Howel Gwyn of Dyffryn, Neath. (*The Cambrian*, 30 June 1882) Built in Early English Gothic style. Cruciform in plan consisting of chancel with vestry, with heating chamber below, nave, transepts, choir under central tower, and north porch. Constructed of Welsh Pennant sandstone with Bath stone dressings. Chancel built in form of an octagon with east window of two lights with plate tracery above. Woodwork used in interior of pitch-pine, which included open benches accommodating 300 worshippers. Chancel roof pyramidal in design and nave roof of open timber arrangement, of which principal rafters were of red deal. Central tower had three belfry lights on its cardinal faces with a pyramidal roof. Walls of tower supported by two-stage solid buttresses on north and south sides. Nave lighted by single and paired lancet windows with hood moulds. Transepts lighted by pairs of broad lancets with oval apertures above. North porch had high-pitched gable and shafted and moulded doorway. Cost £1,800. Cost of tower defrayed by J. T. D. Llewelyn of Penllergare and Howel Gwyn, Dyffryn, Neath. Consecrated on 17 August 1883. (*The Cambrian*, 24 August 1883)

Comments: The design of Holy Trinity Church by Edward Bath was indeed unusual, if not idiosyncratic, with its octagonal chancel and pyramidal roof. The Committee of Architects of the ICBS made strong objections to the design, especially the chancel, and stated that 'the chancel is much too narrow and much too small in every way and the external gabled cants of the octagon are very objectionable. The roof framing is unsatisfactory and the scantlings of the timbers too light. The porch is too small and pinched in width.' (ICBS file no. 8792 (1881)) As a result the Society refused a grant. However, the incumbent, Revd J. W. Jones, succeeded in building the church with the help of the local landowning gentry without changing the idiosyncratic design of the chancel.

ST JOHN THE DIVINE'S CHURCH, GOWERTON

1880–2: New church built on new site given by Sir J. T. D. Llewelyn of Penllergare as chapel of ease to St Michael's Church, Loughor. Erection of church in this part of parish of Loughor at Gowerton needed because of its distance, some 2½ miles, from parish church at Loughor and because road to it was often impassable owing to tidal conditions prevailing in Burry Estuary. Evident that new church would have to serve a population of about 2,000 parishioners. (ICBS file no. 8522 (1880)) Foundation stone laid on 5 August 1880 by Lady Julia Llewelyn of Penllergare. (*The Cambrian*, 6 August 1890) Built in simple form of Decorated Gothic style by John Bacon Fowler of Swansea and Brecon. (*Bldr*, 4 September 1880) Church consists of chancel with vestry and organ chamber, nave, south porch, and western bellcote, which is carried on relieving arch of west window which springs from inner side of massive, single-stage buttresses. Constructed of Welsh Pennant sandstone with Bridgend stone for internal dressings. Interior fittings, including open benches to seat a congregation of 264 worshippers, are in varnished pitch-pine. East window consists of three cinquefoiled lights and west window of two cinquefoiled lights with a quatrefoil in apex. Nave lighted by single, double and triple cinquefoiled windows under square heads. Single-stage buttresses support chancel and nave walls, with massive corner buttresses to south porch. Chancel and nave have arch-braced roofs with iron ties. Octagonal font. Contractors: Messrs Thomas, Watkins & Jenkins, Swansea. Cost £2,900. Sir J. T. D. Llewelyn, Penllergare £1,000. ICBS grant £150. Messrs Wright, Butler & Co. Gower Road £300. Bishop of St David's £25. Consecrated on 5 September 1882. (*The Cambrian*, 8 September 1882) **1886:** Chancel beautified and three stained glass windows inserted by Colonel Sir J. Roper Wright. (*Kelly's Directory of South Wales*, 1926, 453) **1900:** Chancel lined with Italian marble and marble reredos erected at cost of £1,000, the gift of Colonel Sir J. Roper Wright. Dedicated February 1900. (Hywel Rees, *St John's Church, Gowerton* (1996), 9)

Comments: Ewan Christian, consulting architect to the ICBS, made some objections to John Bacon Fowler's plan. He stated that the groin dressings shown were in most cases 'exceeding miserable and useless in respect of strength'. He recommended the use of local stone with a straight arris and greater length of bond and the use of dressed stone for the mullions of the side windows. Furthermore, he recommended that the principal rafters of the nave roof should be framed into wall beams at the bottom and should be secured to the collars by bolts. (ICBS file no. 8522 (1880)) The bell gable is clearly the architect's principal statement and he envisaged the structure as a whole from top to floor. The massive buttresses support the west wall of the nave and enclose the west window. The relieving arch of the bellcote springs from inside the buttresses. The buttresses then continue upwards as engaged pinnacles, which in practice actually serve to enhance and balance the base of the bellcote.

ST LLEURWG'S CHURCH, HIRWAUN

1857–8: New church built on new site given by marchioness of Bute. Building work commenced on 27 April 1857. (*The Cambrian*, 23 July 1857) Built in Early English Gothic style by Alexander Roos, architect to the Bute estate, consisting of

19. St Lleurwg's Church, Hirwaun. Real Photo Series. W. L. Mason, Cynon Terrace, Hirwaun (Source: Geoffrey R. Orrin: Postcard Collection of Glamorgan Churches)

chancel with north vestry, nave with west gallery, two-storeyed south porch with upper room lighted by trefoil light, and western bellcote. (ICBS file no. 5035 (1856)) Constructed of Welsh Pennant sandstone with Bath stone dressings. East window of three lights. Nave lighted by broad lancets between single-stage buttresses. West gable pierced by two single lancets flanking a two-stage central buttress, above which is a single bellcote incorporating chimney stack. Corner buttresses to west wall of nave on north and south sides. Nave has roof of open timber construction. Total seating capacity 350 worshippers. Contractor: William Dork, Cardiff. Cost £1,680. ICBS grant refused due to poor design; LCBS grant £50; LDCES grant £100. Church opened for divine worship on 20 July 1858. (*CMG*, 24 July 1858)

1883–4: Church enlarged by new chancel and south chapel. Seating capacity increased by fifty sittings. Architect: E. M. Bruce Vaughan, Cardiff. Cost £735. ICBS grant £20. (*Ch. Bldr* (1883), 82)

Comments: The correspondent in the *Church Builder* for 1883 (p. 82) stated that 'the church was built A.D. 1858; application was then made to the Society, but the plans were so bad that aid could not be given'. The ICBS file reveals that the Society's Committee of Architects reported that 'the roof is objectionable and should be differently constructed. The society's instructions have not been adhered to, as respects the height and span of the walls.' Roos replied by saying that the roof of All Saints' Church, Cardiff and several other ecclesiastical buildings had been built on the same principle and were not found objectionable. He complained that to modify the design, by increasing the height of the walls and adding common rafters and tie-beams to the roof to prevent lateral pressure on the walls, would cost an additional £200. Despite Roos's protests the Committee of Architects remained adamant and insisted that the design be modified accordingly. Roos was unable to modify the design due to restricted funds and therefore forfeited the award of a grant. (ICBS file no. 5035 (1856)). It is evident from a visual examination of the roof structure that at some time since 1858 the roof has, in fact, been modified by the addition of common rafters and tie-beams in order to prevent lateral pressure on the walls. Alexander Roos's plan is most unusual with its two-storeyed porch and chimney stack as an integral part of the west bellcote.

In the years 1907–8 the church was restored and enlarged by the construction of a new and enlarged vestry, new organ chamber and north aisle. Seating accommodation increased to 243 sittings. Cost £900. Architect: George E. Halliday, Cardiff. (LL/F/349. New vestry, organ chamber and north aisle. Faculty dated 26 July 1907)

ST ILLTYD'S CHURCH, ILSTON

1847: Restoration of church carried out during incumbency of the Revd John Collins, rector of the parish from 1810 to 1854. Sir Stephen Glynne on his visit in August 1847 described the church as 'an interesting specimen of a church of Gower, lately put into a state of order and repair . . . The chancel arch is pointed and springs immediately from the wall without moulding. The west end of the nave has a middle-pointed window of two lights . . . The east window has three lancet lights beneath a pointed arch, the hood having crowned heads for corbels . . . The roofs are newly slated, and there is a very good cross on the east gable and on the west . . . The whole interior is very neat, with new open benches, and the general appearance of this church contrasts agreeably with the neglected state of most churches in Gower.' (Sir Stephen R. Glynne: 'Notes on the older churches in the four Welsh dioceses', *Arch. Camb.* (1897), 293) At the restoration many of the internal features of the church such as square double pews were removed and replaced by free open benches. A watercolour sketch of the church before the restoration (now displayed in the nave) shows the chancel arch to be round (now pointed) and a large tall pew in the chancel formerly occupied by major Penrice of Kilvrough. Pew removed and chancel refurbished. New east and larger window of three

lights in the Early English Gothic style replaced a smaller two-light window. (Geoffrey R. Orrin, *The Gower Churches* (Penmaen, 1979), 34–7) *The Cambrian* newspaper reported that 'On Sunday last (21 November 1847) the church of Ilston in Gower was reopened for divine service. The Revd W. Collins officiated in the morning and the Revd John Collins preached in the evening to respectable and numerous assemblages. The edifice is now in a comfortable state of repair and will contain a goodly number of persons . . . Collections to defray the expenses of the alterations were made at the close of services.' (*The Cambrian*, 26 November 1847) On 3 December 1847 Revd John Collins wrote to ICBS for grant aid to pay for the expense for rearranging the seating accommodation in the church. 'I have had a church rate granted for absolute necessary repairs only, I have collected subscriptions for the amount of £50 which with the rate of £30 will make £80 and probably I may collect £20 so as to make £100, but this will not defray the expense of the improvements we contemplate . . . to throw part of the belfry into the church by an arch and to pew that space with single seats to the extent of ten or twenty additional free seats and by making all the pews single instead of double we shall gain about 12 additional seats making on the whole 30 additional free seats. The estimated expense will be £50 to which sum we cannot raise, unless the Society for Promoting the Enlargement, Building and Repewing Churches, will kindly assist us, £20 would be thankfully received. We need not pressure to ask for more as I well know that the Society has similar claims.' (ICBS file no. 3988 (1847)) In the Religious Census of 1851 the Revd John Collins made the following declaration. 'The sittings are now all free or open sittings: it having been newly pewed about four years ago: with open seats instead of square double pews, which were allocated by one or two Farm Houses. Now they are all free to the Parishioners in general, tho they nicely keep to old stations. Total sittings 120.' (Ieuan G. Jones, *The Religious Census of 1851: A Calendar of the Returns relating to Wales, Vol. 1: South Wales*, edited by Ieuan G. Jones and D. Williams (Cardiff, 1976), 268)

1883–4: During the incumbency of the Revd Sterling Browne Westhorp, rector of Ilston from 1855 to 1885, church reseated and interior refloored. (*GCM*, July 1904)

Comments: The ICBS file on the rearrangement of seating in 1847 contains no responses from the Society, no application form nor other correspondence. In all likelihood the deficit on the Church was defrayed by the new patron of the living and owner of Kilvrough, Thomas Penrice (d. 1897), who became a generous benefactor in the parishes of Ilston and Pennard. The east window of the church, as it is today, of three lancet lights beneath a pointed arch with crowned heads as label stops was described accurately by Glynne in 1851 and therefore belongs to the 1847 restoration and not as John Newman suggests to 'later in the nineteenth century'. (Newman, 366) The restoration of the church considerably improved the fabric and fittings of the church early in the Victorian period. Although the architect is not recorded, the restoration of the church was in keeping with the new interpretations of the liturgy of the Anglican Church. This showed that the church was restored by an architect of some discernment, who had come under the influence of the Oxford Movement and Cambridge Camden Society. It is the opinion of the author that the architect responsible for the work of restoration was John Prichard of Llandaff since the Middle-Pointed or Decorated Gothic style described by Glynne is indicative of the architect's favourite idiom. Furthermore, in 1846 shortly before the restoration at Ilston was contemplated Prichard was restoring the chancel of Penrice church nearby.

ST MARY MAGDALENE'S CHURCH, KENFIG

1878–9: Restoration of church by John Prichard. (ICBS file no. 310 (1877)) Sir Stephen Glynne, who visited Kenfig Church in September 1848, described it as 'A rude church of the South Wales stamp . . . there is little distinction of an architectural character . . . The chancel is also very low.' (Sir Stephen R. Glynne, 'Notes on the older

churches in the four Welsh dioceses', *Arch. Camb.* (1901), 254) Petition for faculty to restore church in 1878 stated 'that the parish church of the said parish of Pyle and Kenfig is in a very dilapidated condition and almost unfit for services to be conducted therein'. Accordingly, faculty granted in November 1878 'to refloor and reseat the said church of Kenfig, to place a heating apparatus therein and to put a new pulpit and reading desk there, to build three new windows and an entirely new roof, to lay down drainage all round the church and to pick the plaster and point all the outside walling of the said church'. At this time font moved to a new position under tower where it was provided with new base. Seating accommodation increased to eighty-eight by an additional twenty-eight seats. Cost £550. (LF/F/696. Repair and improvements in church. Faculty dated 1 November 1878)

1894–5: Rebuilding of chancel by Frederick William Waller, diocesan architect, Gloucester. Dilapidated chancel demolished and rebuilt on larger scale. Arch of chancel enlarged and solid buttress placed on south side. Chancel extended three feet eastwards with small projection on south-west side sufficient to accommodate a seat and also to erect a small organ chamber and vestry on north side. Choir stalls erected in chancel. Miss Emily Talbot paid cost of rebuilding work, which amounted to £440. (LL/F/698. Repair of chancel, organ chamber and vestry. Faculty dated 7 September 1894)

Comments: John Prichard's restoration of St Mary Magdalene's was concerned with the restoration of the dilapidated fabric of the church and the re-ordering of the interior. It was a conservative affair. The rebuilding of the chancel by Waller of Gloucester was undertaken after the architect's report on the church stated that 'the chancel is without archaeological or architectural interest of any kind. It is in a very bad state of repair as regards walls, roof and floors, and in fact, its condition is such that nothing less than its entire removal and reconstruction is recommended.' As for the chancel arch, he reported that 'the chancel arch is much out of shape and defective, it is very narrow and low and this shuts off the chancel from the rest of the church and as it possesses little archaeological interest it is suggested that the arch be enlarged, so as to throw open the chancel to the church.' (LL/F/698M. Mawdlam (i.e. Kenfig) Church notes for a faculty required for the rebuilding of the chancel and chancel arch and erection of vestry, etc. dated 7 September 1894) Although the restoration and rebuilding of the chancel might be regarded outwardly as a destructive restoration, the structure was so crude, as witnessed by Glynne, and in such a poor state of repair after years of neglect by C. R. M. Talbot, the lay impropriator, that Waller was forced to rebuild it. By doing so, he was able to build a chancel and chancel arch that expressed the Tractarian sympathies of the patron, Miss Emily Talbot, with its organ and choir stalls providing music for the ritualism of High Church practices.

ST THEODORE'S CHURCH, KENFIG HILL

1888–9: New church built on new site as mission church. Prior to erection of this church, divine service held in a schoolroom and large congregation brought together in a district with population of 1,500 and rising. Parish church at Tythegston, near Bridgend was three and a half miles away. (*Ch. Bldr* (1888), 96) Foundation stone laid on 19 September 1888 by Miss Emily Talbot of Margam Abbey. (*The Cambrian*, 7 December 1888) Built in Early English Gothic style by George E. Halliday, consisting of chancel, nave, north porch and western bellcote. Constructed of local Pennant sandstone with Bath stone dressings. Interior of Bridgend and Bath stone intermixed. East window of three grouped trefoiled lancets with common hood mould. Chancel and nave have arch-braced roofs of pitch-pine with principal rafters supported on massive, carved stone corbels. Roof is covered with Broseley tiles. (*BN*, 8 March 1889, 334) Nave walls pierced with single, trefoiled

20. Church of St Theodore, Kenfig Hill, Glamorgan, Halliday & Anderson, archts, Cardiff (Source: *The Building News*, 8 March 1889, p. 334)

lights with quatrefoils in head between two-stage buttresses. West end of nave lighted by two single trefoiled lights beneath a quatrefoil in apex of west wall. Open benches of pitch-pine. Seating accommodation for 152 worshippers. Gangway paved with red tiles and area under seats floored with wooden boards of deal. Contractor: John Haines, Cardiff. Cost £800. LDCES £100; Bishop of Llandaff's Fund £200. Church dedicated on 10 June 1889. (*The Cambrian*, 14 June 1889)

Comments: It was Halliday's original intention to build St Theodore's in the early Decorated style, but to limit the cost of the structure he built it in the Early English Gothic style. (*W. Mail*, 20 November 1888) The church was built mainly by the generosity of Miss Emily Talbot and its dedication to St Theodore was in memory of her brother, Theodore, who died after a hunting accident in 1876. St Theodore's was originally a simple structure, but the rapid rise in the population caused Miss Talbot to contribute substantially to its enlargement in 1909.

In the years 1908–9 the church was enlarged by the addition of a south aisle, a vestry and organ chamber with heating chamber underneath and the lengthening of the nave westwards by a single bay. Additional accommodation for 161 persons. Cost £1,430, of which Miss Emily Talbot subscribed £1,200. Architects: Cook & Edwards, Bridgend. Contractors: Knox & Wells, Cardiff. (*W. Mail*, 21 January 1909)

ST DAVID'S CHURCH, LALESTON

1871: Restoration of church. When Sir Stephen Glynne visited Laleston Church on 24 September 1847 he wrote, 'The chief features seem to be Third Pointed; but the windows throughout the chancel and nave are modern, and closed with shutters . . . Most of the northern windows are closed . . . There is an ugly west gallery.' (Sir Stephen R. Glynne, 'Notes on the older churches in the four Welsh dioceses', *Arch. Camb.* (1901), 254–5) The restoration, carried out in 1871, included much needed improvements such as refenestration in the Perpendicular style, the

original style of architecture indicated by Glynne. Old west gallery removed and church reordered in keeping with new ideas in Anglican liturgy. Wagon roof of porch and nave restored and old rood-loft door exposed to view high on north side of nave. Cost of restoration £700. Church rate £193. (Revd Colin M. David, *Some Notes on the Church of St David, Laleston, Bridgend, Glamorgan* (1958), 10)

Comments: Although no architect is recorded for the restoration of St David's in 1871, John Newman suggests that it may well have been John Prichard and calls our attention to the 'refined mouldings of the chancel rere-arches' which may well be attributed to Prichard's fine detailing. (Newman, 36) Whoever the architect was, it appears that the church was restored in a conservative manner in 1871, which rendered its structure fit for another hundred years.

ST LAWRENCE'S CHURCH, LAVERNOCK

1852: David Jones of Wallington visited St Lawrence's on 30 September 1888 and gave this description of the church: 'This seems to have been "carefully rebuilt" (upon old lines and features probably) but was restored some twenty years ago and is a thoroughly neat and perfectly uninteresting building – nave with slim western bell turret and small south porch, chancel with priest's door on South side. All small. Churchyard ditto. Not a single old inscription to be discovered.' (David Jones of Wallington, *Notes and Transcripts of David Jones of Wallington*, Vol. 1, 23ff) According to Howard J. Thomas of Barry, formerly of RCAHM, St Lawrence's was totally rebuilt in 1852, the only part surviving being the single bell, cast by Thomas Bayley of Bridgwater, 1747. According to Ewen's guide, it was 'a neat little Church recently restored at the expense of the marchioness of Bute, in which service is performed every Sunday, alternately, morning and evening by the Rev. R. Jones'. (James Ewen, *Ewen's Guide and Directory for the Town of Cardiff and its Environs . . . for 1855* (Cardiff, 1855), 88) Rebuilt of local lias limestone in fourteenth-century style. Nave windows are of two cinquefoiled lights under square head. Only window in chancel is of similar pattern, but consisting of one single light. East window of two cinquefoiled lights with quatrefoil above. No windows on north or west walls of church. Chancel arch is plain pointed, springing from simple imposts. Nave has an arch-braced roof, plastered between rafters. Open benches of pitch-pine in nave. Simple wooden pulpit on south side of chancel arch. (Personal observation)

Comments: The rebuilding of St Lawrence's in 1852 was carried out by the marchioness of Bute, who became the patron of the church after her husband's sudden death in 1848. The rebuilding was probably carried out by the architect to the Bute estate, Alexander Roos. The new church was a simple and austere building, probably a facsimile of the old structure with its typical lack of windows on the north and west walls of the church, which was a common feature of most medieval churches in Glamorgan. Nevertheless, it provided seating accommodation for sixty worshippers in a new building at no cost to the diocese of Llandaff.

ST JAMES' CHURCH, LECKWITH

(Church in ruins)

1866: Rebuilding of church. (*Kelly's Directory of South Wales*, 1926, 494) In 1866 St Dochdwy's, Llandough-juxta-Penarth, built in 1848 under the superintendence of J. S. Corbett, was found to be too small for the rapidly increasing population of Llandough. (*Bldr*, 1 January, 1848, 59) Consequently, new church built at Llandough-juxta-Penarth, south of site of old church. (*CMG*, 13 July 1866) Local tradition has it that the old Llandough Church, built in 1848, was taken down and removed stone by stone to rebuild St James', Leckwith in 1866. Two photographs of old Llandough Church, in the possession of Miss B. Corbett of Cogan Pill, show remarkable similarities in design both churches. Both churches consisted of chancel, nave, south porch and double bellcote. There was a large three-light window under a square head on south side of both old Llandough Church and St James' and double

bellcotes were of identical design at west end of two churches. At that time old Llandough Church was held in plurality with Leckwith Church. (Personal information from Revd Dr Brian Lodwick, rector of Llandough-juxta-Penarth and Leckwith)

Comments: It is unfortunate that no documentary evidence for the rebuilding of St James' can be found in contemporary newspapers or parish documents. Herbert M. Thompson writes that 'the present church is very prettily built (Prichard, architect) in Decorated style'. (H. M. Thompson, *Old Churches in the Vale of Glamorgan* (Cardiff, 1935), Vol. 1, 96) Photographs taken before Leckwith became a ruin show that the east window was of five lights with Decorated tracery in the head. However, the circumstantial evidence is quite conclusive in stating that the old Llandough Church, a comparatively new building, was taken down and rebuilt, wholly, or partly, at Leckwith in 1866. The most convincing evidence is contained in the fine nineteenth-century photographs used as illustrations 155 & 156 by Roy Thorne in his book *Penarth: A History*, Vol. 1 (Risca, 1975), 128.

ST DENYS' CHURCH, LISVANE

1878: Restoration of church. At vestry meeting held in Lisvane on Easter Monday 1878 it was resolved by Revd Thomas Rees and other members of the church present that St Denys' be thoroughly repaired and the bells recast if vicar could obtain funds through voluntary contributions. Restoration commenced on 23 April 1878 under supervision of vicar. Work comprised thorough repair of roofs of nave, porch, transept and tower. New lead flashings put between chancel and nave and between nave and tower. New iron chutes put all around eaves, downpipes fitted and new earthenware pipes laid down for drains. New windows inserted in chancel and north lancet opened out, which had previously been walled up and plastered out of sight. Chancel excavated and concreted, new steps built and chancel floor paved with new encaustic tiles from Godwin's of Lugwardine. Fresh flue made for stove, and new pulpit and reading desk provided. New wooden floors laid down in transept and nave, and new windows inserted. New doors fitted to tower and new louvred windows opened out on west and east sides of tower which had been previously blocked up. Cost £500. Church reopened after restoration on 9 October 1878. (Dewi-Prys Thomas, *The History and Architecture of Lisvane Parish Church* (Cardiff, 1964))

Comments: After an era of neglect and decay during the incumbency of Revd Benjamin Jones, vicar of the parish from 1820 to 1861, St Denys' was restored in 1878. The restoration was clearly carried out by a sensitive architect, who resisted the temptation of carrying out a harsh Victorian restoration. Apart from inserting new windows he resisted any attempt to alter the structure of the medieval church.

ST JOHN THE BAPTIST'S CHURCH, LLANBLETHIAN

1859: Chancel repairs carried out by Ecclesiastical Commissioners. Cost £51. Architect: Ewan Christian, London. Contractor: W. James, Cowbridge. (RBCW, Eccl. Comm. file no. 10711)

1896–7: Restoration of church by Charles Busteed Fowler of Kempson & Fowler, Llandaff as a result of dilapidated condition of building. Work comprised: removal of old square box pews and replacement with open benches; laying down new wood-block floors; opening out south chapel; and removal of low plaster ceilings from nave, south chapel and chancel, thus exposing to view original medieval oak roofs, with arch-braces, wind-braces and a collar purlin of the local type. All roof timbers were carefully restored. Original low chancel arch demolished and replaced by new one in Decorated Gothic style. Old interior stonework completely repointed. Roofs covered with green Bangor slates. (LL/F/373. Restoration of church. Faculty dated 12 August 1896) New stone pulpit of pink Penarth alabaster and red Forest of Dean stone and Quarella stone with columns of red Irish marble, carved by William Clarke and erected as

21. St John the Baptist's Church, Llanblethian (Photo: W. P. Pring, L.R.P.S.) (By kind permission of D. Brown & Sons Ltd, Cowbridge)

memorial to Revd Thomas Edmondes, vicar of the parish from 1835 to 1883. (*Bldr*, 22 May 1897, 465) During restoration work a vaulted crypt, used as an ossuary, discovered under south chapel, approached by flight of steps down from crypt. Over a hundred human skeletons found therein were reverently reburied in a large common grave in the churchyard. (Charles B. Fowler, 'Discoveries at Llanblethian Church, Glamorganshire', *Arch. Camb.* (1898), 121–31) Contractor: W. A. James, Cowbridge. Cost £1,200. Church reopened after restoration on 5 May 1897. (*W. Mail*, 6 May 1897)

Comments: John Newman's comment on the 'over-restoration' of the interior of St John the Baptist's by Fowler in the years 1896–7 is true in some respects. (Newman, 371) The most controversial aspect of his restoration was the removal of the original thirteenth-century chancel arch, but a photograph taken before the restoration clearly shows that the interior of the nave was dark and dreary and typical of the Georgian period of ugliness. Consequently, Fowler was compelled to demolish this very low arch and replace it with an arch of larger span and greater height. Furthermore he had to reorder the eighteenth-century 'prayer-book' interior with its low plaster ceilings and square box pews. However, he was negligent in removing the plaster from the walls of the church and wall paintings were probably destroyed by this act of destructive restoration much to the displeasure of the Society for the Protection of Ancient Buildings, the 'anti-scrape brigade'.

In 1907 the tower was completely restored at a cost of £550. The buttresses were replaced, the four floors repaired and the foundations strengthened. (*Bldr*, 12 October 1907, 372) In 1911 a new reredos of Austrian oak was erected in the sanctuary in memory of F. W. Dunn (1844–1911), people's warden for 20 years. It depicts a scene from the Supper at Emmaus. Carved by William Clarke. Cost £125. (LL/F/374. Reredos. Faculty dated 5 December 1911)

ALL SAINTS' CHURCH, LLANBRADACH

(Church in ruins)

1896–7: New church built on new site given by Miss Clara Thomas of Llwynmadoc, Breconshire. Llanbradach, in parish of Ystrad Mynach, was a new colliery district which came into existence about 1891. The population numbered about 2,500. Services first conducted in a cottage and from 1892 in corrugated iron mission church. (*Ch. Bldr* 1897, 1–2) Built in Early English Gothic style by E. M. Bruce Vaughan. Constructed of local Pennant sandstone with Bath stone dressings. Nave and aisles and west narthex with entrances on north and south sides and west bellcote above were first parts to be erected. Nave aisles consisted of five transverse gabled bays lighted by a pair of trefoiled lights with quatrefoil in apex. West window of five elongated lancets. Seating accommodation for 350 worshippers. Cost £2,000. ICBS grant £150; donation of £1,000 from Miss Clara Thomas. Church opened and dedicated on 2 June 1897. (*W. Mail*, 4 June, 1897) Consecrated on 1 July 1903. (Revd Handel Thomas, *Llanbradach and its Church: A Short History of All Saints Church* (Cardiff, 1947), 7–8)

Comments: As John Newman says, it was not the original intention to build the tower, since Llanbradach was built in 1897 with a bell turret above the west gable. (Newman, 373) However, the growth of the population of Llanbradach in the Edwardian era required additional church accommodation and a new chancel with vestries provided more space in the nave for the congregation. The church was unique in having a western bell turret as well as a south-east tower. All Saints' was larger than the norm for Bruce Vaughan, who was accustomed to building cheap utilitarian churches in mining communities in the south Wales coalfield. It was, in fact, larger than his church at Cymmer, Porth and it also boasted a substantial tower, an unusual feature for his churches. The whole structure of the church was only made possible by the generosity of Miss Clara Thomas of Llwynmadoc, a generous benefactor of the Anglican Church in Glamorgan.

ST CADOC'S CHURCH, LLANCARFAN

1876–7: Restoration of church. When Sir Stephen Glynne visited the church on 24 July 1871 he stated that 'The interior is untidy and neglected, though some faint symptoms of restoration appear in the chancel.' (Sir Stephen R. Glynne, 'Notes on the older churches in the four Welsh dioceses', *Arch. Camb.* (1901), 255–7) In July 1875 an appeal in the form of a printed letter was made by the vicar of Llancarfan, Revd Alfred T. Hughes, to restore the church. He noted that 'the whole of the interior is in a very dilapidated state and requires entire renovation. The cost of doing this as well as of repairing the exterior, will amount to more than one thousand pounds . . . There are no resident gentry, and the consequences of this state of things is that I have been unable to procure from the landowners of the parish, to whom I, in the first instance, applied, a sufficient sum to carry out the proposed restoration; and I am therefore compelled, however, unwillingly, to appeal to the public to assist me in preserving a church the present conditions of which contrasts most unfavourably with that of other churches in the diocese.' Funds were evidently found and church underwent considerable repairs and renovation. During this restoration all colour-wash was removed from inside of church walls revealing stencilled stars. On south wall of aisle a large stencilled figure of the Virgin Mary was uncovered but then painted over with whitewash since it was thought to be Roman Catholic. (*MCVG*, 189) Reopened after restoration on 17 May 1877. (*W. Mail*, 21 May 1877)

1890: Tower restored and rebuilt. Cost £570. (Bridgend Reference Library: Roderick Williams. Manuscript Notes on Llancarfan Church, 10)

Comments: Despite the fact that Llancarfan Church was one of the finest medieval churches in the Vale of Glamorgan with a history reaching back to the dawn of Christianity in Glamorgan, it was a poor church during the nineteenth century. The vicar, Revd Alfred T. Hughes, found great difficulty in raising funds to restore the old church since there were no resident gentry in the parish.

Consequently, he had to make a broad appeal to churchgoers throughout the diocese for assistance in restoring the church. As a result the church was spared any drastic restoration and the work carried out in the late Victorian period was simply a reparation of the fabric of the medieval church. Therefore the church retains many ancient features such as the Apostles' Creed on the south wall of the nave, as directed to be set up in the seventeenth century, and the holy-water stoup near the south door.

In 1907 the church was restored again. Repairs were carried out to the roof of the tower and to weatherproof the building. Architect: Frederick R. Kempson. (*W. Mail*, 13 September 1907) Contractor: Mr Shepton, Cardiff. Cost £325. Ecclesiastical Commissioners £50; LCBS £20. Reopened after restoration on 5 November 1907. (*W. Mail*, 7 November, 1907)

ALL SAINTS' CHURCH, LLANDAFF NORTH

(Formerly known as Llandaff Yard. Church destroyed in blitz on 2 January 1941)

1890–1: New church built on new site given by Lord Windsor and designed by Kempson & Fowler, Llandaff. Intended as daughter church of Llandaff Cathedral for a populous district separated from rest of parish of Llandaff by River Taff. Prior to erection of new church, services held in a licensed schoolroom. (*Ch. Bldr* (1891), 27) Foundation stone laid on 27 June 1890 by Mrs Lewis of the Palace, Llandaff. (*W. Mail*, 28 June 1890) Built in Perpendicular Gothic style consisting of nave (51ftx25ft), a choir (25ft wide and 15ft deep) and chancel (14ftx12ft 6ins). Choir separated from nave by large arch in centre and small arch at each side. There was also an arch between choir and sanctuary. (*BN*, 6 February 1891, 217) Vestries and organ chamber formed out of the quasi-transepts by open screens with crimson hangings at back. Tower with spire placed at south-west corner; upper part of tower built of teak and spire of cleft oak shingles. Principal entrance to church through south door in tower. Constructed of Pontypridd stone with Bath stone dressings and roof covered

22. Llandaff Yard Church. Kempson & Fowler, archts, Llandaff (Source: *The Building News,* 11 April 1890, p. 334)

with green Welsh slates. Seats, roofs, screens, etc. all of pitch-pine, with lectern and altar of oak. Floors of chancel and choir laid with marble inlay in cement, patented by J. Hartnell of Cardiff. Church, which was fitted with very comfortable seats without bench ends, accommodated 250 parishioners. Church lighted with very powerful oil lamps fitted into wrought-iron coronas hung ingeniously in pulleys to balance each other. (*Bldr,* 7 February 1891, 100) Contractor: W. Thomas & Co, Cardiff. Cost £1,820. ICBS grant £50; Ecclesiastical Commissioners £50; Bishop of Llandaff's Fund £150; LDCES grant £50; LCBS grant £20; Dean & Mrs Vaughan £320. Consecrated on 28 January 1891. (*W. Mail,* 29 January 1891)

Comments: Kempson & Fowler built All Saints' in the Perpendicular Gothic style, a style that continued to be popular towards the end of the nineteenth century. The church consisted of a nave, a choir the same width as the nave, divided from it by a large open arch. The sanctuary was separated from the choir by a sanctuary arch, a rare feature in a small district church. By adopting this plan of a broad nave and choir almost all the

congregation and choir could see the altar and pulpit. This spatial handling of the interior of the church by the architects was in keeping with the late Gothic form of architecture employed at that period.

In 1914 the church was deemed too small for the spiritual needs of the community. (*Ch. Bldr* (1914), 48) Church enlarged by extending the nave westwards and adding a north aisle (70ftx13ft) and new vestry on north side of chancel. The organ chamber was re-erected on the south side. Nave divided from north aisle by new arcade of six bays. Seating accommodation increased to 445 sittings. Cost £2,500. ICBS grant £80. Architect: Frederick R. Kempson. New additions dedicated on 15 December 1914. (*BN,* 19 June 1914, 889)

ST DAVID'S CHURCH, LLANDDEWI

1876: Restoration of church. As early as 1804 Revd John Collins, rector of Oxwich, described St David's as in 'bad repair especially the chancel and altar'. This neglect continued for much of early part of nineteenth century until 1869, when it was agreed that a church rate of 1s in the pound be collected 'only when the church is restored'. (Michael Gibbs, 'Yesterday and the day before (at Llanddewi, Gower)', *Gower Journal*, Vol. 22, 1971, 54–7) When Sir Stephen Glynne visited the church on 2 August 1871 he noted, 'A small neglected church, much out of repair . . . the tower is very low, of very rude construction, and little architectural character . . . The chancel arch is very rude and of obtuse form; but one half has mouldings, the other not.' (Sir Stephen R. Glynne, 'Notes on the older churches in the four Welsh dioceses', *Arch. Camb.* 1897, 298–9) Eventually the church underwent a drastic restoration in 1876 paid for by patron of living, C. R. M. Talbot. This over-thorough restoration destroyed all traces of the famous Henllys Seat or Squire's pew, which was 7ft high, 8ft long and 5ft broad. (Geoffrey R. Orrin, *The Gower Churches* (Penmaen, 1979), 39)

Comments: The drastic restoration of St David's, undertaken in 1876, was the result of years of neglect and piecemeal, churchwardenized repairs carried out during the early part of the nineteenth century. Although this ensured that the church remained fit for divine service for years to come, it was regrettable that a fine example of seventeenth-century craftsmanship in Gower, the Henllys seat, should have been lost to posterity. No architect is recorded, but Talbot employed John Prichard at that period on other churches where he held the patronage in Glamorgan.

In 1905 the church was restored. All the old mortar on the outside walls of the church was picked out and replaced with cement. The tower was repaired and two new windows were placed in the south and north walls and all the other windows substantially repaired. Cost £200. Reopened after restoration on 27 June 1905. (*GCM*, no. 67, July 1905)

ST DAVID'S CHURCH, LLANDDEWI, RHONDDA (GYFEILLON)

1853–4: New church built on new site at Cwm Rhondda given by Lewis Morgan Esq. of Hafod Fawr, near Pontypridd. (*The Cambrian*, 17 January 1851) Petition of consecration stated 'that in consequence of the great increase of population within the Parish of Llanwonno, by reason of many collieries . . . having been established there, many of the inhabitants thereof are prevented or deterred from attending Divine Service in the said Parish Church on account of its distance and . . . accommodation for only a small portion of the population and it has been deemed necessary to provide additional church accommodation in the said Parish.' (LL/C/129. Petition of consecration dated 16 May 1854) Built in Early English Gothic style by Charles E. Bernard, Cardiff, consisting of chancel (17ft 6insx13ft 6ins), nave (45ftx24ft), west gallery, south porch and western bellcote. Constructed of Pennant sandstone, furnished from quarries of Lewis Morgan, with Bath stone dressings. Church was perfectly plain and simple in its internal arrangements. East window of three grouped lancets and nave lighted by tall paired lancets. Arch-braced roofs of pitch-pine to chancel and nave. Buttressed walls. Seating capacity for 263 worshippers. Contractor: William Morgan, Pontypridd. Cost £1,050. Church Commissioners' grant £60; LDCES grant £100; Nash Edwards Vaughan, Rheola £100. Consecrated on 16 May 1854. (*CMG*, 19 and 26 May 1854)

1897–8: Enlargement of church by demolition of old nave and construction of new one. Old chancel allowed to remain and new nave built on to it. Seating capacity increased from 263 to 530 persons. (*Ch. Bldr* (1897), 31) Architect: E. M. Bruce Vaughan, Cardiff. Cost £2,700. ICBS grant £130. (ICBS file no. 9967 (1897)) New nave opened for divine worship on 30 March 1898. (*W. Mail*, 31 March 1898)

Comments: The original Commissioners' church of St David's, Llanddewi, Rhondda, built in 1854, was a poor structure. It was designed by Charles E. Bernard, a civil engineer of Cardiff, who was unaccustomed to building churches. This was the only church he built in Glamorgan. The church owes its present appearance to rebuilding in 1897 and later in the following century. The original structure, though crudely designed and poorly built of cheap materials, served its purpose for nearly fifty years as an Anglican place of worship in the spiritual wilderness of the Lower Rhondda.

In 1910 Revd T. E. Griffiths, the new vicar of Llanwonno, realized the extreme contrast between the new nave and the old chancel. He resolved to demolish the old chancel and build a new structure in its place. The new chancel and nave were consecrated on 4 March 1912. (LL/C/130. Sentence of consecration. Dated 4 March 1912)

ST TEILO'S CHURCH, LLANDEILO TAL-Y-BONT

1859: Late medieval church, which consisted of chancel, nave with south aisle and transept called the Gronw Chapel, repaired and renovated through liberality of Revd Thomas Clarke and his parishioners in 1859. Great credit was due to Mr Davies of Talyvan and Mr D. Lewis of Llandeilo Tal-y-bont, who collected subscriptions and superintended repair of ancient and venerable structure. Church retained its three-decker pulpit and high-backed square box pews. Beams of Irish oak were coupled not by nails, but by wooden pegs or dowels. Reopened after restoration on Sunday 26 June 1859. (*The Cambrian*, 1 July 1859)
1877: Although regular church services did not take place after 1861, repaired in 1877 at a cost of £91.
1900: Repaired at a cost of £100. Church disused except for occasional service during summer to maintain tradition of Anglican worship in the church. (*Kelly's Directory of South Wales*, 1926, 793)

Comments: The church fell into disuse after the erection of St Teilo's, Pontardulais in 1851, because of the shift of the population to the village of Pontardulais and its difficult situation on the edge of the River Loughor surrounded by marshes, which were impassable in times of flood or high tides. The bishop of St Davids, Connop Thirlwall,

felt that the church should be allowed to fall into a ruin, but due to the efforts of successive rectors, including the energetic Revd William Morgan, the 'Old Church' was saved from ruin and decay well into the twentieth century.

Abandoned in the 1960s, the church was scheduled as an ancient monument by Cadw: Welsh Historic Monuments. Since the church could not be saved *in situ*, permission was granted by Cadw in 1985 to dismantle it and re-erect it at St Fagans at a later date. After several years of intensive preparatory work for its re-erection, work began in January 2003 and is still in progress. Sioned Wyn Hughes, assistant curator at the Museum of Welsh Life, St Fagans wrote that 'The re-erection and refurbishment of the medieval church of St Teilo from Llandeilo Tal-y-bont is one of the Museum of Welsh Life's most ambitious projects to date.' (Sioned Wyn Hughes, 'St Teilo's Church, Llandeilo Tal-y-bont: Interpreting a Late Medieval Church', *Amgueddfa* 2 (1998–9), 8–11)

ST DOCHDWY'S CHURCH, LLANDOUGH-BY-COWBRIDGE

1869: Restoration of church by Charles Buckeridge of Oxford. South wall of chancel rebuilt and three lancet windows inserted in place of old wooden-framed window, with modern sedilia, credence and piscina forming part of new sanctuary window. Three-light window with trefoil heads replaced two-light window in east wall. On north side of chancel a doorway was opened into new organ chamber and vestry. Triple-pointed arcade, resting on double arrangement of pink Radyr shafts, separates organ chamber from chancel. Chancel roof entirely replaced and slated, the part over sanctuary being boarded, but woodwork of cradle-roof of nave was left untouched. Dressings used in restored church of green Bridgend Quarella stone. New copings of Forest of Dean stone placed on gables and bell-turret, with crosses and weather-cock. (*BN*, 14 January 1870, 35) Sir Stephen Glynne visited Llandough Church on 18 August 1869, when restoration of church was nearing completion, so we have an accurate account of work carried out at that time. He described it as 'A small church undergoing a complete restoration . . . The original chancel arch, said to have been very small and narrow, in a large mass of wall, has been replaced by a new Pointed one upon marble shafts and a new low stone screen has been added across it.' (Sir Stephen R. Glynne, 'Notes on the older churches in the four Welsh dioceses', *Arch. Camb.* (1901), 258) Restoration of nave consisted of new windows, stone pulpit, floor of encaustic tiles by Godwin of Lugwardine and open benches instead of old-fashioned square box pews. Cost £862. Reopened after restoration on 30 December 1869. (*CGG*, 31 December 1869)

Comments: As a High Churchman the Revd Stephen Nicholl commissioned the ecclesiastical architect, Charles Buckeridge (1823–73), a pupil of Sir George Gilbert Scott, to restore Llandough-by-Cowbridge Church. Thomas Christopher Evans known as 'Cadrawd', an antiquary and folklorist, writing in the 1880s stated: 'The chancel arch, which the original builder had not required to give more than convenient access to the chancel and which was not calculated to display to well effect the "restored" ritual of the English Church, has been replaced by one of requisite height and span and is now an irreproachable example of what such an arch ought to have been in a thirteenth-century church.' (Cardiff Central Library MS. 4.304. T. C. Evans (Cadrawd) – 'A history of the parish of Llandough', 1902) That the church was heavily restored in keeping with the new ideas in the Anglican liturgy was undoubtedly due to the Tractarian persuasion of the Anglo-Catholic rector and the architect.

In 1912 a single-manual organ, built by Positive Organ Co Ltd, was installed. (*MCVG*, 193)

ST DOCHDWY'S CHURCH, LLANDOUGH-JUXTA-PENARTH

1848: Llandough Church was twice rebuilt during nineteenth century, the first time about 1848, during incumbency of Revd James Evans through generosity of marquess of Bute and under superintendence of J. S. Corbett, churchwarden.

(*Bldr*, 1 January 1848, 8) Sir Stephen Glynne, who visited the church on 8 August 1853, described it thus: 'This small church seems to have been almost wholly rebuilt and presents a neat though modern appearance. It has a chancel and nave only with a bell-turret over the west end for two bells.' (Sir Stephen R. Glynne, 'Notes on the older churches in the four Welsh dioceses', *Arch. Camb.* (1901), 258–9)

1865–6: Rebuilding of church. Despite fact that original medieval church had been replaced *c.* 1848 by modern structure, by 1865 this church was found to be totally inadequate to meet spiritual needs of increased population of this parish near new dock and harbour at Penarth. Consequently, old church taken down and new church erected on east side of former structure. (*CMG*, 13 July 1866) Built to designs and specifications of Samuel Charles Fripp of Bristol. Constructed of Leckwith stone lined with bricks, with Bath stone used for the windows, doorways and pillars. Church consists of chancel, nave with north and south aisles, saddleback tower on south side of chancel and west doorway. Style of architecture is Decorated Gothic freely treated. East window of four lights, west window of five lights, both Decorated Gothic. Chancel of red brick with subtle patterns of black brickwork below a moulded string. The columns, separating nave from aisles, are finely executed, although square capitals are of plain character. Interior walls lined with red brick relieved with cross crosslets of constructional polychromy in black and yellow brickwork. Nave has arch-braced roof with collar purlin of stained pitch-pine. Old Norman chancel arch with chevron mouldings from former church, almost entirely restored, re-erected at east end of south aisle, but heightened by insertion of square imposts. Church furnished with open benches of stained pitch-pine. Seating accommodation for 300 parishioners. Contractor: David Jones, Penarth. Cost £2,600. (*BN*, 20 July 488) Consecrated on 12 July 1866. (*Cardiff Times*, 13 July 1866)

Comments: The interior of Llandough-juxta-Penarth Church is an example of Butterfieldian constructional polychromy, a typical feature of the High Victorian period. It is, however, greatly subdued compared with the interior of the neighbouring church of St Augustine's, Penarth, built at the same time and designed by William Butterfield himself. The constructional polychromy extends into the nave arcade of Bath stone, into which have been inset short unconnected runs of red bricks around the head of each arch. This is purely a decorative feature, picking up the red brickwork of the spandrels. Although the heavy square abaci of the pillars appear to indicate a French Gothic influence, what they do convey are more classical proportions generally than one would usually find in a church of the Victorian Decorated period. The odd feature of the church is the heavily restored Norman chancel arch with chevron moulding taken from the twelfth-century church, which has been placed at the east end of the south aisle. This preservation of Norman architectural features was a typical ploy of Victorian architects who rebuilt and restored churches in the Vale of Glamorgan. Similar notable examples exist at the churches of St Bride's-super-Ely and St Mary Hill.

In 1906 an oak reredos was erected in the church as a memorial to John Stuart Corbett, people's warden for more than thirty years and Mary Stuart Corbett, his daughter, people's warden for ten years. Architect: Frederick R. Kempson, Cardiff. Work executed by William Clarke, Llandaff. (LL/F/396. Reredos. Faculty dated 25 July 1906)

HOLY TRINITY CHURCH, LLANDOW

1889–90: When chancel was restored in 1712, as recorded on tablet inscribed in Latin on south side of chancel wall, the builder was faced with problem of preserving east wall of nave, since broad and lofty chancel arch was sagging to a serious extent, giving it an almost horseshoe-like appearance. He preserved lower part of chancel arch with its interesting features, but had to rebuild higher part of structure. In addition, he placed external buttresses of great solidity at the threatened points because north and south walls were bulging alarmingly. (H. M. Thompson, *Manuscript Notes on the Old Churches of Glamorgan* (1935)) Victorian restoration of church

23. Interior of Holy Trinity Church, Llandow, showing 'horseshoe' chancel arch (Photo: W. P. Pring, L.R.P.S.) (By kind permission of D. Brown & Sons Ltd, Cowbridge)

was carried out in latter part of nineteenth century by Kempson & Fowler. Restoration included refurnishing chancel with new clergy seats, prayer-desk, lectern, chancel seats and altar table of oak. Stone pulpit erected on north side of nave. Contractor: John Morgan, Llantrisant. Cost £550. (*Bldr*, 2 November 1889, 317)

Comments: It was the restoration of the church in the early eighteenth century which preserved the building from collapse. The restoration carried out in the years 1889–90 by Kempson was simply a refurbishment of the chancel with new fittings and furnishings. As a result, Holy Trinity avoided any drastic Victorian restoration and retains many of its medieval features.

ST TYFODWG'S CHURCH, LLANDYFODWG

1870: Nave, which was in a dilapidated condition, restored by John Prichard. (Personal information from Howard J. Thomas, formerly RCAHM (Wales))

1892–3: Restoration of chancel and tower arch by George E. Halliday. Work included following: repair and restoration of chancel arch which was partially built up; reroofing chancel with oak roof; insertion of an east and two south chancel windows of suitable character; restoration of priest's door together with other architectural remains found; relaying of chancel and sanctuary floor levels and retaining original floor level of sanctuary; restoration of chancel steps and provision of choir seats, altar rails, etc.; draining and removal of soil accumulation against church walls; fixing of a new cross over chancel arch gable; replastering of walls and reglazing windows; and general reparation so as to leave chancel in a good and lasting condition. Entire cost of this restoration borne by Miss Olive Talbot of Cavendish Square, London. Contractor: John W. Rodger, Cardiff. (LL/F/401. Restoration of chancel and tower. Faculty dated 31 October 1892)

Comments: Halliday restored the chancel in the Perpendicular Gothic style, his favourite idiom in the late Victorian period. He took great care to preserve the three steps leading to the altar by restoring them. Since the early credence was in its right position, these steps were in all probability of late fourteenth-century date. The sepulchral slab of fourteenth-century origin of a pilgrim was also preserved in the chancel. St Tyfodwg's was one of six Glamorgan churches undergoing restoration at this time at the hands of Halliday and all the restoration and rebuilding work was paid for by Miss Olive Talbot, who was a generous benefactor of the Anglican Church in Glamorgan in the final decade of the nineteenth century. (*The Daily Graphic,* 12 November 1892: 'Church Restoration in South Wales')

ST CYNON'S CHURCH, LLANFABON

(Church demolished 1989)

1861–3: New church built on new site donated by Baroness Windsor as chapel of ease to St Mabon's Church, Llanfabon, because parish church was situated in remotest corner of parish and population was centred around new collieries at opposite end of parish. (*CMG*, 26 November 1859) Foundation stone laid on 16 July 1861 by Bessie Shepherd, daughter of Thomas Shepherd of Navigation House. (*CMG*, 20 July 1861) Built in early Geometrical Gothic style by John Pollard Seddon of Prichard & Seddon. (*Bldr*, 27 July 1861, 515) It consisted of chancel, nave, north porch and western bellcote. Constructed of blue Pennant sandstone from Park and Pandy quarries of William Davies, Graig House, Graigberthlwydd. Dressings were of Bath stone. (John T. Arnold, *The Story of St Cynon's Church* (Pontypridd, 1963), 3) East window of three trefoil-headed lights with octofoil in head and polychromatic hood mould achieved by use of light and dark masonry. Nave lighted on south side by pair of two-light trefoil-headed windows and single trefoil-headed window west of porch. Similar arrangement on north side. West window of two trefoil-headed lights with Geometrical traceried head. High-pitched gable to north porch which exhibited moulded arch to south doorway. Interior fittings of Memel and pitch-pine. Open timber roofs to chancel and nave. Seating accommodation for 202 worshippers. Contractor: Messrs Mathias Bros, Abercynon. Cost £1,200. ICBS grant £200; LDCES grant £100; LCBS grant £25; trustees of marquess of Bute £100; Baroness Windsor £100; Lord Dynevor £100. (GRO: D/D PL/817/41. List of subscriptions) Opened for divine worship on 10 July 1862. (*CMG*, 10 July 1862) Consecrated on 27 March 1863. (LL/C/134. Sentence of consecration dated 27 March 1863)

1889–90: Erection of organ chamber and enlargement of choir involved opening up an arch between chancel and vestry. Architect: John Pollard Seddon of Seddon & Carter, Llandaff. Cost £84. ICBS grant £25. (ICBS file no. 9339 (1889))

Comments: St Cynon's was only one of two churches designed in Glamorgan by John Pollard Seddon, Prichard's partner for ten years. The other church, built by Seddon at about the same time, 1862, was St Margaret's Church, Mountain Ash. St Cynon's was built in a Geometrical Gothic style, while St Margaret's was designed in a French Gothic style. Both churches contained sculpture above the south doorway, that at St Cynon's showed Christ as the Good Shepherd, while the porch at St Margaret's shows the enthroned and crowned Christ.

ST MABON'S CHURCH, LLANFABON

1836–8: In August 1836 a decision was made to enlarge and repair church by erection of a gallery and rearrangement of pews at cost of £106 8s 0d. Plan not proceeded with. (ICBS file no. 2063 (1836))

1846–7: In February 1846, the architect, John Prichard advised rector and churchwardens that St Mabon's was not worth restoring and recommended that church be rebuilt from its foundations. (*Bldr*, 8 August 1846, 380) Petition requesting faculty to rebuild church, dated 24 March 1846, stated 'that their Parish church is in a state so deplorable and insecure as to render it impossible . . . to attempt to repair and therefore it hath been proposed that it be taken down and rebuilt according to a plan set forth for that purpose . . . at the costs and charges of the parishioners of the said parish.' (LL/C/403P. Petition dated 24 April 1846) Rebuilt on site of old church in Neo-Norman style consisting of chancel with north vestry, nave, south porch and west doorway below western bellcote. Built of Pennant sandstone with Bath stone dressings. East window of three widely spaced round-headed broad lights. Nave lighted by narrow round-headed lights deeply splayed internally and by broad rounded-headed window at west end. Moulded round-headed chancel arch of two orders, springing from rectangular moulded abacus with foliated capitals on engaged shafts. Open timber roof to chancel with arch-braces and tie beams. Similar roof construction in nave with ceiling plastered between

rafters. Round-headed arch to south doorway decorated with billet moulding supported on scalloped capitals on nook shafts. West doorway adorned with chevron moulding and pellet motifs. (Personal observation) Seating capacity increased by forty-five sittings to 175 seats. Consecrated July 1847. Cost £607. ICBS grant £50. (ICBS file no. 5765 (1846))

Comments: St Mabon's, a medieval upland church, was Prichard's first building commission in 1847. He carried it out in a Neo-Norman style. It was the only time that he used this idiom during his career and he probably chose this style because it was briefly popular in the 1840s, the high tide of revived Norman church building. In fact, some 200 churches out of 800 built during this decade were in the Neo-Norman style throughout England and Wales compared with 600 Gothic-style churches. The main features of the church are the rounded chancel arch springing from foliage capitals on engaged shafts, the west doorway adorned with chevron moulding and pellet motifs, and the round-headed south doorway with billet moulding supported on scalloped capitals on nook shafts. The latter feature is very similar in some respects to the south doorway at Holy Trinity Church, Marcross.

ST BRYNACH'S CHURCH, LLANFRYNACH

1848: That St Brynach's did not become a complete ruin was due mainly to efforts of a local antiquary, Dr William Salmon of Penlline Court, who had developed a strong personal interest in the old church and restored it mostly at his own expense in 1848. *The Cambrian* of 1 September 1848 reported that: 'The opening of Llanfrynach Church took place according to announcement on Sunday last when the first regular service was performed after a period of nearly one hundred and fifty years. The ancient building has been restored through the liberality of William Salmon, Esq. Penlline Court.' Restoration preserved rood-loft staircase and stone benches which are found on inside walls of church. Large window in nave inserted during this restoration. Fine, late medieval oak roof carefully restored. It is of open arch-braced collar truss type with curved windbraces between purlins and principal rafters. Latter extend a short distance down nave walls to rest on rough stone corbels.

1882: David Jones of Wallington reported that there was 'a judicious and moderate restoration' at this date. (Cardiff Central Library: MS.1.187 – David Jones of Wallington, 'Notes on some old Glamorgan churches', 1889)

Comments: St Brynach's fell into disuse owing to its remoteness from the modern village. The old chapel, which stood at the entrance to Penllyn, was rebuilt and beautified in 1850 at the cost of the Homfray family. St Brynach's Church is of crude workmanship and, despite Dr Salmon's generosity in restoring the church to some extent in 1848 by making it wind- and weatherproof, it remains a rather plain and abject structure. Regular services have long ceased to be held in Llanfrynach, but occasional summer services are held to keep up the tradition of Christian worship.

ST CANNA'S CHURCH, LLANGAN

24. Interior of St Canna's Church, Llangan (Photo: W. P. Pring, L.R.P.S.) (By kind permission of D. Brown & Sons Ltd, Cowbridge)

1860–1: Rebuilding of church. Following notice appeared in *The Cambrian* for 11 May 1860: 'To Builders and Contractors: Llangan Church. Persons desirous of contracting for the restoration of this church can see the plans and specifications at Mr Randall's office, Bridgend; to whom sealed tenders must be sent on or before the 26th inst. The lowest or any other tender will not necessarily be accepted.' (Henry John Randall was the agent for the Dunraven estate during the years 1859–89.) (Personal information from Hilary M. Thomas, local historian and former archivist) Only other reference relating to 'restoration' of St Canna's occurs in J. M. Wilson, *The Imperial Gazetteer of England and Wales embracing Recent Changes in Counties, Dioceses and Parishes* (London, 1869), Vol. IV, 108 which states: 'Llangan . . . The church was rebuilt in 1861.' One of Wilson's sources was the *1859 Home Office Report on Church Rates: Diocese of Llandaff*, which gives the state of repair of most churches in the country; Llangan is described as 'dilapidated'. Therefore St Canna's more or less entirely rebuilt with just a few features such as original chancel arch and rood-loft staircase, preserved from the old structure. Sir Stephen Glynne visited the church on 18 August 1869 and noted: 'It is doubtful whether any part of the present church is ancient: the whole seems to have been recently rebuilt, yet possibly some portions of the walls may be old. It has a chancel and nave, with south porch; and over the west end a bell-gable for two bells in open arches. On the north side may be seen the projecting rood-staircase, with the upper and lower doors opening within. The chancel arch is Pointed, with continuous moulding, perhaps original . . . the southern windows are all new; the east window has three lights, with trefoil ogee heads. The seats are all open; and there is a neat new font, in Norman style, having a circular bowl on an octagonal stem.' (Sir Stephen R. Glynne, 'Notes on the older churches in the four Welsh dioceses', *Arch. Camb.* (1901), 259–60)

1881: Large vestry, used as schoolroom in late nineteenth century, erected in 1881. (*MCVG*, 213)

Comments: Several dates have been given by various writers for the rebuilding of St Canna's, but detailed research now shows that the church was partly rebuilt in the years 1860–1. Although no architect is recorded for the work of rebuilding, it seems highly likely that it was John Prichard. Since the old church was in such a dilapidated state, as indicated above, Prichard had no alternative but to rebuild most of the decayed structure, yet retaining important features such as the fifteenth-century chancel arch and the walling containing the rood-loft staircase. The trussed rafter roof with diagonal braces and the circular font indicate Prichard's involvement in the restoration. The reference to 'Mr Randall' implies that St Canna's was rebuilt by the Dunraven family, who were generous bene-factors of the Church in Glamorgan.

ST CEINWYR'S CHURCH, LLANGEINOR

1892–4: Restoration by George E. Halliday. Petition for faculty to restore church stated that 'the chancel is unfit for worship and that the tower is in ruins'. (LL/F/315P. Faculty dated 5 February 1892) Furthermore, additional choir accommo-dation was required in chancel for ten men and six boys. Consequently, chancel enlarged to provide room for choir stalls. New steps introduced leading to altar, and nave floor lowered to restore it to its original level. Floor of sanctuary paved with encaustic tiles. Chancel walls raised, and new oak wagon roof with moulded ribs with carved bosses at intersections placed over sanctuary. Modern tracery windows of Perpendicular Gothic style erected in nave and rood-loft window restored. Wood-block floors laid down under seats in nave and passages tiled. All old features retained, such as chancel arch, squints on each side of chancel arch and holy-water stoup. Upper portions of tower rebuilt with new belfry windows and parapet. Modern brick screen filling up tower arch removed and replaced by oak screen in character with building. Figure of St Ceinwyr over south porch entrance restored. Accommodation for worship-pers in church increased from 125 to 141 as result of restoration work. Contractor: John W. Rodger, Cardiff. Cost £3,000, defrayed by Miss Olive Talbot, Cavendish Square, London. (*Bldr*, 21 July 1894, 45) Reopened after restoration on 9 July 1894. (*W. Mail*, 10 July 1894)

Comments: St Ceinwyr's was one of six churches at that time undergoing restoration under the supervision of the architect, George E. Halliday, and at the expense of Miss Olive Talbot. Halliday's thorough restoration of the church was in fact a remodelling of the old fifteenth-century church in order to return to a more elaborate form of ceremonial worship with more emphasis on ritual. The enlargement of the chancel to introduce a church choir of men and boys was indicative of High Church practices first advocated by the Ecclesiologists. Also it revealed the influence of Miss Olive Talbot's Tractarian sympathies and that of her architect, Halliday, a devout Roman Catholic. The new liturgical arrangements of St Ceinwyr's Church introduced in 1894 provided a modern Victorian setting for divine worship.

ST CENNYDD'S CHURCH, LLANGENNITH

1848: When Sir Stephen Glynne visited St Cennydd's on 24 September 1848 he wrote that 'the roof of the chancel is in very bad order, and there is no pavement, but the bare earth in great part of church. The outer walls have been partly whitewashed.' (Sir Stephen R. Glynne, 'Notes on the older churches in the four Welsh dioceses', *Arch. Camb.* (1897), 299–300)

1881–4: Restoration of church by John Bacon Fowler of Swansea and Brecon. In 1881 church found to be in very decayed and ruinous state. Tower considered to be in dangerous condition, roofs of nave and porch let in wind and rain, and pews so worm-eaten as to be uncomfortable. First stage of restoration comprised work on tower which was partly pulled down and rebuilt stone by stone. (SD/F/361. Faculty dated 19 July 1881) Two years later in 1883, when more funds were available, restoration of nave undertaken. (SD/F/362. Faculty dated 15 March 1883) Work consisted of new roof, new open benches of pitch-pine, restoration of some of nave windows which had been replaced by wooden casements, opening of two blocked-up windows in chancel and new floors and tiling throughout. (*BN*, 27 April 1883, 567) Most significant feature of restoration was raising of floor level by four feet. Centuries of soil deposit outside church due to erosion of higher slopes had made this alteration necessary. (Geoffrey R. Orrin, *The Gower Churches* (Penmaen, 1979), 40–4) Expense of work in the chancel undertaken by lay rector, C. R. M. Talbot of Margam Abbey, the remainder being raised by parishioners. Contractors: Messrs Henry & George Rosser, Reynoldston. Cost £1,100. Reopened after restoration on 20 March 1884. (*The Cambrian*, 21 March 1884)

Comments: John Bacon Fowler carried out a conservative restoration of St Cennydd's at this time. He was careful to preserve the essential features of the Gower church by rebuilding the tower to its original saddleback design as well as reordering the interior of the nave to meet the liturgical requirements of the Anglican Church.

ST GIWG'S CHURCH, LLANGIWG (LLANGUICKE)

25. St Giwg's Church, Llangiwg (Llanguicke) (Source: J. H. Davies, *A History of Pontardawe and District from Earliest to Modern Times* (Llandybïe, 1967), p. 123) (By kind permission of Christopher Davies)

1812: Inscription on outside of south wall of the church reads: 'This church was new roofed and considerably altered in A.D. 1812.'

1844: Although Llangiwg Church had been restored in 1812, by 1844 the fabric of the church was described by the churchwardens in their replies to the questionnaire sent out by the bishop of St David's prior to his visitation as in a bad state of repair with poor fittings. Even the Bible, Common Prayer Book and altar cloth were decayed. (SD/QA/75/76. Bishop's Visitation Returns for the Archdeaconry of Carmarthen:

answers of clergy and churchwardens, Llanguicke, 1845)

1882: Restoration of church. Caernarvon slates replaced stone slats and formed a lighter and better roof. (J. H. Davies, *A History of Pontardawe and District from Earliest to Modern Times* (Llandybïe, 1967), 123) It was probably at this time that level of church floor from inside doorway was raised nine inches and chancel raised to a level with tops of pews, 3ft 4ins above ground. (W. Ll. Morgan, *Antiquarian Survey of East Gower* (London, 1899), 52)

Comments: At the beginning of the nineteenth century the parish of Llangiwg was mainly agricultural, and the population of about 500 inhabitants was widely scattered. With the development of iron works and coal mines there was an influx of people into the parish, who settled in the Swansea valley. In 1862, St Peter's was built in Pontardawe since Llangiwg was inadequate for the needs of the increased population in the parish and too far away from the new centre of population of Pontardawe itself. As a result, although Llangiwg remained the parish church, it was in a poor state of repair throughout the nineteenth century. Only a minor restoration in 1882 preserved it from further decay. The north wall remains windowless, which is a good indication of the absence of any major restoration during the Victorian era.

ST CYNWYD'S CHURCH, LLANGYNWYD

1891–3: Restoration of church by George E. Halliday at expense of Miss Olive Talbot. (*Bldr*, 18 July 1891, 30) Repairs carried out in 1873 inadequate to prevent building's deterioration, and after 1877 its condition was so dilapidated that it was no longer used for regular services other than monthly Holy Communion. (D. R. L. Jones, *The Restoration of Llangynwyd Church, 1891–93* (Maesteg, 1993), 3–12) Faculty for restoration of church issued in July 1891 and work began immediately. (LL/F/416. Restoration of church. Faculty dated 9 July 1891) Work included taking down and rebuilding portions of walls on new foundations and removal of unsafe west gallery. Old chancel arch, which was only architectural feature of note remaining of thirteenth-century church, replaced by larger pointed arch. New east window inserted in chancel and new windows in nave in Perpendicular Gothic style. Chancel paved with tessellated tiles bearing arms of bishop of Llandaff. New roofs of solid oak raised in chancel and nave. New oak pulpit replaced old three-decker pulpit, and new choir stalls and altar table replaced old pews in chancel. Porch of more suitable design built with arches of massive blocks of Quarella stone from Bridgend. West tower, 69ft high, restored and ornamented by four pinnacles with carved crockets. Aisles boarded, and benches of solid oak to seat 160 persons erected in nave. Reredos made of oak from old rood-loft carved with panels of sacred subjects. Heated by a Porritt's hot-air apparatus. Contractor: William Clarke, Llandaff. Cost £3,000. (*Bldr*, 13 May 1893, 374) Reopened after restoration on 3 May 1893. (*GG*, 12 May 1893)

Comments: The restoration of St Cynwyd's was hailed by contemporary newspapers as a great success. The *Glamorgan Gazette* regarded it as a 'Royal Work' and stated 'that the greatest care has been bestowed upon every detail of the architecture and furniture, both as to material and design by Mr. Halliday of Llandaff, the architect'. Even T. C. Evans (Cadrawd), who had expressed serious reservations about the work of restoration, wrote that the church had been 'magnificently restored'. Nevertheless, he was reported to have regretted some features of the work, but never expressed his views in public. There is no doubt that the restoration of St Cynwyd's in 1891–3 altered the appearance and character of the church, which was inevitable in the light of the Gothic Revival and its influence upon the architecture of churches. It was a remodelling and reordering of the interior of the church according to the new spirit in the Anglican Church. Halliday 'recast' the church completely in the Perpendicular style in keeping with the rebuilding of the church in the fifteenth century. Whatever the merits or demerits of the restoration it was to give the church a long lease of life instead of allowing it to fall to total ruin.

SS. JULIUS' AND AARON'S CHURCH, LLANHARAN

1858–9: New church built on or about site of old medieval church which had fallen into a state of dilapidation. Designed by John Prichard of Prichard & Seddon and built in early Decorated Victorian Gothic style consisting of chancel, nave, north transept and south porch. Western gable surmounted by square turret with short spire. Constructed of grey, green, and brown local Pennant sandstone laid in thin courses, which contrasts well with ashlar bands and quoins of buff-coloured Bath stone. Roof covered with slates. (ICBS file no. 5066 (1857)) East window of three trefoiled lights with Geometrical-style tracery in head surmounted externally by hood mould with carved heads as label stops. External relieving arches of windows as well as arch of south porch constructed of polychromatic stonework. Chancel has arch-braced roof with curved windbraces between wallplate and purlins, and principal rafters descend some distance down chancel wall to be supported on carved stone corbels. Chancel lighted by four lancet windows, one on north side and three on south. Chancel arch pointed and springs from moulded capitals. Nave has trussed rafter roof with diagonal braces. West end of nave lighted by pair of two-light trefoil-headed windows with trefoil in apex. Nave walls pierced by four two-light trefoil-headed windows with cinquefoils in apex and external hood mould with foliated label stops. Open benches of pitch-pine. (Personal observation) Accommodation for 120 parishioners. Contractor: John Rees, Watertown, near Bridgend. Cost £1,058. ICBS grant £80; LCBS grant £35; LDCES grant £50; Church rates £234. (*CMG*, 24 September 1859) Consecrated on 16 September 1859. (*B. Chr*, 30 September 1859)

Comments: Llanharan Church was one of Prichard's fine village churches. His architectural ability was such that he was able to transform what would outwardly appear to be a simple structure into an outstanding work of art with his fine detailing of the architectural features and his original treatment of the bell turret. The church was too small to have carried off a steeple, but this is what the bell turret over the west gable is intended to represent. It undoubtedly achieves that effect when viewed from a distance. Prichard took great pains to ensure that it was a very detailed structure and that its proportions were correct. He built a broach spire in miniature, with gabled spire lights on the cardinal sides and with the top of the spire terminated by a finial. It is furnished with a moulded parapet and on each face of the square tower below there is a pair of trefoil-headed bell openings beneath a continuous hood moulding with a string below the windows to the apex of the roof. The various elements that make up the turret, such as the spire, spirelets, belfry stage and lower stage, are all well proportioned and the whole feature is in harmony with the nave and lower chancel. In the rest of the church, Prichard confined himself to the strictest early Decorated Geometrical style. The fine detailing of the three-light Geometrical-style east window allows the inclusion of a couple of extra trefoils by the continuation of the tracery into the head.

ST ILLTYD'S CHURCH, LLANHARRY

1868: Restoration and rebuilding of church by David Vaughan of Bonvilston. Churchwardenized repairs carried out in first part of nineteenth century inadequate to arrest decay of structure. Consequently, by 1868 the medieval church was so dilapidated that it had to be virtually rebuilt, with only fifteenth-century chancel arch and octagonal font surviving from old church. Built in a Transitional style between late Early English and early Decorated Gothic consisting of chancel, nave, south porch and western bellcote. Constructed of Pennant sandstone and Bath stone dressings. (*Kelly's Directory of South Wales*, 1926, 609) Architect has incorporated blocks of pink conglomerate in masonry of church. East window of three trefoiled lights beneath large sexfoil encased in plate tracery. Externally, this window has a hood mould with polychromatic masonry in relieving arch above. Chancel lighted on south side by two trefoiled lights with hood moulds. Nave lighted by five windows, two, east of porch, of twin trefoiled lights with quatrefoil set in plate tracery with hood moulds, and single trefoil light with hood mould west of porch. West end of nave lighted by two trefoiled lights with quatrefoil set in plate tracery with similar hood

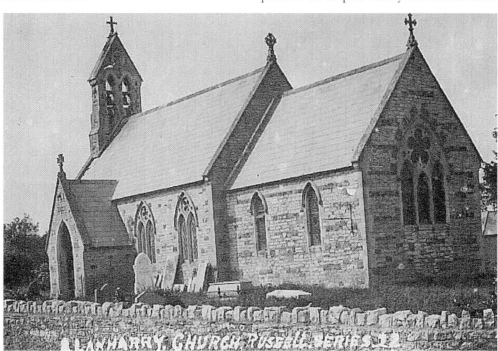

26. Llanharry Church (Source: Geoffrey R. Orrin: Postcard Collection of Glamorgan Churches)

mould. Pointed Perpendicular chancel arch with continuous mouldings from medieval church remains *in situ*. Chancel roof has scissors-beam arrangement springing from the common rafters partway along their length. Because of distance above longitudinal wallplate, diagonal rafters act as braces between wallplate and common rafters. Nave roof has a similar arrangement. Open benches of stained pitch-pine. Seating accommodation for 150 worshippers. Cost £1,565. (GRO, D/DV 53/1–12. David Vaughan Drawings Collection: Llanharry Church, 1868)

Comments: David Vaughan's rebuilding of St Illtyd's in 1868 was similar in some respects to Prichard's rebuilding and restoration of St Mary the Virgin's Church, Bonvilston in 1863. Both retained the fifteenth-century chancel arch, but whereas Prichard rebuilt Bonvilston in a severe Early English style Vaughan chose a slightly later period. His sensitive polychromatic treatment of the exterior of the church with blocks of pink conglomerate incorporated in the Pennant sandstone walls is in keeping with the architectural style of the High Victorian period.

ST ILID'S CHURCH, LLANILID

27. Pencil sketch by Charlotte Louisa Traherne of Llanilid Church, before restoration in 1883 (By kind permission of National Museums and Galleries of Wales, Cardiff)

1882–3: Restoration of church by John Prichard. In his application to ICBS dated 12 June 1882, the rector of Llanilid, Revd John Morgan, stated 'I beg leave to bring before you the deplorable condition of the parish church and tower of Llanilid. In its present condition it is most unfit for the celebration of Divine Service . . . and unless substantially repaired threatens before long to become an utter ruin.' (ICBS file no. 8753 (1882)) Successful appeal for funds to restore church was made in and beyond the parish. Accordingly, faculty issued on 28 August 1882 empowered rector 'to take down the present roof and put a new roof to and generally restore the nave; to re-floor, re-roof and reseat the nave, to re-floor, re-roof and reseat the chancel and put a new roof to the porch and tower of the said church of Llanilid'. (LL/F/423. Restoration of church. Faculty dated 28 August 1882) In addition, new stone steps and footpace placed in sanctuary and stonework of windows repaired with new internal arches. Masonry of tower substantially repaired and all windows in church reglazed. Old-fashioned square box pews removed and replaced by open benches of pitch-pine instead of individual chairs as indicated by architect in his epitome of work of restoration. Seating capacity of church increased by thirty-two seats to seventy sittings. Contractor: Thomas & William Cox, Llandaff. Cost £875. ICBS grant £20; LCBS grant £25; Lord Dunraven £200. Reopened after restoration on 13 September 1883. (*W. Mail*, 14 September 1883)

Comments: Prichard's thorough, yet conservative, restoration of St Ilid's was quite remarkable as it replicated very closely the character of the old building, as illustrated in the early nineteenth-century pencil sketch of this church by Charlotte Louisa Traherne in the Coedrhydglyn Collection in the National Museums and Galleries of Wales, Cardiff. Fortunately no major structural rebuilding was found necessary, but even so the total cost of restoration work amounted to £875.

ST ILLTYD'S CHURCH, LLANILLTERNE

1862–3: Church rebuilt on same site, the old building being much dilapidated, with walls having large cracks from the ground to the roof which was beginning to fall in. The original intention was to restore the old building, but when the architect examined the walls they were found to be in such a ruinous state that it was decided to demolish the old structure and build a new church from the foundations. (*BN*, 9 October 1863) Built in Early English Gothic style by George Edmund Street of London, consisting of chancel, nave and western bellcote with polished marbles of different colours inlaid with various devices. Chancel floor laid with ornamental encaustic tiles with a ground of black and red. Prayer desks of oak, which stand one on each side of chancel arch, carved with coats of arms of Lewis family. Massive altar table is of oak. Both chancel and nave have arch-braced roofs plastered between rafters. Nave furnished with open benches of oak accommodating forty parishioners. West wall has Rose window of unusual design and is surmounted by small bellcote. Crest of roof is of red tiles with high ridge perforated with holes. Nave floor consists of plain black and red tiles. Contractor: Thomas Williams, Cardiff. Cost £500, defrayed by Baroness Windsor, St Fagans. Reopened after rebuilding on 25 September 1863. (*CMG*, 2 October 1863)

Comments: It was Street's intention to give the exterior of the church a rustic appearance. He achieved this by building the walls of uncoursed, roughly squared Pennant sandstone with individual blocks interspersed in a random fashion, which gave it not only a mottled but also a slightly polychromatic effect. His treatment of the interior of the church, especially the chancel, was characteristic of his enthusiasm for the Ecclesiologists. The sanctuary is particularly well ornamented for a country church. This is all in great contrast to the outside with the plainest thirteenth-century style single bell gable, which is constructed as an extension of the west wall, not even corbelled out.

ST ISAN'S CHURCH, LLANISHEN

1854: Addition of north aisle. Architect: John Prichard, Llandaff. (ICBS file no. 7195 (1870))

1872: Enlargement of nave and aisle and restoration of church. Work included new windows to north aisle and new west window. Columns of aisle renewed. Reseating of nave. Old structure, which had a barn-like roof spanning nave and north aisle, replaced by new one with boarded ceiling divided into longitudinal and transverse moulded ribs with appropriate cornices, carved patera being placed at intersection of those ribs. Chancel floor paved with Godwin's encaustic tiles. Architect: John Prichard. Contractor: William Parry, Llandaff. Cost £950. ICBS grant £30. (*W. Mail*, 31 October 1872) Reopened after restoration on 28 September 1872. (*Cardiff Times*, 2 November 1872)

1873: Restoration and reseating of chancel. Chancel rendered in keeping with rest of church. Architect: John Prichard. Contractor: William Parry, Llandaff. Cost £300. Colonel C. K. Kemeys-Tynte and George T. Clark, Talygarn £200.

1893: Restoration of church. Work comprised construction of new organ chamber for organ which had formerly occupied a position in body of church; reflooring of centre of nave; and removal of old screen close to west wall. By moving organ into new organ chamber, additional seating accommodation provided for sixty-one parishioners. (LL/F/429. Restoration of church. Faculty dated 11 August 1892) Architect: Charles B. Fowler, Llandaff. Contractor: William Williams, Llanishen. Cost £200. (*BN*, 19 May 1893, 690) Reopened after restoration on 10 May 1893. (*W. Mail*, 11 May 1893)

Comments: After its enlargement it is structurally two churches in one, the original church prior to 1908 and now incorporated into the present building, and basically comprising the fifteenth-century tower, the south aisle, which was formed by the old nave and the Lady Chapel plus the additions carried out partially in the years 1872–3 and mainly in 1908. Blessley constructed the walls of the new chancel and nave in multicoloured stonework in keeping with parts of the old structure.

At Easter 1904 a reredos, depicting in the centre panel 'The Supper at Emmaus', was erected in the chancel. Designed by George E. Halliday. Executed by William Clarke. (LL/F/431. Reredos. Faculty dated 14 January 1904)

In the years 1907–8 the north aisle and vestry were demolished. New nave (48ft 2insx17ft 5ins) was built extending towards the west to within six inches of the face of the tower. New chancel (30ft x 17ft 5ins) with a priest's and choir vestry on the east end built. North wall of old chancel taken down and replaced by two arches. The old chancel remained as a morning chapel on the south side of the church. Organ removed to new organ chamber and pulpit removed to north side of new chancel arch. The proposed enlargement of the church provided additional accommodation for 150 parishioners. Architect: W. Douglas Blessley, Cardiff. Cost £2,000. (LL/F/433. Extension of church. Faculty dated 10 August 1907) Reopened after enlargement on 11 May 1908. (*W. Mail*, 12 May 1908) The church was finally completed by the addition of a narthex given by Captain and Mrs David Owen of Llanishen at a cost in excess of £600 and dedicated on 10 July 1921. (John Parry, *The Church of St Isan, Llanishen: Handbook* (1991), 5–6)

ST MADOC'S CHURCH, LLANMADOC

1865–6: Restoration and rebuilding of church by John Prichard. (ICBS file no. 6130 (1863)) At this time, the church was in a deplorable state and Revd John David Davies, rector of Llanmadoc and West Gower historian, described it to the diarist Kilvert as 'meaner than the meanest hovel in the village'. (F. G. Cowley, *Llanmadoc and Cheriton: Two North Gower Churches and their Parishes* (Llanmadoc and Cheriton, 1993), 20) Visitation returns of 1860 confirmed poor state of church at time: 'Very much out of repair. The roof is not secured. Doors very much out of repair, pews in a most dilapidated state. There are no seats in the chancel, earth allowed to lie against walls and there are no spouts or drains to carry off the water. . . A church rate has been made this year, for the first time during several years.' (SD/QA/87. 1860 Visitation: questions and answers of churchwardens) Much of south side of nave, portion of upper part of tower and greater part of chancel's east wall taken down and completely rebuilt. Rebuilt in Early English Gothic style. Reconstruction of chancel arch necessitated by rise in floor level of nave by as

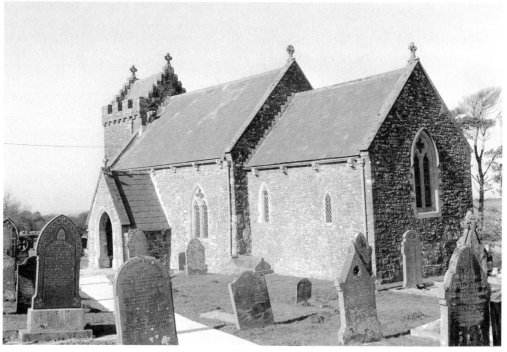

28. St Madoc's Church, Llanmadoc (Photo: Geoffrey R. Orrin)

much as four feet as result of centuries of burials in churchyard. New windows inserted in east end of chancel and south side of nave. New floor of red and black Staffordshire tiles laid down in diamond shape. New roof of red pine raised and pulpit of pitch-pine, inlaid with walnut, installed. New south porch built. (*Bldr*, 2 June 1866, 414) Contractors: Woodwork executed by Messrs Henry and George Rosser, Reynoldston. Freestone work by Rees Roderick, Port Talbot. Cost £585. ICBS grant £30; C. R. M. Talbot £100; Revd J. D. Davies £124. Reopened after restoration and rebuilding on 26 April 1866. (*The Cambrian*, 4 May 1866)

Comments: As an Anglo-Catholic and a fervent follower of the Ecclesiological Society Revd J. D. Davies commissioned John Prichard to restore and rebuild St Madoc's. As a result of Prichard's drastic restoration of 1866, the building bore the appearance of a new structure. The reopening ceremony which took place on 26 April 1866 was performed with such ritual style, including the use of a surpliced choir, a procession of clergy wearing hoods and coloured stoles, and candles and flowers on the altar, that it caused great controversy among Low churchmen and Nonconformists at this time. Subsequently, a long and impassioned debate followed in the correspondence columns of *The Cambrian* newspaper over the following two months.

ST CADOC'S CHURCH, LLANMAES

1857: Restoration of church during incumbency of Revd David Parry Thomas, rector of Llanmaes from 1850 to 1871. Fabric of church had fallen into such a state of decay that chancel and considerable part of nave had to be completely rebuilt. New roof raised over nave with exception of principal rafters, which were retained and restored. Open benches of simple design erected in nave in place of old-fashioned, high-backed pews. Consequently, seating accommodation increased to 100 sittings. Old, medieval oak screen freed from its thick coating of paint and thoroughly repaired. South porch rebuilt and repairs carried out on tower. Cost £510. Trustees

of marquess of Bute £190. Church rates £20. Reopened after restoration on 4 November 1857. (*CMG*, 14 November 1857)

1882: New window of two lights with pointed heads and dripstone with carved heads as label stops inserted in north wall of nave. The two single lights are separated internally by single slender shaft with round moulded caps and astragal and vertical fillet. The arches above, which are returned on half-caps set in side wall, are decorated by continuous bands of nineteenth-century approximations of Early English leaf forms. Window with stained glass erected as memorial to Canon William Leigh Morgan (d. 1876), rector from 1871 to 1876 and his wife Elizabeth (d. 1878). Structure of window designed by John Prichard. (LL/F/448. Cutting the church wall for erection of stained glass window. Faculty dated 19 September 1882)

1898: Restoration of tower. (*Kelly's Directory of South Wales*, 1926, 616)

Comments: Unfortunately Sir Stephen Glynne made no notes on St Cadoc's and, as no application was made to the ICBS for a grant towards restoration, no file exists in Lambeth Palace library recording the details of the restoration. The only reliable information is to be found in a local newspaper account of the reopening of the church after restoration. Like many other ancient churches in the Vale of Glamorgan, Llanmaes had fallen into a state of decay by the mid-nineteenth century. Fortunately the manor of Llanmaes was held by the trustees of the marquess of Bute. They contributed a large proportion of the cost of the restoration, while the remainder was found by the levying of a church rate and public subscriptions. Although no architect is recorded, it is probable that the architect to the Bute estate, Alexander Roos, was responsible for the restoration.

ST MICHAEL'S AND ALL ANGELS' CHURCH, LLANMIHANGEL

1888–9: Restoration of church by Frederick R. Kempson of Llandaff. (ICBS file no. 9229 (1888)) The correspondent in the *Church Builder* reported that 'the church is very dilapidated, no repairs having been done during this century. Parish is a small one and contains no resident landowner. Thirty-two seats will be added.' (*Ch. Bldr* (1888), 70) New roofs of oak covered with felt and Westmoreland tiles. Chancel roof boarded in oak within, also part of nave above rood-loft similarly treated. Walls renewed in places and chancel walls raised by three feet all round. Insertion of new east window of three lights, old east window moved to north wall of chancel, and old window opened out in south wall of chancel. New open seats of red deal, oak stalls for chancel, oak altar table, reading desk and lectern and stone pulpit installed. New floors put down in chancel and nave – partly coloured tiles and partly red deal blocks. Three new steps introduced from nave to altar. Contractor: John Morgan, Pontyglyn (Pontyclun). Cost £671. ICBS grant £15. Lord Dunraven, patron of the living, made a substantial contribution to restoration fund, while Colonel M. Franklen and Colonel and Mrs J. P. Turbervill assisted generously. (*CGG*, 10 May 1889) Reopened after restoration on 7 May 1889. (*BNC*, 10 May 1889)

Comments: Kempson's restoration of Llanmihangel Church in 1889 was a rather conservative affair. Its objectives were twofold. Firstly, the fabric of the church was restored and repaired, which he did by rebuilding crumbling walls and replacing decayed timber. Secondly, he devoted the other part of the restoration to an ecclesiological reordering of the interior of the church by inserting a larger window to lighten the chancel and to removing the old square box pews and refurbishing the church with modern Victorian church furniture and fittings, which were fundamental to the new liturgical changes in the Anglican Church. He raised the chancel above the nave by three stone steps and distinguished the chancel, where the Holy Eucharist was celebrated, by a more dignified roof. Finally he was careful to preserve the ancient mural monuments of the Edwin family in the chancel.

In 1909 a turret staircase was constructed on the north side of the tower because the upper part of the tower could only be reached through a doorway by means of a ladder placed against the west wall of the nave. It was designed by Edward Jenkin Williams of Bruton & Williams, Cardiff. (LL/F/451. Improvement of tower. Faculty dated 27 July 1909)

ST ILLTYD'S CHURCH, LLANRHIDIAN

1856–8: Rebuilding of nave by Richard Kyrke Penson, 'honorary' diocesan architect. Nave of church completely demolished and rebuilt from foundations. (*The Cambrian*, 17 April 1857) New windows of nave constructed of Bath stone. North wall strengthened by two-stage buttresses. Accommodation provided in church to seat 282 worshippers on modern pews of pitch-pine. West gallery under tower built exclusively for use of children of parish. (ICBS file no. 4965 (1856–8)) Contractor: John Williams, Leason, Llanrhidian. Cost £1,496. ICBS grant £150; C. R. M. Talbot, Margam Abbey £100; H. H. Vivian, Singleton Abbey £50. Reopened after restoration on 6 October 1858. (*The Cambrian*, 29 October 1858)

1899–1901: Chancel refurbished with new oak roof, carved oak altar, chancel rail of oak with iron and brass standards, choir seats of oak and teak, and floor of encaustic tiles. (The oak roof was an exact reproduction of an older structure put up in 1720 by Miss Talbot's ancestor, Lord Mansel.) New chancel windows inserted made by Jones & Willis of Birmingham. New ceiling to nave of pitch-pine with 324 ceiling bosses carved by Revd J. D. Davies of Llanmadoc. Cornice of nave and poppy heads of choir stalls carved by Mr Daniel, Singleton Street, Swansea, and internal decoration tastefully carried out by Thomas Dartnell of Cheriton. (*GCM*, June 1901, 4) Open joints of tower repointed with Portland cement. Contractors: John Daniel, Swansea, John Williams, Llanrhidian and Thomas Dartnell, Cheriton. Cost £350. Miss Emily Talbot, patron of living, bore entire cost of the restoration. (Geoffrey R. Orrin, *The Gower Churches* (Penmaen, 1979), 49) Reopened after restoration on 14 May 1901. (*The Cambrian*, 17 May 1901)

Comments: Penson rebuilt the nave, retaining the rural character of the building by the simple manner in which this was done. He inserted small two-light windows of Bath stone with the external arches formed of stones, without hood mouldings or dripstones, giving them the appearance of plate tracery with hardly a hint of mouldings and only very depressed and conservative quatrefoils in the heads. Penson chose paired lancets with the exception of a single trefoil-headed light in the north side of the nave to conform with the old windows in the chancel. He rebuilt the nave in the Early English style, quite simply because it was a small and plain church. He was forced to alter the original design slightly at the west end of the nave where he raised the tower arch to provide additional seating in a tiered gallery under the tower for the exclusive use of children of the parish. The south porch, which was rebuilt at the same time, is typically Victorian with its steeply gabled roof and pointed arch of Bath stone surmounted by a relieving arch of hammer-dressed stone done in a medieval style.

ST SENWYR'S CHURCH, LLANSANNOR

1853: Partial repairs carried out on nave at cost of £200. Reseating of nave. (ICBS file no. 8154 (1878))

1878: A printed leaflet, written by Revd David N. Llewelyn, stated that 'considerable portions of the Parish Church of Llansannor being in a miserable and even dangerous condition, efforts are now being made to raise the necessary funds for repairing the fabric . . . The carrying out of the whole of the work will require an outlay of about £500 . . . plans have been drawn up by J. Prichard, Esq., Diocesan Architect, Llandaff.' (ICBS file no. 8154 (1878) Miscellaneous material) Contract for restoring chancel, porch and rebuilding new chancel arch was £285, but total expenditure was £376 13s 3d. Amount raised by subscription £391 12s 5d, with balance of £14 19s 2d intended to form nucleus of fund for repairing tower, reseating nave, furnishing chancel, and supplying church with a heating apparatus. (ICBS file no. 8154 (1878): Statements of accounts dated 18 March 1880) Work confined to restoration of chancel and rebuilding of churchyard

walls. Contractor: John Rees, Bridgend. ICBS grant £20; LDCES grant £15; trustees of Sir Joseph Spearman, Bt. £100; Sir Ivor B. Guest, Bt. £20; Charles Aubrey Aubrey £10; G. T. Clark, Dowlais House £10. Reopened after restoration on 17 September 1878. (*W. Mail*, 19 September 1878)

Comments: St Senwyr's was restored twice during the Victorian period. So restricted were incumbents by the lack of adequate church funding that many of the Vale of Glamorgan churches suffered serious dilapidation. Therefore, at Llansannor only the nave could be repaired and reseated in 1853, and the restoration of the chancel had to be postponed until 1878. This was typical of old parish churches in Glamorgan, where appeals for substantial subscriptions, notably from landowning gentry and wealthy church-people, to restore decaying structures had to be made in and beyond the boundaries of parishes.

In the years 1909–10 the church was restored again. The work comprised the removal of the old pulpit made of deal and all the pews of the same material and their replacement with a new pulpit, choir stalls and pews throughout the church constructed of oak. The entrance of the rood-loft was exposed. Entrance to old rood-loft exposed. Additional 20 sittings provided. Restoration work was carried out under the supervision of William Clarke, Llandaff. (LL/F/453. Removal of pulpit and other improvements. Faculty dated 20 December 1909)

SS ILLTYD'S, TYFODWG'S AND GWYNNO'S CHURCH, LLANTRISANT

1871–4: A printed circular dated 11 July 1868 stated that 'the church being much out of repair and as regards the roof in a dangerous state of dilapidation, steps should be forthwith taken completely to restore it.' (ICBS file no. 7101 (1871)) Accordingly, interior of church rebuilt, including demolition of 'Norman' style arcade which Prichard replaced by a new, lofty and pointed arcade of Early English Gothic style. (*CMG*, 18 July 1871) All chancel and nave windows replaced, chancel arch rebuilt, new roofs raised and vestry added on north side of church. Prichard transformed whole of interior from Norman to Early English Gothic style. Contractor: Rees Roderick, Margam. Cost £2,257. ICBS grant £35. (*CMG*, 28 October 1871)

1893–4: West end of church restored. Work consisted of rebuilding upper part of tower and putting on a new lead roof, renewal of the four lofts, installation of new ringing chamber, and rehanging bells. In addition, restoration included provision of new seating accommodation and construction of a baptistery in white marble under floor of choir vestry in tower and reopening built-up tower arch which was replaced by oak screen. Seating accommodation provided for 317 parishioners. Architects: Seddon & Carter, Cardiff. Contractor: Charles Cooksley, Pontyclun, Llantrisant. Cost £2,000. ICBS grant £45; LDCES grant £35. (LL/F/463. Restoration of tower and improvement of church. Faculty dated 19 April 1892) Reopened after restoration on 9 April 1894. (*GG*, 13 April 1894)

Comments: Prichard's restoration of Llantrisant Church caused a certain amount of controversy, not just locally but also in the national architectural press. Many Victorian architects showed a complete disregard for restoration work carried out in previous centuries, and this was demonstrated by Prichard's demolition of the five-bay Norman-style arcade of the nave with its cylindrical columns and its replacement with an Early English-style arcade of alternate round and octagonal pillars. However, when the nave was pulled down, Prichard's assumption about the date of the nave arcade was proved correct for the date 1640 was found carved on one of the principals of the nave roof. As there was no doubt that the arcades were erected for the specific purpose of fixing the roof in its present position, it was inferred that the date 1640 on the principal indicated the year of the erection of the arcades. Apart from the controversy over the nave arcade, Prichard was attacked and accused of vandalism in the architectural press for his intention to remove the old dilapidated roof of the nave and not to replace it with an identical structure. He replied to this criticism by stating that his practice was to 'preserve an old roof if possible; failing this make a

close copy of the original, but if funds should hopelessly fail, then put up the most appropriate roof under the circumstances'. (*BN*, 27 September 1867, 675) Lack of funds prevented the restoration of the west end of the church until 1893–4.

ST ILLTYD'S CHURCH, LLANTRITHYD

1828: Church reroofed at cost of £30 13s 5d raised by a local church rate. (ICBS file no. 2539 (1839))

1839: Church was repewed to provide additional seating accommodation for twenty-one parishioners. Architect: David Vaughan, Bonvilston. ICBS grant £25. (ICBS file no. 2539 (1839))

1882: 'A fine open timber roof was placed over the nave and chancel under the direction of John Prichard.' (GRO: D/D Au 303/3. Records of the Aubrey family of Llantrithyd: Llantrithyd Parish Church. George Eley Halliday's report on the condition of the church. 1896)

1897: Restoration of church by George E. Halliday. The correspondent in the *Church Builder* reported that 'with the exception of the nave and chancel roofs, the church is now in a very bad state of repair'. (*Ch. Bldr* (1897), 50) Church restored during incumbency of Revd Evan Lodwick Ellis in 1897. (ICBS file no. 9972 (1896)) Work of restoration as follows: new open benches of pitch-pine installed; new wood-block floors laid under seats; and ground floor of tower repaved. West gallery and its external staircase, erected in restoration of church in 1711, removed, roof of south porch renewed and a new altar, altar rails and stone pulpit erected in church. Bells in belfry rehung, cracked bell recast and four louvred belfry windows inserted in tower. Rood-loft entrance doorway removed from its place in north wall of nave and built into tower wall. Tower reroofed with lead, and two new doors put to tower. Chancel screen restored by William Clarke of Llandaff. Nave and chancel roofs, designed by John Prichard, were in an excellent state of preservation and were in no way interfered with. New Porritt's heating apparatus installed. Finally, church reglazed throughout. Seating accommodation increased from 84 to 113 sittings. (LL/F/468. Restoration of church. Faculty dated 13 April 1897) Contractor:

W. A. James, Fonmon. Cost £795. ICBS grant £40. Reopened after restoration on 25 August 1897. (*W. Mail*, 26 August 1897)

Comments: St Illtyd's underwent restoration during the nineteenth century under three different architects, David Vaughan, John Prichard and George E. Halliday. Halliday's major restoration of the church in 1897 was a thorough reparation of the tower which had been neglected over a period of some years. The restoration of the nave was essentially a reordering of the pre-ecclesiological arrangement with its square box pews and west gallery which had survived almost to the end of the nineteenth century. The only insensitive part of the restoration, which was unusual for an architect of Halliday's standing and Tractarian sympathies, was his disregard for the old rood-loft entrance doorway which he relegated to a place in the tower wall. As a result all traces of the rood-loft arrangements were swept away during the Victorian period.

ST ILLTYD'S CHURCH, LLANTWIT FARDRE

1854: Restoration of church at cost of £560.
1894: Church renovated and memorial windows erected at a cost of £300. At this time church consisted of chancel, nave, vestry, south porch and western tower. (*Kelly's Directory of South Wales*, 1926, 634)

Comments: The church was drastically remodelled and enlarged towards the south in the years 1972–4. As a result, much of the work of Victorian architects was swept away. No records or documents exist relating to the Victorian restorations and no parish guide or history has apparently ever been written.

ST ILLTYD'S CHURCH, LLANTWIT-JUXTA-NEATH

1858–9: According to a report in a local newspaper 'the church had long fallen into a very dilapidated state and become totally unworthy of its sacred purpose'. (*The Cambrian*, 10 December 1858) In 1856

parishioners resolved to levy church rate of 1s in the pound for 'rebuilding the body of the church'. (Llantwit-juxta-Neath Church Vestry Book) By September 1858 tenders sought for carrying out work under direction of the architect David Vaughan. Work comprised: rebuilding of south wall and repairs to north wall; tower arch restored, and whole of walls raised by 21ins; roof restored using Memel timber and covered with copper-coloured slates 24ins by 12ins. Tower repaired and parapets replaced. New windows constructed of 'the best Combdown Bath stone'. New open benches of Memel timber and new pulpit erected. Floor raised 18ins resting upon oak sleepers with dwarf walls. Whole of woodwork stained and varnished. Vestry panelled with old pew timber. Architect: David Vaughan, Bonvilston. Cost £560. LCBS grant £55; LDCES grant £95; church rates £120. Reopened after restoration on 7 July 1859. (*The Cambrian*, 15 July 1859)
1876: Further restoration. Church roofs stripped, with lath and plaster entirely removed and replaced by ¾in. red matched boarding and new lath for slates. Part of chancel wall rebuilt, new window inserted in chancel and chancel floor paved with encaustic tiles. Whole of building repointed. New Bath stone coping on pine end of chancel corresponding with church roof. Contractor: John Thomas, Neath. Cost £250. (D. Rhys Phillips, *The History of the Vale of Neath* (Swansea, 1925), 99)
1898: Restoration of tower. Architect: Charles Busteed Fowler, of Kempson & Fowler, Llandaff. Contractor: W. A. James, Cowbridge. (*Bldr*, 7 May 1898, 448)

Comments: The most controversial aspect of Vaughan's restoration was his design of the windows that he inserted in the north and south walls of the nave and which Newman described as 'rough-and-ready round-headed windows belonging to the drastic restoration of 1858–9 by Mr. Vaughan'. (Newman, 457–8) One would have expected Vaughan to have designed Gothic-style pointed windows in the spirit of the Gothic Revival, which had been approved in the middle of the nineteenth century even in the remote parts of Glamorgan. Instead, he chose to model the round-headed windows on the original Norman chancel arch (which he carefully preserved in the church) and the Norman inner and outer arches of the south doorway of the porch. However, he added a shoulder-arched doorway in Bath stone and placed above it an inscription in Welsh recording the restoration of the church in 1859. David Vaughan was the only architect to restore a church in Glamorgan using Neo-Norman fenestration during the High Victorian period of church restoration.

ST ILLTYD'S CHURCH, LLANTWIT MAJOR

29. Llantwit Major Church – the chancel arch *c*.1899 with the Carne hatchment in its original position (By kind permission of the Revd David Jenkins, rector of Llantwit Major)

1888: Restoration of church by George Fenton Lambert of Bridgend. Church partially restored in 1888 with restoration recommenced in 1899 and finally completed in 1905. Primary objective of work carried out in 1888 according to a contemporary local newspaper account was to preserve everything worth preserving and to remove all that was objectionable through decay or unsightliness. (*BNC*, 8 June 1888) Work at this time comprised reroofing of nave and aisles of eastern church with deal and pitch-pine and restoration of nave walls to reveal medieval wall paintings. Temporary floor laid down in western church and new seats provided. Seating of nave rearranged and varnished, and belfry repaired. Chancel refurbished with new choir stalls. Contractor: Richard Price, Llantwit Major. Cost £1,000. Reopened after restoration on 4 June 1888. (*W. Mail*, 6 June 1888)

1899–1900: Restoration of western church and south porch by George E. Halliday. A national newspaper reported in 1898 that 'Llantwit Major Church, one of the most interesting churches in south Wales, is sadly in need of repair, and the vicar, the Revd E. W. Vaughan, is making strenuous efforts to obtain the sum of about £1,000, which is required for the purpose.' (*The Daily Graphic*, 22 October 1898) West doorway and most of windows had been built up with masonry for many years and fine tracery of windows broken. Earthen floor was paved, roof timbers repaired and roof reboarded with oak and reslated. Stonework of windows restored and windows reglazed. South porch reroofed and new floor laid down in parvise. Earth, which had accumulated on south side of church causing considerable dampness, removed. All walls repointed internally and externally, and all pre-Norman stones placed in western church. Contractor: William Clarke, Llandaff. Cost £1,100. (LL/F/479. Restoration of part of church. Faculty dated March 1899) Reopened after restoration on 30 July 1900. (*GG*, 3 August 1900)

Comments: In its report for 1888 the Society for the Protection of Ancient Buildings, which had taken great interest in St Illtyd's, severely criticized the restoration work carried out at the church because the architect had not heeded the advice or followed the recommendations given by the Society. For instance, black mortar had been used to point the tower which made it look smaller and less impressive and roofs requiring recovering had not been dealt with in the way specified by the Society. The old stone tiles had been removed and substituted with poor quality slates and the wooden 'V' lead-lined gutters recommended by the Society were not used. Deal or pitch-pine had been mostly used for the roof timbers in the nave and aisles instead of oak, again contrary to the Society's advice. Finally, the Society complained that the iron tie rods specified by their architects for the prevention of further bulging of the south wall of the nave had been omitted altogether. (SPAB – Annual report, 1888, 40–1) However, Halliday's restoration of the western church in the years 1899–1900 was well received. The reporter in the *South Wales Daily News* stated: 'it is gratifying to find that the work has been carried through in no vandal spirit. The pre-Gothic and Early English architecture has been restored as closely as possible to the likeness of the original.' (*SWDN*, 31 July 1900)

In 1905 the correspondent in the *Church Builder* stated that 'in addition to the seating of the aisles and providing chairs for the Western Church, a considerable amount of necessary repairs to the fabric and tower are absolutely necessary'. (*Ch. Bldr* (1905), 7) At this time the eastern church was restored. The arcade of the south aisle was found to be in a dangerous condition. Foundations of piers of south arcade rebuilt and arcade supported by four flying buttresses across south side with external buttresses to take thrust. Chancel restored by Ecclesiastical Commissioners as lay impropriators under direction of their architect, W. D. Caröe. Late fourteenth-century stone reredos repaired. Roof covered with oak boards and re-slated. Tower found to be in very dangerous condition, the bases of piers being very much out of perpendicular. Foundations of piers relieved of as much weight as possible by laying new concrete footings under each arch. Tower shored up by massive square timber supports while new foundations of concrete, six feet deep in places, were laid. Once weight was relieved all loose stonework removed and reset in cement. Walls of sacristy repaired and new roof raised. Walls underpinned and cellar formed to receive heating apparatus. Architects: George E. Halliday & John W. Rodger, Cardiff. Contractor: William Clarke, Llandaff. (*Bldr*, 22 July 1905, 100) Cost £1,300. Reopened after restoration on 14 July 1905. (*W. Mail*, 15 July 1905). The restoration of St Illtyd's in 1905 undoubtedly saved the imminent collapse of the tower. J. P. Seddon, Prichard's former partner, who examined the state of the tower on behalf of the LDCES, advised the building committee to take it down and rebuild it from the foundations. However, the vicar of Llantwit Major, Revd Henry Morris, appointed Halliday to take charge of the restoration of the tower. Together with the assistance of the experienced William Clarke they saved the tower from collapse and a great deal of cost to the parish. Fortunately for St Illtyd's, the restorations were carried out at the end of the nineteenth century and during the Edwardian era when attitudes to church restoration had changed considerably from the early Victorian period.

ST GWYNNO'S CHURCH, LLANWONNO

1893–4: Restoration, enlargement and partial rebuilding of church by George E. Halliday. (*Bldr*, 21 July 1894, 45) Church guide states that 'until 1893 the church resembled a barn from the outside with an appendage containing the chancel and a porch leading from the south wall. Inside the church, the pulpit, a three-decker was situated on the north wall; the pews were interlocked and ran from east to west.' (J. Gwyn Davies, *A Brief Account of the Church of St. Gwynno* (1967), 2) Petition for faculty to restore church stated 'that it is proposed to restore, enlarge and partly rebuild the above named church, which is now in a dilapidated condition'. (LL/F/490P. Petition for faculty. Dated 19 January 1893) Restoration included raising of new oak barrel-shaped roof over chancel and insertion of elaborately carved east window of three cinquefoiled lights with flowing Decorated style tracery in head. Nave floor lowered to its original level and new two-light windows inserted in nave walls, all of Decorated Gothic design. Old dilapidated roof of nave replaced with one of oak with arched braces and decorated with gilded bosses. Old-fashioned square box pews removed and replaced with open benches of oak. Three-decker pulpit removed and church completely refurbished with choir stalls, altar table, lectern and pulpit of teak with red Dumfries stone base. South porch rebuilt in Decorated Gothic style with effigy of patron saint in niche above doorway. Western elevation is most striking, comprising a bell turret surmounting the west gable supported by buttresses with set-offs flanking a two-light west window and forming western entrance to church at its base which is supported by corner buttresses. Seating accommodation doubled from fifty-five to 110 places. Porritt's heating apparatus installed. Contractor: John W. Rodger, Cardiff. Cost £3,000, defrayed by Miss Olive Talbot. (LL/F/490.

Restoration and rebuilding of church. Faculty dated 10 February 1893) Reopened after restoration on 13 July 1894. (*W. Mail*, 14 July 1894)

Comments: Halliday's costly and over-enthusiastic restoration of St Gwynno's in 1894 destroyed much of the historical interest of the building with its old three-decker pulpit and square box pews, which had survived well into the late Victorian period. However, as a result of its remodelling and refurbishment with standardized Victorian church furniture and fittings, it now had a much more imposing appearance, placing it firmly as a good example of fine Decorated Gothic church architecture.

ST ANDREW'S CHURCH, LLWYNYPIA

1877–8: New church built on new site given by De Winton family of Brecon by Walter Douglas Blessley, Cardiff. Foundation stone laid on 29 October 1877 by Miss Eliza Agnes Walker Hood, daughter of Archibald Hood of Glamorgan Coal Company. (*W. Mail*, 30 and 31 October 1877) Built in Early English Gothic style. Constructed of Welsh Pennant sandstone with Bath stone dressings. Cruciform in plan having a simple nave with centre aisle and transepts, the provision of a chancel having had to be postponed for lack of funds. (*BN*, 2 November 1877, 446) Nave has curved-braced roof with decorated tie-beam and decorated wall plates. At west end is a typical single bellcote above west gable. Circular, geometric window beneath encloses seven cinquefoils. Single lancets flank the porch and above standard pointed doorway are three square-headed lights. All windows of church have polychromatic heads. Open benches of pitch-pine. Seating accommodation for 500 worshippers. Contractor: Thomas White, Swansea. Cost £1,960. ICBS grant £120; LDCES grant £100. (*W. Mail*, 25 October 1878) Opened for divine worship on 24 October 1878. (*Cardiff Times*, 26 October 1878) Consecrated on 18 December 1878. (T. J. Prichard, 'The Anglican Church in the Rhondda from the Industrial Revolution to Disestablishment' (unpublished

Ph.D. thesis, University of Keele, 1981). Appendix 5. Building grants 1851–1920. (Ystradyfodwg))

1886–7: Chancel added, with vestry on south side and organ chamber on north side. East window of three trefoil-headed lights, the middle higher than others with round trefoils in spandrels. Chancel arch tall and moulded, the stops on hood moulding are, as are corbels and stops generally, conservative and understated. Only corbel to chancel arch has a flourish; floriferous stiff-leaf encompassing a carved head. Roof of chancel has braced scissors-beam arrangement with boarded decorated ceiling. Architect: E. M. Bruce Vaughan, Cardiff. (*Ch. Bldr* (1886), 64) Cost £525. ICBS grant £40. (ICBS file no. 8044 (1886))

Comments: St Andrew's was the first permanent stone-built church erected by Revd Canon William Lewis in the parish of Ystradyfodwg. William Lewis chose Walter Douglas Blessley of Cardiff as his architect, and thereafter he relied on the services of Bruce Vaughan. The ICBS and the Ecclesiastical Commissioners objected to the plans drawn up by Blessley. The Society criticized the lack of space at the west doorway, the orientation of the nave seats westward of the pulpit and reading desk, and the general terms in which the specification was cast, if it was to be the basis of the contract. They recommended six specific structural directions for inclusion in a new specification. The objections of the consulting architect to the Ecclesiastical Commissioners are not to be found in the ICBS file, but a covering letter from the Commissioners stipulated that his suggested alterations be adopted and also dealt with matters concerning pew rents, patronage and parochial status of the new church. Amended plans were approved by all parties in February 1877. William Lewis found the building of his first permanent church at Llwynypia a difficult proposition. However, there were extenuating circumstances, for Lewis's brother died prematurely in 1877 whilst the building was in process of being constructed, and at that time the Rhondda experienced the onset of a deep depression in the coal trade which lasted from 1875 to 1879. Lack of funds at that time prevented the building of the chancel which was added ten years later.

In 1904 the church was renovated and enlarged by the addition of a south aisle. Reopened and dedicated on 17 October 1904. (LL/F/498. Repair and enlargement of church. Faculty dated 20 July 1904)

ST TYDFIL'S CHURCH, LLYSWORNEY

1894: Rebuilding and restoration of church by Bruton & Williams of Cardiff. (*Bldr*, 27 December 1890, 502) The correspondent in the *Church Builder* reported: 'This church is now in a very dilapidated state. The tower requires thorough repair and a new roof over nave and chancel in addition to renewing all the windows. It is at present almost the only one in the Vale of Glamorgan which has not received a thorough restoration beyond necessary repairs in the course of this century.' (*Ch. Bldr* (1894), 124) Llysworney was a poor agricultural parish, and it appears that last documented occasion, on which church was considerably repaired and reseated, was in 1774 when faculty was granted to sell two bells, which 'since time immemorial were broken and useless' to provide new seats and pews in the church. Petition for faculty records that a considerable sum was spent at that time repairing nave and tower. (LL/F/367. Sale of bells to pay for improvements in church. Faculty dated 6 January 1774) As a result of granting of faculty in March 1894, new roofs raised over church, all defective walling pulled down and rebuilt and new floors laid down. Old-fashioned square box pews removed and replaced with open benches of red deal, and new pulpit erected. New vestry constructed on north side of chancel and turret-staircase built on north side of tower, leading from vestry to belfry. Several windows were renewed, constructed of Bath stone, and all reglazed. Soil, which had accumulated on south side of church, removed to prevent dampness in church. (LL/F/369. Restoration of church and erection of vestry and stairway. Faculty dated 16 March,1894) Contractors: Hatherley & Carr, Bristol. Cost £1,100. ICBS grant £30. Reopened after restoration on 6 June 1894. (*GG*, 15 June 1894)

Comments: As John Newman says the work of restoration carried out by Bruton & Williams in 1894 was insensitive. (Newman, 414) The architects restored the church simply as a work of reparation and reconstruction without any coherent plan as to what form the restoration should take. As a result the old medieval church was transformed into a heterogeneous structure of differing styles of architecture, including Early English, Tudor and nondescript Victorian Gothic represented by the mustard-coloured Bath stone.

ST MICHAEL'S CHURCH, LOUGHOR

1868: Vestry held on 22 July 1868 reported that 'the ancient church is found upon examination to be in a most dilapidated condition and unfit for worship especially during the winter months . . . It was proposed that the present building be erased and a new structure be built instead of it.' (*The Cambrian*, 7 August 1868) However, since no restoration of church took place until 1884 it must be assumed that since Loughor was a poor colliery district with no resident gentry it was unable at this time to raise the necessary funds to rebuild the church.

1884–5: Original intention was to restore church, but on removing battens and plaster it was discovered that walls were unsafe and dangerous in some places. Thus decided that walls should be pulled down and nave rebuilt upon old foundations. Architect: James Buckley Wilson, Swansea. (SD/F/466. Restoration of church. Faculty dated 20 August 1884) Foundation stone laid on 19 September 1884 by Mrs J. R. Wright of The Mount, Loughor. (*The Cambrian*, 26 September 1884) Church rebuilt in Early English Gothic style using local Welsh sandstone with Bath stone dressings. Walls of chancel retained and chancel raised above nave by two steps constructed of Forest of Dean stone and chancel floor laid with encaustic tiles. Chancel window of three lights, west window of two lights and nave and chancel lighted by single lancets, all glazed with Cathedral glass. West gallery, erected *c*.1802, removed, and open benches of pitch-pine with red deal ends replaced high-backed, square box pews. Ponderous three-decker pulpit removed from nave and replaced with modern one of pitch-pine. New Communion table, choir stalls, prayer-desks, lectern, faldstool, credence table, sedilia and small aumbry in south wall introduced in chancel. New vestry built on north side of chancel. Open timber roofs of pitch-pine raised on nave and chancel supported on Bath stone corbels. Church walls strengthened by two-stage buttresses. Accommodation for 300 worshippers. (WGRO: P/112/CW/29. Agreement for restoring St Michael's Church, Loughor) Contractor: William Brown, Swansea. Cost £1,884. Reopened after rebuilding on 20 August 1885. (*W. Mail*, 22 August 1885)

Comments: James Buckley Wilson's rebuilding of the nave and restoration of the chancel of St Michael's transformed the old early nineteenth-century auditory church, which had survived into the late Victorian period, into a modern Victorian Gothic church with its liturgical emphasis manifestly towards the chancel and altar, and away from the pulpit. Wilson rebuilt and restored the church in the Early English style, the original style of the medieval church. The church is distinguished by its oversized western bellcote, which towers above the rest of the structure.

ST DAVID'S CHURCH, MAESTEG (MAESTEG EPISCOPAL CHAPEL)

1852–3: New church built on new site given by Traherne family as chapel of ease to Llangynwyd parish church. Architect: Egbert Moxham, Neath. Work on church commenced in May 1852. (ICBS file no.4473 (1852)) Original intention was to build church seating 1,000 worshippers, parsonage house, schoolroom and establish an endowment to provide a stipend for a clergyman, estimated altogether at £6,000. Subscription list opened in 1840, and Maesteg Works promised to pay £550 towards cost. Scheme proved impractical when Maesteg Company failed in 1847, and project lay dormant until 1852 during incumbency of Revd Richard Pendrill Llewelyn, when a more realistic estimate of £1,000 was set for erection of Anglican

church in Maesteg. (*The Cambrian*, 27 June 1840) Built in Early English Gothic style consisting of chancel, nave, west gallery, vestry and north porch. Western gable surmounted by single bellcote. Constructed of local Pennant sandstone with Bath stone dressings. East window of three widely spaced lancets surmounted by three trefoils. Chancel arch is pointed and springs from capitals above pendant corbels, and its outer moulding ends in rectangular label stops. Chancel and nave have trussed rafter roofs of red deal. Ground woodwork all of pitch-pine, including open benches which seat 221 parishioners. West end of nave lighted by three widely spaced lancets between tall two-stage buttresses. Single and double lancet windows with hood moulds pierce walls of nave. Pipe organ in low west gallery. Font with octagonal bowl with scalloped underside linked by succession of octagonal mouldings by way of a collar to a well-proportioned stem and moulded base at west end of nave. Contractors: Morgan Evans and Rees Jones, Maesteg. Cost £1,045. Church Commissioners grant £100; ICBS grant £105; LDCES grant £100; dowager countess of Dunraven £100. (*CMG*, 11 November 1852) Opened for divine worship on 27 March 1853. (D. R. L. Jones, *Richard and Mary Pendrill Llewelyn: A Victorian Vicar and his Wife* (Maesteg, 1991), 17)

1900: Removal of pipe organ from west gallery to newly constructed organ chamber on north side of chancel. (David Thomas, *Eglwys Dewi Sant, Maesteg: Dathliad Canmlwyddiant yr Eglwys, 1852–1952* (1952), 11)

Comments: St David's, Maesteg, or Maesteg Episcopal Chapel, as it was known in the nineteenth century, is typical of a Commissioners' church built in the simple 'lancet' style with little ornamentation, to accommodate as many worshippers as possible with a pre-ecclesiological low west gallery to seat the children. The depressed moulded arch above inset columns, which enclose the window, is wide and unsightly. The pendant corbels beneath the chancel arch are simple but effectively eye-catching, yet strange in that they are not repeated elsewhere in the church, where they would have been more effective than the plain rectangular blocks that terminate the outer chancel arch moulding. St David's is much inferior in design and execution to Moxham's church at Skewen, but we must remember that he was not completely responsible for the design there and gained more credit than he deserved by modifying another architect's original plan. Much credit must be accorded to Revd Richard Pendrill Llewelyn in building the church under difficult circumstances. As a result, the Anglican Church was able to gain a visible foothold in the centre of the developing town of Maesteg, which was dominated by Non-conformity at that time.

ST MICHAEL'S AND ALL ANGELS' CHURCH, LLANGYNWYD, MAESTEG

30. Church of St Michael, Llangynwyd (Source: *The Builder*, 21 December 1894, p. 857)

1895–8: New church built on new site given by Miss Olive Talbot of Cavendish Square, London. Original plan, drawn up by George E. Halliday of a church designed in Perpendicular Gothic style, had to be abandoned due to high cost estimated at £9,465. New plans drawn up by Halliday in 1894 for

a church seating 529 persons and costing £4,725 approved by Miss Talbot, who promised £1,000 towards cost, but she died in October 1894 and St Michael's and All Angels' Church erected as memorial church to her. (ICBS, file no. 9772 (1895)) The correspondent in the *Church Builder* reported that 'Maesteg is sadly in want of greater church accommodation. Rapid progress is being made in church work and to meet this a commodious church is wanted immediately. This district is a stronghold of Nonconformity; there being in the same about seventeen Dissenting Chapels. The inhabitants are all poor miners and tradespeople.' (*Ch. Bldr* (1895), 73) Foundation stone laid on 7 October 1895 by Mrs Margaret Leighton, Miss Talbot's niece. (*W. Mail*, 8 October 1895) Built in Early English Gothic style, its plan is somewhat unusual. Nave is 37ft wide and designed so that practically every member of congregation can see Communion table. (*Bldr*, 22 October 1895, 364) On either side of nave is fine arcade with clerestory above. Choir is well raised above body of church with seating accommodation for 100 persons. Ground floor of tower on north side of chancel provides organ space with choir vestry, and large clergy vestry in tower basement. The tower, when eventually completed, would rise to a height of 100ft with access by way of an octagonal staircase on the north-east side. Constructed of coursed ashlar-faced local Pennant sandstone with hard green Bridgend stone dressings, cement pointed throughout, while internal dressings of green Bridgend stone as are arcades, chancel and arches. (*Bldr*, 29 January 1898, 113) Stones from the old iron works used for construction of church by permission of Talbot family and special track laid down from Neath Road station to bring stones to site. Owing to exposed situation of building a damp-proof course was introduced throughout west wall. Open timber roof, seats and choir stalls of pitch-pine left free of stain or varnish. Tripartite chancel arch springing from bell-shaped capitals on tall, slender shafts, and inner sanctuary arch. Pulpit of dark green Bridgend stone with bands of pink alabaster with Irish red marble shafts. At west end of nave there is a baptistery for total immersion. Church accommodates 600 worshippers. Contractor: William McGaul, Bridgend. Cost £5,600. ICBS grant £100; LDCES grant: £60; Bishop of

Llandaff's Fund £400; Miss Emily Talbot £500; Mrs Bertha Fletcher of Saltoun Hall £300. Consecrated on 19 January 1898. (*W. Mail*, 20 January 1898)

Comments: Had the church been built to Halliday's original design in the Perpendicular Gothic style it would doubtless have been regarded as one of the finest churches in the diocese, but the amended design is, as John Newman says, 'of a drastic simplicity the architect usually preferred to avoid'. (Newman, 418) The intended upper stage of the tower was never built in the Victorian era and the church had an unfinished appearance at its consecration in 1898. As such it was hardly a fitting memorial to Miss Olive Talbot by her family in the light of the lavish funds she had expended on church building and church restoration in the county during her lifetime.

The tower was finally built in 1956 at a cost of £14,000 and dedicated on 26 November 1958. (Revd M. J. Mainwaring, *The Church of St Michael and All Angels, Maesteg: 75th Anniversary* (1973), 14–15)

ST PETER'S CHURCH, SPELTERS, MAESTEG (NANTYFFYLLON)

1886–7: New church built on new site given to Ecclesiastical Commissioners jointly by J. G. R. Homfray of Penllyn Castle and Revd Robert C. Lynche-Blosse of Stinchcombe, Gloucestershire. Architect. E. M. Bruce Vaughan. Prior to building of church, Anglican Church services held as early as 1851 in licensed room in Metcalfe Street in district known as Spelters. Spelters' Mission Church lay in parish of Llangynwyd and was situated four miles from parish church. Development of Spelters district as colliery township hastened building of new church in area. Erection of a permanent stone church had been contemplated for many years, but nothing done until Revd Samuel Jones started a building fund in 1884. Work of building church commenced in September 1886. (Clive Smith, *St Peter's Church, Nantyffyllon, Parish of Caerau, 1887–1987: Centenary Souvenir* (1987), 3–6) Built in Early English Gothic style consisting of chancel, nave, organ recess, vestry on north side of chancel, south porch and western bellcote. Built of local Welsh

sandstone with yellow brick dressings. East and west windows of three grouped broad lancets. Floors of sanctuary, chancel and centre aisle paved with Godwin's encaustic tiles; some of those in chancel emblazoned with coat of arms of bishop of Llandaff. Nave is a continuation of chancel, there being no interposing chancel arch. Church has an arch-braced roof of pitch-pine whose principal rafters are supported on large stone corbels. Nave lighted by four broad lancets on south side and five on north. South wall of nave strengthened with solid two-stage buttress. Nave furnished with open benches of pitch-pine, stained and varnished and seating 200 parishioners. Floor of nave under seats boarded with deal. Crest of roof of red tiles with high ridge perforated with holes. (*CGG*, 15 July 1887) Contractor: John Haines, Cardiff. Cost £1,000. Bishop of Llandaff's Fund £300; LDCES grant £80; Earl of Dunraven £50; C. R. M. Talbot £50. Opened for divine service on 13 July 1887. (*B. Chr.*, 15 July 1887)

Comments: Bruce Vaughan built the church in the less expensive Early English Gothic or 'lancet' style. It is a fairly plain and simple structure and the nave is a continuation of the chancel with no interposing chancel arch. Even yellow brick dressings were used in place of the usual Bath stone to cut costs. St Peter's was one of the first churches to benefit from a substantial grant from the newly inaugurated Bishop of Llandaff's Fund. Its aim was to provide plain, but comfortable, churches in the industrial areas, such as Spelters, in the diocese of Llandaff. Strangely, John Newman makes no reference to this church in his book, although he has a section on Nantyffyllon.

HOLY TRINITY CHURCH, MARCROSS

1893–4: Restoration of church by Kempson & Fowler, Llandaff. New roofs raised: barrel roof on chancel and arch-braced roof with curved wind-braces between purlins and wallplate on nave. South porch completely rebuilt with typical high-pitched Victorian gable. New pulpit, lectern, Communion table, altar rails and chancel seats installed. New east window of three trefoiled lights with external dripstone with scrolled label stops inserted in chancel. The two side lights are markedly less high than middle one, above which is plate tracery in form of two small trefoils on either side. New window inserted on north side of church and two new windows in south side. Blocked-up window in west wall of tower opened out. In north wall of nave, fourteenth-century tomb with arched recess opened up and preserved. Also thirteenth-century incised sepulchral slab of Sutton stone unearthed by workmen and carefully preserved in chancel floor. Repairs also carried out on tower. Earth, which had accumulated on south side of church above floor level, removed and new drain laid to keep building free from dampness. (LL/F/506. Restoration of church. Faculty dated 11 March 1893) Contractor: W. A. James, Cowbridge. Cost £875. Miss Olive Talbot made a substantial donation and Mrs Mary Stradling and Mrs Ella Pownall, St Donat's, made valuable contributions to restoration fund. (*CGG*, 26 January 1894) Reopened after restoration on 16 January 1894. (*W. Mail*, 22 January 1894)

Comments: Kempson & Fowler, who showed a reverential regard for the churches they restored in Glamorgan, carried out a sensitive restoration of Holy Trinity in 1893. They preserved many interesting architectural features of the medieval church, such as the chancel arch with its chevron moulding and the south doorway with its billet-moulded outer arch with grotesque heads as label stops together with nook shafts. The architects retained the corbels of the rood-loft and the rood-loft doorway with its four-centred arch and brattishing along the top of the lintel of the old rood-loft arrangement. They restored the church in the Early English Gothic style with simple lancets, the style of architecture of the late-twelfth and early thirteenth centuries to which the church basically belonged.

ST MARY'S ABBEY CHURCH, MARGAM

1805–9: North and south aisles of St Mary's Abbey Church rebuilt by the architect Charles Wallis of Swansea. The major work, which altered exterior appearance of church considerably, was re-modelling of west facade according to plan by a 'Mr. Heverfield'. Although most of original work between buttresses remained unaltered, that above triplet of late Norman windows entirely rebuilt, roof lowered and bellcote replaced by modern gable. Buttresses were extended upwards and capped by Italianate campaniles, the flanking aisle sections being pierced by Neo-Norman windows. Cost £6,490 5s 11d. (D. John Adams, 'The restoration of Margam Abbey Church in the nineteenth century', *Transactions of the Port Talbot Historical Society,* III (3) (1984), 61–5)

1872–3: Restoration of church. During incumbency of Revd John Owen Evans (1872–80) a major restoration of church took place inspired by C. R. M. Talbot's son, Theodore, a devout Christian, who was a churchwarden at Margam. Fine wood-panelled ceiling superseded earlier one of lath and plaster which was gradually disintegrating, and pulpit of Caen stone with green serpentine marble pillarets and circular base replaced old three-decker pulpit. (Leslie A. Evans, *Margam Abbey* (Port Talbot, 1958), 117) Old-fashioned high-backed pews also removed and replaced with open benches seating 350 parishioners. When workmen began to dismantle church, Theodore Talbot was reported to have said, 'Let us begin by demolishing the Squire's and Parson's pews; there must be no vested interest here.' Highly polished marble font of crinoidal limestone placed at west end of south aisle replacing former font installed in earlier restoration of church in 1805–9. Numerous coats of whitewash and plaster covering original Norman pillars and west wall removed. Theodore Talbot donated the seven lamps positioned before the altar and which were replicas of those used in St Alban's Church, Holborn where he spent years assisting Father Stanton in social work in the parish. (D. John Adams, op. cit., 65–6)

1899: Roof of church repaired at cost of £1,000 by Miss Emily Talbot. (Ibid.)

Comments: The radical rebuilding of Margam Abbey Church at the beginning of the nineteenth century was due to the perpetual curate, Revd John Hunt (1794–1816) and his influence with Thomas

Mansel Talbot (1747–1813) of Margam Abbey. It was inevitable that Theodore Mansel Talbot's Tractarian influence, which derived from his early association with Father Stanton of St Alban's Church, Holborn, was reflected in the restoration of Margam Abbey Church in the the years 1872–3. There is no doubt that the strong Tractarian character of Margam Abbey Church, which remains in the church to this day, is attributable to the Victorian restoration by him.

In 1904 choir seats, consisting of rush-bottom chairs and desk of deal, were replaced with new choir seats and clergy seats constructed of teak, which were Norman in character. Memorial marble tablet erected to C. R. M. Talbot. Woodwork and sculpture by William Clarke. Cost £550, defrayed by Miss Emily Talbot. (LL/F/508. Reseating; memorial tablet. Faculty dated 2 June 1904)

MARGAM CHAPEL OF EASE (TAIBACH)

1827: New church built on new site given by C. R. M. Talbot as chapel of ease to Margam Abbey Church. Phillip Jones, manager of Taibach Copper Works, took active part in building of chapel in order to satisfy spiritual needs of his workforce and their families. Revd William Bruce Knight, vicar of Margam, was also instrumental in effecting erection of Margam chapel of ease at a time when community of Taibach was rapidly expanding. Built in early Decorated Gothic style according to plans and specifications drawn up by Edward Haycock of Shrewsbury. Cruciform in plan consisting of chancel, nave, transepts and bell turret. Constructed of local Pennant sandstone with Bath stone dressings. Corner or clasping buttresses to walls of church, surmounted by shouldered ends to gables. Marble font donated by Bishop Van Mildert stood before altar, in front of which were pulpit and reading desk. Rose window at west end of nave. Seating accommodation for 500 persons, 430 of which were free and unappropriated. (ICBS file no. 529 (1824)) Consecrated on 15 September 1827. Cost £1,600. ICBS grant £400. (*The Cambrian*, 21 September 1827)

31. Margam Chapel of Ease, Taibach (Photo: Geoffrey R. Orrin)

1831: Gallery erected at west end of nave to accommodate choir and orchestra. (Parish of St Theodore, Port Talbot Archives)

1860: New organ installed in west gallery, which had to be extended by three feet to house it. Organ subsequently taken down from gallery and placed in north transept on east side of alley running through middle of that transept leaving just enough room between it and north wall for use as vestry. Theodore Talbot was responsible for this move in 1873. (Ibid.)

1880: Choir vestry erected under south side of west gallery. (Ibid.)

1901: In 1901 church was transferred from parish of Margam to that of St Theodore's, Port Talbot and it became known as Holy Cross Church, Port Talbot.

Comments: Externally the church has an unusual appearance with its segmental pointed windows with slender mullions as well as transoms. The gable ends together with their shoulders are corbelled out above the corner buttresses which die into the walls beneath. The gables of the transepts with their square pinnacles are most unusual. Inside, the church resembles a typical Anglican church of the period with its austere seating arrangements fitted out as an auditory church with high pulpit, reading desk and font placed in the chancel in front of the altar. Margam chapel of ease was built ten years before the beginning of the Victorian period at the same time as St John's Church, Dowlais. It provided much needed accommodation in the Victorian era, which was an intense period of church building and restoration in Glamorgan. It was rather unusual in that it did not undergo any dramatic Victorian restoration.

In 1903, when the church was used for the Welsh-speaking population of Port Talbot, the church underwent renovation under the direction of George E. Halliday. At this time the west gallery was removed, and a fine Perpendicular-style s creen was erected by William Clarke, Llandaff. Contractors: Messrs Hill & Sons, Port Talbot. Cost £986. (*SWDP*, 2 October 1903) Reopened after renovation on 1 October 1903. (*The Cambrian*, 2 and 9 October 1903)

ST DYFAN'S AND ST TEILO'S CHURCH, MERTHYR DYFAN

1857: Restoration of church by John Prichard of Prichard & Seddon. At this time church was found to be in sad and ruinous state and its lamentable state of decay made it unfit for performance of divine worship. During incumbency of Revd Charles Herbert Jenner, rector of parish (1834–68), church was restored. Portions of dilapidated walling rebuilt and additional windows inserted. Walls plastered and painted. New open timber roof raised on nave and several gables coped with stone and provided with gable crosses. Chancel refurbished with properly vested altar table standing upon footpace, and with stalls for officiating clergy. New screen erected at chancel arch with lectern. Old fashioned, high-backed pews removed and interior of nave refurnished with individual purpose-built chairs. Old stone font-bowl mounted upon new base and steps and fitted with oak cover with ornamental wrought ironwork. New south porch constructed with pointed archway with hood mould and rectangular label stops, surmounted by medieval-style relieving arch. Cost £427. Church first opened for divine worship on 10 May 1857 when after sermon a collection was made amounting to nearly £15, which with previous subscriptions, produced the sum of £312 16s 11d, leaving a debt of £114 11s 3d. It was partly with a view to liquidating this debt that the bishop consented to preach and officially reopen the church on Monday, 21 September 1857. (*CMG*, 26 September 1857)

Comments: The work of restoration carried out by John Prichard at Merthyr Dyfan Church clearly shows the influence of the Ecclesiological Society, of which he was an enthusiastic follower, in the rearrangement and ecclesiological reordering of the church to suit the new ideas in the Anglican liturgy. He removed the old-fashioned square box pews and instead of installing the low open benches, which was his custom, he refurnished the nave with purpose-built individual chairs. This was certainly an innovation at that period, particularly in a small village church in Glamorgan. The present character of the interior is due to a reconstruction by the architect George Pace of York in the years 1972–4.

In 1909 the tower was restored. (*Kelly's Directory of South Wales*, 1926, 671)

ST TEILO'S CHURCH, MERTHYR MAWR

1849–51: New church built on site of old church – north wall of old church being line of south wall of new one. Architects: Benjamin Ferrey, London, assisted by John Prichard, Llandaff. Erected at expense of patron of living, Rt Hon. John Nicholl of Merthyr Mawr House. (*Bldr*, 8 December 1849, 581) Petition for faculty to take down old church stated that 'this particular church is very ruinous and in great decay and that it is inexpedient to repair it and it hath been proposed that it should be taken down and a new church built on a more commodious site near the present church yard'. (LL/F/521. Demolition of old church and erection of new church. Faculty dated 25 May 1848) Foundation stone laid on 13 November 1849 by Lady Mary Cole. (*CMG*, 17 November 1849) Built in Early English Gothic style consisting of chancel, nave and south porch. Western gable surmounted by lantern bell turret with spirelet, supported on pillar corbel. Constructed of local Pennant sandstone with Doulting stone dressings and inside of church lined with bricks. East window of three widely spaced lancets, deeply recessed and separated internally by three continuous pointed arches, which spring from bell capitals above slender marble shafts. Chancel lighted on south side by two lancets between south door and two-stage buttresses. Chancel raised on one step above nave and the sanctuary on two steps. Both chancel and nave have arch-braced roofs of Memel timber with curved windbraces supported on stone corbels. Moulded chancel arch springs from decorated capitals on polygonal columns. Pulpit of white statuary marble with serpentine marble columns. Whole floor of church paved with Minton's encaustic tiles of various patterns. Medieval font preserved and stands in its traditional position at west end of nave near south door. It is raised on dais of three stone steps, floor of which is covered by blue and yellow encaustic tiles representing the Holy Spirit given at baptism. West end of nave lighted by pair of single lancets above western doorway. Nave walls pierced by six lancets between two-stage buttresses with gablets. Gables of nave and chancel surmounted with stone gable crosses. Low open benches of pitch-pine for 100 parishioners. Contractor: William Parry, Cowbridge. Cost £1,167. Consecrated in June 1851. (GRO: Merthyr Mawr MSS. E/187/1–50. Correspondence, design and building of Merthyr Mawr Church, 1845–51)

Comments: St Teilo's was a church which exemplified many of the principles of the Ecclesiologists, both in its structure and internal fittings and furnishings. It was a competent essay in Early English Gothic Revival. The bellcote is an unusual design for a Glamorgan church. The piece is similar to the bellcote of Leigh Delamere Church, Wiltshire, and also to St Nicholas' Church, Biddestone in the same county. Brian Lodwick said that 'the design and furnishings of this church are of a type which has become very familiar. It is easy to forget that it contains many features which were innovations at the time and that they were designed for a type of worship which would today seem ordinary, but which then seemed very advanced.' (B. M. Lodwick, The Oxford Movement and the Diocese of Llandaff during the Nineteenth Century. Unpublished M.Phil. thesis, University of Leeds, 1976, 226) Several architectural historians, including John Newman, give the impression that John Prichard designed some of the architectural features of St Teilo's, but Prichard stated rather reluctantly in a letter to Benjamin Ferrey that 'I willingly accede to the proposals you make, although you will readily understand my feeling when I say it is not interesting to execute another man's design, but I may except yours, certainly for I look upon myself as a humble imitator of your style and shall feel myself under an obligation to you for the knowledge I acquired in your office.' (GRO. Loc. cit. E/187/6. Letter from Prichard to Ferrey, 19 February 1846) It is abundantly clear, therefore, that Prichard executed the work but Ferrey designed it. The rebuilding of Merthyr Mawr Church in the years 1849–51 was indeed a most remarkable piece of work since Ferrey designed a correct, archaeologically detailed Puginesque church. It was the first of its kind to be built in Glamorgan.

CHRIST CHURCH, CYFARTHFA, MERTHYR TYDFIL

1856–7: New church built on new site at Cae Nanty-gwennith given by Lord Dynevor and E. P. Richards of Plasnewydd, Cardiff. As early as 1844 the rector of Merthyr, Revd J. C. Campbell, had written to the Church Commissioners asking for aid 'to relieve the spiritual destitution of the place'. The part of the parish to which he particularly referred was Cyfarthfa, where many of the inhabitants worked in the nearby Cyfarthfa ironworks. It was thus decided to erect a church in the part of Merthyr Tydfil, known as Georgetown, a district, named after a member of the Crawshay family of Cyfarthfa Castle. (F. L. G. Bevan, *History of Christ Church, Cyfarthfa, Merthyr Tydfil* (1957), 11) Built in a Geometrical Gothic style, Christ Church is cruciform in plan consisting of chancel, nave with aisles and clerestory, transepts, west and south porches and belfry crowned with spire. Architect: James Smyth Benest, Norwich. (ICBS file no. 4608 (1853)) Constructed of purple rag stone from neighbourhood with Bath stone dressings. Voussoirs of arches are alternated with light blue Pennant sandstone and dark rag. Arches of nave supported on Bath stone columns, alternately circular and octagonal with carved capitals. Bands of polished slate introduced in columns with good effect. All interior dressings and arches of Bath stone. Pulpit and reading-desk of Memel deal, stained and varnished, with Bath stone diapered panels. Altar and pulpit railings of wrought-iron and sanctuary paved with Minton's tiles. Galleries for children in transepts. Whole of woodwork, including open benches which seat 595 worshippers, stained and varnished. Roofs of chancel and nave arched-braced, springing from massive decorated stone corbels. East window of four cinquefoiled lights with Geometrical-style tracery in head, and west end lighted by large Rose window with similar tracery. Clerestory windows consist of sexfoils. Contractors: William Daniels, Abergavenny and P. Rees, Merthyr Tydfil. Cost £2,677. ICBS grant £275; LDCES grant: £100. Anonymous donation £1,000. (*Bldr*, 9 May 1857, 266) Consecrated on 30 April 1857. (*CMG*, 2 May 1857)

Comments: Christ Church stands as a remarkable monument to an anonymous benefactor. A lady, whose name remains unknown, with the aid of a friend of the bishop of Llandaff, placed at his lordship's disposal the sum of £1,000 to be used at his discretion in the erection of a church in one of the populated parts of the diocese 'where it is most needed and where infidelity is most prevalent'. (*Bldr*, 3 April 1852, 213) The church's exterior shows a certain irregularity and lack of uniformity, which was characteristic of the High Victorian Gothic 'muscular' buildings of the 1850s. The windows have thick, flat mouldings and rather eccentic geometric designs in the window tracery. The west doorway is shaped rather like a horseshoe – a most unusual feature of ecclesiastical architecture. Above is a Rose window of considerable geometric complexity giving it almost a primitive, non-religious appearance and, above it all, a single bell turret with spiracle is supported on wasp-nest corbels. The interior is infinitely superior after the eccentricity of the exterior. John Newman describes the architecture of the church as 'florid geometrical', an expression prompted by the ubiquity of the red decoration throughout the interior of the church. (Newman, 437) The red ceiling, for example, is an inspiration against the dark brown beams of the roof timbers, and the red decoration around the windows picks them out to great effect. Bands of polished slate have been introduced in the alternately circular and octagonal Bath stone columns of the nave arcade to good effect. Despite the fact that James Benest was formerly the surveyor to the Board of Health in Merthyr Tydfil and not a church architect of any standing, he produced nevertheless a reasonably competent design for the Anglican Church in Cyfarthfa.

ST DAVID'S CHURCH, MERTHYR TYDFIL

1846–7: New church built on new site as chapel of ease to parish church, St Tydfil's. As early as March 1840 an appeal had been set up by the Provisional Building Committee to provide a new church to accommodate the ever-increasing population of Merthyr Tydfil. Another reason for building St David's was to provide church accommodation for English-speaking Anglicans in Merthyr Tydfil, since St Tydfil's was a Welsh-speaking church. Designs drawn up by the architect David Vaughan, who proposed a Grecian-style church, rejected in favour of new Gothic-style design by Wyatt & Brandon, architects of London. (ICBS file no. 2725 (1841)) Foundation stone laid on 24 March 1846 by Lord James Stuart, MP. (*CMG*, 11 September 1847) Built in Early English Gothic style consisting of chancel, nave, aisles, clerestory, west gallery, south and west porches, and western bellcote. Constructed of Welsh Pennant sandstone with Bath stone dressings. Total length of church 138ft and width 58ft. Nave divided from side aisles by arcades of pointed arches springing from decorated capitals on clustered columns, with clerestory above pierced by twin lancets. East window is triplet of grouped lancets and at west end is spacious gallery for 300 children. Interior of nave lighted by two-light windows with plate tracery in apex. Chancel has arched-braced roof and nave has tie-beam roof, both plastered between rafters. Open benches of deal seat 1,200 worshippers. Contractor: Joshua Daniel, Crickhowell. Church Commissioners' grant £1,204. ICBS grant £700. LCBS grant £30. Cost £4,110. Consecrated on 8 September 1847. (*CMG*, 11 September 1847)

1868–9: Restoration of church. Architect: Edward Brigden. Large organ chamber built on north side of chancel, which was considerably enlarged and filled with stalls. Organ, installed in 1854 in west gallery, removed to new organ chamber. Whole of church paved with encaustic tiles. Space under gallery converted into lobby. Lighting improved by installation of brass coronae. Gurney's heating stoves installed. Cost £700. Lord Dynevor £100; Lady Windsor £100. Reopened after restoration on 24 January 1869. (*CMG*, 30 January 1869)

Comments: Wyatt & Brandon chose a severe Early English style for St David's Church, as expressed in the cluster of slender shafts that form the pillars of the arcades with their plain moulded bell capitals and necking, the heavily undercut stiff-leaf foliage beneath the chancel arch and the plate tracery with most trefoils in the head of the windows. The window arches show both the prevailing forms in Early English works – lancets on the exterior and segmental pointed in the interior. When the church was built it occupied a corner site, so that the architects were inspired to put up an imposing west facade; a shafted west doorway, and a shafted two-light window, the centrepiece of a shafted arcade. However, the whole insertion appears too heavy and might have been improved had the blind arcading also been pierced with lights. This may be due to the fact that the original plans were 'watered down' to meet the economic strictures imposed on the building. It is interesting to note that this was one of the first town churches in Glamorgan to be built with a clerestory to provide more light in the main body of the church, which was surrounded by other high buildings, a principle later advocated by Street in the 1850s.

ST TYDFIL'S CHURCH, MERTHYR TYDFIL

(Church now closed and used only for funerals)

1897–1901: By 1890 church was found to be in very dilapidated condition with nave roof near to collapse and tower battlements loose and falling. Following petition from parishioners for restoration in 1894 it was decided to restore church by rebuilding and lengthening chancel by adding an apsidal east end and building vestries and organ chamber, by removing unsightly galleries blocking interior of church, and by restoring nave and west tower. (LL/F/537. Restoration and extension of church. Faculty dated 23 April 1897) Application for grant aid from ICBS stated that chancel was only ancient part of structure, but of no architectural interest. Nave built 100 to 150 years earlier. John Loughborough Pearson, the architect, planned to rebuild and lengthen chancel and restore nave by retaining side walls and rebuilding and restoring tower. Although plans approved in May 1894, work not completed until 1901 as result of mounting cost of work, which had to be done in three stages. (ICBS file no. 9785 (1894)) Rebuilt in a Burgundian Romanesque style and body of church divided into nave and four-bay aisles with arcades of tall pillars and capitals with water-leaf decoration. Part of south aisle set aside for use as chapel dedicated to St Mary. Chancel apsidal in shape and lighted by seven round-headed lancets. Round-headed windows also light nave. Stone transverse arches to nave and groined aisles, groined chancel and flat cemented ceiling to nave. West wall of nave and west tower partly rebuilt and restored. Local Pennant sandstone and Bath stone dressings used in restoration, interior of church plastered and roof covered with slates. Contractor: Messrs W. Cowlin & Sons, Bristol. Cost £8,000. ICBS grant £60. (*Bldr*, 22 June 1901, 612) Reopened after restoration on 13 June 1901. (*W. Mail*, 14 June 1901)

Comments: Apart from the apse this was an uncharacteristic design for John Loughborough Pearson, whose favourite idiom was the Early English style. As John Newman says, he probably chose this style 'to accommodate the simple classicism of the surviving nave', built nearly 150 years previously. (Newman, 435) However, he retained the flat ceiling of the old Georgian church. The groined vaults of the aisles are characteristic of Pearson's architectural skill in designing vaulted ceilings, as exemplified at St Theodore's, Port Talbot, built at the same time.

ST MICHAEL'S AND ALL ANGELS' CHURCH, MICHAELSTON-LE-PIT

1864: According to entry in *Llandaff Diocesan Church Calendar*, church restored in 1864 at cost of £550. (*Llandaff Diocesan Church Calendar*, 1884–5, 89) Structural examination of building revealed that two windows are nineteenth-century insertions, presumably belonging to Victorian restoration. Large west window of three trefoiled lights is a combination type which includes ogee arch in same tracery as more formal panel-style tracery

lights which were a feature of early Perpendicular work. Other nineteenth-century insertion is in south wall of chancel. It is a two-light pointed window with trefoil-headed lights beneath ogee arches, which continue straight into head with elongated quatrefoil between, and is done in fourteenth-century style. (*MCVG*, 275–9) Nave roof also renewed at this time; it is a simple arch-braced roof with crenellated wallplate. Old three-decker pulpit, which was retained, skilfully adapted to local conditions. It is the only such pulpit in Vale of Glamorgan and dates from the early eighteenth century. Across aisle from pulpit is typical box pew of coeval date used by Cwrt-yr-Ala family. All four pews in transept and one in chancel itself face west towards pulpit with backs towards altar. Also Ten Commandments inscribed on stone tablets each side of altar indicate Low Church persuasion of rector during Victorian restoration. Central tower remains untouched by Victorian restorer and dates from early fourteenth century. Ancient Early English font carefully preserved togther with the holy-water stoup. No traces remain of former rood-loft arrangements. (Chrystal Tilney, *A History of the Parishes of St Andrew Major and Michaelston-le-Pit* (Penarth, 1960), 49–56)

Comments: As John Newman says, the eighteenth century three-decker pulpit and pews are 'altogether a remarkable survival from pre-ecclesiological days'. (Newman, 449) This indicates that the Victorian architect who restored the church in 1864 was a conservative restorer who simply renewed the decaying fabric of the church and inserted two new windows, but preserved its interesting fittings and furnishings.

ST MICHAEL'S CHURCH, MICHAELSTON-SUPER-ELY

1842–3: Churchwardens' account book for these years indicates substantial work carried out on church. Total sum paid to various craftsmen amounted to £191 19s 9d, no small sum for parish to spend at that time. (Michaelston-super-Ely Church: Churchwardens' Accounts, 1842–3)
1864: Restoration of church by David Vaughan of

32. Interior of St Michael's Church, Michaelston-super-Ely (Photo: W. P. Pring, L.R.P.S.) (By kind permission of D. Brown & Sons Ltd, Cowbridge)

Bonvilston. Vaughan's report on state of church said that 'the walls to the church are in a good state with few exceptions, the windows on the south side I propose to take down . . . the walls of the tower are thick and of a strong character and will require new quoins and the modern roof taken off the walls and put a new roof on same. The whole of the inside requires new seats, floors and also the plastering to be redone. The windows to be repaired and three new ones of the same character as the present ones.' (GRO: D/D.V/58/1. Report on Michaelston-super-Ely Church by David Vaughan, 1862) Work consisted of removing two-light window from south wall and inserting same in north-east corner of nave. Vaughan inserted two single lancets in place of two-light window removed from chancel's south wall and one single lancet on north side, all deeply splayed. Former chancel arch, described by G. T. Clark as 'narrow, rude Norman, quite plain with imposts', removed and replaced by pseudo-Norman arch with chevron and bead decoration. (NLW MS5212 E Glamorgan Manors,

Vol. IV, Description of Michaelston-super-Ely Church by G. T. Clark, 1863) Height of tower increased by 10ft and additional apertures provided. New luffers fitted to north and south sides of tower. West door fitted. Roof of transept raised and gabled south face with modern window added. Three large box pews removed, two from nave, one from transept. (Walter B. Vile, *A History and Description of the Parish Church of St Michael, Michaelston-super-Ely* (rev. edn 1981), 3–8) Cost £700, completely defrayed by Mrs Charlotte Louisa Traherne of Coedriglan. Reopened after restoration on 20 July 1864. (*CMG*, 20 July 1864)

Comments: Besides its thoroughness, David Vaughan's restoration of Michaelston-super-Ely Church was also rather intrusive with his removal of a window from the south wall of the chancel to the north wall of the nave. By inserting two single lancets in the south side of the chancel and another on the north side he obviously felt that the chancel should have the appearance of an Early English-style church. His corruption of the chancel arch with a stylized Neo-Norman arch was inappropriate. As John Newman perceptively points out, 'The Norman character of the C19 chancel arch reflects the existence, but not the ambition of a C12 predecessor.' (Newman, 449) In his disjointed report on St Michael's to the rector, Revd Lewis Anthony Nicholl (1837–67), Vaughan proposed the entire removal of the diminutive south transept, but was evidently overruled. Vaughan preserved the stone benches in the north-west corner, but he replaced those in the south-west corner with replicas. Although his restoration of the church was quite radical and intrusive in many respects, Vaughan nevertheless made the structure visually more effective from an exterior point of view and in keeping with other Vale of Glamorgan churches.

In 1908 the church was restored by Frederick R. Kempson. The work included the removal of soil from the exterior of the chancel, which centuries of burial had brought about. An arch was formed on the north side of the chancel, with a view to the erection of a vestry at a future date. The interior walls were replastered, the windows reglazed and fitted with gun-metal casements, and the floor of the chancel laid with marble mosaic and marble steps. All the new wooden fittings, such as the altar, stalls, pulpit and lectern, were of oak. Contractors: Messrs Shepton & Son, Cardiff. Reopened after restoration on 11 February 1909. (*LDM*, Vol. 6, 1909–10, 30–1)

ST MICHAEL'S CHURCH, MICHAELSTONE-SUPER-AVON

1835–6: Register for the years 1813–47 records the following entry: 'On 8 June, 1835 the lightnings struck against the church and shattered about 7ft of the top of the spire which was just finished and the electric fluid entered the church at the west end wall and tore open the laths and plastering work to the ground with a part of two seats on the north side. The tower was erected and finished last May by John Vigers, Esq. proprietor of the tinworks. This event is recorded June 15, by me, David Griffiths, minister.' (Michaelstone-super-Avon Church: Parish Registers, 1813–47)

33. St Michael's Church, Michaelstone-super-Avon: exterior view taken from south-east and interior view showing Prichard's controversial timber arcade to the north aisle built in 1851 (Photos: Geoffrey R. Orrin)

1850–1: Rebuilding and enlargement of church by John Prichard. As result of large increase in parish population, which numbered nearly 6,000 inhabitants at that time, Revd William Thomas felt it necessary to restore and enlarge parish church. His letter to ICBS, dated 2 April 1851 and requesting further grant aid, stated that 'the cost of enlarging the church at Michaelstone-super-Avon will exceed the sum I first intended to expend by full £400 – I find the walls and roof of the nave and chancel in so decayed a state that I am compelled to rebuild it all except the steeple (tower) – the cost will be about £1,100.' (ICBS file no. 4316 (1850)) Consequently, nave and chancel taken down and church was rebuilt on old site with addition of north aisle and with chancel extended eastwards. (J. O'Brien, 'Cwmavon and St. Michael's Church', *Transactions of the Aberafan and Margam District Historical Society*, 1929, 50) Additional accommodation of 238 seats provided, of which 119 free and unappropriated. Reopened after rebuilding on 16 May 1851. Cost £900. ICBS grant £100; English Copper Company £800. (*The Cambrian*, 23 May 1851)

Comments: When John Prichard rebuilt and enlarged this church he was young and inexperienced, and this resulted in some aspects of his design provoking criticism. Firstly, Prichard indulged himself, as Newman says, in designing some rather eccentric Perpendicular-style windows on the south side of the church – three cinquefoiled windows surmounted by a row of quatrefoils in circles in the nave and triangular arches with rectilinear tracery in the chancel. This was strange since the east windows of the church conform quintessentially to the Perpendicular period with cinquefoiled lights with standard panel tracery above. Secondly, the economical use of a timber Tudor-style arcade to the north aisle was most unorthodox and incurred the displeasure of the consulting architect to the ICBS. He made the following comment: 'The mode of dividing the nave and new aisle is singular, 4 arches with low pillars might be constructed of stone, the more churchlike and durable.' (ICBS file no. 4316 (1850)) Revd William Thomas replied to this admonition in a letter, dated 27 November 1850, that 'the wood pillars have been prepared under the advice and direction of the Diocesan Architect, Mr Prichard, and it would cost more than £100. Now to alter them – we were so anxious to proceed that we lost no time in getting everything ready we could. Hoping therefore that you will rescind that portion affecting the material of the pillars and also increase the grant.' Thomas did not obtain an increase in the grant, but there was no further objection to the timber arcade and a grant of £100 was voted. Although John Newman dates the spire to the mid-eighteenth century, it is quite clear from the entry in the Parish Registers quoted above that the 'steeple' was in fact built in 1835 and repaired in 1836 after the lightning strike. (Newman, 337)

ST MARY'S CHURCH, MONKNASH

1860: Restoration of church. Work comprised rebuilding of east wall of chancel and insertion of new east window in Decorated Victorian Gothic style. East window of three trefoiled lights cusped with reticulated-style tracery in head enclosed by ogee curves which blend elegantly into window

34. St Mary's Church, Monknash (Photo: W. P. Pring, L.R.P.S.) (By kind permission of D. Brown & Sons Ltd, Cowbridge)

arch. Hood mould of two different coloured stones gives polychromatic effect. Architect: John Prichard of Prichard & Seddon. (J. M. Wilson, *Imperial Gazetteer of England and Wales Embracing Recent Changes in Counties, Dioceses and Parishes* (London, 1865–9), Vol. IV, Monknash, 362)

1869: When Sir Stephen Glynne visited the church in August 1869 he found a low, plain stone screen across chancel arch, which probably resembled the arch at Marcross church nearby. But now there is no trace of it. 'The church has been restored and is in good case.' (Sir Stephen R. Glynne, 'Notes on the older churches in the four Welsh dioceses', *Arch. Camb.* (1901), 261)

1891: Restoration of church during incumbency of Revd William Joseph Edwards. Petition for faculty stated that 'the parishioners attend the church at risk of their health'. This was a reference to dilapidated state of roof. Work of restoration included reroofing chancel, but nave roof only repaired with raw, unstained and unvarnished timber. Open benches replaced old-fashioned, high-back pews to accommodate a congregation of eighty worshippers. Wooden structure also constructed about 5ft from end of west wall of nave for use as vestry instead of the former curtain. Font removed from middle of aisle to its traditional position near south doorway. New altar rails installed and walls replastered. New stone pulpit erected on north side of nave, access to which gained by steps which formerly led to the rood-loft from within chancel. (LL/F/550. Restoration of church. Faculty dated 5 February 1891)

Comments: St Mary's underwent two restorations in the Victorian era. The first, in 1860 by John Prichard, was to rebuild and repair parts of the decayed structure of the chancel. The second restoration, in 1891, was basically a crude repair of the roof of the nave, and the ecclesiological re-ordering of the interior of the church to bring it into line with the changes, which had occurred earlier in the century, in the Anglican Church liturgy.

ST MARGARET'S CHURCH, MOUNTAIN ASH

35. St Margaret's Church, Mountain Ash. *c.*1890 (Source: David Yeoman, *The Parish of Mountain Ash: An Illustrated Guide.* 2nd edn (Mountain Ash, 1990), inside cover photograph) (By kind permission of the Vicar and Churchwardens, Mountain Ash Church)

1861–2: New church built on new site by John Pollard Seddon, of Prichard & Seddon. (ICBS file no. 5659 (1861)) Built in French Gothic style consisting of nave with south aisle and small chancel with three-sided apse, small vestry on north side of nave with slender octagonal bell turret over west gable. South aisle gabled transversely with four gables, westernmost of which, formed a porch. Porch, approached by seven steps, is in character with French Gothic architecture of building. (*Bldr,* 30 August 1862, 624) Seating accommodation for 400 parishioners. Contractor: H. Williams, Llandaff. Cost £2,527. ICBS grant £300; John Bruce Pryce, Duffryn £2,000; LDCES grant £50. Consecrated on 14 August 1862. (*CMG,* 16 August 1862)

1883–4: Enlargement of church by addition of north aisle and construction of new vestry by John Prichard. (ICBS file no. 5659 (1883)) Additional

seating accommodation for 152 parishioners. Contractor: William Cullis, Hereford. Cost £1,000. ICBS grant £40. (*Ch. Bldr* (1883), 82) Consecrated on 20 March 1884. (*W. Mail,* 21 March 1884)

1897–8: Enlargement of church by E. M. Bruce Vaughan. The correspondent in the *Church Builder* reported that 'the population of the parish has been and is still growing at a rapid rate and it is most difficult to provide adequate accommodation for the people, who are almost exclusively of the collier class'. (*Ch. Bldr* (1897), 53) Enlarged by construction of new chancel, organ chamber, vestries and tower on north-east side of chancel. Chancel same width as nave with wagon-shaped roof, panelled with gilded bosses at intersections. It is divided from nave by rich moulded arch. Label stops of north and south arches in chancel carved to represent Lord Aberdare and Lady Aberdare and are excellent likenesses. Also carved bosses representing bishop of Llandaff and Queen Victoria and a well-carved figure of patron saint in east gable, representing St Margaret triumphant over Satan. Sculpture by William Clarke. Additional accommodation for 250 persons. Contractor: Messrs Charles Jenkins & Sons, Porth. Cost £3,300. ICBS grant £60. (*Bldr,* 19 February 1898, 188) Reopened after enlargement on 8 February 1898. (*W. Mail,* 9 February 1898)

Comments: The original church built in 1862 was only one of two churches designed by John Pollard Seddon in Glamorgan. The French Gothic style, freely treated, adopted by Seddon predominates throughout the church. The apsidal form of the east end was characteristic of French churches and the use of plain cylindrical shafts in place of compound clustered shafts was employed by Seddon to emulate French Gothic architecture. The French Gothic style at St Margaret's is exemplified by the south porch with its richly carved sculpture. Seddon's church, with its mixture of French Gothic and Italian-influenced constructional polychromy in the relieving arches of the porch and windows, is a striking example of the trend to mix both styles in the same building in the 1860s. Prichard's enlargement of the church in 1883 provided additional seating for 152 worshippers in the new north aisle. In addition, the chancel was improved by repaving the floor with

36. St Peter's Church, Nantymoel (Photo by Morley from the Parish Archives) (By kind permission of the Vicar and Churchwardens of Nantymoel Church)

encaustic tiles of better quality and elevating the altar above the chancel floor level. However, St Margaret's owes its present appearance to a further enlargement of the church in the years 1897–8, which radically altered the whole aspect of the east end of the building. Bruce Vaughan evidently tried to follow the thirteenth-century style of the original building by designing the additions in the Early English style. The design of the original building was regarded by *The Ecclesiologist* as having 'too much eccentricity about it' (*Eccl.*, 21 (1860), 323–4), and the remodelling of the east end of the church in the late Victorian period by Bruce Vaughan has compounded this description. The eastern and western extremities of the church are clearly the work of two different architects. Apparently the uniformity of the design was sacrificed by the urgent need of the Anglican Church in the diocese of Llandaff to provide additional accommodation for the growing population of Mountain Ash.

In 1904 a reredos was erected in the sanctuary. It is Early English in character in keeping with the architecture of the chancel and is executed in Caen stone. The spandrels between the gables of the central portion and the arches of the wings are of selected alabaster, the columns being of red Ogwell and Irish green marble. The plinth, immediately under the bases of the arcade in wings, is in red Mansfield stone. Design by Bruce Vaughan. Cost £250. Dedication of reredos on 10 November 1904. (LL/F/556. Reredos. Faculty dated 18 October 1904)

ST PETER'S CHURCH, NANTYMOEL
(Church demolished *c.*1960)

1887–90: New church built on new site as chapel of ease to St Ceinwyr's, Llangeinor. Built in Early English Gothic style by E. M. Bruce Vaughan, consisting of chancel, nave, south porch and western bellcote. Constructed of blue-grey, rock-faced Welsh Pennant sandstone laid in random courses with Bath stone dressings. East window of three lights, with centre placed higher than two flanking lights. Walls of church lighted by narrow lancets with slender hood moulds. Massive stone buttresses to west wall of nave, which was of considerable height due to slope of ground towards west end. (Personal observation from photograph of St Peter's Church by Morley) Seating accommodation for 214 worshippers. Cost £1,137. ICBS grant £50; Bishop of Llandaff's Fund £250. (ICBS file no. 9190 (1887)) Opened for divine worship on 10 March 1890. (*GG*, 14 March 1890)

Comments: Another very cheap church built at the head of the Ogmore Valley for a small mining community. Funds were restricted so that the windows have minimal Gothic tracery. This was part of Bishop Richard Lewis's strategem to build 'plain and comfortable churches' as a means of providing church accommodation in the industrialized parts of the diocese of Llandaff. Newman's description of St Peter's actually refers to St Peter's and St Paul's Church, Nantymoel, which was in fact built in 1909 and dedicated at that time simply to St Paul. (Newman, 455)

ST CATHERINE'S CHURCH, MELINCRYDDAN, NEATH

1889–91: New church built on new site given by Edward Evans of Eaglebush. Since 1850 church-goers had had to be content with a small mission church, but in late 1880s Miss Catherine Place promised £500 towards building a new stone church. Foundation stone laid by Miss Catherine Place of Neath on 21 March 1889. (*W. Mail*, 22 March 1889) Built in Early English Gothic style by John Coates Carter of Seddon & Carter, Cardiff and London. It consists of chancel, nave with north and south aisles, vestries and bell flèche over chancel arch. (ICBS file no. 9279 (1888)) Constructed of local blue rock-faced Pennant sandstone with Bath stone dressings. Contract, valued at £2,000, was entered into with Benjamin

Thomas of Neath for building of church. Thomas got into financial difficulties and subsequently died, so that the Committee was placed in an unenviable position. Subcontractor appointed under supervision of resident architect, D. M. Davies of Neath. Work, which Thomas had commenced in professional fashion, was further stopped for six months due to error in deed of conveyance. (*GG*, 24 April 1891) Arcades of nave and aisles formed of timber arcading springing from short stone pillars. Chancel roof, differentiated only by a flèche, is continuation of nave with tie-beam, collar and kingpost arrangement below three-tiered barrel roof. Aisles paved with red Staffordshire tiles, herringbone pattern in nave and lover's knot in chancel. Open benches of varnished pitch-pine. Fenestration of church consists of series of elongated lancets. Seating accommodation for 550 worshippers. Pulpit of Devonshire marble. Font of Caen stone with pillars of Devonshire marble. Heated by Messrs King's of Liverpool high pressure hot-water system. (*BN*, 23 January 1891, 128) Contractor: Benjamin Thomas, Neath. Cost £3,000. ICBS grant £200; Bishop of Llandaff's Fund £250; LDCES grant £80; LCBS grant £20. Consecrated on 23 April 1891. (*W. Mail*, 24 April 1891)

Comments: The unusual feature of John Coates Carter's design of St Catherine's is its economical use of timber arcading, by which nave and aisles are formed, with the use of short stone pillars, giving more light and also an uninterrupted view of the chancel and altar, which now became the focal point of the congregation. With his economical use of materials, Carter was able to provide a large church seating more than 500 parishioners. The use of short stone pillars supporting the timber arcade of the nave may well be based on a similar design by John Prichard in St Clement's Church, Briton Ferry, erected in 1866. The design of St Catherine's exhibits Carter's spatial handling, which became a feature of late Victorian churches.

37. Interior of St David's Church, Neath (Source: Geoffrey R. Orrin: Postcard Collection of Glamorgan Churches)

ST DAVID'S CHURCH, NEATH

1864–6: New church built on new site presented by Howel Gwyn of Dyffryn as church for English services. Foundation stone laid on 22 September 1864 by Mrs Howel Gwyn. (*The Cambrian*, 23 September 1864) Built in Early English Gothic style with French treatment of ornament and detail by John Norton, London. Cruciform in plan consisting of nave (101ftx31ft 8ins and 61ft high to ridge), north and south aisles (13ft wide and 12ft high to wallplate), north and south transepts (20ft 9ins wide and 50ft high to ridge), with north transept aisle used as vestry, chancel with semi-circular apse (40ftx9ft and 56ft to roof), tower: the lowest stage of which forms organ chamber, south porch and narthex or western porch. (ICBS file no. 6339 (1865)) Constructed of local blue Pennant sandstone with Bath stone dressings and with bands of red sandstone introduced. Lined internally with red bricks in diaper patterns with bands of blue Staffordshire bricks and with stone and brick arches. Columns of nave arcade are alternately of circular and quatrefoiled design, with richly moulded bases and capitals. (*Bldr*, 13 June 1868, 430–1) Ten couplet trefoiled windows with geo-metrical-traceried heads run round apse, the arches internally carried by columns with carved capitals. Chancel opens from nave by arch of fine proportions and formed of richly moulded rim of stone (with two more above of coloured stone) and red and blue bricks enclosed with a moulded label and supported by dwarf columns with moulded bands and bases and carved capitals. Low stone screen defines more clearly division between chancel and nave. Clerestory windows are of type rarely met with in England, but to be seen in France, consisting of two trefoiled lights with large foliated circle in head. West window consists of four lights with elaborate geometrical tracery in head, comprised within deeply recessed and moulded pointed arch. The Vaughan tower, named after Rheola family who paid for the structure, 152ft high to vane, is placed at south-west corner of chancel. It consists of four stages surmounted by low pyramidal spire, covered with tiles with elaborate pinnacles around it. Each stage clearly defined by broad bands of coloured stone. Of rather uncommon design, being square in plan and rising to a height of 88ft without break or buttress. At this point projects a bold, battlemented cornice, from which gradual slope of stonework leads up to series of low arches, supported by columns, which carry the spire. Massive pinnacles of square outline, with deeply recessed panels, surmounted by figures of the four Evangelists, stand at the corners. Roofs of Memel timber covered with Broseley tiles in bands. Principals supporting roof are segmental arches of brick and stone springing from side walls. South porch, which is width of one bay, projects 10ft from aisle rising into gable with carved finial and summit. It is entered by double doorway divided by a trumeau or central pillar. Figure of patron, St David, stands in canopied niche over south doorway. Western narthex extends whole width of nave under west window and is entered by series of pointed arches at west and north-west sides. Whole of pavement of church covered with tiles, the chancel and apse of rich design. Seats of deal, stained and varnished. Seating accommodation for 1,200 worshippers. Heating apparatus installed by Haden's of Trowbridge. Wrought-iron gas fittings, consisting of coronae, executed by Hale's of Bristol. (*SGH*, 5 December 1866) Contractor: Messrs Jones & Son, Gloucester. Cost £6,400. ICBS grant £400; E. N. Vaughan, Rheola £1,300; Lord Dynevor £500; Howel Gwyn, Dyffryn £250. Consecrated on 29 November 1866. (*The Cambrian*, 30 November 1866)

1868: New organ built by Messrs Davies & Sons, London installed, the gift of James Kempthorne at cost of £400. (*The Cambrian*, 31 January 1868) Organ opened by W. Gilbertson on 30 April 1868. (*The Cambrian*, 1 May 1868)

1883: Pulpit of Caen stone, resting on Devonshire and Cornish marble pillars, presented by congregation and erected in church. Designed and executed by T. R. Williams of Neath (formerly of Manchester). Also polished brass lectern donated. (*BN*, 18 May 1883, 687)

Comments: St David's is regarded as John Norton's masterpiece in Glamorgan. It was common in the 1860s for French Gothic to form a basis of a style mixed with Italian or Ruskinian-influenced constructural polychromy and English Gothic. The interior of St David's is a striking feature of this new trend. This is apparent in the lining of the walls with red bricks with bands and diaper patterns of blue Staffordshire bricks with stone and brick arches. It is an example of strident polychromy at its best. The French Gothic influence is exemplified by the apsidal end to the chancel, a common feature of French churches. The French Gothic influence is also manifested in the circular heads of the windows of the clerestory and apse with their multifoils. In thirteenth-century France, decoration was obtained by the use of richly carved sculpture of the type manifested in the south porch, especially in the tympanum where a vesica piscis contains the figure of St David, the patron saint. The tower with its campanile-like structure is influenced by Street's Italian campanile at St James the Less Church, Westminster. Apart from the square abaci, which are again indicative of the French Gothic influence, the nave arcade is basically Early English with stiff-leaf foliage to the capitals and low round or groups of engaged shafts and simple moulded, lancet shapes. The reviewer in *The Ecclesiologist* stated that 'this is work of much merit and originality' and also complimented the architect on the correct observance of the ritual arrangements of the church, where the altar was raised on no fewer than eleven steps above the nave and a low chancel screen stood below the chancel arch. (*Eccl.*, 26 (1865), 51–2) St David's was clearly built by Norton as a landmark church.

ST MATTHEW'S CHURCH, DYFFRYN, NEATH

1870–1: New church built on new site by Howel Gwyn, Dyffryn. Expansion of coal-mining operations in Bryncoch area and subsequent increase in population was one of the main reasons that led Howel Gwyn (1806–88), philanthropist and church stalwart, to build St Matthew's. Foundation stone laid on 10 December 1871. (*Bldr*, 17 December 1870, 1014) Built in Early English Gothic style by John Norton, consisting of chancel (27ftx21ft), nave (62ftx25ft), organ chamber and vestry on north side of chancel, and south-west tower, the base of which forms a south porch. Constructed of local Pennant sandstone from one of Gwyn's quarries, with Bath stone dressings. Walls of interior of church stuccoed and both chancel and nave have roofs of teak panels. East window of chancel of

38. St Matthew's Church, Dyffryn (Neath) (By kind permission of Dr Tom Davies, Blaendulais, Neath)

century'. (*The Cambrian*, 29 September 1871) Norton submitted a plan of this description which met with Gwyn's approval. The nave was given a plain appearance, owing to the absence of aisles and a clerestory in keeping with Gwyn's conception of an early Welsh church. But here the similarity ends, for twelfth-century Glamorgan church architecture was hardly so advanced. Had Norton really wanted to retain the early appearance of the church he might have used plate tracery in the large windows. Instead, he opted for bar tracery and a fairly common nineteenth-century Early English-style east window, deeply recessed and moulded with slender shaft and foliated capitals to enhance its appearance. The upper stage of the tower with its cornice of stiff-leaf foliage was obviously very much done for overall effect rather than according to archaeological authencity of style. Furthermore, the interior boasts a higher decorative standard than most churches of its time with intricate scroll work around the walls together with sentences from the psalms in ornate black lettering. However, all this was in keeping with the nineteenth-century Gothic stylized treatment of churches in the Victorian era.

three trefoil-headed lights with sexfoil enclosing a circle in head. Nave lighted both north and south by plain, single and double lancet lights. Intricate scroll work stencilled around walls; each window and door with wide decorative borders and sentences from psalms in ornate black lettering decorate interior. Nave covered with open benches of varnished pitch-pine. Seating accommodation for 300 parishioners. Entrance porch below tower has Gothic doorway, which is surmounted by carved stone statue under gabled canopy of patron, St Matthew. Floor paved with Godwin's tiles while steps leading to altar and dais are of Kilkenny marble. Font of Bridgend stone and pulpit carved of same stone with crosses of alabaster in panels. (*Bldr*, 14 October 1871, 812) Contractor: Rees Roderick, Margam. Cost £4,500, defrayed by Howel Gwyn. (*The Cambrian*, 29 September 1871)

Comments: According to a report in *The Cambrian*, St Matthew's was built 'to be as purely as possible a type of the Welsh Church of the twelfth

ST THOMAS' CHURCH, NEATH

1839: New west gallery erected and vestry room built. Architect: William Richards, Swansea. Cost £310. (D. Rhys Phillips, *The History of the Vale of Neath* (Swansea, 1925), 101–2)

1841: *The Cambrian* reported that 'On the 19 inst. (September), our church was reopened for divine worship after having undergone a satisfactory condition of repair. No expense has been spared either in decorating the Lord's House, or in making it more capable of accommodating the numerous worshippers desirous of treading her courts. Our organ has been tuned and handsomely ornamented, the pews painted throughout, two galleries raised and the coverings for the altar and the reading desk and pulpit furnished with the richest crimson velvet fringed with gold.' (*The Cambrian*, 25 September 1857)

1856–7: An announcement in the *Cardiff & Merthyr Guardian* reported: 'We are glad to find that the inhabitants of Neath will be spared the infliction of another church rate contest, it having been resolved at a full vestry, held on Easter Monday, "the church having been in a great measure restored during the past year, that no rate for the maintenance of public worship and the incidental expenses of the church should at present be applied for in the parish of Neath", but that "contributions should be made by the congregation for paying off existing debts and defraying the current expenses".' (*CMG*, 9 May 1857) Contract for reslating and repairing fabric given to William Davies, Neath. (*The Cambrian*, 25 June 1856) Old chandelier, which was rendered useless for many years by introduction of gas, taken away and pulpit removed to a more convenient spot in church. Improvements carried out under superintendence of churchwardens, Alexander Cuthbertson and Rees Morgan. (*The Cambrian*, 22 May 1857)

1873–4: Restoration of church by John Bacon Fowler of Swansea and Brecon. Huge gallery, which blocked westernmost bay of nave and entirely filling tower arch, removed and tower arch opened out. West window of tower replaced by new one of Perpendicular Gothic style, of four lights with traceried head. East window enlarged by piercing the two side-lights, which were formerly blank, and filling them with stained glass. Aisle windows taken out and replaced by new stone ones of two lights with plain roundel in head. Old fashioned, high-backed pews removed and new boarded floors laid and open benches of pitch-pine installed in nave. Chancel, tower and nave passages paved with encaustic tiles by Godwin's of Lugwardine, but side aisles covered with Vals de Travers asphalt. Chancel cleared of its old fittings, including an unsightly, high-backed pew and refurbished with choir stalls in pitch-pine with brass gas standards by Mr Shrivell of Castle Street, Neath. Nave roof stripped of its plastered ceiling and boarded under principals according to its original design. Organ deposed from its former position in west gallery was re-erected in north aisle. Parapet of tower, which was rebuilt and raised to make room for town clock, to detriment of original design. Contractor: John Thomas, Neath. Cost £1,300. (*BN*, 4 September 1874, 298) Reopened after restoration on 27 August 1874. (*W. Mail*, 28 August 1874)

Comments: The main restoration work, carried out in the 1870s, was considerably difficult on account of the peculiar character of the building and the limited funds at Fowler's disposal. Nevertheless, he transformed what was basically a church remodelled in the classical style of the eighteenth-century auditory church into a church restored and reordered, with its standardized Victorian fittings and furnishings, for the fit and proper service of divine worship according to the new liturgical arrangements of the Anglican Church.

ST JOHN THE BAPTIST'S CHURCH, NELSON

1888–9: New church built on new site as chapel of ease to St Mabon's, parish church of Llanfabon. Foundation stone laid in July 1888. Built in Early English Gothic style by E. H. Lingen Barker of Hereford. Original design cruciform in plan consisting of chancel, nave with short transepts, western narthex with baptistery in north end and porch in south end, and western bellcote. However, transepts and western narthex not built until 1908. (ICBS file no. 9189 (1887)) Constructed of Welsh Pennant sandstone laid in thin courses with Bath stone dressings. East window of three plain lancets with sexfoil in apex in form of plate tracery beneath recessed arch. Chancel roof barrel-shaped with curved principal rafters and plain cornice. Chancel arch is broad and plain pointed without mouldings. Nave has an arch-braced roof with scissors-beam arrangement at its apex. Principal rafters supported on large stone corbels with naturalistic foliage. Nave lighted on either side by five two-light lancets with plate tracery above in form of cinquefoils surmounted by hood moulds whose label stops terminate in foliated ends. Open benches of pitch-pine, stained and varnished. Seating accommodation for 267 worshippers. Circular font of Bath stone on circular stem and base. (*Cardiff Times*, 16 February 1889) Cost £1,500. ICBS grant £100; Bishop of Llandaff's Fund £300; LDCES grant £50. Consecrated on 3 June 1889. (*Pontypridd Chr.*, 7 June 1889)

Comments: Initial plans for St John the Baptist's were drawn up by the surveyor, R. J. Mathias of Navigation, who was also churchwarden at the parish church. However, when the plans were submitted for approval to the ICBS they were sent back for amendment. As a result of this rejection, the building committee decided to commission the architect, E. H. Lingen Barker of Hereford to design the new church. However, the Society's Committee of Architects also raised several objections to his scheme, with regard both to the structural soundness of the building and also to its embellishment, asserting that 'the whole design is pretentious in character and unsuitable for the proper simplicity of a village church'. (ICBS file no. 9189 (1887)) Barker responded by claiming that his plans were exactly similar to those he had put into effect at Brynaman, Carmarthenshire in 1880 when the Society made a grant without raising any objection – a claim which the Society contested. (ICBS file no. 8480 (1880)) It later emerged, after extensive correspondence, that differing interpretation of the drawings submitted by Barker had led to misunderstandings over some of these points and he eventually agreed to modify the plans in line with the Society's requirements. In 1889 it was a very plain structure and its only concession to embellishment was the naturalistic foliage of the large stone corbels supporting the principal rafters of the roof with its scissors-beam arrangement and the polychromatic effect achieved by the architect's skilful arrangement of different coloured stonework in the hood moulds of the windows of the church.

In 1908 the church was enlarged by the addition of north and south transepts, south porch, extension of nave to the west by 18ft and west tower. Corsham stone for internal dressings. Box Ground stone for external dressings. Architect: E. M. Bruce Vaughan. Cost £1,200. Increased accommodation by 177 to 477 sittings. (LL/F/405. Enlargement of church. Faculty dated 4 March 1908)

ST JOHN THE BAPTIST'S CHURCH, NEWTON NOTTAGE

1860–1: In 1860 *The Cambrian* announced that following tenders had been received for restoration of Newton Nottage Church: Rees & Roderick £935; Jarvis £654 18s.; James £610. (*The Cambrian*, 10 August, 1860) Work comprised reseating and general repair of fabric. Old-fashioned, high-backed pews replaced by open benches of pitch-pine, stained and varnished. Accommodation increased in the church by 135 seats. Architect: John Prichard, Llandaff. Contractor: W. A. James, Cowbridge. Cost £610. ICBS grant £50. (ICBS file no. 5627 (1860))

1885: Restoration and enlargement of church by John Prichard. When Revd William Jones became rector in 1873 he petitioned for faculty to increase accommodation for worshippers in church. Church bazaar held on 27 and 28 August 1884 to raise funds for proposed restoration. (*CGG*, 29 August 1884) Accordingly, faculty issued in September 1885. Work included construction of organ chamber on north side of chancel to house organ which former rector, Revd Robert Knight, had installed behind west door. By moving organ from base of tower, west door was made available for use of worshippers. An entrance from organ chamber to vestry, which was constructed by lowering floor of the latter, made doorway through north wall unnecessary. Also a window in north wall of chancel was opened out and rood-loft doorway exposed to view. Timbers of chancel ceiling exposed by removal of plaster covering, and internal walls of church received a new coat of plaster. Piscina in chancel also exposed to view and walling, which had blocked up the two squints on either side of chancel arch, removed. Enlargement provided additional accommodation for sixty worshippers. Cost £200. (LL/F/599. New organ and organ chamber and repair of fabric. Faculty dated 8 September 1885)

Comments: Although the restoration of the church in the years 1860–1 included an ecclesiological reordering of the interior to meet the new liturgical arrangements of the Anglican Church, John Newman states that 'the nave was severely restored in 1860–61'. (Newman, 473) While this might suggest that the nave was in a dilapidated state requiring some rebuilding, Sir Stephen Glynne made no mention of the poor state of the fabric when he visited the church on 24 September 1847. (Sir Stephen R. Glynne, 'Notes on the older churches in the four Welsh dioceses', *Arch. Camb.* (1901), 264–5) However, the sum of £610 was a substantial amount to spend on the church at that time. Many schemes for the repositioning of the organ, either from a west gallery or from the west end of the nave, as this particular church, took place in the Victorian era. In the latter part of the nineteenth century many organs were moved to a chancel aisle or a custom-built organ chamber to be near the choir at a time when choral services were an important part of the ritual and ceremony of the Victorian Church.

In 1903 the tower, which was in a ruinous condition, was restored. Work comprised the repair of the parapets, the reopening of the blocked doorway on the west face, as well as of the filled-in slit windows with wide splays (reminiscent of the earlier church) and repointing tower walls. Architect: George E. Halliday, diocesan surveyor. (Charles D. Davies, *The History of the Church situate at Newton, Porthcawl in the Parish of Newton Nottage* (Cowbridge, 1938), 30)

ST NICHOLAS' CHURCH, NICHOLASTON

1893–4: Rebuilding and restoration of church by George E. Halliday. Miss Olive Talbot had the church more or less rebuilt at her own expense in memory of her father, C. R. M. Talbot of Margam Abbey and 'Father of the House of Commons'. Old church demolished with exception of chancel arch (a small round-headed opening), portion of south wall of chancel with deeply splayed window and south-east corner containing piscina. In taking down old walling many fragments of carved stone were found built in, showing that church had undergone rough handling at some earlier period. Old church had existed for centuries in an almost primitive state, which, but for its belfry, resembled an old farm building. New church built of carboniferous limestone from hillside at Cefn Bryn together with dressed stone of a hard, green colour from Bridgend, known as Quarella sandstone. (*The Cambrian*, 19 May 1893) This little church, one of the smallest in Glamorgan, measures only 50ft from east to west. (*BN*, 21 December 1894) When Sir Stephen Glynne visited the church in July 1836 he described it as 'An extremely small church, with only a diminutive low nave and chancel, and a bell-gable over the west end. There is a large south porch. The west window, a single lancet now closed; the eastern, a double lancet . . . The chancel arch rude and pointed, upon imposts.' (Sir Stephen R. Glynne, 'Notes on the older churches in the four Welsh dioceses', *Arch. Camb.* (1897), 300) Built in Early English Gothic style consisting of chancel, nave, vestry on north side of church, south porch and western bellcote. East end, reredos and chancel windows of polished pink alabaster. New vestry was only addition to building. Exquisite reredos of pink alabaster, with red and green Irish marble shafts, consists of five niches – in the centre is found the Blessed Virgin with the Holy Child on her knee, angels with censers are in adjoining niches, and prophets in outer ones. Figures of reredos carved in white lias with gold mosaic background. Three-light Early English window above reredos, the inner arches of which correspond to reredos. Cross, candlesticks and sanctuary lamps of highly polished brass. Church paved throughout with black and white Numidian and Devonshire marbles. Steps leading to altar of polished white statuary, Brèche sanguinaire and Belgian black marble consecutively. Roof of oak and cornice elaborately carved with figures of angels with musical instruments. Stone corbels supporting roof represent Our Lord, the Blessed Virgin, the Four Evangelists and cherubs. Rest of woodwork is teak. Pulpit, reached from chancel by groined staircase, depicts figures of Pusey, Keble and Liddon. Prayer desks of teak are splendid examples of carver's art. Inner doorway and doorway to vestry are both elaborately carved with polished marble shafts. Above south door on inner side are heads of twelve apostles, each a study of stone carving in miniature. Arch above vestry filled with sculptured figures, representing on one side four great fathers of Eastern Church and on other those of Western Church. Font has every appearance of belonging to Norman period – circular bowl and circular stem are carved from single block of stalagmite. In a niche over porch is figure of St Nicholas, patron saint of fishermen, in act of benediction. Fisherman with his net forms one of gable corbels. Exterior of church is in keeping with interior. This little church seats only fifty worshippers. The metal work, a most noticeable feature in church, supplied by Singer's of Frome and Messrs Morgan & Williams of Cardiff. Marbles supplied by Blacker's of Torquay. Contractor: William Clarke, Llandaff. Sculpture and carving throughout church executed by William Clarke. Cost £6,000. (Geoffrey R. Orrin, *The Gower Churches* (Penmaen, 1979), 50–3) Consecrated on 6 December 1894. (*The Cambrian*, 14 December, 1894)

Comments: St Nicholas' was described by Revd J. D. Davies in 1894 'as the most elaborately treated ecclesiastical building in Wales, if not in the West of England'. (J. D. Davies, *A History of West Gower*, Vol. IV (Swansea, 1894), 410) Miss Olive Talbot chose her favourite architect, George E. Halliday, to design her church. He built the church in an embellished Early English Gothic style, so that we have a perfect example of thirteenth-century Gothic architecture at its best. The figures of Pusey, Keble and Liddon, in the niches of the pulpit reflect the Tractarian sympathies of both the Talbot family and Halliday, a Roman Catholic. St Nicholas' stands today as a typical period piece of late nineteenth-century ecclesiastical architecture with finely crafted Victorian church fittings and furnishings. No regard was paid to the cost of the building, which incorporates fine oak and teak and costly marbles and alabaster, as well as wrought ironwork and polished brasswork. Miss Olive Talbot died in October 1894, a few months before the completion of the church in December 1894, and as a mark of respect and gratitude the parishioners erected a plaque in her memory in the nave.

ST DAVID'S CHURCH, TYNEWYDD, OGMORE VALE

1879: New church built on new site given by earl of Dunraven as chapel of ease to St Ceinwyr's, Llangeinor. Inhabitants of area mostly employed in collieries which had sprung up in the parish. Prior to erection of this church, nearest church was the parish church of Llangeinor, situated about four miles away. However, church people attended services in a school-church in Tynewydd called Graig-rhiw-Glyn, which had been built by Mrs J. Blandy Jenkins. Built in Early English Gothic style consisting only of nave, south porch and western bell turret. Foundations for chancel and vestry laid, but not built due to lack of funds. (ICBS file no. 7970 (1876)) Constructed of local Pennant sandstone laid in thin courses with Bath stone dressings. Nave lighted by pairs of two-light trefoiled windows between two-stage buttresses, and pulpit lighted by single trefoiled lancet. West end of nave lighted by a pair of two-light trefoiled windows with quatrefoils in apex between a central four-stage buttress below a wooden bell turret. Roof of nave is of open timber construction and woodwork consists of red pine, stained and varnished. Open benches of pitch-pine, stained and varnished, seat 205 worshippers. Lamps and heating apparatus supplied by Messrs Singer and Buckley of Bridgend. Contractor: William Howell, Nantymoel. Cost £1,785. ICBS grant £120; LDCES grant £100; Mrs Blandy Jenkins, Llanharan House and the Aber Colliery Company also made substantial contributions to building fund. (*CCG*, 26 December 1879) Consecrated on 19 December 1879. (LL/C/136. Sentence of consecration dated 19 December 1879)

1884: Chancel built with vestry on north side by John Prichard. East window of five pointed lights with large cinquefoil within a circle in apex flanked by two roundels. Sanctuary paved with encaustic tiles. Cost £800. ICBS grant £120. Mrs Blandy Jenkins, Llanharan House and Messrs John & William Nicholson, Aber Colliery Company also made large contributions to cost of erection of chancel. Mrs Blandy Jenkins's total commitment to the church amounted to £1,600. (*CCG*, 19 September 1884) Consecrated on 18 November 1884. (*W. Mail*, 19 November 1884)

Comments: John Prichard designed St David's in the Early English Gothic style, which seemed most appropriate for a small mining community. Although he designed a church whose original plan included nave, chancel, vestry and south porch at an estimated cost of £1,785, only the nave with its bellcote and south porch were actually built in 1879. This was another instance where Prichard exceeded the estimated cost of the church so that the chancel could not be built until five years later in 1884. The cost of the nave amounted to £1,600, almost the total estimated cost of the entire church. Prichard failed to keep within the estimated cost of the building because he could not adapt his high architectural standards to building a cheap church for a poor mining community. This was the last church that Prichard built in an industrial area. By way of contrast, Bruce Vaughan's architectural style was admirably suitable to building cheap utilitarian churches in the south Wales coalfield at an average cost of £1,500.

ST ILLTYD'S CHURCH, OXWICH

1891–2: Restoration of church by Frederick William Waller, diocesan architect, Gloucester. Waller produced detailed report on St Illtyd's dated 19 February 1891, in which he drew attention of Miss Emily Talbot, patron of living, to state of church and his plans for its proposed restoration. 'It is to be regretted that some very badly designed modern windows have been inserted in the walls of the nave and also that the old roofs of both nave and chancel have disappeared and been replaced by common barn-like roofs of deal covered with blue slates . . . the nave roof appears to be fairly sound except at the west where some of the timbers have decayed, but the chancel roof is in a very bad state.' Furthermore Waller said that 'Before giving any suggestion as to the best method to be adopted for the repair and re-arrangement of the church may I be allowed to express my opinion that other parts of the building should be left untouched, except where repair is absolutely necessary and in fact that the whole treatment of this interesting little church should be conservative as possible.' (GLRO: D2593/2/3Y/ R4. Report on St Illtyd's Church, Oxwich, 1891 by F. W. Waller) Accordingly, application made for faculty to restore church, which was granted in early part of 1892. (SD/F/525. Restoration of church. Faculty dated 13 February 1892) Outer walls not touched in any way except, where it was necessary to insert three new windows, one in chancel and two in nave. Vestry added on south side of chancel. New roofs raised on chancel and nave. Roof of tower renewed and two new floors placed in belfry. New floor of herringboned wood-blocks laid down in nave and aisle paved with decorative red bricks. Nave reseated with chairs. New altar table carved from teak by Revd J. D. Davies, rector of Llanmadoc and Cheriton. New altar rails with wrought-iron standards erected in chancel. Church was previously somewhat damp due to exhalations from vaults beneath the floor and fact that soil had been allowed to accumulate against exterior walls. This was remedied by a layer of concrete being laid down throughout church, soil removed and drainage around church improved. During work of restoration two incised, sepulchral stones inscribed in Lombardic figures discovered, one lying face downwards in nave and other face upwards near inner doorway, bearing names of two former rectors of fourteenth century. Both stones were placed each side of interior walls of porch in 1892. Prior to 1890, circular font bowl, hewn from block of Sutton stone, built into wall in south-west corner of church, but then taken out and placed on tall, smooth shaft rising out of an oblong base. Seating accommodation for 120 worshippers. Contractor: Messrs Bevan & Gibbs, Horton. Cost £1,000. Restoration carried out at sole expense of Miss Emily Talbot. (Geoffrey R. Orrin, *The Gower Churches* (Penmaen, 1979), 53–6) Reopened after restoration on 17 August 1892. (*The Cambrian*, 19 August 1892)

Comments: Waller carried out a sensitive restoration of St Illtyd's in 1892, leaving the walls of the church untouched except where it was necessary to insert or open out blocked windows. He carefully preserved the Tudor windows of the nave and added new ones as required. The work was essentially a careful and thorough reparation of the structure, which had long been in need of repair, caused no doubt by its close proximity to the wind and waves of the Bristol Channel.

39. All Saints' Church, Oystermouth, as proposed to be enlarged and restored. North-west view and north-east view. R. Kyrke Penson, Archt (By kind permission of the Vicar and Churchwardens of Oystermouth Church)

ALL SAINTS' CHURCH, OYSTERMOUTH

1835: When Revd Samuel Davies, perpetual curate at that time, wrote to ICBS in March 1832 for grant aid towards repairs he described church as follows: 'The Church is in a most comfortless condition, it being neither ceiled nor paved – having only an earthen floor which is necessarily damp, cold and unhealthy and deters many persons from attending divine service.' In 1835, £100, most of which was raised by levying a rate of 1s 2d in the pound for purpose of 'ceiling and otherwise repairing and flooring the church', was spent on repairs to church fabric. New gallery built to accommodate fifty-seven additional parishioners at west end of church for sum of £61 10s 0d. ICBS grant £60. (ICBS file no. 343 (1832))

1859–60: Restoration of church and addition of north aisle with west gallery with external access. Architect: Richard Kyrke Penson, 'honorary' diocesan architect. Repairs of 1835 insufficient to arrest decay of structure, and in 1857 application made to ICBS for grant to restore and enlarge church. In 1856, church accommodated 416 parishioners (289 in nave, 27 in chancel, 50 in east gallery erected in 1821, and 50 in new west gallery).

Accommodation further increased by 253 seats, so that total seating capacity amounted to 669 seats. Penson's original drawings for restoration and enlargement of All Saints' included spire crowning tower, but this was never built. New portion of building constructed of Clyne-wood sandstone with Bath stone dressings. Restored in Early English Gothic style. Floored with black and red Staffordshire tiles. Chancel windows restored to their original state – three narrow Early English lancets with deep splays. New chancel arch constructed. Tower repaired. Galleries removed from nave together with old three-decker pulpit. New Communion table, altar rails, oak pulpit. Drainage around church improved. During restoration, greatest care taken to use as much as possible of old materials, such as doors, windows, etc. and, where rebuilding absolutely necessary, old style closely imitated and preserved as far as possible. (*Bldr*, 11 August 1860, 517) West gallery constructed in north aisle, access to which was by means of external staircase at west of aisle. (Geoffrey R. Orrin and F. G. Cowley, *A History of All Saints' Church, Oystermouth* (Llandysul, 1990), 42–9) In a letter to IBCS, Penson stated that 'the west gallery has been forced upon me for a peculiar reason. A portion of the congregation is given to inordinate spitting and with a view to accommodating this section the vicar insisted upon a gallery with an external approach. (ICBS file no. 5136 (1857)) Contractor: Joseph Holtham, Bath. Cost £2,100. ICBS grant £165. Reopened after restoration on 2 August 1860. (*The Cambrian*, 3 August 1860)

1873: New organ chamber and vestry built. New organ, built by Robert Postill of York, installed. (SD/F/526. Taking down vestry and building organ chamber. Faculty dated 26 January 1873) Reopened after restoration on 17 April 1873. Architect: Thomas Lewis Jowett, Langland, Swansea. Benefactor: Henry Crawshay, Langland. Cost £590. (*The Cambrian*, 18 April 1873)

Comments: Before its restoration in the years 1859–60, All Saints' was typical of the early nineteenth-century auditory church with the focus of the congregation directed at the three-decker pulpit against the north wall of the nave and galleries at the east and west ends of the nave. The restoration and enlargement of the church changed all this, and the emphasis was redirected at the chancel and altar where the Holy Eucharist was celebrated. Richard Kyrke Penson had a reputation for being a radical church restorer. This is illustrated by the antiquarian George Grant Francis's manuscript notes written at the back of his personal copy of Baker and Francis's *Surveys of Gower and Kilvey* (now deposited at Swansea Museum). At the time, he wrote, 'when it was necessary to enlarge the church it was proposed to remove it entirely, but by a timely interference I got only so much of the old structure removed as was absolutely necessary and I succeeded in getting the old stonework of the windows, the Norman font and pillar piscina, the water stoup, etc. retained instead of the new, which had been designed and approved'. As a result of this timely intervention and the great concern shown by the Cambrian Archaeological Association in their influential journal *Archaeologia Cambrensis*, Penson took much care to preserve the many features of the medieval church. When rebuilding and enlargement was necessary he closely imitated the Early English style of the medieval church and made as much use as possible of the old materials.

In 1915 the church was enlarged by building a new chancel, nave and vestries on the north side and the old thirteenth-century nave of the old church acted as a south aisle with the former chancel becoming a Lady Chapel. Architect: Leonard William Barnard of Prothero, Phillott and Barnard, architects of Cheltenham. Foundation stone laid on 10 June 1915. (*The Cambrian*, 11 June 1915) New church built in Perpendicular Gothic style of architecture. Seating accommodation for 815 persons. Cost £8,305. ICBS grant £150. (SD/F/ 527. Restoration of church. Faculty dated 9 April 1915) Consecrated on 7 September 1916. (*W. Mail*, 8 September 1916) The church was not finally completed until 1937 when the nave was extended westwards. It owes its present appearance to the erection of a new church of 'Cathedral-like' proportions built under the direction of Revd Harold Williams.

ST PETER'S CHURCH, NEWTON, OYSTERMOUTH

1901–3: New church built on new site as chapel of ease to All Saints', Oystermouth. Architect: E. M. Bruce Vaughan, Cardiff. (ICBS file no. 10,255 (1900)) Revd Harold Williams, vicar of Oystermouth, felt new church necessary to serve growing population of districts of Caswell, Langland and Newton. The correspondent in the *Church Builder* reported 'that the present church accommodation is totally inadequate. The parish church is filled morning and evening. In the summer months when there are often 1,000 visitors, hundreds of people have to be turned away. It is very urgent that in a place such as this there should be ample church accommodation.' (*Ch. Bldr* (1901), 76) Foundation stone laid on 19 September 1901 by Mrs Ella Miller on behalf of Miss Emily Talbot, who was indisposed. (*OCM*, October 1901, 4) Built in Decorated Gothic style consisting of chancel (37ftx 25ft), broad nave (28ft 4ins wide by 82ft long), north and south aisles (76ftx11ft 4ins), clerestory, choir vestry and clergy vestries, organ chamber, base of tower and north porch. Total inside breadth of church 56ft and length 119ft, height of wallplate 31ft and to apex of roof 48ft. Constructed of hammer-dressed, green and white Quarella stone from Bridgend with Bath stone dressings. (*BN*, 27 September 1901, 417) East window of five cinquefoiled lights with late Decorated-style traceried head. Chancel has wagon roof panelled with gilded bosses at intersection of purlins and common rafters. Sedilia with cinquefoiled arches and credence table with niche on south side of chancel. Nave divided from aisles by arcades of three pointed arches springing from moulded capitals on round and octagonal columns. Nave has open timber hammer-beam roof with principal rafters supported on pillar corbels. Clerestory windows square with traceried heads. Aisles lighted by two-light windows with Decorated-style traceried heads between slender buttresses capped with gablets. West window of five cinquefoiled lights with late Decorated-style traceried head. Accommodation provided on individual chairs for 634 worshippers. Contractors: A. J. Howell, Cardiff and Venning & Gaen, Cardiff. Cost £7,619. ICBS grant £150; Miss Emily Talbot £400. (*The Cambrian*, 20 November 1903) Consecrated on 19 November 1903. (*W. Mail*, 20 November 1903)

Comments: St Peter's, built in the Decorated Gothic style, was an ambitious design for Bruce Vaughan who, with the notable exception of St James' Church, Cardiff, had been accustomed to building cheap churches in the south Wales coal-field. At Newton he had funds to demonstrate his mature architectural ability, which is reflected in the well-appointed and finely executed traditional Victorian Church, built in a late Gothic form. The chancel is particularly well executed with its three sedilia beneath cinquefoiled arches springing from slender pillars with caps and bases and a credence table with niche on the south wall. The wagon roof, panelled with gilded bosses at the intersections of the purlins and rafters, is also well crafted. The east window of the chancel with its intricate rectilinear-style tracery in the head is a particularly fine feature of the church. Bruce Vaughan's design, intended to be carried out in two stages, was unfortunately only partially fulfilled since the south-east tower was never built, the structure only reaching to the height of the roof.

A new organ, presented by Arthur Gilbertson, was dedicated on 10 October 1907. (Jean Haines (ed.), *St. Peter's Church, Newton: History and Guide* (Swansea, 1984), 6–7)

CHRIST CHURCH, PANT

40. Christ Church, Pant (By kind permission of Merthyr Tydfil Library)

1894–6: New church built on new site given by Edward Davies, The Garth, Bassaleg, Newport. Foundation stone laid on 4 October 1894 by bishop of Llandaff, Rt Revd Dr Richard Lewis. (*Merthyr Times*, 11 October 1894) Built in Perpendicular Gothic style by E. M. Bruce Vaughan, consisting of chancel with vestry, nave, organ chamber and west porch. Bellcote above chancel arch. Constructed of blue Llancaiach sandstone with Bath stone dressings. East window of three cinquefoiled lights with panel tracery in head. Altar surrounded by oak panelling. Piscina in south wall of chancel under three pointed arches. Nave has hammerbeam roof of pitch-pine supported on stone corbels. Plain quarried windows in nave and porch of red tinted pale stained glass. Carved oak pulpit and brass eagle lectern stand on each side of chancel arch. Open benches of pitch-pine. Seating accommodation for 280 worshippers. Gable crosses on roof gables. Contractor: Edward Lumley, Merthyr Tydfil. Cost £1,400. LDCES grant £50; Bishop of Llandaff's Fund £200; William Jenkins, former manager of Consett Ironworks, Durham £500. Dedicated on 11 June 1896. (*Merthyr Times*, 18 June 1896)

Comments: Christ Church was part of a project to build three new churches in the district, which was to include St Michael's Church, Pengarnddu, which was built as a mission church. The third proposed church was never built. It is a large church designed in the Perpendicular Gothic style, a late Gothic form. The chancel arch is surmounted by a well-designed bellcote in the style of the fifteenth century. Inside its fine fifteenth-century-style hammerbeam roof is an unusual feature for a church built in a mining community by Bruce Vaughan.

ALL SAINTS' CHURCH, PENARTH
(Destroyed by fire in April 1926)

1890–1: New church built on new site given by Lord Windsor. Built to provide additional accommodation for large and ever-increasing population in western part of town and parish. Foundation stone laid on 1 October 1890 by Lady Windsor.

(*Bldr*, 4 October 1890, 274) Built in Early English Gothic style freely treated by John Coates Carter of Seddon & Carter, Cardiff. (ICBS file no. 9362 (1885)) It consisted of nave (73ft long by 25ft wide between the arcades and 55ft between the aisle walls) with chancel (33ftx25ft), making a total length of 106ft, with organ chamber and vestries on south side of chancel. Principal entrance to church through west doorway between flat buttresses. Octagonal bell turret with flèche over chancel arch. Constructed of Newbridge stone laid in uniform courses and hammer-polled, with Bath stone dressings. Roofs covered with Whitland Abbey slates. Each bay of aisles had transverse roof ending in gable over tall window. Side aisles were nearly same height as nave, from which they were separated by arcades of five bays, the columns and arches growing richer in decoration towards east end. Chancel same height as nave and divided into three bays, those on north side each containing a three-light window with Geometrical stone tracery in head. On south side, easternmost bay alone contained similar window. The other two, consisting of arches, supported by moulded column opened into upper part of vestry and also enclosed organ pipes. East window of six lights. Heating done by John Grundy. Church accommodated 500 parishioners on oak benches. Contractor: L. Purnell, Penarth. Cost £6,300. No ICBS grant made; Lord Windsor £3,000; LDCES grant £60; Bishop of Llandaff's Fund £100. (*BN*, 26 June 1891, 874) Consecrated on 31 October 1891. (*W. Mail*, 2 November 1891)

1895: New porch built, new stone pulpit erected and organ installed in church. Improvements made to seating arrangements. (LL/F/629. New porch, pulpit and organ. Improvements. Faculty dated 26 October 1895)

Comments: John Coates Carter, the architect of All Saints', had just designed and built St Paul's, Grangetown, Cardiff, and All Saints' was almost an exact replica of St Paul's. At Grangetown Carter used the warm pink Penkridge sandstone instead of the greyish blue Pennant sandstone. Also he used a single doorway with flat buttresses topped by octagonal pinnacles instead of the triple doorway with rectangular buttresses at Penarth. As at St Paul's, the chancel was the same height as the nave and divided into three bays. In addition, each bay of the side aisles had a transverse roof ending in a gable with a tall window. Both churches included in their design octagonal bell turrets with a flèche over the chancel arch. Thus, apart from the use of different coloured varieties of sandstone and roofing materials for their construction and minor variations in the design of their west fronts, both churches displayed a remarkable affinity with each other despite the fact that they were situated within a comparatively short distance of each other. Had All Saints' not been destroyed by fire in 1926 and once again after its rebuilding razed to the ground by the blitz of 1941 it would have been regarded, with St Paul's Church, Grangetown, as one of the finest late Victorian churches in Glamorgan.

ST AUGUSTINE'S CHURCH, PENARTH

1865–6: New church built on extended site of old one. Revd Charles Parsons, vicar of parish from 1863 to 1889, instigated movement for new and larger church soon after his appointment 1863. Baroness Windsor, who was sympathetic to rector's grandiose plans for new church worthy of new town, promised £7,000 for erection of new church. Foundation stone laid on 8 June 1865 by Baroness Windsor. (*CMG*, 9 June 1865) Petition for faculty to build new church stated that 'the said church of Penarth was in a state of decay and much too small for the accommodation of the parishioners in consequence of the great increase of population there and that it had become necessary to take down the present church and erect a new church upon the present and more extended site'. (LL/F/612P. Demolition of old parish and building of new one. Petition dated 22 April 1865) Built in Early English Gothic style somewhat freely treated by William Butterfield. It consists of chancel, nave, north and south aisles, clerestory, and transepts, with saddleback tower

41. St Augustine's Church, Penarth: interior (Photo: Geoffrey R. Orrin)

90ft high at south-west corner of building. Constructed of grey-white Leckwith limestone with Bath stone dressings. West entrance approached by flight of stone steps and there is another entrance on north side. Roofs covered with red Staffordshire tiles and tower has a saddleback roof in imitation of old church. Nave is 87ft long and chancel 37ft, both internal measurements. Width of nave and aisles 51ft. Massive pillars which form nave of pink Radyr sandstone and yellow Bath stone in alternate bands. Between arches in spandrels are eight quatrefoil panels in each of which is painted a Beatitude. Red brickwork filled with black and white diaper work is used for the facings of the walls. East window of three lights and west window of four, both with Geometrical tracery in heads. Reredos of coloured marble with sacred monogram IHS inlaid. Within altar rails are sedilia and piscina. Floor of chancel laid with red and black stone and patterned tiles. Chancel approached by flight of steps made of stone from Pentrebach quarry. Seating accommodation for 800 worshippers. Contractor: Webb's of Birmingham. Cost £7,550. LDCES grant £100. (*BN*, 14 September 1866) Consecrated on 11 September 1866. (*CMG*, 14 September 1866)

Comments: Butterfield had originally designed a square embattled tower more in keeping with Victorian taste, but when his plans were publicized there was great opposition to his design from mariners and channel pilots since the saddle tower of the old church was marked on admiralty charts. Accordingly Butterfield bowed to public demand and altered his design to incorporate instead a traditional Glamorgan saddleback tower. He thus built a 90ft tower, copied from the existing building, which served as a prominent landmark to mariners in the Bristol Channel. The church is now regarded as Butterfield's boldest asymmetrical composition. This is achieved externally by the powerful vertical form of the saddleback tower, balanced by the equally strong horizontal form of the north porch. Inside, this is achieved by the simple circular and octagonal pillars and the splayed intrados of the arcade which emphasize weight and mass. The brilliant constructional polychromy of the interior provides a striking

contrast to the austere grey-white Leckwith limestone of the exterior. The interior of the church is one of Butterfield's finest creations, probably only surpassed by All Saints' Church, Babbacombe in the provinces and All Saints' Church, Margaret Street, London.

ST GWYNOUR'S CHURCH, LLANYRNEWYDD, PENCLAWDD

1850: Petition of consecration stated 'that the old chapel of ease of Llanyrnewydd alias Penclawdd in the parish of Llanrhidian had become dilapidated and unfit for use and that a new chapel had been erected on or near the site of the old one'. (SD/C/179. Petition of consecration, dated 17 December 1850) Accordingly, old church pulled down in 1846 and appeal made for subscriptions to build new church for growing population of district which numbered 2,000 inhabitants at that time. Appeal for funds in local newspaper in 1849 reported that although 'the building is now in course of erection, sufficient funds to complete it have not been obtained'. (*The Cambrian*, 31 August 1849) New church built in 1850 in Early English Gothic style consisting of small chancel, nave and western tower with spire. Principal entrance through west end of tower, lower part of which forms a porch. Constructed of local Pennant sandstone with Bath stone dressings. Nave has a collar-beam roof of Memel timber. Two-stage west tower with stone broach spire. Open benches of pitch-pine. Seating accommodation for ninety-five worshippers. ICBS grant refused on grounds that Phillip Evans, churchwarden, of Brynhir House, had neglected to apply for grant before erecting church. Contractor: George E. Strawbridge, Swansea. (ICBS file no. 4241 (1850)) Consecrated on 17 December 1850. Cost £700. Phillip Evans, Brynhir House £300. (*The Cambrian*, 20 December 1850)

1886: Restoration of church by James Buckley Wilson, Swansea. Stone spire taken down and completely rebuilt with new stonework and belfry windows. Entrance archway through west porch under tower fitted with oak door, whole of windows reglazed with Cathedral glass and walls and ceiling replastered. Exterior walls carefully repointed with Aberthaw mortar. New Porritt's heating apparatus installed. Contractor: Messrs Thomas, Watkins & Jenkins, Swansea. Reopened after restoration on 9 December 1886. Architect: James Buckley Wilson, Swansea. (*Bldr*, 18 December 1886, 893)

Comments: St Gwynour's was built in a pre-Puginesque style. The church has no particular claim to architectural merit and is built in the less expensive Early English Gothic style. It is a plain rustic church, built for a poor community of working-class people. Its interior, furnished with crudely constructed open benches of pitch-pine and simple collar-beam roof, is plain and austere. The poor coursing of the stonework and the rough quoining, the appalling keystones and the dreadful infill between the windows must dismay anyone considering the church purely from an architectural point of view. However, the two-stage tower is well proportioned, although the broach spire might have been a little taller in keeping with the Early English style as well as in relation to the height of the tower. Sound buttresses with gablets turn the tower into the porch it is, which saved the expense of a separate structure. Unfortunately, no architect is recorded for the design the church, but it was in all probability the work of the builder George E. Strawbridge.

ST CADOC'S CHURCH, PENDOYLAN

1855: Church restoration. In 1854 church found to be in very dilapidated and ruinous state and thus thoroughly restored the following year at sole expense of Rowland Fothergill, Hensol Castle. Cost £1,100. Principal work of restoration included refenestration of church and raising of new roofs. All traces of rood-loft, which once extended across chancel arch, swept away at this time. (T. J. Hopkins, 'The Village and Parish of Pendoylan', in Stewart Williams (ed.), *History on My Doorstep* (Cowbridge, 1959), 80)
1870: Following grant of faculty in 1867, Hensol burial vault constructed in 1870 by Rowland Fothergill for himself and his family in chancel.

(LL/F/640. Construction of family vault in chancel of church. Faculty dated 18 July 1867) Construction of vault resulted in collapse of chancel wall, which had to be rebuilt and strengthened by two-stage angle buttresses. (T. J. Hopkins, op. cit., 80)
1891: Chancel repaired by Ecclesiastical Commissioners as titular rectors. Cost £6. Architect: Ewan Christian, London. Contractor: John Phillips, Aberthin, Cowbridge. (RBCW. Eccl. Comm. file no. 66494)
1893: Restoration of church by Bruton & Williams, architects of Cardiff. (*Bldr*, 15 July 1893, 55) Tower rebuilt, four bells recast and two new bells added. Seating rearranged to secure additional accommodation for forty worshippers. New pulpit erected on north side of chancel arch in nave and new oak lectern on opposite side. Tower screen heightened to fill tower arch completely. Font moved to fill space under tower wall. New oak reading desk placed on south side of chancel. Contractor: Messrs J. R. Haines, Cardiff. Cost £800. (LL/F/640. Restoration of tower and bells; rearrangement. Faculty dated 21 February 1893) Reopened after restoration on 13 June 1893. (*W. Mail*, 15 June 1893)

Comments: The main purpose of the restoration of St Cadoc's in 1893 was twofold: firstly, the reconstruction of the dilapidated medieval west tower and, secondly, the rearrangement of the interior of the church to provide additional accommodation. At the same time the interior of the auditory church underwent a late ecclesiological reordering, being provided with standardized Victorian fittings and furnishings in keeping with the new liturgical arrangements of the Anglican Church.

ST DAVID'S CHURCH, PENLLERGAER

1837–8: Built on new site by John Dillwyn Llewelyn of Penllergare as chapel of ease to St Cyfelach's, Llangyfelach. Nearest church was at Llangyfelach, where family worshipped. At this time services also held in servants' hall, conducted by Revd Ben Thomas, who travelled from Llanon. However, John Dillwyn Llewelyn realized need for

42. New chancel, Penllergare Church: James Buckley Wilson, archt (Source: *The Building News*, 5 March 1886)

roof timber pitch-pine, unvarnished and in its natural state from carpenter's bench. Principal rafters over sanctuary supported by columns running from floor to roof, with moulded Early English Gothic-style capitals. Chancel lighted by Early English-style triple lancet window with four columns supporting interior arches above. Floor of chancel laid with encaustic tiles. On north and south sides of chancel are two long lancet windows, the base of that on south side is formed by sedilia. Deeply moulded chancel arch of red bed Farleigh stone divides chancel from nave. Old doors to porch removed and substituted with new oak doors. Hot-water apparatus for heating purposes supplied and fixed by Mr Bennet, Swansea. Contractor: Messrs Thomas, Watkins and Jenkins, Swansea. Cost defrayed by J. T. D. Llewelyn. (*Bldr*, 31 July 1886, 182) Reopened after restoration for divine worship on 25 July 1886. (*The Cambrian*, 23 July 1886)

Comments: St David's was the first church to be built in the Victorian era in the Glamorgan part of the diocese of St David's. At that time St David's was an example of the auditory church with strict emphasis on the pulpit and sermon. The church continued in this condition until 1886, when John Talbot Dillwyn Llewelyn – like his father before him an active participant in the church extension movement in Swansea of the 1880s – decided to restore the nave and build a new chancel. The construction of the chancel in that year transformed the old auditory church, which had survived well into the late Victorian period, into a typical Anglican Church with the focus now directed away from the pulpit and towards the altar, where the Holy Eucharist was celebrated with all the ritual and ceremony. So well was Wilson's design of the chancel received by the architectural press that a photolithograph of the structure appeared in *The Building News* for 5 March 1886.

church near at hand and decided to build, with bishop of St David's permission, a chapel at Penllergare with 200 sittings. Foundation stone laid in 1837 by John Talbot Dillwyn Llewelyn (later Sir John), the year-old son of John Dillwyn Llewelyn. (Margaret Williams, *St David's Church, Penllergaer, 1838–1988* (Swansea, 1988)) Church consisted entirely of nave and small vestry on north side and opposite it a doorway for people of Penllergare House. Below west gallery stood main doorway. Altar stood in small bay with font and immediately in front of it and on either side stood oak pulpit and clerk's reading desk and seat. Congregation seated in old-fashioned high-backed pews, each with its separate entrance. (*HOW*, 6 November 1937)

1886: Church restored and enlarged by addition of chancel (37ftx18ft), together with organ chamber and vestry. Architect: James Buckley Wilson, Swansea. (*BN*, 5 March 1886, 181) Whole of nave reseated with open benches of pitch-pine. Six steps lead up to altar table. Roof of chancel of pitch-pine of late thirteenth-century style; in fact whole of

PENLLYN CHAPEL, PENLLYN

1842–50: The correspondent in *The Cambrian* reported that 'Penllyne Chapel, in this county, which has remained ever since its first conversion about a century ago, from a "Parish House" into chapel of ease to Llanfrynach Church, a mile distant, in a very unprotected state is now happily undergoing considerable improvements; towards which sacred object the ever-charitable Lord Bishop of the Diocese, and the highly respected Conservative Member for the County, Lord Adare, have most liberally contributed five pounds each, in addition to donations of most of the landed proprietors of the parish. The first stone of a new wall to enclose the chapel and grounds adjoining was laid by Mrs Salmon of Penlline Court on Tuesday last the 25th January . . . It is hoped that the chapel, which now wears the exterior semblance of a white-washed barn, will, in a few short years . . . be no less an ornament to the peaceful village than in cheerful, but serious keeping with its holy Protestant character.' (*The Cambrian*, 29 January 1842)

In 1850 John Homfray rebuilt Penllyn Chapel and at same time incorporated it into entrance to Penllyn Castle grounds. (J. B. Davies, 'The parish of Penllin', in Stewart Williams (ed.), *Saints and Sailing Ships* (Cowbridge, 1962), 97) Structural examination of building reveals that it was built in Decorated Gothic style in 1850 consisting of chancel and nave, south porch and western bell-cote. Its east window displays fourteenth-century-style reticulated tracery reminiscent of east window in Stradling Chapel at St Donat's Church. Inner arch springs from engaged shafts with bell caps and round bases. Chancel is continuation of nave with a ceiled barrel roof with common rafters and purlins. West window of two cinquefoiled lights with quatrefoils in head. Nave and chancel windows all of two cinquefoiled lights with stylized fourteenth-century tracery in apex. Above west gable is single bellcote. Oak panelled walls of chancel done at post-Victorian date.

Comments: Although originally built as chapel of ease to St Brynach's, Penllyn Chapel has reversed its role in recent years. Anglican worship is now regularly conducted at Penllyn Chapel, while apart from burials, only occasional services are conducted during the summer months at St Brynach's to keep up the tradition of Anglican worship. It is to the care of John Homfray and his descendants that Penllyn Chapel owes its existence today as a well-cared-for and attractive church.

ST JOHN THE BAPTIST'S CHURCH, PENMAEN

1847: Church repaired at cost of £118 raised by church rate. (ICBS file no. 4712 (1854))

1854–5: Restoration and enlargement of church by Richard Kyrke Penson. Local newspaper described condition of church prior to its restoration as 'a cold damp, dilapidated crumbling relic of olden times'. (*The Cambrian*, 29 June 1855) When Sir Stephen Glynne visited church on 30 August 1861, he wrote 'This church has been almost wholly rebuilt, but in a meritorious manner, not out of keeping with the prevailing character of the district. It has now a nave, with short north aisle (which is a recent addition), and chancel and south porch. Over the west end a pretty new bell-cot. The walls are old.' (Sir Stephen R. Glynne, 'Notes on the older churches in the four Welsh dioceses', *Arch. Camb.* (1887), 288–9) Parts of church rebuilt with local Pennant sandstone with Bath stone dressings. New roof covered with Bangor slates. East window of three trefoil-headed lights, the mullions of taller central light continue into the head forming tracery with a pointed trefoil. In the spandrels on each side are round trefoils. West window of nave is of two lights with cusped trefoils and circular trefoil in head. Both have dripstones with heads as label stops. Arcade to north aisle has two pointed arches springing from octagonal pillar. Bellcote, surmounting chancel arch, has gabled buttresses rising above usual set-offs, which form shoulders. Enlargement of church doubled its seating capacity to 152 sittings. Contractor: George Strawbridge, Swansea. Cost. £500. ICBS grant £50. (Geoffrey R. Orrin, *The Gower Churches* (Penmaen, 1979), 61–3) Reopened after restoration on 26 June 1855. (*The Cambrian*, 29 June 1855)

43. Interior of Penmark Church showing Transitional pointed Norman chancel arch decorated with chevron mouldings on its face (Photo: W. P. Pring, L.R.P.S.) (By kind permission of D. Brown & Sons Ltd, Cowbridge)

Comments: Revd Edward Knight James's initial application to the ICBS requesting grant aid was refused on the grounds that he employed a building contractor, George Strawbridge of Swansea, to draw up plans and specifications, instead of a professional architect. Accordingly, James commissioned Richard Kyrke Penson, the 'honorary' diocesan architect, who resubmitted a design for the proposed work of restoration to the Society. The Society's Committee of Architects made several objections stating that 'the main roof looks rather heavy as compared with that of the aisle'. Furthermore, the committee suggested that 'as many as possible of the seats in the new aisle should face east – at least all the adult sittings should be so placed', and also that 'the buttress forming the southern abutment of the chancel, having great stress, taking the weight of the bell turret, might with advantage be somewhat larger'. (ICBS file no. 4712 (1854)) Penson evidently complied with these suggestions, for the ICBS voted a grant of £50. One cannot deny that certain features of the old Gower church were

lost for ever. However, Penmaen lost its uncared-for and dilapidated appearance and became a fitter and more seemly place for divine worship as a result of its restoration in 1855.

ST MARY'S CHURCH, PENMARK

1858: Restoration of chancel, comprising insertion of large Perpendicular-style windows in east and south walls. Cost £528. George T. Clark and Robert Oliver Jones noted that 'It [the church] stands in Penmark village near the northern edge of the parish ... It is of large size, handsome, it has recently been restored in good taste, and is well kept. It is composed of a tower, nave, south porch and chancel.' (George T. Clark and Robert O. Jones, 'Some account of the parish of Penmark', *Arch. Camb.* (1861), 5) The correspondent in the *Church Builder* reported that 'the church was built in the thirteenth century and substantial repairs to some portions were carried out in 1858'. (*Ch. Bldr* (1893), 83)

1893–4: Restoration of church by Seddon & Carter of Cardiff. (ICBS file no. 9710 (1898)) The correspondent in the *Church Builder* reported that 'the present application is for much needed renovation of the interior and the repair of the tower and roof'. (*Ch. Bldr* (1893), 83) Work of restoration confined to thorough structural repair of tower and reflooring and reseating of nave and chancel. Old-fashioned, high-backed pews in nave entirely removed and nave furnished with modern oak pews, every second pew supporting three-branched candle-pole. Accommodation increased by an additional twelve seats to 182, of which twelve were free. Altar, dated 1709, replaced by new and larger one of oak and raised above level of sanctuary by several inches. New oak choir stalls, richly carved by William Clarke, installed to provide better accommodation for choir. In relaying floors special care taken to preserve ancient monumental tombstones thereon. Ringing gallery erected at level of sill of Perpendicular west window and approached by wooden staircase from vestry beneath through trap door in floor. Warm-air underground stove erected near entrance of south porch and existing flue and stack in north wall utilized for carrying off smoke. Plaster stripped from part of barrel roof to expose principal rafters and main braces. (LL/F/643. Restoration of church. Faculty dated 6 December 1892) Contractor: J. S. Shepton, Penarth. Cost £600. ICBS grant £15. (*W. Mail*, 20 June 1894)

Comments: St Mary's was yet another church situated in the depths of the Vale of Glamorgan where the liturgical arrangements and 'prayer-book' interior of the eighteenth and nineteenth centuries had survived intact until the last decade of the Victorian era, despite a restoration of the chancel in 1858. Consequently, apart from structural repairs to the tower, the restoration carried out in 1894 was essentially an ecclesiological reordering of the interior of the old auditory church with its emphasis on the three-decker pulpit and sermon, and the replacement of the outdated interior arrangement with the modern standardized fittings and furnishings of the Anglican Church in the late Victorian period.

ST MARY'S CHURCH, PENNARD

1847: Church restored by Thomas Penrice of Kilvrough, patron of living. (Olive Phillips, *Gower* (London, 1956), 45) Date of restoration, 1847, recorded above south porch doorway. Sir Stephen R. Glynne, who visited the church in August 1851, wrote, 'This church is more modernised than most others in Gower. It has only a chancel and nave, a small north transept, with a small steeple at the west end . . . There are no windows on the north of the chancel and those on the south of the nave are modernised . . . The roofs are modern and slated; and the whole is in a neat state.' (Sir Stephen R. Glynne, 'Notes on the older churches in the four Welsh dioceses', *Arch. Camb.* (1897), 296) With reference to Glynne's description of church four years after restoration and a visual examination of structure, it is apparent that church underwent a thorough restoration in 1847 when roofs were replaced and slated, interior rearranged with modern benches in place of the square box pews, and new windows with Y-tracery inserted in south wall of nave.

1899: Vestry constructed on north side of chancel in 1899. (SD/F/549. New vestry room. Faculty dated 21 June 1899) William Douglas Caröe, an eminent London architect, who made a report on the church in 1929 described it as 'a flimsy and ill-designed vestry of 1899', and recommended its rebuilding. (St Mary's Church, Pennard, Parish Records: W. D. Caröe, Pennard St Mary: Report and plans, 13 May 1929)

Comments: It appears that both St Mary's, Pennard and St Illtyd's, Ilston, were restored in 1847, a year after the death of Major Thomas Penrice. He was succeeded by his nephew of the same name. Thomas Penrice was obviously concerned as patron of both livings at the poor state of these churches and took immediate steps to restore both churches. When wealthy members of the landed gentry restored churches at their own expense in the nineteenth century they rarely made an application to the ICBS in London for grant aid. Consequently, there are no records in the Society's archives at Lambeth Palace library or in the Church in Wales archives in the National Library of Wales giving detailed information about the work of restoration. Fortunately, Sir Stephen Glynne made visits to both churches in August 1851 and we can deduce from his accurate accounts of the structures what actually occurred.

ST WINEFRED'S CHURCH, PENRHIWCEIBER

1883: New church built on new site given by Major A. Vaughan Lee. The correspondent in the *Church Builder* reported that 'The population of this parish has increased by 4,000 in the past ten years. A new coal-pit has just been sunk in the district where this church is to be erected, and a population of 1,000 has already gathered around it, and is expected to grow at a great rate. For some time past divine service has been carried on in a cottage, the only building available, but wholly inadequate to the wants of the people. This church will serve as a chapel of ease.' (*Ch. Bldr* (1882), 35) Architect: Thomas Nicholson, Hereford. (ICBS file no. 8687 (1882)) Foundation stone laid on 29 March 1883 by Lady Aberdare. (*W. Mail*, 30 March 1883) Built in Early English Gothic style consisting of chancel, nave, south porch and western bellcote. Constructed of Welsh Pennant sandstone with external dressings of Ombersley stone from the Bromsgrove quarries and internal dressings of Bath stone. Roof over chancel and nave of hammerbeam type and constructed of pitch-pine left in its natural state. Trusses dividing nave from chancel are more ornate than others. Portion of roof over sanctuary is semicircular with moulded ribs divided into panels. Roofs covered with Pelton blue slates. East window of three widely spaced lancet lights and separated internally by three continuous trefoiled arches which spring from round caps and shafts on round bases. Aisle laid with encaustic tiles whilst rest of church floor composed of Gregory's patent wood blocks. Chancel seated with well-designed oak chairs and accommodation for parishioners in nave provided on 265 individual chairs. Pulpit constructed of Bath stone. (*Bldr*, 22 December 1883, 843) Contractor: William Cullis, Hereford. Cost £1,900. ICBS grant £100; LDCES grant £50; Lord Aberdare £50. Opened on 18 December 1883. (*W. Mail*, 19 December 1883) Consecrated on 12 November 1884. (*W. Mail*, 13 November 1884)

1888–9: Church enlarged by addition of south aisle and transept on south side and vestry on south side of chancel. Additional seating provided for 140 parishioners. Work completed April 1889. Cost £800. ICBS grant £40; Bishop of Llandaff's Fund £150. (ICBS file no. 8687 (1888))

Comments: St Winefred's stands out among the mediocre church architecture of other neighbouring mining communities, partly because of its superior design and partly because Nicholson chose to use external dressings of Ombersley stone from the Bromsgrove quarries as a contrast to the drab Welsh Pennant sandstone. Thomas Nicholson, was an architect of some distinction, which is reflected in certain features of the church. The east window of three single lancets with cusped trefoil heads separated by two slender shafts springing from bell capitals with moulded bases is a particularly fine feature of the church. This cusping of the trefoil heads is depicted also in the outline of the north doorway. Because funds were restricted the architect did not build a chancel arch to distinguish the nave from the chancel. However, he made the distinction between them by making the trusses more ornate at this point. Furthermore, he distinguished the sanctuary and rest of the chancel by erecting a semicircular roof with moulded ribs divided into panels. The other part of the roof of the chancel and that of the nave was of a hammerbeam construction, an unusual type of roof for a church in the south Wales coalfield.

In 1911 the *Church Builder* announced that 'the population had doubled during the last ten years, and 250 more houses are being built. It is proposed to enlarge the church by the addition of one western bay to the nave and aisle providing 72 additional seats, making in all 465: all free, at an estimated cost of £735. £30 voted by ICBS.' (*Ch. Bldr* (1912), 18) Architect: Charles Henry Elford, Aberdare. (ICBS file no. 11091 (1911–12))

ST ANDREW'S CHURCH, PENRICE

1846: Restoration of chancel. Architect: John Prichard, Llandaff. Revd J. D. Davies wrote that 'some few years ago the chancel was restored from plans by John Pritchard [*sic*] of Llandaff'. (Revd J. D. Davies, *History of West Gower*, Vol. IV (Swansea, 1894), 58)

1893–4: Restoration of church by Frederick William Waller, diocesan architect, Gloucester. In 1893 dilapidated condition of church attracted attention of its patron, Miss Emily Talbot, of Penrice Castle, and she immediately set about restoring it. New roof of Memel timber replaced old oak roof which was in decayed condition. Nave reseated with open benches in place of old-fashioned panelled box pews. New wood-block floors of red deal laid down beneath seats in nave and chancel and set in asphalt; the remaining floors paved with Maw's tiles except those of porch and tower where some of old paving stones put down. New larger windows of Bath stone in the Perpendicular Gothic style inserted in nave. West gallery in nave removed, together with its external stone staircase. New oak choir stalls and prayer-desk erected in chancel. Whole of stonework of walls repointed and stonework of tower repaired, and renewed where necessary. Tower reroofed. New pulpit erected in nave and new font placed in baptistery in north transept. New oak door fitted from nave to porch. Windows reglazed with Cathedral glass. Contractor: Messrs Bevan & Gibbs, Horton. Cost £1,000, defrayed by Miss Emily Talbot. (GLRO: D2593/2/VK/S37. Penrice Church Restoration) Reopened after restoration on 24 July 1894. (*The Cambrian*, 27 July 1894)

Comments: Waller's restoration of St Andrew's was in fact a careful reparation of the fabric, which had been neglected over a long period of time. He inserted Perpendicular-style windows in the nave to replace modern ones of bad design which had been put in at an earlier period. During the course of the restoration the rood-loft opening was discovered blocked up with rubble, but instead of opening it out to view Waller chose to plaster it over. This was contrary to the practice carried out in other churches in Glamorgan. He was careful, however, to preserve the Jacobean cornice of the nave and chancel and

44. Saint Peter's Church, Pentre (Source: *The Builder*, 24 October 1891)

especially the Norman chancel arch. No structural alterations were carried out on the fabric of the church.

ST PETER'S CHURCH, PENTRE

1888–90: New church built on new site as chapel of ease to St John the Baptist's Church, Ystradyfodwg by Frederick R. Kempson of Birchyfield, Herefordshire. Built in Early English Gothic style consisting of chancel with transeptal aisles having upper floors in each for organ or auxiliary choir, and nave with arcade of five bays surmounted by clerestory. There are side aisles to nave, western tower and large south porch. On south side of chancel is a morning chapel. There are clergy and choir vestries and connecting passage between east wall of chancel gives direct access between clergy vestry and morning chapel. Bellcote over chancel arch. Free use made of constructional colour in a variety of different kinds of stone, brickwork, alabaster, marbles, mosaic and tiles. Composition of east end occupies whole of space from floor to roof. First 15ft taken up by reredos constructed in alabaster

132

combined with marbles, mosaic and sculpture. On either side of altar are wall arches elaborately moulded and carved and above these are figures in niches of the four great prophets and four evangelists. Above reredos is great triplet occupying width of chancel. Chancel floors paved with tiles and marble of rich colour and chancel fittings of oak. Pulpit in stone of different colours and font of richly coloured marble. Open benches of oak. Seating accommodation for 800 worshippers. Contractor: Thomas Collins, Tewkesbury. Cost £20,000. (*BN*, 1 August 1890) Cost defrayed by Griffith Llewellyn (d. 1888) and after his death by his widow, Mrs Madelina Llewellyn, Baglan Hall. Consecrated on 28 July 1890. (*W. Mail*, 29 July 1890)

Comments: Griffith Llewellyn's original intention was to provide the bare structure of the building, but unfortunately his sudden death in 1888 deprived him of seeing the project completed. His widow, Mrs Madelina Llewellyn, amended her husband's original plan of St Peter's, and when this fine building was finally completed at a cost of £20,000 in 1890 it had been lavishly decorated with marble and alabaster with mosaics, sculpture and stained glass such as had never been seen in the Rhondda. Appropriately it has been called the 'Cathedral of the Rhondda'. The predominant aspect of the church is the pink and buff poly-chromatic banding of the stonework inside, and on the dressed stone outside. John Newman calls the execution of the Early English style as 'surprisingly restrained'. (Newman, 510) Even if we ignore the style of the polychromy, which can be described as restrained, there are so many features of the church which are clearly of Early English character that Newman's description is rather inappropriate. The building of St Peter's marked Mrs Madelina Llewellyn's entry into the sphere of church extension in the Rhondda. From that time onward, until her death in 1903, she was a warm, loyal and generous benefactor of the Anglican Church in the diocese of Llandaff.

ST JAMES' CHURCH, PENTREBACH
(Demolished in 1980)

1900–1: New church built on new site for Welsh services by Penry Williams, Merthyr Tydfil. (*Bldr*, 13 April 1901, 374) For many years, need for more convenient place of worship felt by church people in Pentrebach district; until 1901 services conducted in school building of Upper Pentrebach. Decided that new church be provided in Lower Pentrebach in central position for both old district and fast increasing new district of Taibach and Dyffryn. Built in Early English Gothic style consisting of chancel, nave, aisle, western bellcote and south porch. Constructed of local Pennant sandstone with red brick dressings. Entire woodwork of pitch-pine. Internal arrangements plain and simple. Seating accommodation for 312 worshippers. Contractor: John Griffiths, Merthyr Tydfil. Cost £1,200. Sir W. T. Lewis, Bt £20. Dedicated on 22 March 1901. (*Merthyr Times*, 23 March 1901)

Comments: St James' was a cheap and simple structure built to accommodate the Welsh-speaking population of Pentrebach. It was built by the Anglican Church in the diocese of Llandaff to provide separate church accommodation for Welsh-speaking church people, who had long called for their own church building. It was plain structures such as this that helped the Anglican Church to combat the drift of church people to Welsh-speaking chapels.

ST CATTWG'S CHURCH, PENTYRCH

1857: Church rebuilt on site of old dilapidated structure in Decorated Gothic style with flowing tracery by John Prichard of Prichard & Seddon. New structure replaced former ancient church, which had for some years been in state of dilapidation and therefore quite inadequate for spiritual needs of parishioners in a rapidly expanding industrial district. Advantage taken of rapid fall of ground to east to obtain considerable height for eastern end, which faces road. Church consists of nave (50ftx26ft), with an octagonal turret (70ft high) at south-west corner of church, surmounted by a spire with open traceried belfry stage, south porch, chancel (25ftx15ft) with vestry adjoining. Constructed of Welsh Pennant sandstone with Combe Down Bath stone dressings. Building rises from bold spur base and buttressed at corners only by somewhat peculiar sloping buttresses set diagonally to walls. East window of three traceried lights and west window of four lights moulded and recessed with flowing tracery. Roofs all constructed of stained Memel timber and ceiling, which is panelled between rafters, tinted blue. Roofs covered with Bangor slates of purple and blue, arranged in bands of these colours. Whole of gables coped with freestone. Turret is octagonal in plan, with a buttress on four sides, terminating with a pediment beneath the belfry stage. The latter consists of a moulded two-light traceried window under a crocketed canopy, on each fall of the octagon forming a light open crown. From this springs a tapering spire, banded with alternately some with plain courses of masonry, and some with slightly projecting weathering. Interior of church, which seats 200 worshippers, fitted with open benches of stained Memel. Passages paved with red and black Staffordshire tiles. Chancel furnished with carved benches placed longitudinally as stalls. Step at chancel arch and two steps before altar rail which is of oak supported on illuminated wrought-iron standards, the latter and wrought-iron hinges of oak doors made by Messrs Skidmore of Coventry. Sill of easternmost window of chancel carried down to form sedilia. Caen stone font with pillars of Devonshire marble with wrought-iron cover. Pulpit also of Caen stone. (*Bldr*, 5 December 1857, 709) Contractor: Norman Brown, Cardiff. Cost £1,339. ICBS grant £80; LDCES grant £100; LCBS grant £50; church rate £709 8s 7d; W. T. Booker Blakemore £500. Consecrated on 26 November 1857. (*CMG*, 28 November 1857)

1901: Completion of church. Work of carving corbels and other minor works, not completed in 1857, carried out. Architect: Edward Henry Bruton, Cardiff. Contractor: William Clarke, Llandaff. Cost £90. (LL/F/651. Completion of church. Faculty dated 5 November 1901)

Comments: At St Cattwg's, John Prichard seems to have embraced the Decorated period with rather more enthusiasm than usual, particularly in the four-light west window with its rich flowing tracery, where he placed his personal stamp on the ornamentation. Prichard's design of the windows of the church demonstrates his desire to deviate from the strict Geometrical style. It was in this spirit of restrained freedom that the design of the turret at the south-west corner of the church was conceived. The turret with its spire, rising to a height of 70ft from the ground, is the outstanding feature of the church and contributed to Prichard's growing reputation as the leading church architect in south-east Wales. Inside the church, all the internal arrangements and fittings are consistent with the principles of the Ecclesiological Society, including the Middle Pointed style of the church itself.

ST JOHN'S CHURCH, PENYDARREN

1858: New church built on new site to serve rapidly growing population of Penydarren by Edward Brigden of Dowlais. Built in Early English Gothic style consisting of nave and western bellcote. Constructed of grey Pennant sandstone in random courses of rubblework with Bath stone dressings. Plain building almost devoid of ornament. West gable surmounted by bellcote rising 16ft from ridge of roof and 60ft from ground. Three-stage corner buttresses support west wall. Roof is reddish slate, which contrasts well with grey stonework. Externally, length of church is 91ft, width 32ft and height to ridge of roof 44ft. Nave lighted by four windows with dressed stonework with two at each end, one surmounted by a quatrefoil, the other of more elaborate Geometrical tracery. Interior is open from end to end and pulpit and lectern, which in other churches interrupt view of chancel, are here placed at sides – pulpit on north side and lectern on south side. Timber roof is open to ridge and principal rafters supported on Bath stone corbels. Small organ gallery at west end of nave is only other feature of note. Seating accommodation for 300 worshippers provided on open benches of pitch-pine. Contractor: John Gabe, Merthyr Tydfil. Cost £900. LDCES grant £100. (*Bldr*, 29 May 1858, 379) Opened for divine service on 20 May 1858. (*CMG*, 22 May 1858) Consecrated on 16 November 1870. (*CMG*, 19 November 1870)

1900: Iron tie bars inserted about this time to cope with walls of nave which were some twelve inches out of perpendicular. Massive buttresses of solid stonework built to support south side of nave. Reason for this defect was due entirely to improperly framed principals of roof. (Joseph Gross, 'St John's Church, Penydarren', *Merthyr Historian* 3 (1980), 23–32)

Comments: Edward Brigden submitted two designs for the church, the one simple, the other ornate. Preference was of course given to the simpler structure. This plain building was typical of church accommodation at that time in industrial areas of the diocese of Llandaff. Lack of funds was the main reason for building a simple nave only, as was the case in other Glamorgan churches during that period. It was only in the Edwardian period that a chancel was eventually added.

In 1904 plans were made to demolish the nave and build a new parish church, but lack of funding again thwarted this intention. Instead the nave was retained and the church was enlarged by the addition of chancel, south chapel, vestries and organ chamber. Architect: E. M. Bruce Vaughan. Contractor: Messrs Gough Bros, Cardiff. Cost £2,200. Dedicated on 6 October 1908. (LL/F/656. Enlargement of church. Faculty dated 4 January 1908)

ST PETER'S CHURCH, PETERSTON-SUPER-ELY

1860: Rearrangement of seating to provide additional accommodation for sixty-four worshippers. Restoration of roof and window mullions. Removal of whitewash. Architect: David Vaughan, Bonvilston. Cost £420. ICBS grant £50. (ICBS file no. 5670 (1860))

1870: Construction of family vault for Edward Turberville Llewellin and his wife in chancel floor. (LL/F/659. Construction of vault. Faculty dated 13 May 1870)

45. St Peter's Church, Peterston-super-Ely (Photo: W. P. Pring, L.R.P.S) (By kind permission of D. Brown & Sons Ltd, Cowbridge)

1891: Restoration of church by Kempson & Fowler, Llandaff. (*BN*, 7 November 1890, 669) Work included raising east window and insertion of two-light window in south wall of chancel; new oak choir stalls and altar, fine oak chancel screen and pulpit, all carved by William Clarke. Mosaic floor laid down in chancel and west door of nave renewed. Tower refaced, new buttresses put in and new parapet constructed. Bells recast and rehung by Taylors of Loughborough. New heating apparatus installed. Font moved to traditional position near south door. Contractor: William Morgan, Canton, Cardiff. Cost £1,400. Charles Aubrey Aubrey £200; Revd J. Owen Evans £100; Col. A. R. M. Lockwood £50. (LL/F/660. Repair and restoration of church. Faculty dated 5 February 1891) Reopened after restoration on 23 July 1891. (*W. Mail*, 24 July 1891)

1893: Two-manual organ, built by Alexander Young & Sons Manchester, installed in memory of Robert Francis Langley (d. 1892). (*MCVG*, 308)

Comments: The work carried out on St Peter's in 1860, and churchwardenized repairs in the following years, were insufficient to arrest the decay of the whole structure of the church, so that by 1891 the tower and chancel had begun to show signs of age and the elements. When Revd John Owen Evans was appointed to the living in 1890, he undertook immediately the task of obtaining the necessary funds to restore the church. Although

Kempson & Fowler's restoration was a thorough affair involving a large sum of money for a village church to find, it was, in fact, simply a reparation of the ruined portions of the tower and complete refurbishment of the chancel. However, the architects were careful to preserve the essential character of the church by faithfully replicating the Perpendicular Gothic style of the building when they inserted a new window in the south side of the chancel.

ALL SAINTS' CHURCH, PONTARDAWE

1885–6: New church built on new site presented by Herbert Lloyd, Plas Cilybebyll. (*The Cambrian*, 28 August 1885) Erected as private chapel and as memorial to William Gilbertson, Pontardawe by his son Arthur Gilbertson, Glanrhyd, Pontardawe. Plans prepared by Arthur Gilbertson. (*Bldr*, 5 September 1885, 340) Built in Early English Gothic

style consisting of chancel, nave, west porch and belfry over organ chamber. Constructed of hammer-dressed Welsh sandstone with Bath stone dressings. Owing to difficulty of site All Saints' was built in north-east direction instead of usual east to west. Reredos against east wall of chancel is of Caen stone and richly carved with five Gothic arches of pink Penarth alabaster carried on Irish green marble columns. White marble figures of Christ and his Four Evangelists seated under canopies of arches. Chancel rails are brass and beautifully ornamented. Group of five lancet windows lights chancel while north wall of nave pierced by Rose window. Roof over sanctuary is barrel-shaped while that of nave is of fine hammer-beam construction. Chancel divided from nave by low stone screen decorated with trefoil arches. Pulpit of Caen stone, admirably carved, and all interior woodwork in pitch-pine. Three-manual organ installed, built by V. G. Vowles of Bristol. Seating accommodation for 300 worshippers. (J. H. Davies, *A History of Pontardawe from Earliest to Modern Times* (Llandybïe, 1968),

46. All Saints' Church, Pontardawe (Photo: Geoffrey R. Orrin)

138–9) Contractor: John Griffiths, Pontardawe. Cost £2,440. Opened for worship on 2 September 1886. (*W. Mail*, 3 September 1886)

Comments: All Saints' is exquisitely appointed. The outstanding feature of the lavish chancel is the reredos of Caen stone richly carved by William Clarke. This was another instance where the private benefaction of the Glamorgan gentry furthered the cause of church extension in the county by building well-appointed churches at their own expense. Built as a private chapel, its consecration took place when the trustees transferred it to the Representative Body of the Church in Wales. All Saints', when officially opened in September 1886, was in the parish of St John's Clydach, but on 25 June 1903, the parish of Llangiwg annexed it.

ST PETER'S CHURCH, PONTARDAWE

1858–62: New church built on new site given by J. E. Lloyd, Plas Cilybebyll. Before Industrial Revolution, parish church of Llangiwg was positioned centrally, but with development of iron works and subsequent rapid increase in population concentrated at Pontardawe it became necessary to build new church in more convenient place. Foundation stone laid on 13 May 1858. (*The Cambrian*, 21 May 1858) Built in Decorated Gothic style by John Henry Baylis of Swansea, consisting of chancel, nave with north and south aisles and clerestory, and western tower with spire. Constructed of Pennant sandstone with Bath stone dressings, but main quoins of building and whole of spire built of Portland stone brought up Swansea canal in barges. Length of church, clear of walls internally, 111ft and width of nave and side aisles together 54ft. Height of nave from pavement to tie-beams of roof 35ft and to top of roof (which is open timber structure of pitch-pine, stained and varnished) 54ft. Width of chancel 22ft and height 28ft. Height of tower and spire, from base to top of fleur-de-lis crowning spire 192ft. Chancel roof is barrel-shaped. Organ loft screen, pulpit, reading desk and font of Caen stone elaborately carved in high relief. Nave divided from side aisles by six pointed arches springing from clustered columns

whose capitals are carved with imitation natural foliage. Open benches of pitch-pine, stained and varnished. Seating accommodation for 730 worshippers. Contractor: Joseph Holtham, Bath. Cost £5,347. William Parsons, Ynysdrew House, Pontardawe paid entire cost of church. (*Bldr*, 9 August 1862, 572) Completed in July 1860. (*The Cambrian*, 13 July 1860) Consecrated on 31 July 1862. (*The Cambrian*, 1 August 1862)

1894: Chancel improved by Arthur Gilbertson in memory of his parents, William and Eliza Gilbertson. Chancel raised and new floor laid with polished Belgian marble, reredos of Caen stone erected, and new choir stalls and altar installed. Architects: Wilson & Moxham, Swansea. Contractor: William Dodd. Cost £250. (*The Cambrian*, 20 July 1894)

Comments: The Swansea architect, John Henry Baylis, whose sympathies were clearly with the purest style of Gothic architecture according to Pugin, built the church in the Decorated style. The tower, with its ornate Decorated Gothic-style buttresses, is the main feature of the church. The five-sided buttresses beautifully worked in stages, carrying their own strings, as well as those which encompass and connect them to each stage of the tower, have gabled canopied niches. These protrude from the surfaces of the buttresses. Parsons's inspired purpose was to build the church higher than the stacks of industry, which he achieved, for the tower rises to a height of 192ft. The interior of the church is lavishly appointed. The fact that so much of the sculptured work was carved in Caen stone imported from Normandy indicates that the work of the interior of the church was done on an unusual scale for a Swansea Valley church. The interior of the church shows particularly the sumptuous refinement of the work of a nineteenth-century Decorated Gothic-style church, built with no regard to expense. Overall the impression we have in this church is what one would expect to find in a large city, not a church in the parish of Llangiwg.

In 1907 a marble font in the form of a kneeling angel holding a shell, a copy of Thorvaldsen's font in the Church of Our Lady, Copenhagen, was erected in memory of Sarah Griffiths (d. 1899), wife of Revd James Griffiths, vicar of Llangiwg (1881–92). (*The Cambrian*, 26 July 1907)

47. Photograph of construction of the west window of St Michael's and All Angels' Church, Pontardulais, c.1900 (By kind permission of the Vicar and Churchwardens of St Michael and All Angels' Church, Pontardulais)

ST MICHAEL'S AND ALL ANGELS' CHURCH, PONTARDULAIS

1900–1: New church built on new site donated by Joseph Edward Moore-Gwyn of Dyffryn. (*CDL*, 12 July 1901) The correspondent in the *Church Builder* reported that 'this is a large bilingual parish, with a population of upwards of 6,000 souls, and rapidly increasing, and consisting of exclusively wage-earning class. There are no landed proprietors or resident gentry in the parish. This permanent new church, which is in course of erection, will meet a long-felt want of having the means of Grace administered in English and Welsh in decent buildings. At present we hold Welsh and English services alternately in the parish church . . . The people are very eager for their new church and are subscribing liberally and cheerfully, so much per month in aid of the Building Fund.' (*Ch. Bldr* (1900), 116) Built in Perpendicular Gothic style by E. M. Bruce Vaughan. (ICBS file no. 10,218 (1900)) Cruciform in plan consisting of chancel with vestry and organ chamber in transepts, nave, south porch and bellcote. Constructed of grey Pennant sandstone and window and door dressings as well as copings to gable all executed in Box Ground stone. Double bellcote, surmounting the chancel arch, chiefly of Box Ground stone. Nave

walls on north and south side strengthened by two-stage buttresses. Roof of chancel wagon-shaped but nave roof of open timber construction with arched braces, all of pitch-pine. Open benches of pitch-pine. Seating accommodation for 302 parishioners. Nave and organ chamber and vestry walls pierced with two-light traceried windows, west wall of nave with a five-light and east wall of chancel with a three-light window. (*Bldr*, 27 July 1901, 85) Contractor: Messrs John Thomas & Sons, Pontardulais. Cost £2,600. ICBS grant £110. Consecrated on 11 July 1901. (*W. Mail*, 12 July 1901)

Comments: Bruce Vaughan built the church using cheap materials such as the local Pennant sandstone and Box Ground Bath stone together with the ubiquitous pitch-pine, as was his normal practice. However, he indulged himself by designing a church in the Perpendicular Gothic style instead of his usual Early English or 'lancet' style. This made a considerable difference to the visual appearance of the church, as demonstrated by his fine five-light cinquefoiled west window with intricate shapes such as rectilinear and dagger tracery in the head. In the late Victorian period, Perpendicular Gothic architecture had become an accepted and fashionable idiom for churches. Bruce Vaughan had previously confined his church building activities in Glamorgan to the diocese of Llandaff and this was a rare appearance in this part of Glamorgan.

ST TEILO'S CHURCH, PONTARDULAIS

1850–1: New church built on new site given by Howel Gwyn of Dyffryn, Neath, patron of living. Built to replace medieval parish church of St Teilo, Llandeilo Tal-y-bont situated on the edge of the River Loughor and surrounded by marshes which were impassable in times of flood or high tides. Its accommodation was inadequate for population of parish, which had increased to 1,408 by 1850. Foundation stone laid on 29 August 1850 by Howel Gwyn. (*The Cambrian*, 6 September 1850) Built in Early English Gothic style by William Richards of Swansea. (ICBS file no. 4300 (1850)) It consists of chancel, nave, west gallery and western tower with spire. Principal entrance to church is through west end of tower, the lower part of which forms a porch. Constructed of Welsh Pennant sandstone with Bath stone dressings and roof covered with Caernarfon slates. East window of three trefoiled lights with plate tracery in head. Nave lighted on its north and south sides by five lancet windows between slender buttresses. Both east and west walls of church supported by corner buttresses. Low plaster ceiling covers timbers of nave roof. West gallery supported on stone pillars with bell-shaped capitals. Three-stage west tower with full width set-offs to each stage of tower and stone broach spire. Clasping buttresses to angles of lower stage of tower. Seating accommodation for 340 parishioners. Cost £988. ICBS grant £180. Consecrated on 30 October 1851. (*The Cambrian*, 31 October 1851)
1879: Restoration and reseating of church. Cost £550. (*Kelly's Directory of South Wales*, 1926, 793)

Comments: William Richards had originally designed a west porch, but the Committee of Architects of the ICBS objected and it was removed from the design. However, the architect neglected to send the amended plans to the Society, so that Richard Kyrke Penson, in his capacity of 'honorary' diocesan architect, was asked to inspect the church on the Society's behalf. Penson reported that the architect had complied with its instructions and recommended the award of a grant, which was accordingly made in November 1851. The only redeeming feature of an otherwise austere church with short chancel and plain nave is the three-stage tower with clasping buttresses to the corners of the lower stage only. The full-width sets-offs to each stage are unusual and there is a short broach spire. As John Newman says 'only the three-stage tower, with strong set-offs and stone broach spire acknowledges the new ideas in church design'. (Newman, 517)

ST TYFAELOG'S CHURCH, PONTLOTTYN

1863: New church built on new site given by William Williams, Maesrhudid. Prior to erection of new church, inhabitants of village of Pontlottyn, some seven miles distant from parish church at Gelligaer, had worshipped for previous three years in a stable loft, rented at a cost of ten shillings a month. (*Ch. Bldr* (1864), 77) Foundation stone laid on 27 April 1863 by Mrs Clark of Dowlais House. (*CMG*, 1 May 1863) Built in Early English Gothic style by Charles Buckeridge of Oxford consisting of nave (56ftx20ft), north and south aisles (8ft wide), apsidal chancel (26ft 6insx18ft), south chancel aisle, vestry on north side of chancel with heating chamber beneath and western porch. (ICBS file no. 6025 (1862)) Bellcote over chancel arch. Constructed of local sandstone with red brick quoins and windows, with bands of red brick at intervals. Internally, nave arcades consist of three wide arches on each side of red and white bricks resting on Bridgend stone cylindrical shafts with Bath stone caps and bases; chancel and other arches being treated in similar way. Chancel lined with red and white bricks and floor laid with encaustic tiles. Owing to peculiarity of site, chancel is of great height externally as ground falls 7ft from west to east so that sill of east window is 20ft above ground. Chancel raised on steps. Another rise of a single step reaches sanctuary level, on which again stands footpace of two steps. Chancel provided with choir stalls, sedilia, credence table and altar rails, and altar and superaltar 8ft long on a footpace. Beside font is baptistery provided for immersion of adults. It is approached by steps and floored with Godwin's tiles. Circular pulpit of Bath stone with open arcade of green Bridgend stone shafts. Roofs of stained and varnished deal and covered with local stone tiles. Roof of nave is of four bays, whose principals rest on stone corbels. Chancel roof is coved and boarded and aisle roofs are lean-tos. Open benches of deal. Seating accommodation for 350 parishioners. Contractors: Messrs James & Price, Cardiff. Cost £2,252. ICBS grant £350. (*Bldr*, 9 May 1863, 337) Consecrated on 11 November 1863. (*CMG*, 13 November 1863)

Comments: Andrew Saint, professor of architecture at Cambridge University, said of the church when writing about Charles Buckeridge in 1973, 'Better in, than out.' (Andrew Saint, 'Charles Buckeridge and his family', *Oxoniensia*, 38 (1973), 371) Obviously Saint meant that the standard of polychromatic design inside the church was superior to that without. The interior of the church has nave arcades of three wide arches, constructed of red and white brickwork, resting on Bridgend stone cylindrical shafts with Bath stone caps and bases. The chancel arches are similarly treated. The whole of the polychromatic construction of the interior derives its effectiveness from its initial impact as one enters the church. On the other hand, one might argue that the choice of building materials and the way they are used gives the exterior a subtle charm and cohesion which suggest promise and is much preferred to the polychromatic explosion within which is overt. The correspondent in *The Ecclesiologist* reported that 'It is a good design altogether. The level of the ground slopes rapidly from the west to the east; accordingly, the east end has much external dignity.' (*Eccl.*, 24 (1863), 190)

ST PAUL'S CHURCH, PONTYCLUN

1894–5: New church built on new site as chapel of ease to Llantrisant Parish Church. The correspondent in the *Church Builder* reported that 'The parish of Llantrisant is a very extensive one . . . The need for increased church accommodation is urgently felt for the rapidly growing wants of the parish, which measures twelve miles by four along the nearest roads. In the district where the proposed new church will be built, services have for some time been held in a school-room which is overcrowded, besides being uncomfortable and

48. St Paul's Church, Pontyclun (Source: Geoffrey R. Orrin: Postcard Collection of Glamorgan Churches)

unsuitable for divine service.' (*Ch. Bldr* (1894), 165) Foundation stone laid by Miss Masters of Lanelay on 15 August 1894. Built in Perpendicular Gothic style by E. M. Bruce Vaughan, consisting of chancel, nave, vestry, south porch and bellcote over chancel arch containing two bells. (ICBS file no. 9787 (1894)) Constructed of local grey Pennant sandstone with Bath stone dressings and roof of green slate with red tile ridges. Nave has arch-braced roof of unvarnished pine, but chancel roof is boarded and formed into panels by moulded fillets. All windows traceried and nave walls supported by slender two-stage buttresses. Open benches of pitch-pine. Seating accommodation for 306 worshippers. Contractor: John Morgan, Llantrisant. Cost £1,500. ICBS grant £70, but lapsed in 1909 as church was not consecrated. (*Bldr*, 13 July 1895, 35) Opened and licensed for divine worship on 27 June 1895. (*W. Mail*, 28 June 1895)

Comments: Although limited by a budget of £1,500, E. M. Bruce Vaughan was able to design a church in the Perpendicular style which was infinitely superior to the majority of his churches built in the south Wales coalfield area in his accustomed Early English or 'lancet' style. The bellcote, above the chancel arch, is a fine feature with its gabled, moulded buttresses and finely moulded bell openings executed in a fifteenth-century Gothic style.

ST THEODORE'S CHURCH, PONTYCYMMER

(Demolished 1979)

1893: New church intended for Welsh services built on new site given by J. Blandy Jenkins, Llanharan. Foundation stone laid on 11 February 1893 by Miss Fletcher, niece of Miss Emily Talbot of Margam Abbey. (*W. Mail*, 13 February 1893) Built in Decorated Gothic style by Bruton & Williams, Cardiff, consisting of only nave (70ftx24ft) and western bellcote. (*BN*, 17 February 1893, 255) Chancel and south aisle never built. Constructed of Welsh Pennant sandstone with Bath stone dressings. Seating accommodation for

250. Contractor: Messrs Hatherley and Carr, Bristol. Cost £2,500. LDCES grant £50; Bishop of Llandaff's Fund £300; Miss Emily Talbot and Miss Olive Talbot also made substantial donations to building fund. (*Bldr*, 9 September 1893, 195) Opened on 4 September 1893. (*W. Mail*, 5 September 1893)

Comments: The architects, Bruton & Williams of Queen Street, Cardiff, who had already built St James' Church, Blaengarw and St Mary's Church, Pont-y-Rhyl, earlier in the decade, were commissioned to build St Theodore's in Pontycymmer. However, their design for the new church was rather ambitious, particularly for a church in a small mining community. It included a chancel with organ chamber and vestries, nave with clerestory, south aisle and western bellcote. Furthermore, instead of designing the church in the less expensive Early English or 'lancet' style, as they had done in their other churches, they decided to build the church in the more expensive Decorated Gothic style. As a result of their over-ambitious design, the chancel and south aisle were never built and the church consisted simply of a nave. The estimated cost of £3,250 proved too much for a small mining community to raise.

ST MARY MAGDALENE'S CHURCH, PONTYGWAITH

1894–6: New church built on new site at Penrhys Isaf donated by Mrs Madelina G. Llewellyn. Foundation stone laid in 1894 by Mrs Llewellyn. Built in Early English Gothic style by George E. Halliday, consisting of chancel with vestry on north side, bellcote with double openings with hood moulding, moulded caps and well-proportioned shafts above chancel arch, and nave. Constructed of rock-faced blue Pennant sandstone overall, inside as well as outside, with Doulting stone dressings. Roof covered with Belgian green slates. East window of three grouped lancets with roll mouldings, and lancet windows of sanctuary also lavishly provided with roll mouldings or shafted. Sanctuary arch spans whole width of chancel. Chancel arch flanked by low, acutely pointed passage arches. Chancel has boarded wagon roof. Nave lighted by elongated lancets with hood moulds between typical external Early English-style buttresses and at west end by a pair of two-light windows and quatrefoil, a typical Victorian device, in west gable. Nave roof has curved brace arrangement. Pulpit an font of green Bridgend stone. Church accommodates 370 worshippers on open benches. Contractors: Messrs Knox & Wells, Cardiff. Cost £4,000. Building erected at entire expense of Mrs Madelina G. Llewellyn. (*Cardiff Times*, 11 July 1896) Consecrated on 6 July 1896. (*W. Mail*, 7 July 1896)

Comments: Mrs Madelina G. Llewellyn, the principal benefactress of church extension in the Rhondda in the late Victorian period, chose George E. Halliday, the diocesan surveyor, to build her church at Pontygwaith in 1896. The east window of three grouped lancets with roll mouldings and the tall lancet windows of the sanctuary are lavishly shafted. Undoubtedly, these are the finest windows in the church. Halliday was remarkably sympathetic in his design of the window dressings, doorways, and archways, which he treated in exactly the same way throughout the church. Plain chamfers, incised mouldings, and no overt decoration to detract from the overall effect of an integrated design. All the arches die into the walls without the use of stone corbels. The bellcote over the chancel arch is well designed and executed with its double opening with hood moulding, moulded caps and bases and well-proportioned shafts and Early English-style buttresses for good effect. However, the outstanding feature of Halliday's design is the full-width sanctuary arch, which is a rare feature in any church, and all the more so in a church built in a small mining community. It is obviously a decorative feature to enhance and emphasize the sanctity of the sanctuary, where the ceremony of the Holy Eucharist was celebrated. It is indicative of the Tractarian sympathies of both Halliday and Mrs Llewellyn.

ST CATHERINE'S CHURCH, PONTYPRIDD

49 St Catherine's Church, Pontypridd (Source: Geoffrey R. Orrin: Postcard Collection of Glamorgan Churches)

1866–9: New church built on new site given by Thomas family of Ystrad Mynach. Foundation stone laid on 13 November 1866 by Miss Clara Thomas of Llwynmadoc. (*Cardiff Times*, 16 November 1866) Built in Decorated Gothic style by John Norton consising of chancel (35ftx22ft and 43ft high), nave (71ft 6insx24ft 9ins and 53ft high to ridge), south aisle, vestry and tower with spire. Constructed of Newbridge sandstone with Bath stone dressings and lined internally with red brick banded in patterns of blue. Floors laid with plain and ornamental encaustic tiles. Nave separated from south aisle by arcade of five bays supported by circular columns over which is clerestory of circular windows with Geometrical plate tracery. In west wall is a lofty four-light traceried window and underneath is western doorway, richly moulded with banded shafts, carved caps and moulded bases. Aisles lighted with single and double light windows with circles in heads. Chancel opens from nave by lofty arch of brick and stone in consecutive rims, sub-arch supported by coupled dwarf columns and space over arch richly diapered with cross enclosed in circle and other devices, the alpha and omega occupying spandrels. (*BN*, 14 December 1866, 841) East window of three traceried lights. Tower projects from south aisle, of four stages and 76ft high, with spire 160ft to vane. Nave and chancel roofs of open timber stained in imitation of oak. Open benches of pitch-pine, stained and varnished. Seating accommodation for 400 worshippers. Contractor: William Morgan, Pontypridd. Cost £4,800. LDCES grant £100. (*Bldr*, 29 December 1868, 963) Opened for divine service on 7 September 1869. (*W. Mail*, 8 September 1869)

1883–4: New north aisle built and church roof repaired. Foundation stone of north aisle laid on 9 July by Miss Clara Thomas. Additional seating accommodation for 120 worshippers. Cost £1,600. Architect: Peter Price, Cardiff. Contractor: W. Seaton. (*W. Mail*, 20 July 1883) New north aisle consecrated on 8 March 1884. (*Pontypridd Chr.*, 15 March 1884)

1890: Spire of church underwent extensive restoration. Framework and wallplates at the bottom which had perished were reinstated, all slates removed and whole spire newly slated. Four new stone gables constructed on lower part of spire, in which clock was placed. Architects: Kempson & Fowler, Llandaff. Contractor: Messrs William Thomas & Co., West Bute Docks, Cardiff. Cost £650. (*Bldr*, 12 July 1890, 33)

Comments: The tower of St Catherine's is the dominant feature of the church. With its elegant proportions, it is virtually a detached tower with spire of which there are very few and it is obviously a porch tower of which there are not many. The niche above the doorway is occupied with the figure of the patron saint, and as such is quite noteworthy since most other Victorian attempts at interpreting the Decorated period in Glamorgan stopped short of actually providing figures for the niches they created, as was the case at St Peter's, Pontardawe. The three-stage buttresses with their shallow set-offs are exceptionally elegant, and the architectural features of the top stage of the tower are particularly well crafted. The detailed arch ordering to the belfry, with pointed arches as acute

as those in the doorway below, shows considerable attention to detail. Norton has accentuated this feature by adding the little corbel table and giving the belfry lights a masonry frame. Inside the church there is strident constructional polychromy as at his church at Neath. The nave has a number of symbols of Christianity, a cross crosslet, a saltirewise cross, whereas opposite these are the Greek Cross with splayed ends next to a Trinity star or Star of David. These devices are repeated around the nave. The nave arcade, with its alternating round and square capitals with heavily cut stiff-leaf foliage, is indicative of French Gothic influence. The chancel arch, with its cut brick outer orders to the arches and incised patterns, is obviously influenced by Street's Church of St James the Less, Westminster. The chancel, which was similarly treated by Norton with strident constructional polychromy, 'was drastically toned down' by Sir Giles Gilbert Scott in 1919. (Newman, 521)

ST MARY'S CHURCH, PONT-Y-RHYL

(Made redundant in 1986, now in ruins)

1891–2: New church built on new site as chapel of ease to parish church of St David's, Bettws. The *Church Builder* announced that 'Pontyrhyl in the Garw Valley is a very important place now. The population is 2,000. There are four large collieries and at present the church accommodation is inadequate.' (*Ch. Bldr* (1890), 71) Site for new church conveyed to Ecclesiastical Commissioners on 31 December 1890. Foundation stone laid on 11 May 1891 by Miss Emily Talbot of Margam Park. (*BN*, 22 May 1891, 727) Built in Early English Gothic style by Bruton & Williams, Cardiff. (ICBS file no. 9438 (1890)) Lancet-shaped windows filled with square leaded lights and Cathedral glass. Constructed of local Pennant sandstone with dressings of Doulting stone supplied ready for fixing by Messrs Charles Trask & Sons of Shepton Mallet. Pulpit and font also of Doulting stone. Building consists of nave (51ftx27ft) and chancel (17ftx13ft) both under one roof but divided internally by arched-open timber screen which was continued on north and south sides of chancel behind choir stalls, forming a vestry and organ chamber. Above Communion rail was lofty stone arch, dividing chancel from sanctuary which is 13ft wide by 9ft 6ins deep containing altar table on raised stone floor. Sanctuary floor and that of chancel tiled as was that of passage in centre of nave, with floors of vestry and organ chamber of woodblocks. Whole of church warmed by hot air on Porritt's system. Open benches of pitch-pine. Seating accommodation for 260 worshippers. Contractor: John Hall, Cardiff. Cost £1,200. ICBS grant £35; LDCES grant £50; Bishop of Llandaff's Fund £300. (*Bldr*, 23 May 1891, 417) Consecrated on 13 June 1892. (*W. Mail*, 14 June 1892)

Comments: Bruton & Williams designed St Mary's, which was intended for a poor mining community, in the less expensive Early English style. It was rather a simple structure consisting of nave and chancel under one continuous roof, but divided internally by an arched timber screen which was continued on the north and south sides of the chancel, forming an organ chamber on the north side and a vestry on the south. Above the communion rail was a lofty stone arch dividing the chancel from sanctuary – a rare feature in a Glamorgan church, particularly so here, in a mining community.

ST THEODORE'S CHURCH, PORT TALBOT

1895–7: New church built on new site for services in English. Phenomenal growth of Port Talbot during 1880s and envisaged increase in population due to future development of new docks and railway company made building new church an absolute necessity. Margam chapel of ease (now known as Holy Cross), built in Taibach in 1827 and accommodating 500 parishioners, overcrowded and uncomfortable. When approached by vicar of Margam, Revd Z. P. Williamson about new church, Miss Emily Talbot agreed to build St Theodore's Church as a memorial to her brother Theodore (d. 1876) and her sister Olive (d. 1894). Built near small

mission church erected in 1887, which together with Margam chapel of ease served the church people until 1897. Decided to use chapel of ease for Welsh services and a mortuary chapel. (*The Cambrian*, 6 August 1897) Built in Early English Gothic style by John Loughborough Pearson of London, consisting of nave, chancel, morning chapel, north and south aisles, transepts, north and south porches, vestries and organ chamber, and small bell turret. Building measures 147ft in length, 76ft in width and 60ft in height. Constructed of local Pennant sandstone from nearby Constantinople Quarry. Dressings of Bath stone and interior lined throughout with the same stone. Nave roof is an open one of oak and rest of ceilings are beautifully groined. Chancel arch is a lofty span placed over flight of four steps. Gangways tiled with common black and red tiles, and chancel and morning chapel laid with rich encaustic tiles. Floor beneath seats laid with wood blocks. Nave, which was built in three stages – arcade, triforium and clerestory – seated with teak benches, and chancel stalls are also of teak, richly carved. Remainder of church seated with chairs. Seating accommodation for approximately 1,000 worshippers. Sanctuary approached by one step and altar, built of teak and marble, by three. East and west windows are triplets of large dimensions and clerestory windows are couplets. Pulpit of Portland stone with Purbeck marble shafting. Shafting of chancel also in Purbeck marble. Massive brass eagle lectern by Potter of London. Church heated on the Perkin's high-pressure system. Contractor: Messrs Shillitoe & Sons, Bury St Edmunds. Cost £25,000, borne entirely by Miss Emily Talbot. Consecrated on 5 August 1897. (*W. Mail*, 6 August 1897)

Comments: John Loughborough Pearson had built several churches in Wales, including the recently erected church of St Matthias at Treharris in the parish of Merthyr Tydfil. He designed St Theodore's in the Early English style, a style which he used consistently and with great effect throughout his later period. The main body of the church was built in three stages: nave with its acutely pointed arches, triforium with its blind arcading and plate tracery and clerestory with its two-light windows. The roof of the nave is a fine structure of oak with its tie-beams and arch-braced collars, supporting crown posts and secondary collars. The pillars of the nave are typically Early English with detached shafts. Apart from the nave and transepts, the ceilings of the church have quadripartite rib-vaults. The Early English style detail and ornament consist almost entirely of fine mouldings. In designing St Theodore's, Pearson was greatly influenced by his work at Truro Cathedral, and the beauty of his architectural design increases as one passes from the nave into the chancel and from there into the sanctuary. In place of the proposed tower, which was never built, Pearson placed a Breton-style bell turret over the chancel arch to provide a Celtic touch to his magnificent church.

ST CATTWG'S CHURCH, PORTEYNON

1861: Restoration of church. West gallery in nave completely removed and west end enlarged to accommodate growing population of parish. Prior to restoration chancel arch was obtuse and ill-shaped. Minute, signed by Revd William Melland (rector of Porteynon, 1867–1901) and written in Porteynon Church vestry book, records that 'Porteynon was restored and enlarged at the west end in the year 1861, chiefly at the expense of Christopher Rice Talbot, Esq. M.P.' Statement confirmed by Colonel C. D. Morgan, who wrote in 1886 'that the church . . . is of modern date, having recently undergone a thorough renovation. The old structure was mostly pulled down and the fabric enlarged to suit the growing population of the neighbourhood. C. R. M. Talbot, Esq., M.P. with his characteristic liberality laid out his hundreds with a willing hand. If I err not, the total cost was defrayed by that gentleman with little exception. The church is now an interesting structure, but nothing remains, with the exception of the Norman archway at the entrance and the font in the porch.' (C. D. Morgan, *Wanderings in Gower* (Swansea, 1886), 35)
1868: Roof of nave and chancel boarded up owing to plaster falling down, rafters being too wide apart. (Geoffrey R. Orrin, *The Gower Churches* (Penmaen, 1979), 74)

1901: Restoration of church. Stone entrance replaced by one of cement and church partially refloored. New carved oak altar designed by Jones & Willis, Birmingham, presented by Miss Emily Talbot. Reopened after restoration on 25 July 1901. (*GCM*, July 1901, 9)

Comments: No architect is recorded for the restoration of the church in 1861, but it is possible that it was carried out by Richard Kyrke Penson, who restored several churches in Gower. Although the Norman south doorway was retained in its original form, the chancel arch described by Sir Stephen Glynne in 1848 'as very low, rude, obtuse and ill-shaped springing from imposts with a considerable space of wall', was altered to a plain pointed arch in keeping with the architectural practice of the period. (Sir Stephen R. Glynne, 'Notes on the older churches in the four Welsh dioceses', *Arch. Camb.* (1897), 295)

The restoration of St Cattwg's in 1861 revealed the destructive nature of some of the Victorian restorers, who failed to preserve ancient features of the medieval church but who were determined to provide more accommodation by enlarging the church without due respect to the ancient fabric of the building. The restoration, carried out in 1901 by parishioners and friends of Revd William Melland, was 'to perpetuate the deep and lasting affection cherished by them for their dear departed minister', a sentiment inscribed on a memorial plate in the church.

ST PAUL'S CHURCH, PENRHIWGWYNT, PORTH

1886–7: New church built on new site given by trustees of estate of late Major A. Vaughan Lee. The correspondent in the *Church Builder* reported that 'Porth is a rapidly growing centre of mineral and railway traffic. The nearest church is two miles and a half distant. The feeling in favour of the Church is strong and earnest. It is almost a certainty that the proposed new church will be at once filled with a zealous and grateful congregation. The bulk of the inhabitants are miners. There are eight Non-conformist chapels in the town.' (*Ch. Bldr* (1886),

64) Foundation stone laid on 5 August 1886 by Miss Davies, Glynrhondda House. (*Pontypridd Chr.*, 16 August 1886) Built in Early English Gothic style by E. M. Bruce Vaughan. (ICBS file no. 9091 (1886)) It consists of chancel, nave, south porch and western bellcote. Constructed of Welsh Pennant sandstone with Bath stone dressings. East window of three trefoiled lancets with Geometrical-style tracery in head. Wide moulded chancel arch springs from moulded capitals set upon twin pillarets. Nave lighted by single lancet windows, deeply splayed between solid two-stage buttresses with prominent set-offs, while chancel lighted on the south side by two-light trefoil-headed window. West end of nave lighted by pair of two-light trefoiled windows with quatrefoil in apex. Chancel and nave have simple arch-braced roofs of pitch-pine. Open benches of pitch-pine accommodate 305 worshippers. Font has octagonal bowl with circular moulded stem and base resting on rectangular plinth. Contractors: Messrs Thomas & Morgan, Porth. Cost £1,228. ICBS grant £100; LDCES grant £100; Bishop of Llandaff's Fund £300. Opened for divine worship on 2 June 1887. (*Pontypridd Chr.*, 4 June 1887) Consecrated on 22 May 1888. (*The Parish of St Paul: Centenary, 1887–1987* (1987), 1)

Comments: St Paul's is characteristic of Bruce Vaughan's cheap, utilitarian churches built for mining communities. John Newman gives the impression that the 'short unbuttressed tower' on the south side of the chancel, e.g. 'with its bellstage of timber', was part of Bruce Vaughan's original building erected in 1887. (Newman, 527) However, the tower was not added until 1935.

In the years 1909–10 the church was enlarged by the addition of a north aisle. Seating capacity increased by ninety sittings. Cost £1,131. (LL/F/6 81. Enlargement of church. Faculty dated 10 August 1909)

ST CURIG'S CHURCH, PORTHKERRY

1867: Restoration of church. J. Romilly Allen, of Porthkerry House, writing in 1876, stated that 'The present building was repaired and reroofed in the year 1867. The wall between the nave and the chancel was found to be in such a dangerous condition that it had to be entirely rebuilt. The old chancel arch was of Tudor shape, without moulding of any kind, and in pulling it down a pewter chalice, associated with a skeleton, was discovered buried beneath the floor; this chalice, now engraved, is carefully preserved at Porthkerry House [the home of the Romilly family, whose tomb is in the church in the shape of a great block of marble]. The church is at present fitted with open seats which were added at the same time as the other repairs. The only new part added was a vestry at the north side of the nave.' (J. Romilly Allen, 'Notes on Porthkerry Church, Glamorganshire, with special reference to the churchyard cross', *Arch. Camb.* (1876), 45–8)

Comments: The restoration of St Curig's, carried out by the Romilly family who were patrons of the living in the nineteenth century, was a sensitive affair. The old chancel arch was only rebuilt because of its dangerous condition. The church was reseated with open benches in keeping with the new liturgical arrangements of the Anglican Church and to provide additional accommodation for the parishioners.

ST JAMES' CHURCH, PYLE

1876–7: Reseating of church and repairs to fabric of building. Work commenced on 5 April 1877 by John Prichard. Church reseated providing additional accommodation for seventy-three parishioners, thus increasing total number of seats to 153 seats, all of which were free and unappropriated. All dilapidated old pews, including large square pew belonging to C. R. M. Talbot, the lay rector, removed from chancel and replaced by chairs. Repairs also carried out to old well-moulded oak roof and walls of church. The *Cardiff Times* reported that 'Owing to the energy and perseverance of the Revd Watkin Davies, vicar, and to the cordial co-operation of a few influential inhabitants, but more especially to the countenance and support of the lord lieutenant of the county (Mr. Talbot, M.P., Margam), great improvements have been effected in church affairs in the parish.' (*Cardiff Times*, 14 September 1877) Cost £848. ICBS grant £25. (ICBS file no. 8017 (1876)) Reopened after restoration on 13 September 1877. (*Cardiff Times*, 14 September 1877)

1891: Restoration of chancel by Frederick W. Waller, diocesan architect, Gloucester. Repairs carried out to stonework of chancel walls and windows. Chancel roof replaced by new structure and floor paved with encaustic tiles. New organ chamber constructed on north side of choir. Floor of organ chamber laid down with wood-blocks. Organ removed from its original position at south-east corner of nave to new organ chamber. New seats erected in space formerly occupied by organ, providing additional accommodation for forty parishioners, thus increasing overall capacity to 260 sittings. Cost £450, entirely defrayed by Miss Emily Talbot, patron of living. (LL/F/697. Organ chamber and removal of organ repair and improvements. Faculty dated 3 November 1891)

Comments: John Prichard's restoration of St James' Church in 1877 was fundamentally an ecclesiological reordering of the interior, which had retained its eighteenth-century liturgical arrangement well into the latter part of the nineteenth century. The *Cardiff Times* announced that 'Archaeologists and the few who, very properly advocate the strictest conservatism in church restoration, will be pleased to hear that the roof is not new, but is a fine specimen of a well-moulded oak roof, and that it has been faithfully repaired.' (*Cardiff Times*, 21 September 1877) Although the lay rector, C. R. M. Talbot, felt unable at that time to restore the chancel, which was his responsibilty, he permitted all the dilapidated square box pews to be removed and replaced by chairs. Waller carried out a thorough restoration of the chancel in 1891. The main reason for transferring the organ to a custom-built organ chamber in the chancel was to comply with the liturgical arrangements of the Anglican Church revival. Organs situated in the nave were transferred to the chancel to accompany the choir in the choral worship and ritual of the Victorian Anglican Church. In addition, they provided much needed extra seating accommodation in the area formerly occupied by the organ.

ST JOHN THE BAPTIST'S CHURCH, RADYR

1869–70: Restoration of church by John Prichard. Work comprised renewal of roofs of chancel and nave and present east window was substituted for old one which was a triplet of grouped lancets. Old lofty three-decker pulpit with massive sounding board suspended over it together with two old-fashioned high-backed pews in nave replaced with new pulpit and open benches of pitch-pine. Exterior of church considerably altered when walls were faced with polychromatic random rubble-work. Over west gable was a bell turret, square in plan with gabled sides and with roof ridges running at right angles to each other, symbolically in shape of cross. Benefactress: Lady Mary Windsor Clive, St Fagans. Cost £1,050. (*Radyr Parish Notes*, November 1895, no. 5)

1897–8: Further restoration to church carried out: vestry extended eastwards; west wall lined on inside with brickwork so as to form a cavity in view of its very damp condition; heating system improved; roof water drained more efficiently; and inside of church decorated throughout. There was a proposal at this time for chancel arch to be widened and raised, but when application made for faculty to carry out work the bishop made a personal visit to the church and decreed that as arch was probably of thirteenth-century date it should not be altered. Architect: George E. Halliday, Llandaff. Contractor: W. Couzens, Cardiff. Cost £800. Reopened after restoration on 19 June 1898 (*Radyr Parish Magazine*, December 1897/July 1898)

Comments: John Prichard retained the fourteenth-century chancel arch with double chamfers springing directly from the side walls, and although he replaced the east window to provide more light in the chancel he retained also the medieval fenestration in the chancel and nave. However, the most controversial aspect of his restoration was the alteration of the exterior walls, which he faced with polychromatic random rubblework. What John Newman says about 'the polychromatic crazy-paving of the walls' is quite a valid description and is to a degree underlined by the extraordinary number of different colours in the stonework. It may seem strange that Prichard, having carefully preserved the thirteenth-, fourteenth- and fifteenth-century features of the church, should face the walls with polychromatic random rubblework, thus destroying the authenticity of a medieval Glamorgan church. However, it can be argued that polychromatic decoration was popular during the last decade of the High Victorian Victorian and that Prichard chose to express this fashionable idiom at Radyr. His originality of expression was also demonstrated by his idiosyncratic design of the bell turret over the west gable, which can only be described as a 'towerlet'. It was fortunate that the bishop of Llandaff made a personal visit to Radyr Church in 1897 when the church was being renovated and decreed that the thirteenth-century chancel arch should remain *in situ*.

ST DAVID'S CHURCH, RESOLVEN

1850: New church built on new site given by Nash Edwards Vaughan of Rheola, Neath. Built in Early English Gothic style consisting of chancel, nave, west porch and bell turret over west gable. Constructed of Welsh Pennant sandstone and Bath stone dressings. East window of three widely spaced lancets, deeply recessed and separated internally by three continuous pointed arches which spring from bell capitals and slender shafts on square bases. Outer moulding ends in floriated stops in surface of east wall. Arch-braced roof of chancel has curved windbraces and is plastered between rafters. Nave also has simple arch-braced roof of pitch-pine plastered between common rafters and with principal rafters springing from stone corbels. West window in shape of a cinquefoil set high in west wall of nave. Chancel and nave lighted by simple lancets. Castellated bell turret with spirelet and corbels above west gable. Open benches of pitch-pine. Seating accommodation for 214 worshippers. Cost £1,300. Entirely defrayed by Henry J. Grant, The Gnoll, Neath and Nash Edwards Vaughan, Rheola. (*CMG*, 1 June 1850) Consecrated on 29 May 1850. (*The Cambrian*, 31 May 1850)

Comments: St David's was built in the pre-Puginesque Gothic style of the Early English Gothic or 'lancet' design. The thirteenth-century-style bell turret is both incongruous and striking, for it is the only exterior piece of discernible embellishment. It is strange that the architect, who is not recorded, should have erected such a castellated structure with spirelet and corbels when a simple gabled bellcote would have been more in keeping with the exterior and in a more archaeologically correct style. The only striking feature of the interior is the east window of three spaced lancets, deeply recessed and separated internally by three continuous arches springing from slender shafts on round bases. Consequently, apart from the embellishment of the two features referred to above, the architect was severely restricted by the amount of money he was allowed to spend on the building.

In the years 1903–4 the church was restored and a new vestry erected. A new vestry was constructed on the south side of the chancel, and the floors of the vestry and the aisles were retiled. Four additional seats were provided in the chancel, and a new heating apparatus of high-pressure hot water was installed in place of the obsolete stove, formerly on north side of nave. This improvement of the church provided an additional fifty-six sittings in the nave. Architect: J. Cook Rees of Neath. Cost £347. (LL/F/713. Restoration and improvement of church. Faculty dated 28 December 1903)

ST GEORGE'S CHURCH, REYNOLDSTON

1861–7: New church built on site of former church. During incumbency of Revd John Davies (1834–73), plans were drawn up to rebuild church from foundations. Firm of Prichard & Seddon of Llandaff commissioned to draw up plans and specifications for new church. In 1861, population of Reynoldston parish comprised 279 persons and ten sittings in old church were appropriated to Colonel John Nicholas Lucas (1784–1863) of Stouthall. Remaining sittings were free. John Pollard Seddon, Prichard's partner at that time, examined the old church and stated that 'the existing church is a mere barn without any architectural pretensions and contains 37 sittings'. (ICBS file no. 5837) In his booklet Robert Lucas notes that 'In 1756 the seating capacity of the Church was improved by the erection of a gallery across the west end of the nave. This gallery was entered from a door high up in the wall of the nave, reached by an outside flight of stone steps on the west side of the porch. The work was paid for by the Revd Thomas Talbot.' (Robert Lucas, *A History of Reynoldston Church* (1978)) St George's, like many other Gower churches, had fallen into a state of dilapidation as Revd Davies stated in his application requesting grant aid from ICBS. C. D. Morgan described the church in 1862 as 'dreadfully dilapidated. The interior is even worse than the exterior, pits and holes in the floor, rotten old seats and crumbling timbers. It is the worst church in Gower, quite a ruin – if we except the chancel, which has been put in good order at the expense of the very worthy clergyman the Revd J. Davies. This gentleman has done all he could to have a new church built.' (C. D. Morgan, *Wanderings in Gower* (Swansea, 1862), 90–1)

Estimated cost of new building according to Prichard & Seddon was £1,200 plus their professional fees and travelling expenses of £75. According to rector, £800 had been promised in subscriptions leaving a deficiency of £475, a considerable sum of money for a poor parish to find in 1861. As result of deficit, scheme to rebuild church postponed for five years until 1866 when work actually began on the building. Towards end of 1866, old Reynoldston Church pulled down and rebuilt on its former site and on much the same plan, although nave was slightly longer and probably much wider. Foundations laid to an average depth of three feet and soil of site was loam. Decided not to construct crypt under church as had originally been intended. Transept added on north side to take place of modest extension built by John Lucas in eighteenth century (Robert Lucas, *A History of Reynoldston Church*, 3) Built in early Decorated Gothic style consisting of chancel, nave, north transept and western bellcote. Constructed of reddish-coloured, hammer-dressed Pennant sandstone from local quarries on Cefn

Bryn. East window of two trefoiled cusped lights with quatrefoil in head. Chancel arch pointed and there is another low pointed arch on south side of it leading to stone pulpit. Roofs of nave and north transept are of scissors-beam construction and spring in transept from massive rectangular stone corbels. Roofs framed with Memel timber and covered with slate. Nave lighted by a three-light and a two-light cusped window on south side and a two-light cusped window on north side. Aisle paved with black and red Staffordshire tiles and floor under seats boarded with deal. On south side of nave the stone pulpit, with its ballflower decoration on cornice, has a statue in a niche of St George, patron saint of England, slaying the dragon, which symbolizies the dedication of church. Open benches of pitch-pine accommodate 142 parishioners. Only remaining feature of old church is built-up obtuse lancet in south wall of chancel. Architect: John Prichard of Prichard & Seddon. Contractors: Messrs Henry & George Rosser, Reynoldston. Cost £1,500, defrayed by Starling Benson of Fairyhill with assistance of Wood family of Stouthall and public subscriptions. (Personal information from Robert Lucas, Reynoldston) For some obscure reason no ICBS grant was made. Church opened for divine worship on 3 November 1867. (Geoffrey R. Orrin, *The Gower Churches* (Penmaen, 1979), 74–7)

Comments: The architect of the church was an enigma for some time. However, as this book went to press, the author discovered the presence of the ICBS file no. 5837 in Lambeth Palace Library, which gave information on the rebuilding of the church. Nevertheless, the scissors-beam construction of the roof of the nave and transept, the circular pulpit with its ballflower cornice and particularly the finely executed bellcote with its moulded and gabled decorative buttresses are all features which can only be attributed to John Prichard. Finally, the church is built in the Decorated Gothic or Second Pointed Style of the Victorian era, an idiom most favoured by the architect.

In the years 1905–6 the west window was inserted, the gift of Mrs F. M. Crawshay in memory of her parents, Colonel Edward R. Wood and Mrs Mary Wood of Stouthall. A vestry was built on the north side of the nave and a heating apparatus installed. (SD/F/571. New west window, vestry and heating apparatus. Faculty dated 29 May 1905)

ST MARY THE VIRGIN'S CHURCH, RHOSSILI

50. Rhosilly Old Church, previous to restoration. Sketch by W. W. Goddard (Source: J. D. Davies, *Historical Notices of the Parishes of Llangenydd and Rhosili in the Rural Deanery of West Gower* (Swansea, 1885), facing page 157)

1855–6: Restoration of church. When Sir Stephen Glynne visited Rhossili Church on 24 September 1848 he stated that 'the roofs are open, the floor is bare clay'. (Sir Stephen R. Glynne, 'Notes on the older churches in the four Welsh dioceses', *Arch. Camb.* (1897), 303) Revd J. D. Davies, historian of west Gower, wrote that 'In or about 1856, the church, which had got into a very dilapidated condition, was restored by the joint liberality of C. R. Mansel Talbot, Esq., M.P. of Margam Park and Mrs Charlotte Traherne of Coedriglan'. (Revd J. D. Davies, *Historical Notices of the Parishes of Llangynwydd and Rhosili in the Rural Deanery of West Gower* (Swansea, 1885), 160) The correspondent in the *Church Builder* reported that 'The church was erected in the 12th century and was last repaired in 1856 at the expense of £500.' (*Ch. Bldr* (1890), 69)
1890–1: Restoration of church by Ewan Christian of London. (ICBS file no. 9435 (1890)) New roofs raised and new south porch built. New oak chancel furniture and open benches of pitch-pine to accommodate 120 parishioners installed. New altar, gift of Miss Emily Talbot, patron of living. Floor of encaustic tiles laid down in chancel and new cylindrical-shaped altar rail of oak supported on massive brass pillars erected. Ground floor of

tower made into vestry and new window inserted. Two new windows inserted in nave, one on south side, other on north side. Norman doorway improved by exposure of bases, which had been buried under soil of porch for many years. Also soil which had accumulated against walls on south side of church removed. Low-side or 'lepers' window which was formerly blocked up, glazed with Cathedral glass. Contractor: Messrs Bevan & Gibbs, Horton. Cost £700. ICBS grant £20; Miss Emily Talbot £550. (*W. Mail*, 29 June 1891) Reopened after restoration on 27 June 1891. (*The Cambrian*, 3 July 1891)

Comments: Although Rhossili Church underwent a thorough restoration in 1856, which made the church wind and water tight, it failed to arrest the decay of the structure caused through age and its exposure to the full force of the prevailing south-westerly winds at the western extremity of the Gower Peninsula. Therefore, during the incumbency of Revd Ponsonby Lucas (1855–98), a thorough restoration was carried out by Ewan Christian, the architect to the Ecclesiastical Commissioners. His restoration of the church, although very thorough, was carried out in an unobtrusive way. He preserved the essential character of the church by not making any structural alterations to the fabric of the building. A correspondent, who gave a contemporary account of the restoration work in a local newspaper said, 'What more could be wanted for the renovation of the building (except the demolition of the four walls) it is hard to conceive.' (*W. Mail*, 29 June 1891)

ST JAMES' CHURCH, RUDRY

1885–6: Restoration by John Prichard. Church as it stands today is largely result of major restoration carried out in 1885. Citatory decree stated that 'the parish church of St James, Rudry having from age and other causes become dilapidated and out of repair and unfit for the performance of divine worship that the petitioners were desirous of restoring the same'. (GRO: P/5/CW.23. Restoration of church. Citatory decree dated 21 March 1885) Work of restoration commenced in May

51. St Andrew's Church, St Andrew's Major (Photo: W. P. Pring, L.R.P.S.) (By kind permission of D. Brown & Sons Ltd, Cowbridge)

1885 and comprised rebuilding, using hammer-dressed stonework, certain parts of church walls on east and south sides and in north-east corner as well as porch. Church roofs replaced with Memel timber, stained and varnished and covered with Broseley tiles. Floor of nave concreted and boarded, and old-fashioned square box pews replaced with open benches of pitch-pine. New steps of red Forest of Dean stone placed at chancel entrance and to all doorways in church. New floors laid down in belfry and ringing loft. Lancet window inserted in north wall of nave and alterations made to windows in south wall of church. Work also entailed removal of all whitewash from internal and external walls of church and removal of font from its place under chancel arch to new position in north-west corner of nave. Aisles of chancel and nave paved with monumental slabs taken down from walls. Additional accommodation provided for another twenty parishioners. (John R. Guy, *A History of Rudry* (Risca, 1976), 12–13) Contractor: Thomas and William Cox, Llandaff. Cost £610. Reopened after restoration on 1 November 1886. (*Cardiff Times*, 6 November 1886)

Comments: Prichard's restoration of St James' was a conservative affair, since no structural alterations were made to the fabric of the church except where necessary such as rebuilding of decayed stonework. It was basically an ecclesiological reordering of the church and a restoration of the structure which had been neglected during the early part of the nineteenth century, which was quite common in rural Glamorgan.

ST ANDREW'S CHURCH, ST ANDREW'S MAJOR

1860: Description of church by G. T. Clark *c*.1860 said that 'The church is comprised of a tower, nave, south aisle, chancel and south porch . . .The nave has a Decorated south door, and two south windows of two lights and late Perpendicular . . . The roof is modern and bad. The north aisle has two north and a west window probably Jac. I of three lights, cinquefoiled. At the east end is a large arch, now blocked up, what led into the Herbert Chapel, recently pulled down by Mr Lee of Dinas Powis. The roof has good principals, but the rest is modern and bad. The east window of two lights, cinquefoiled is late Perpendicular. The upper part is blocked.' (NLW MS 5215E. Description of St Andrew's Major Church by G. T. Clark c.1860)

1865: Nave reseated and repairs carried out to the fabric of the church. Architect: John Prichard. Cost £400. ICBS grant £20. (ICBS file no. 6389 (1865))

1878: Chancel and belfry restored in memory of Revd Henry Thomas Lee (d. 1877), vicar of Hel-Houghton with South Raynham, Norfolk for twenty-five years, by his wife and children. At this time east window of chancel inserted; it is a copy of original design of former window. Cost £997. (Chrystal Tilney, *A History of the Parishes of St Andrew Major and Michaelston-le-Pit* (Penarth, 1960), 42)

1885: Restoration of church. Chancel arch reconstructed further to east. Chancel paved with Minton's tiles. Wood-block flooring laid down throughout church, but encaustic tiles laid in passage ways. Beautifully carved oak reredos erected by Major-General and Mrs Herbert Henry Lee, composed of three double panels surrounded by concave border of patera with gold and colour-painted motifs. Whole surmounted by brattishing and little shields containing sacred monogram IHC. Central devices contain instruments of the Passion. This Victorian restoration of church swept away many of old monuments, but place of burials beneath floor of sanctuary and the Howel Chapel are marked by series of encaustic tiles bearing date of burial and initials of deceased. (LL/F/889. Improvements to church. Faculty granted 29 April 1885)

1889–91: Chancel beautifully decorated. Barrel roof painted with striped vaulting, panels and walls coloured in red, grey, and gold leaf with sacred monogram IHC dominant. (LL/F/727. Panelling, decoration and improvement. Faculty dated 4 June 1889)

Comments: St Andrew's underwent several restorations in the Victorian period which improved and beautified the church. It was as a result of Major-General Lee's patronage of the church that the sanctuary and chancel were embellished in the late Victorian period. As eldest son of the Revd Henry Thomas Lee, he took a prominent part in the

restoration of the chancel and belfry in 1878 in memory of his father. As lord of the manor and rector's warden he was a generous benefactor of the church during his lifetime and it was appropriate that the old chapel should be restored in his memory in 1922. Thus St Andrew's became whole again as it had been before the neglect of the eighteenth and early nineteenth centuries.

In the years 1921–2 the Herbert Chapel, now known as the Lee Chapel, was restored. At the same time the organ was removed from the east end of the north aisle to the chapel, thus providing an additional thirty-five sittings. Cost £1,000. Architect: Cecil Locke Wilson of Teather & Wilson, Cardiff. (LL/F/731. Restoration of Chapel. Faculty dated 16 September 1921)

ST TATHAN'S CHURCH, ST ATHAN

1888: Restoration of nave and tower. Work of restoration included reroofing and repointing tower. Tower arches opening to chancel and nave were groined in Bath stone. Old-fashioned box pews removed and replaced with open benches and whole of nave refloored. Old windows in north transept replaced by new ones and roof entirely renewed. Three windows inserted in nave, and new vestry built on north side of church. Old stoves removed and new heating system installed throughout church. (*MCVG*, 332)

1890: Restoration of chancel. Work comprised removal of two-light east window which was replaced by larger three-light cinquefoiled window with traceried head. Four lancet windows in south wall restored with Bath stone dressings according to their original design. Sanctuary within Communion rails paved with encaustic tiles and altar steps renewed. Chancel completely reseated and walls relined with oak panelling. Oak reredos also erected in sanctuary. Architect: William Martin, Glamorgan. Cost £1,300. (LL/F/739. Repair, restoration and additions to church. Faculty dated 10 October 1888)

Comments: The writer for *Archaeologia Cambrensis* of 1888 who visited the church as part of the field excursions of the Annual Meeting of the Cambrian Archaeological Association stated that 'the nave has been restored in the worst possible taste and new windows inserted, entirely devoid of architectural character, but the old oak roof has fortunately been spared. The chancel still retains three of the original lancet windows in the south wall . . . The arches under the tower are Pointed, without moulding of any kind. The two opening into the north and south transepts are old, but the other two openings into the nave and chancel have been restored.' (Cambrian Archaeological Association. Report of the forty-third Annual Meeting of the Cambrian Archaeological Association held at Cowbridge on Monday, August 13 1888 and four following days, *Arch. Camb.* (1888), 382) It is curious that the writer stated that the new windows in the nave with Y-tracery were 'entirely devoid of architectural character' as Y-tracery is only a continuation of the Early English arrangement of two lights formed when a single mullion divides into two branches of equal length within the head. It was a form of early Decorated architecture and was not entirely out of keeping with the Decorated style of the church. The architect, William Martin, interpreted the age of the nave as being very early Decorated in style and inserted Y-traceried windows accordingly. As far as the chancel was concerned, apart from replacing the east window of two lights by a larger three-light one as was common practice in nineteenth-century restorations, the architect felt compelled to replace modern windows which had been injudiciously inserted at an earlier date. He was careful to preserve the de Berkerolles tombs and sculpture of the south transept and the wagon roof of the chancel. On the whole it was a rather conservative restoration in keeping with the recent changes in attitude to restoration in the late Victorian period.

ST BRIDE'S CHURCH, ST BRIDE'S MAJOR

1852: Restoration of church by Egbert Moxham, Neath. Moxham reported that church was much decayed and dilapidated, particularly nave and parts of west tower as result of ravages of time and weather. (ICBS file no. 4404 (1851)) Nave entirely rebuilt in Decorated Gothic style. New north porch added. Vestry added on north side of chancel. New west window and west doorway inserted in west wall of tower, done in poor quality sandstone and weathered so as to present a medieval appearance. Nave uniformly seated with open benches of pitch-pine, three-quarters of which were free and unappropriated. Seating accommodation for 240 worshippers. New octagonal pulpit, carved from Sutton stone erected on left side of nave. New open timber roof with massive scantlings raised over nave. Part of chancel provided with stalls for dowager countess of Dunraven and family. (*Bldr* (1852), Vol. X, No. 510, 719) Contractors: John Jenkins, New Inn, Bridgend, David Jones, Briton Ferry. ICBS grant £75. Cost £900, £268 of which raised by parish rate. Dowager countess of Dunraven £200. (*CMG*, 30 October 1852)

Comments: Newman stated that 'the building was seriously compromised by Egbert Moxham's obtrusive restoration in 1851 (*sic*), when many large windows were inserted'. (Newman, 549) However, when Sir Stephen Glynne visited St Bride's Major Church in August 1849, he stated that 'The chancel has on the south, three lancet windows with trefoil heads and one at the north-west. The other windows throughout the church are wretched modern ones.' (Sir Stephen R. Glynne, 'Notes on the older churches in the four Welsh dioceses', *Arch. Camb.* (1901), 272) The octagonal pulpit of Sutton stone, designed by Moxham, may well be excessive, as stated by Newman, in relation to other fittings in the church. However, with its reticulated-style tracery and ogee arches it is representative both of the Decorated Gothic style and of the High Victorian period to which it belongs.

ST BRIDE'S CHURCH, ST BRIDE'S MINOR

1876: Restoration of church. Reroofing and new bellcote. Architect: John Prichard. Cost £650. ICBS grant £20. (ICBS file no. 7994 (1876))

1896: Enlargement of church by addition of north

aisle. During incumbency of Revd Henry Lewis it was the unanimous decision of vestry meeting, convened on 11 March 1896, that 'on account of the growing congregation that we should apply to the Consistorial Court of Llandaff for a faculty to enable us to add a north aisle to the existing church'. Petition for faculty stated that 'in consequence of the inadequacy of the accommodation in the above named church it is proposed to take down the present priest's vestry on the north east side of the Church and also the whole of the north wall of the nave of the church in order to erect a new north aisle and priest's vestry'. (LL/F/753P. Petition for faculty dated 18 March 1896) Accordingly, faculty granted on 13 April 1896 and work commenced on building new north aisle in May 1896. Nave divided from north aisle by three pointed double-chamfered arches springing from simple moulded capitals on plain round columns. North aisle has simple fourteenth-century-style arch-braced roof with braces supported on stone corbels below wallplate. Roof boarded between common rafters which rest on three massive purlins which in turn rest on arch-braces. Priest's vestry formed out of east end of north aisle and separated from congregation by curtain screen. North aisle lighted by three trefoil-headed lights with Decorated tracery lights above in shape of two trefoils and quatrefoil in apex. Seating capacity increased by additional ninety-eight seats to 194 sittings. Architect: George E. Halliday, Llandaff. Cost £625. Mrs Madelina Llewellyn, Baglan Hall £500; Lord Dunraven £125. (LL/F/753. New north aisle and priest's vestry. Faculty dated 13 April 1896)

Comments: John Prichard's restoration of the church in 1876 was to replace the roof, which was at that time in a dilapidated condition, and to construct a new bellcote. Twenty years later, in 1896, Halliday was commissioned to add a north aisle, which extended almost the whole length of the nave, to accommodate more parishioners due to the increased population of the parish. He built the new north aisle in keeping with the old nave by inserting Decorated-style windows with trefoils and a quatrefoil in the apex in the north wall. He divided the nave from the north aisle by a

Decorated-style arcade of three pointed chamfered arches springing from slender capitals on short columns, all executed in Bath stone.

ST BRIDE'S CHURCH, ST BRIDE'S-SUPER-ELY

1849: Restoration and rebuilding of church. Contemporary newspaper account stated that 'the church presents the appearance of a new edifice which virtually it is'. (*CMG*, 15 September 1849) Pseudo-Norman chancel arch constructed between nave and chancel. Norman outer arch with chevron decoration brought from Margam Abbey, discovered when 'a stable abutting on the south side of the old building east of the old almshouses was taken down in March 1840', and placed in south porch doorway. (J. M. Traherne, 'Marginal note' in Revd William Thomas, *Manuscript Account of Margam Abbey* (1787)) Insertion of Perpendicular east window (brought from Chapel of Llanfair Vawr [i.e. Chapel of St Mary] at Sant-y-Nyll, just north of St Bride's). (J. M. Traherne, 'Chapel, of Llanvair Vawr, Glamorganshire', *Gentleman's Magazine*, XXV (1846), 59) Other work included new open timber roofs, new open benches, chancel floored with encaustic tiles, new gable crosses and installation of heating apparatus. Cost £690. Reopened after restoration on 6 September 1849. (*MCVG*, 346)

1901–2: Restoration of church by George E. Halliday. (*Bldr*, 22 March 1902, 296) Tower repaired. Addition of vestry on north side of chancel; wood-block flooring and reseating of nave; erection of glazed screen to tower arch; insertion of new three-light window in south wall of nave and general repair of fabric of church. (LL/F/755. Restoration of church. Faculty dated 8 July 1901) Contractor: Messrs Harries & Davies, Cardiff. Cost £330. Reopened after restoration on 6 March 1902. (*W. Mail*, 7 March 1902)

Comments: The patron of the living of St Bride's-super-Ely Church was Revd John Montgomery Traherne (1788–1860) of Coedriglan, who was a noted antiquary and scholar. As such, he introduced parts taken from other ecclesiastical buildings into St Bride's at its restoration in 1849. He evidently supervised the work of restoration since no professional architect was employed. This most unusual work, which today would not have been approved by any diocesan advisory committee, was aided and abetted by his wife, Charlotte, sister of C. R. M. Talbot, who lived at Margam. Halliday's restoration of St Bride's at the turn of the century was essentially a reparation of the south porch and west tower, which were in need of repairs. The other work carried out at this time was concerned with improving 'the creature comforts' of the congregation seated in the nave by the installation of a simple underground heating apparatus and the erection of a draught-proof tower screen.

ST DONAT'S CHURCH, ST DONAT'S

52. Interior of St Donat's Church, St Donat's (Photo: W. P. Pring, L.R.P.S.) (By kind permission of D. Brown & Sons Ltd, Cowbridge)

1878: Restoration of church by David Vaughan of Bonvilston. Despite fact that church had been subjected to large-scale restoration in 1847, decay of building could not be adequately arrested, so that by 1878 roof and other parts of church in dilapidated condition. Restoration restricted to: placing of roof in an excellent state of repair by inserting new rafters and packing asphalt between timberwork and fresh slates; raising floor a foot higher (with exception of aisle); and staining and varnishing pews. Walls also appeared to have received some treatment at hands of contractor. Contractor: Edward Richards, St Donat's. Cost £155, defrayed by Dr Nicholl-Carne, St Donat's Castle. (*Cardiff Times*, 5 October 1878) Reopened after restoration on 2 October 1878. (*CGG*, 4 October 1878)

1892–4: Restoration of church by George E. Halliday. Work included repair and reslating of roofs of chancel and Stradling Chapel, and re-plastering walls. New oak floors laid down in tower together with new lead roof and repointing of its walls. North chancel window reglazed and new lead gutters fitted to north and south sides of nave and between Stradling Chapel and chancel. Soil, which had accumulated to height of several feet at east end of church, removed. Porritt's heating apparatus replaced old stove in church. (*BN*, 26 August 1892) Contractor: William Clarke, Llandaff. Cost £922. (SPAB (London): St Donat's Church file)

Comments: During the 1878 restoration of St Donat's, David Vaughan took great care not to interfere in the slightest degree with the architectural design of the original medieval church, which still retained its Norman features. By the time of the restoration of the church in 1892, the Society for the Protection of Ancient Buildings was exerting its influence on church restoration in Glamorgan. As part of the St Donat's Castle complex, the estate chapel fell under the watchful eyes of the Society and Halliday thus carried out a sensitive reparation of the church.

In 1907 the church was restored by Morgan Stuart Williams of St Donat's Castle. He did this in return for some concessions by the church authorities on the estate regarding the access road to the church. The post-Victorian work carried out on St Donat's Church in 1907 was by way of improvements to the interior of the church. The work of restoration included the reflooring of the nave with wooden blocks and the restoration of the high altar slab from the sanctuary pavement.

The parapets of the tower were rebuilt and the external walls repointed. Morgan Stuart Williams, patron of the living, bore the entire cost of the work himself and he presented a handsome stone pulpit and had a pseudo-Norman arch constructed to provide access to it from the chancel. He also presented a carved oak prayer desk. Architect: George E. Halliday. Reopened after restoration on 23 April 1907. (*W. Mail*, 24 April 1907)

ST MARY'S CHURCH, ST FAGANS

1859–60: Restoration and enlargement of church by addition of north aisle. When Revd William David was appointed to living in 1858 he found church in ruinous state of decay: mullions had been removed from south windows of chancel and sashes substituted; east window and two windows on north side blocked up with masonry; flooring broken and in many parts worshippers stood on bare earth; roof timbers all decayed; and pews were old high square ones. Rector sought assistance of parishioners and Baroness Windsor to restore church. Petition for faculty stated that 'the parish church of the said parish of St Fagans is in a state of great decay and requires restoration'. (LL/F/ 764. Restoration and enlargement of church. Faculty dated 8 April 1859) Architect: George Edmund Street. Work included erection of new north aisle along full length of nave, with arcade of three pointed arches springing from simple moulded capitals on circular columns with octagonal bases. Aisle lighted by five windows, all in Decorated Gothic style of architecture. In addition, new vestry with high-pitched gable constructed on north side of chancel, new roofs raised, plaster removed from interior walls with repointing inside and outside, old high-backed square pews removed and open benches installed throughout; chancel and aisles floored with Minton's encaustic tiles, and windows of chancel restored. New east window inserted and two other lights placed in south wall of nave; one an exact

53. Interior of St Mary's Church, St Fagans, showing the fourteenth-century chancel beyond the lofty, acutely pointed chancel arch (Photo: W. P. Pring, L.R.P.S.) (By kind permission of D. Brown & Sons Ltd. Cowbridge)

copy of the original fourteenth-century lancet window to west of porch. New choir stalls erected in chancel, new glass screen installed at base of tower to divide it from nave, and new gates placed in south porch. Heating apparatus installed by Rimington & Sons of Halifax. Bells recast by Charles Mears of London. Tombstones of Gibbon family, found under Castle pew, carefully buried beneath tower floor and their position recorded in one of parish registers. Contractor: Thomas Williams, Canton, Cardiff. Cost £2,244, defrayed by Baroness Windsor. (*Bldr*, 15 September 1860, 596) Reopened after restoration on 4 September 1860. (*CMG*, 8 September 1860)

Comments: The reviewer in *The Ecclesiologist* regarded the restoration of St Fagans Church as 'a very properly conservative restoration'. (*Eccl.*, 22 (1861), 205) He expressed this opinion because Street had been careful to preserve the Norman arches, which were discovered when the plaster above the south door of the chancel was removed

during the course of the restoration leaving them in prominent view. This was a good example of how ancient work with later restoration should be preserved and not plastered over or pulled out to be lost to posterity. Furthermore, Street's restoration of St Fagan's Church was a brilliant piece of work, characteristic of the architect's skill in blending new work with old in the Decorated Gothic style, the original style of the architecture of the church. With Baroness Windsor's full support, Street was able to carry out the work of restoration without regard to the cost, as was not always the case in many other parishes in Glamorgan at that time. His restoration of St Fagan's Church in the years 1859–60 is undoubtedly the best example of a properly restored church in Glamorgan during the High Victorian period.

ST GEORGE'S CHURCH, ST GEORGE-SUPER-ELY

54. St George's Church, St George-super-Ely (Photo: W. P. Pring, L.R.P.S) (By kind permission of D. Brown & Sons Ltd., Cowbridge)

1838–9: Restoration of church by Edward Haycock, Shrewsbury. Work included rebuilding of north transept which had been demolished sixty years earlier. Tower also rebuilt completely from foundations and small turret staircase constructed on north side of tower so that bells could be rung without entering church. Chancel roof replaced and supported by single corbel, shaped like octagonal capital, on each side of chancel. East window, which was in dilapidated state, restored. Corner buttresses put to east wall of chancel. New Communion table, which is ornamented with Gothic arches and mouldings, has similar architectural features to those displayed on the pulpit and reading desk. Open benches with Gothic carvings replaced dilapidated old-fashioned box pews. Original roof of nave preserved and ceiling between moulded oak timbers plastered. Exterior arch of south porch rebuilt with freestone. Cost of restoration £500, borne by Revd John Montgomery Traherne, Coedriglan, son of patron of living. (*Glamorgan, Monmouth & Brecon Gazette and Merthyr Guardian*, 19 January 1839) Reopened after restoration on 13 January 1839. (*The Cambrian*, 26 January 1839)

1886–8: Further restoration of church when massive stone altar, work of William Lewis of Cardiff, erected in chancel. (Charles F. Shepherd, *A Short History of St George-super-Ely* (Cardiff, 1933), 13)

Comments: St George's owes its present appearance to the extensive restoration carried out in the years 1838–9 during Edward Copleston's episcopate. Edward Haycock rebuilt the central tower in the Rhenish Romanesque style, an unusual style of architecture for Glamorgan. He was careful to preserve the medieval cradle roof of the nave. When Sir Stephen Glynne visited the church in August 1857, he wrote 'the church has of late years been much renovated. The tower itself has been raised, and gabled on each side; but it rises on four very plain Pointed arches, opening to the chancel, nave and transepts.' (Sir Stephen R. Glynne, 'Notes on the older churches in the four Welsh dioceses', *Arch. Camb.* (1901), 273) Glynne's description of the tower implies that he regarded it as an unsatisfactory feature, a theme taken up by

Herbert M. Thompson, who regarded the tower as a failure due to its lack of height, emphasized by the double-gabling with each of the four gables crowned with a large crocket. He felt that a conventional square tower with battlements and corbel table would have been more appropriate. (Cardiff Central Library: Herbert M. Thompson, Manuscript notes on the old churches of Glamorgan, Vol. 2, 1935)

ST HILARY'S CHURCH, ST HILARY

55. St Hilary's Church, St Hilary. View of east end of church. Photo by Sir T. M. Franklen (Source: By kind permission of the Librarian, Cardiff Central Library)

1861–2: Restoration of church by George Gilbert Scott. All old walls retained, but securely underpinned and drained. Arcade between south (Edmondes) aisle and nave, which was formerly out of perpendicular, forced up into place without taking down. Other principal works included renewing most of fenestration of main body of church. Five-light flowing Decorated east window erected in chancel (designed by Scott) as well as new three-light window in south chancel wall. Four-light Perpendicular Gothic-style window in east wall of south aisle taken down and restored. Two other windows inserted in west and south walls. New roofs of varnished pitch-pine with kingposts and cambered tie-beams raised over nave and south aisle. New south porch with high-pitched gable constructed. (*Bldr*, Vol. XX (1862), 376) Contractor: Messrs James & Price, Cardiff. Cost £2,600, defrayed by Mrs Charlotte Louisa Traherne. Reopened after restoration on 2 May 1862. (*CMG*, 10 May 1862)

1900–1: Whole of nave of church and south aisle reslated with Welsh stone tiles and buttresses on north-west, south-west and south-east corners were rebuilt at expense of Thomas Mansel Franklen, churchwarden. Chancel roof recovered at expense of rector, Revd Henry C. Davies. Architect: William Weir on behalf of Society for the Protection of Ancient Buildings. Contractor: W. A. James, Fonmon. Cost £300. £250 for roof of nave and repair of tower, and £50 for repair of chancel roof. (St Hilary's Church Vestry Book, 1900–1)

Comments: Revd John Montgomery Traherne was in fact drawing up plans for the restoration of St Hilary's Church when he died suddenly in 1860. His widow, Charlotte Louise, daughter of Thomas Mansel of Margam Abbey, decided to carry out the last wishes of her husband and restore the church as a memorial to him. The most controversial aspect of Scott's restoration was his 'gothicky' design of the windows of the church which he replaced or restored entirely. He chose to use reticulated-style tracery, the style of the fourteenth century, in many of these windows and he designed the large six-light east window as a nineteenth-century approximation of flowing Decorated architecture (the form of the original window it replaced according to Glynne). The theme of reticulated-style tracery is repeated in the windows of the south aisle, two of which are square-headed. Scott assiduously followed the original fourteenth-century Decorated style of the original church, but his designs are examples of eclectic architecture of the High Victorian period. In his restoration, he showed a reverential regard for the preservation of all the ancient features of the building, such as the font, the holy-water stoup, the medieval effigies and the remains of the old rood-loft staircase and doorway uncovered during the restoration. Another criticism levelled at him was that he swept away all the woodwork of the church, although efforts had been made in a rather inappropriate way to reproduce features of the original work. Newman pointed out quite rightly that the tie-beam and kingpost pattern designed by Scott for St Hilary's were alien and were 'more at home in the South of England than

in South Wales'. (Newman, 564) When Sir Stephen Glynne visited the church on 17 August 1869, he described it as 'a good parish church, in excellent condition, and having more of good work than the generality of churches in Glamorganshire. The nave is unusually wide; and the whole of the roof both in nave and in chancel, is new, with tie-beams and kingposts. The porch is also new.' (Sir Stephen R. Glynne, 'Notes on the older churches in the four Welsh dioceses', *Arch. Camb.* (1901), 274–5) A contemporary newspaper account of the re-opening of St Hilary's Church reported that 'this venerable church is now added to the already large number of new and restored churches which is destined to mark the Victorian era of architecture as pre-eminent in church history for many years to come'. (*CMG*, 10 May 1862)

ST LYTHAN'S CHURCH, ST LYTHAN'S

1861: In *Archaeologia Cambrensis* for 1862, George T. Clark and Robert O. Jones stated that the church was 'recently repaired in excellent taste by a happy combination between the squire and the vicar'. (George T. Clark and Robert O. Jones, 'Some account of the parishes of St Nicholas and St Lythans, Co. Glamorgan', *Arch. Camb.* (1862), 198) Squire referred to was John Bruce Pryce of Dyffryn St Nicholas and incumbent Revd William Bruce, vicar of parish from 1848 to 1863. It is fairly certain from this article that restoration was carried out in 1861. Work of restoration included insertion of new east window of three trefoiled lights with fourteenth-century-style reticulated tracery, which replaced window described as 'Middle Pointed of two lights, now much mutilated' by Sir Stephen Glynne on his visit to church on 28 August 1849. New windows inserted in north wall of nave and new cusped trefoil-headed belfry lights replaced former narrow apertures in tower. Chancel arch, which Sir Stephen R. Glynne described in 1849 as 'very small and rude pointed,' enlarged and new south porch with wagon roof constructed. (Sir Stephen R. Glynne, 'Notes on the older churches in the four Welsh dioceses', *Arch. Camb.* (1901), 275) New roofs raised in nave and south chapel,

56. Interior of St Lythan's Parish Church (Photo: W. P. Pring, L.R.P.S.) (By kind permission of D. Brown & Sons Ltd, Cowbridge)

and boarding and ribs of chancel roof renewed. New carved altar table and pulpit displaying similar inlaid work installed in church. Architect: John Prichard of Prichard & Seddon. Cost £552, defrayed by John Bruce Pryce, Dyffryn. (Olwen M. Jenkins, 'Illustrated examples of the effect on medieval and later parish church fabric in the post-1844 Archdeaconry of Llandaff of restoration work by John Prichard and John Pollard Seddon'. Diploma in Building Conservation at the Architectural Association, London, 1985, 57–69)

Comments: The restoration of St Lythan's, which was held in plurality with St Nicholas', itself restored in 1860, followed much the same pattern as dictated by the fabric of the church at St Nicholas. The most vulnerable parts of the structure of any church and particularly those in the Vale of Glamorgan, near to the salt-laden rain and winds of the Bristol Channel, were the church roofs. Prichard retained and restored the main principals of the wagon roof of the chancel, but he

replaced the boarding and ribs. He raised a simple, open timber, arch-braced roof over the nave, but chose to follow the example of the chancel and erected a wagon roof formed by a series of closely set arch-braces with crenellated wallplate in the south chapel. The restoration of most medieval churches in the Victorian era usually involved the replacement of the east window and the enlargement of the chancel arch, both of which were usually too small and St Lythan's was no exception. Originally there were no windows in the north wall of the nave, as was common in most medieval Glamorgan churches, so Prichard inserted two windows in this wall, one a trefoil-headed lancet, the other a two-light trefoil-headed window with fourteenth-century-style reticulated tracery in the head matching that of the chancel. The work of restoration of St Lythan's was instigated by John Bruce Pryce of Dyffryn, St Nicholas, a generous benefactor not only of his own parish church but of several churches throughout Glamorgan. It was such persons of

Pryce's stature, the landed gentry, who exerted a significant influence on the building and restoration of churches in Glamorgan during the Victorian era.

ST MARY'S CHURCH, ST MARY CHURCH

1861–2: Church almost entirely rebuilt except for medieval west tower and medieval roofs of chancel and nave, which were retained. Architect: John Prichard of Prichard & Seddon. In his application to ICBS for grant aid in 1861 Revd Edward P. Nicholl stated, 'It [the church] was in a dilapidated state owing to nothing having be done to it for many years.' Furthermore, he wrote, 'Many persons from the adjoining parish of Llandough [held by the same incumbent] who reside nearer to the Church of St Mary Church than to their own parish church are constant attendants in this church. There is no resident squire and the farmers are small holders.' (ICBS file no. 5836 (1860)) Rebuilt in Early English Gothic style consisting of chancel, nave, south porch and west tower. East window of three widely spaced trefoil-headed lights, deeply recessed, and separated internally by three continuous pointed arches. Chancel arch is pointed springing from side walls. Chancel lighted on south side by two trefoil-headed windows separated internally by single slender shaft. Chancel has arch-braced roof with continuous internal curve and curved windbraces between purlins. Part of roof over sanctuary boarded. Floor of chancel and centre aisle of nave covered with encaustic tiles by Messrs Maw & Co., Worcester. Chancel divided from nave by low stone screen with horizontal band of continuous three-lobed leaf decoration. Windows of nave comprise single lancet on north side and on south side a three-light trefoil-headed window. Stone pulpit, integral with chancel arch, decorated with multicoloured banding. Nave has arch-braced roof similar to chancel, with curved windbraces between purlins. Open benches of pitch-pine, free and unappropriated, for ninety-seven parishioners. Contractor: Thomas Williams, Canton, Cardiff. (*MCVG*, 383–6) Cost £585. C. R. M. Talbot, patron of living contributed £300; ICBS grant £35; LDCES

£15; church rate £60. (*Ch. Bldr* (1864), 35) Re-opened after restoration on 29 May (Ascension Day) 1862. (GRO: P/23. Church of St Mary Church Vestry Book)

Comments: John Prichard, who was commissioned by Revd Edward Powell Nicholl to restore the church, had the foresight to retain and restore the fine medieval roofs of the chancel and nave with their archbraces and windbraces. This was done in the light of Glynne's statement when he visited the church on 27 September 1848 that 'There is here some improvement on the usual Glamorgan character of churches . . . the roof of the nave is open and rather a good one . . . The chancel roof much resembles that of the nave.' (Sir Stephen R. Glynne, 'Notes on the older churches in the four Welsh dioceses', *Arch. Camb.* (1901), 277) Prichard divided the chancel from the nave, as advocated by the Ecclesiologists, with a low stone screen. With its polychromatic bands of pink, green and white stone it mirrors the stone banding of the circular pulpit, characteristic of the architect's art. The sedilia on the south side and a medieval-style aumbry on the north side are indicative of a return to the Catholic practices of the Middle Ages. The use of imagery in the sculpture over the south porch outer doorway, together with the holy-water stoup in the porch as well as the design of so many fittings and furnishings associated with the pre-Reformation Church, reflect the influence of the Ecclesiological movement in Prichard's restoration of St Mary's Church.

ST MARY'S CHURCH, ST MARY HILL

1803: A small tablet above the east window records the fact that 'This chancel was rebuilt by Sir John Aubrey, Bart., 1803.' (*MCVG*, 387)

1856: Church partially restored when work on roof carried out at cost of £90. (ICBS file no. 8444 (1879))

1879–81: By 1879 church was in dilapidated condition and successful appeal for grant aid was made by incumbent to ICBS. First stage of restoration carried out during incumbency of Revd Samuel Evans when tower and chancel were restored. (GRO: D/Dra 19/1071. St Mary Hill. Articles of agreement between John Waterton of Coychurch and Revd Samuel Evans of St Mary Hill Church, 6 October 1879) Architect: John Prichard, Llandaff. Contractor: Messrs John & Edmund Rees, Watertown, Bridgend. Cost £471. ICBS grant £25. (ICBS file no. 8444 (1879))

1884–5: Petition for faculty stated that 'the church of St. Mary Hill having from age and other causes become dilapidated is in want of repair and restoration. The tower was some years since during the last incumbency rebuilt and the chancel restored and the present vicar is desirous of executing the works necessary for restoring the nave and porch of the said church.' (LL/F/779. Restoration of church. Faculty dated 10 May 1884) Second stage of restoration carried out during the vicariate of Revd Henry James Humphreys, when nave and south porch were restored. Architect: John Prichard. Contractors: John & Edmund Rees, Watertown, Bridgend. Cost £536. Charles Aubrey Aubrey £300. (*MCVG*, 390–1)

Comments: A decision was taken in 1879 to restore the tower and chancel of St Mary Hill Church in order to avoid the disaster which had befallen the neighbouring parish church of Coychurch by the fall of its tower in 1877. The restoration of the nave was deferred until 1884 when more funds were raised with difficulty by Revd H. J. Humphreys. The writer in *Archaeologia Cambrensis* (1888) stated that 'the recent restoration was a good one except that the chancel arch, a plain, round Norman one, had been removed bodily and built into the north wall of the nave. It is built round the embrasure of a window and is a striking example of the Vale type of contracted arch.' (Sir Stephen R. Glynne, 'Notes on the older churches in the four Welsh dioceses', *Arch. Camb.* (1888), 402) In removing the chancel arch Prichard realized that he would be criticized for 'destructive' restoration, so he compromised by preserving the arch and placing it in the north wall of the nave. The restoration of St Mary's in the years 1879–85 was so thorough that the church has the aspect of a new building.

ST NICHOLAS' CHURCH, ST NICHOLAS

1848: When Sir Stephen Glynne visited church on 27 September 1848 he described it as 'A coarse church, with much of the local character, and rather curiously arranged. The south chapel extends along the whole chancel and part of the nave as far as the porch . . . The south wall of the chapel was rebuilt in 1803 and contains ugly Italian windows . . . The chancel opens to the same chapel by a rude, misshapen arch of great width, and without mouldings and has a debased north window and an ugly one of Strawberry Hill Gothic at the west end.' (Sir Stephen R. Glynne, 'Notes on the older churches in the four Welsh dioceses', *Arch. Camb.* (1901), 276–7)

1859–60: Restoration of church by John Prichard of Prichard & Seddon. Work included completely renewing roofs with Memel timber, that over the chancel having been adapted from old type of roof found in neighbouring church of St Lythan's. Entire church refloored and aisles repaved with tiles from Godwin's of Lugwardine, Hereford-shire. New open benches of pitch-pine, stained and varnished, installed in nave. Prayer desk, new altar rails and holy table of teak, richly carved, were erected in chancel. All windows restored or replaced in Decorated or Perpendicular Gothic style. New teak doors fitted. Traceried screen erected between chapel and nave. Contractor: William Parry, Llandaff. Cost £1,200, defrayed by John Bruce Pryce of Dyffryn, St Nicholas. (*CMG*, 2 June 1860) Reopened after restoration on 24 May 1860. (*CMG*, 26 May 1860)

1880: Stone and marble pulpit erected on south side of nave as it was found too large to go on north side. Pulpit the gift of Mrs Ella Mackintosh of Mackintosh, Cottrell, St Nicholas. (*MCVG*, 395)

Comments: George T. Clark, engineer and anti-quary of Talygarn, writing in 1862 in cooperation with Robert O. Jones of Fonmon, said that 'The church is dedicated to St Nicholas. It has recently been restored in particularly good taste and with great liberality by the patron. It is composed of a tower, nave, south porch, chancel, vestry and south chapel . . . In the restorations of this church Mr

Prichard has regarded the prevailing style of the building as late Decorated passing into Perpendicular and has judiciously worked in this style.' (George T. Clark and Robert O. Jones, 'Some account of the parishes of St Nicholas and St Lythan, Co. Glamorgan', *Arch. Camb.* (1862), 96–7) The patron referred to was John Bruce Pryce of Dyffryn and the rector, who initiated the restoration of the church, was Revd William Coneybeare Bruce, who held the living from 1848 to 1863. As Clark stated above, Prichard regarded the prevailing style of the building as late Decorated passing into Perpendicular. But, although he, in fact, inserted Decorated and Perpendicular Gothic style windows in various parts of the building, as exemplified in the south chapel, he chose in some cases to mix Decorated and Perpendicular motifs in the same window. This juxtaposition of Decorated and Perpendicular motifs is depicted in the east window of the chancel, which for the most part is Perpendicular in style consisting of three cinquefoiled lights below standard panel tracery, but vertical tracery bars continue from the apex of the lights beneath circles enclosing quatrefoils with a quatrefoil above. The circles enclosing quatrefoils represent Decorated-style architecture and appear to be an intrusion into what is basically a conventional Perpendicular-style window. However, in designing the window, Prichard imposed his personal interpretation on the transitional stage from the Decorated to the Perpendicular style of architecture, which was typical of the eclecticism of the High Victorian period, whereby the architect could select motifs and forms from the whole range of historic Gothic architecture.

ST PETER'S CHURCH, SENGHENYDD

1896–7: New church built on new site given by Plymouth estate as stone mission church in parish of Eglwysilan. In early 1890s radical changes associated with incessant search for new coal seams began to take place in area, which transformed district from quiet rural hamlet into industrial mining community. Architect: E. M. Bruce Vaughan, Cardiff. (Revd M. J. Mainwaring, *History of St Peter's Church, Senghenydd, 1895–1945*

(1946), 3) Foundation stone laid on 6 August 1896 by R. Leigh-Thomas, Brynllefrith. (*Y Llan*, 14 August 1896) Built in Early English Gothic style consisting of chancel and nave under one continuous roof with north porch and bellcote at western end. Constructed of local Pennant sandstone. East window of three coupled lancets and west window of two elongated lancets beneath single bellcote. Windows of nave and chancel lighted by two-light lancets under square head. Roof of open timber construction without interposing chancel arch. Seating accommodation for 300 worshippers. Contractors: Messrs Cox & Bardoe, Cardiff. Cost £800. Bishop of Llandaff's Fund £80; LDCES grant £40. (*Pontypridd Chr.*, 26 February 1897) Dedicated on 25 February 1897. (*Y Llan*, 12 March 1897)

Comments: St Peter's, in the extensive parish of Eglwysilan, was typical of the small plain churches built in mining communities in the south Wales coalfield in the last decade of the nineteenth century to meet the spiritual needs of miners and their families who worked in the nearby coal mines. The church costing only £800 was originally a very plain structure, but it served its purpose at that time. It was extended in 1908 to meet the needs of the time. Newman omitted this church from *The Buildings of Wales: Glamorgan*.

ST JOHN THE BAPTIST'S CHURCH, SKEWEN

1849–50: New church built on new site. Designed by Robert Cook Saunders in 1848, but modified and executed by Egbert Moxham, Neath. (ICBS file no. 4026 (1848)) Built in early Decorated Gothic style consisting of chancel, nave, south aisle, south porch and western bellcote. Constructed of Welsh sandstone with Bath stone dressings. Nave of lofty proportions and lighted by narrow clerestory. Length of church inside 80ft and width 37ft and western end surmounted by bellcote. North side left incomplete so as to permit extension of building at later date. East window of three lights, central one cinquefoiled and outer two trefoiled, with Geometrical tracery above. Chancel arch high and pointed. Church has hammerbeam and scissors-beam roofs. Nave divided from south aisle by arcade of five pointed arches springing from alternate octagonal and round capitals supported on similar shafts. Seating accommodation for 252 worshippers in seventy-two square box pews. Cost £1,050, defrayed by second parliamentary grant of £125 and ICBS grant of £150 – with rest made up by public subscriptions. (*The Cambrian*, 6 December 1850) Consecrated on 28 November 1850. (*The Cambrian*, 7 December 1850)

1865–6: North aisle built. LDCES grant £30. Chancel laid with encaustic tiles. Reopened after enlargement on 24 August 1865. (*The Cambrian*, 25 August 1865)

1881: Restoration by E. M. Bruce Vaughan. Alterations and additions consisted of new seating and choir stalls of pitch-pine, new tile pavement, polished marble pulpit and marble font. Church heated by Porritt's hot-air system. Contractor: Messrs Thomas, Watkins and Jenkins, Swansea. Cost £1,300. Reopened after restoration on 6 December 1881. (*The Cambrian*, 9 December 1881)

Comments: Egbert Moxham built St John the Baptist's Church, Skewen from a modified design, originally drawn up in 1848 by Robert Cook Saunders. It is a fine example of a Puginesque church built in the early Decorated Gothic style favoured by the Ecclesiologists. The steeply gabled nave is of lofty proportions with a well-designed, single hammerbeam and scissors-beam roof with long wall posts ending in little decorative features. The unusual height of the nave displays a well-proportioned arcade with alternating octagonal and round pillars with moulded capitals. With its finely detailed row of single trefoils, the narrow clerestory on the south side is a visually pleasing aspect of the church. The tall lancets in the west end appear to be of much earlier date, whilst behind the altar there is Geometrical tracery in its true sense. The head of the east window is an open multi-cusped circle and the flanking spandrels have stylized inverted mouchettes; the central light is a cinquefoil, but outer lights are trefoil-headed. The windows of the south aisle are a representation of early Geometrical architecture. The floor of the church was not paved with Minton's decorative

tiles as at St Teilo's, Merthyr Mawr, but merely covered with rough flagstones. A disappointing feature of an otherwise well-designed and executed church for its date in the county is the lack of good internal fittings and furnishings as seen at Merthyr Mawr. The old-fashioned pews were typical of its status as a Commissioners' church erected with its paltry grant of £125. This was only one of two churches built by Moxham in Glamorgan (the other being St David's Church, Maesteg), and it is apparent that Moxham gained more credit than he deserved by modifying another architect's design.

ST JOHN THE BAPTIST'S CHURCH, SULLY

1833: During incumbency of Revd W. D. Coneybeare (later dean of Llandaff) south aisle demolished, small Norman chancel arch taken down and replaced by present one of poor workmanship, and chancel lengthened. (Marianne Spencer, *Annals of South Glamorgan* (Carmarthen, 1913), 185)

1848: The architect who restored church in 1833 came across old foundations of original east wall. In 1848 Revd Chancellor George Woods became rector of Sully and he had chancel restored to its original dimensions and repaired choir. (Ibid.)

1874–6: Restoration of church. Three-decker pulpit and old high-backed pews removed and replaced with modern pulpit and open benches. New oak altar and font erected in church. Main doorway sited on south side. Reopened after restoration on 31 August 1876. (Glyn M. Jones and Elfyn Scourfield, *Sully: A Village and Parish in the Vale of Glamorgan* (Caerphilly, 1986), 16)

1895: Restoration of church by Seddon & Carter, Cardiff. The correspondent in the *Church Builder* reported that 'the building needs restoration at the present time, the nave roof being quite unsafe and must be taken in hand at once. The present seats are good open benches and it is not proposed to make any alteration in them.' (*Ch. Bldr* (1895), 94) Plaster ceiling in nave removed and new open timber roof of red deal with deal cornices raised. New choir stalls erected in chancel, and sanctuary paved with encaustic tiles. Stone pulpit erected on north side of nave. New stone arches placed internally over two Perpendicular windows on south side of nave in place of wooden lintels. Chancel arch refaced with Bath stone and new dressings put to south door of tower. Cost £550, of which Lord Wimborne, patron of living, contributed £100. (LL/F/792. Restoration of roof and improvements. Faculty dated 26 July 1895) Reopened after restoration on 17 October 1895. (*W. Mail*, 18 October 1895)

Comments: Several important restorations of the church took place in the nineteenth century, three of them during the Victorian era. The earlier restorations were concerned with rebuilding the church to its original proportions and with removing the Glamorgan type of contracted chancel arch and replacing it with one of larger span. The restoration in 1876 was devoted to the reordering and remodelling of the old 'prayer-book' church of the eighteenth century with its high-backed pews and three-decker pulpit to suit the new liturgical arrangements in the Anglican Church. The restoration in 1895 was principally intended to remove the dilapidated eighteenth-century plaster ceiling and restore it to its medieval fifteenth-century state with an open arch-braced timber arrangement. It also improved the internal appearance of the church by refitting and refurbishing the chancel for the ritual and ceremony of the Anglican Church in the late Victorian period.

CHRIST CHURCH, SWANSEA

1871–2: New church built on new site donated by Swansea corporation. During 1860s town of Swansea was rapidly expanding westwards to provide housing for dock workers in port of Swansea in area known as the Sandfields, between St Helens and town centre. J. W. Clark, a generous and devout layman, realized that increasing population needed an Anglican church to counteract the effect of several Dissenting chapels which had been erected in district. Accordingly, he offered to erect a new church at his own expense. (W. H. Trew, *Christ Church, Swansea, 1872–1972: centenary brochure.* 1972) Architect: Thomas Nicholson, diocesan architect, Hereford. Foundation stone laid on 28 June 1871 by Mrs Squire, wife of the then vicar of Swansea, Revd E. B. Squire. (*Bldr*, 15 July 1871, 553) Built in Early English Gothic style consisting of chancel, north and south chapels, nave, north and south aisles, sacristy, and north and south porches. Constructed of local Pennant sandstone with Bath stone dressings, Box Ground being used for all exterior and Combe Down for all interior work. Nave and aisles arranged under triple-ridged roofs of pitch-pine and divided from each other by arcade of three arches on either side supported by moulded pillars with carved foliage capitals. Open seats accommodate 600 worshippers. Triple-gabled south front, double-arched bellcote to centre gable above three-light Geometrical window. (*Bldr*, 29 June 1872, 513) Contractor: Thomas Gough, Bishop's Castle, Salop. Cost £2,800. Church erected at sole expense of John William Clark, Swansea. Consecrated on 13 June 1872. (*The Cambrian*, 14 June 1872)

1883: Enlargement of church. Western portion of church enlarged by extension to boundary of pavement. (SD/F/624. Enlargement of church. Faculty dated 1 September 1883) Foundation stone laid on 27 September 1883 by F. E. Williams, Wind Street, Swansea. Additional 150 sittings. Architect: John Bacon Fowler, Swansea and Brecon. Contractor: Henry Billings, Swansea. Cost £500. (*The Cambrian*, 28 September 1883) Reopened after enlargement on 29 November 1883. (*The Cambrian*, 30 November 1883)

Comments: Thomas Nicholson designed the church in the Early English style. However, when the plans were drawn up it was discovered that because of the shape of the site the church could not, as was customary, be built with the altar in the east. Thus Christ Church was built with the altar in the north making the church almost unique in Glamorgan in this respect. Nicholson arranged the nave and aisles under triple-ridged roofs, divided from each other by a thirteenth-century style arcade of three pointed equilateral arches either side, supported by quatrefoil pillars with carved stiff-leaf foliated capitals. The west gable embraces three gables, the centre one being carried up into double-arched bellcote. The finest feature of the church is its nave roof with finely executed arch-braces and decorated with an embattled moulding, quatrefoils and 'nailhead' motifs. The church built in three stages from 1872 to early in the twentieth century illustrates clearly the growth of the Anglican congregation in this district of Swansea.

In 1912 the church was repaired with the addition of new chancel and Lady Chapel, vestry and south porch. (SD/F/625. Enlarging of church. Faculty dated 28 June 1912) Additional thirty sittings. Architect: E. M. Bruce Vaughan. Cost £3,000. ICBS grant £100. (ICBS file no. 11,130 (1912)) Reopened after restoration on 17 December 1912. (*W. Mail*, 18 December 1912)

HOLY TRINITY CHURCH, SWANSEA

(Church destroyed in blitz, 1941)

1842–3: New church built on new site by Wyatt & Brandon, architects, London. Erection of another church in Swansea urgently needed since population of Swansea, including environs, was not far short of 20,000 inhabitants and existing church accommodation allowed for only 2,100 persons. Built in Early English Gothic style consisting of chancel, nave, aisles with galleries on north and south sides with entrance at west door beneath a bellcote. Constructed of Welsh Pennant sandstone with Bath stone dressings. Church measured 125ft long by 47ft wide. East window of three elongated lancets and nave lighted by long and narrow windows, which gave building a dark and uninviting appearance. Interior of church filled with square box pews and there were a pulpit and reading desk placed ambo-like at front of nave. Church accommodated 1,200 worshippers in box pews and galleries of this auditory church. Contractors: Baker, Crispin & Reid, Bristol. Cost £2,850. ICBS grant £250. (ICBS file no. 2677 (1842)) Consecrated on 26 October 1843. (*The Cambrian*, 27 October 1843)

1882–3: Restoration and repewing of church by Augustus James Schenk, Swansea architect. (ICBS file no. 9822 (1881)) Petition for restoring church stated that 'the parish church of Holy Trinity, Swansea aforesaid is in need of restoration and

repewing . . . a vestry meeting gave its approval on 4 July 1881 and at a meeting held on 27 April 1882 it was resolved that the parish church of Holy Trinity should be restored and repewed as soon as possible'. (SD/F/626. Restoring and repewing church. Faculty dated 1 August 1882) South and north galleries removed and windows replaced, and church recast in the Perpendicular Gothic style. New west window inserted at west end and old belfry replaced by new porch. Tower surmounted by spire erected at north-west corner of church. West gallery erected seating 150 persons. Flooring of church renewed and body of church repewed with modern pews of pitch-pine. Vestry enlarged and aisles laid down with encaustic tiles. Entrance through south porch under tower. New choir stalls erected. Contractor: Thomas Rees, Swansea. Cost £2,000. ICBS grant £130. (*The Cambrian*, 26 January 1883) Reopened after restoration on 1 February 1883. (*The Cambrian*, 2 February 1883)

Comments: In 1843 the interior of the nave of Holy Trinity reflected the Low Church persuasion of the vicar of Swansea, Revd Dr William Hewson, and the services were of the usual order of extreme evangelicalism. Dr F. G. Cowley has said that 'the establishment of Holy Trinity Church in 1843 seems to have owed little to Hewson and was not a strategically wise contribution to church extension anyway'. He felt that it would have been more prudent to have sited a new church to the north or west of the town where the population was spreading rapidly. (F. G. Cowley, 'Religion and education', in Glanmor Williams (ed.), *Swansea: An Illustrated History* (Swansea, 1990), 162) By 1883 the church needed restoring and repewing, and A. J. Schenck took the opportunity to recast the church in the Perpendicular Gothic style which, as a late Gothic form, had now become an acceptable idiom in the late Victorian period. The interior of the church was completely reordered to suit the new liturgical arrangements of the Anglican Church. The restoration of Holy Trinity Church in 1883 not only provided additional church accommodation but its ecclesiological reordering and recasting into the Perpendicular Gothic style improved the visual appearance of the church both internally and externally.

ST GABRIEL'S CHURCH, BRYNMILL, SWANSEA

1888–9: New church built on new site, donated by Lt. Col. William Llewelyn Morgan and Captain Thomas Llewelyn Morgan, of St Helens. The correspondent in the *Church Builder* reported that 'The enormous mother church of St Mary, Swansea has been for a long time greatly in need of church extension. Three new churches have recently been built and three new ecclesiastical parishes separated. A temporary Iron Church for St Gabriel's district was erected in 1886 and is now too small for the requirements of the neighbourhood. The St David's Diocesan Church Building Board strongly recommended this case to the favourable consideration of the Committee.' (*Ch. Bldr* (1889), 2) Foundation stone laid on 27 September 1888 by Lady Vivian of Singleton. (*The Cambrian*, 28 September 1888) Built in Perpendicular Gothic style by Thomas Nicholson & Son, Hereford, consisting of chancel and nave, each with north and south aisles, and south porch with bellcote surmounting gable of chancel arch. (ICBS file no. 9255 (1889)) External walling built of local sandstone arranged as hammer-dressed random course work. Internal walls ashlared with claw-tool Bath stone. Internally, church 95ft 6ins long and 53ft 6ins wide. Arcades of four arches on either side separate nave from aisles, and arcades of two arches divide chancel from side chapels. Four-light window at west end of nave and large five-light window at east end of chancel. Nave aisles lighted by nine three-light windows, chancel aisles by six two-light windows and clerestory by eight two-light windows. Roofs constructed of wrought timber framework, boarded over then overlaid with felt and covered with green Westmoreland slates. Part of roof over sanctuary underceiled with moulded and panelled ceiling. Chancel entered from nave under lofty arch, 28ft high. Crocketed sedilia and piscina in south wall of sanctuary. Chancel floored with Godwin's encaustic tiles. Pitch-pine benches seat 400 worshippers. Woodblock floors – red deal under seats and oak in alleys. Immersion font in south-west part of nave, arranged north–south with steps down at east end. Contractor: Henry Smith, Kidderminster.

Sculpture and carving: Richard L. Boulton, Cheltenham. Cost £6,237. ICBS grant £300; Lt. Col. W. Ll. Morgan, St Helens £2,000; Swansea and East Gower Church Extension Committee grant £500. Consecrated on 18 July 1889. (*The Cambrian*, 19 July 1889)

Comments: St Gabriel's was regarded as one of Nicholson's finer churches. *The Cambrian* reported that 'The whole design and all the arrangements of the church reflect great credit on the architects who have succeeded in erecting by far the best church in Swansea, notwithstanding that the churches which they have already built in the town have been also highly praised.' (*The Cambrian*, 19 July 1889) The reason for the reporter's statement was that St Gabriel's was the first church in Swansea to be built in a late Gothic form, Perpendicular Gothic, as a conscious effort by Nicholson. He designed the church in the early Perpendicular style, which is manifested in the architecture of the chancel and which of financial necessity was interpreted in an austere manner.

In 1931 the church was extended westwards by an extra bay. Cost £3,000, defrayed by a bequest of Colonel Morgan's sister, Miss Catherine Morgan (d. 1930). Dedicated on 30 November 1931. It marked the completion of St Gabriel's Church. However, funds were insufficient to build Nicholson's intended tower. (Paul Reynolds, *St Gabriel's: 1889–1989* (Swansea, 1989), 64)

ST PETER'S CHURCH, COCKETT, SWANSEA

1856: New church built on new site donated by John Dillwyn Llewelyn of Penllergare. Built as chapel of ease to St Mary's, Swansea, some three miles distant. Architect: Richard Kyrke Penson of Ferryside. (ICBS file no. 4938 (1855)) Foundation stone of new church laid on 12 May 1856 by Henry Hussey Vivian of Singleton Abbey. (*The Cambrian*, 16 May 1856) Built in early Decorated Gothic style or Transitional style of thirteenth century immediately following that known as Early English. Church consists of chancel (22ft long by 25ft wide), nave (55ftx25ft), vestry on north side of chancel (12ft 6insx9ft 6ins) and west gallery. Constructed of roughly coursed Pennant sandstone quarried locally, laid in random layers. Church is rectangular in shape and chancel is formed by continuation of nave. Chancel ceiling is boarded in an arched shape. Roof of nave constructed of arch-braced principals open to ridge. Seats all open benches of varnished pitch-pine and there is accommodation, including gallery at west end set apart for children, for 307 worshippers. All seats free and unappropriated. Porch on south side, and vestry with heating chamber beneath on north side. Bellcote corbelled out over west gable. Contractor: Joseph Richards, Swansea. Cost £1,495. ICBS grant £205; grant of £85 from Church Building Commissioners. (*Bldr*, 24 May 1856, 289) Opened for worship on 15 December 1856. (*SGH*, 17 December 1856) Consecrated on 14 April 1857. (*Swansea Journal*, 15 April 1857)

1879: Restoration of roof. Cost £1,400. (ICBS file no. 8582 (1881))

1881–2: Church enlarged by addition of south aisle. Additional seating accommodation for 150 worshippers. The correspondent in the *Church Builder* reported that 'Owing to the increase in the number of worshippers at the church, the enlarging of it has become a necessity. The district is miserably poor containing one or more "pit-villages", as they would be called in the north, but the parishioners are willing and ready to do what they can.' (*Ch. Bldr* (1881), 30) Architect: John Bacon Fowler, Brecon. Contractor: Joseph Gwyn, Sketty. Cost £1,500. ICBS grant £65. (SD/F/641. Enlarging church. Faculty dated 3 August 1881) Reopened after enlargement on 18 April 1881. (*The Cambrian*, 21 April 1882)

Comments: St Peter's was the last Commissioners' church to be built in Glamorgan. This was because the second parliamentary grant of £500,000, made in 1824, was almost exhausted. St Peter's chapel of ease, as it was then known, was typical of a Commissioners' church. The chancel was formed merely as a continuation of the nave, without any intervening chancel arch or screen. The chancel was distinguished only by its more refined treatment of the ceiling which was barrel-shaped and boarded. In sharp contrast, the roof of

the nave is of open timber construction with arch braces and collar braces. Penson was sufficiently acquainted with the principles of the Ecclesiologists to realize that even in a Commissioners' church built with restricted means he had to make some distinction between the chancel and nave. The west gallery was forced upon the architect by the demands to include the maximum amount of sittings. The enlargement of the church in 1882 by the addition of a south aisle was determined by the growth of the population in that district. John Bacon Fowler failed to continue the early Decorated style of architecture of the church by inserting triple lancet windows with engaged shafts in the east and west ends of the south aisle, which are basically Early English in style.

ST LUKE'S CHURCH, CWMBWRLA, SWANSEA

1889–90: New church built on new site by E. M. Bruce Vaughan, Cardiff. (ICBS file no. 9299 (1889)) The *Church Builder* reported that 'The district in which the proposed new church is to be built is increasing very rapidly, and church accommodation is very much needed. The inhabitants of the district are poor and not able to subscribe much towards the expense, but are willing and ready to do what they can. The sub-committee of the St David's Diocesan Church Building Board have examined and approved the plans. The population of the whole parish is 5,600 and of the district 2,600.' (*Ch. Bldr* (1889), 78) Foundation stone laid on 31 October 1889 by Mrs F. Walters Bond. (*The Cambrian*, 1 November 1889) Built in Early English Gothic style consisting of chancel flanked by north organ chamber and south vestry, nave with north and south aisles, and south-west tower with spire. Principal entrance to church through doorway in west front. Constructed of hammer-dressed Welsh Pennant sandstone with Box Ground stone dressings. Wide, almost square, nave separated from aisles by four pointed arches, which spring from circular capitals on round pillars. Nave has open timber roof of pitch-pine whose principal rafters are supported on stone corbels. Chancel arch springs from twin shafts to corbels. Boarded wagon roof to chancel. East window of three lights with traceried head. Aisles pierced by two-light windows with plate tracery. West front with four-light Geometrical window and west doorway with pointed arch under cill band flanked by lancets. Octagonal stair-turret to lower stages of tower, belfry lighted with twin lancets with nook shafts below plain parapet surmounted by pyramidal spire under weather vane. Open benches of pitch-pine, stained and varnished, for 530 parishioners. Contractor: G. Gustavus, Swansea. Cost £2,800. ICBS grant £225. (T. M. Walters, *St Luke's Church, Cwmbwrla, Swansea: Some Highlights of the First Eighty Years* (Swansea, 1970)) Consecrated on 25 September 1890. (*The Cambrian*, 26 September 1890)

Comments: St Luke's was the first church to be built by Bruce Vaughan in Swansea. It was far superior in design and execution to any of Vaughan's churches built in the south Wales coalfield. He was even provided with sufficient funds from public subscription to design and build a short south-west tower with spire. In the latter part of the nineteenth century, the ecclesiastical parish of Cockett extended from Cwmbwrla in the east, in the middle of a large industrial area, right up to the populous village of Waunarlwydd in the west. As a result of the indefatigable efforts of the vicar, Revd Daniel Roderick, by 1890 the populous centres of the parish were served by two new churches at Cwmbwrla (1890) and Waunarlwydd (1888) and an enlarged parish church at Cockett (1882).

ST JAMES' CHURCH, FFYNONE, SWANSEA

1863–7: New church built on new site donated by James Walters, Ffynone, a member of a prominent Swansea family. David Walker has noted that 'the plan to build a new church had been ventilated during the early 1860s'. Once land was known to be available, an architect, Thomas Nicholson of Hereford, was approached and brochure issued laying out advantages of scheme and asking for public support. The necessity for this new church, as brochure claimed, 'must appear to all who are

57. South-east view of proposed new church of St James, Ffynone, Swansea. T. Nicholson, archt., Hereford. The architect's impression of the new church (Source: Canon D. G. Walker, *Saint James' Church, Swansea, 1867–1992* (Swansea, 1992), frontispiece) (By kind permission of the Vicar and Churchwardens of St James' Church, Swansea)

acquainted with the large and continually increasing population of the Parish [of St Mary]'. (David G. Walker, *Saint James' Church, Swansea, 1867–1992* (rev. edn, Swansea, 1992), 6) Foundation stone laid on 3 July 1863 by Mrs E. B. Squire, wife of vicar of St Mary's Church, Swansea. (*The Cambrian*, 10 July 1863) Built in Decorated Gothic style consisting of chancel with north and south chancel chapels, nave with north and south transepts, vestry and south porch. Constructed of local Pennant sandstone with Bath stone for arches and dressings. Total length of building 120ft and extreme width 75ft. Nave separated from aisles by arcade of five pointed arches on each side springing from round pillars with carved capitals. Chancel stalled and well elevated above nave. Wide and lofty arch springing from carved capitals above three pillarets with sculpted figures of angels below separates nave from chancel. West front, transepts and chancel filled with large windows of Geometrical-style tracery, that in chancel being of five lights, those in transepts of four lights each, and that in west front of three lights. Series of three-light windows decorate aisles. Roofs open timbered of interlacing pattern, stained and varnished. Open benches of pitch-pine. Seating accommodation for 600 worshippers. Godwin's tiles used for floors throughout, plain in body of church but ornamented in chancel. Reredos composed of enriched tile work. (*BN*, 12 July 1867, 484) Contractor: Thomas, Watkins and Jenkins, Swansea. Cost £2,500. Consecrated on 21 June 1867. (*The Cambrian*, 28 June 1867)

Comments: St James', designed in the Decorated Gothic style, is characterized by its verticality. A wide and lofty chancel arch separates the nave from the chancel, which is only slightly lower than the nave. The chancel arch, the nave arcading and the windows are in perfect harmony with each other. One unusual feature of the interior is that the arcades of the aisles carry on across the transepts. The best view of the church is from the south-east where the east window of the chancel is filled with graceful Geometrical tracery and the corner or clasping buttresses of the Decorated period are worked in stages. The figures in the east window are circles within arches; lancets with elongated cinquefoils, trefoils above and diamond shapes above those. The fine proportions of the west window exhibit slender mullions, slender tracery, figures within figures, trefoil-headed lights with inverted daggers and quatrefoils higher still. Nicholson's attention to detail makes the church a building of considerable quality. As Newman says, St James' Church was built with the clear intention of dominating its surroundings on its island site, but it failed to do so, since the proposed south-west tower and spire were never built. (Newman, 584)

ST JOHN THE BAPTIST'S CHURCH, HAFOD, SWANSEA

1878–80: New church built on new site by Vivian family for their workers at Hafod Copper Works. Architect: Henry Woodyer, Guildford. (ICBS file no. 8216 (1878)) Foundation stone laid on 29 August 1878 by Sir Henry Hussey Vivian of Singleton Abbey, who donated the site. (*The Cambrian*, 30th August 1878) Built in Perpendicular Gothic style consisting of chancel, nave, south

aisle and western bellcote. Principal entrance to church through west doorway in south aisle. Built of local Pennant sandstone with rubblework facings with Bath stone dressings and roof covered with slates. East window of seven cinquefoiled lights with rectilinear-style tracery in head. Chancel formed by continuation of nave, and principally distinguished by panelled arch over chancel responds. Furnishings of chancel include highly carved Gothic choir stalls, and altar rail is of oak from Baltic. Woodwork of interior – pews, roof etc. – of pitch-pine, while that of roof enriched with Gothic ornamentation. Nave divided from south aisle by arcade of six pointed arches springing from octagonal pillars. Open timber collar-beam roofs of nave and south aisle have ornamented tie-rods, moulded purlins and windbraces. West end of nave lighted by pair of four cinquefoiled lights with rectilinear-style tracery between centre buttress. Walls of nave and south aisle pierced by pairs of two-light windows with Y-tracery. Open benches of varnished pitch-pine. Seating accommodation for 650 worshippers. Contractor: David Morgan, Swansea. Cost £5,000. ICBS grant £180. Consecrated on 30 March 1880. (*The Cambrian*, 2 April 1880)

Comments: The building of St John the Baptist's Church, Hafod, in the years 1878 to 1880 removed an anomaly which had existed in Swansea for some time, namely that the parish of St John's-juxta-Swansea was virtually without a parish church. The old church of St John's-juxta-Swansea in High Street had caused great difficulty because it was situated some distance outside the extreme boundary of its parish and within the parish of St Mary's, Swansea. Therefore in 1878 on the erection of St John's Church, Hafod, it was divested of its parochial rights to the vicar of St Mary's, Swansea, to serve as a parish church for a new ecclesiastical district. In 1886 St John's-juxta-Swansea became St Matthew's Church. Sir Henry Hussey Vivian chose Henry Woodyer, who had built the Vivian estate church at Sketty in 1850, to build their new church at Hafod. The church was built in the Perpendicular Gothic style, a style of architecture that was soon to become fashionable in the late nineteenth century, but not one favoured by the

Surrey architect. The explanation was that the church was a Vivian benefaction and that Vivian had conceived the idea of building a church here for his workers at the Hafod Copper Works, modelled on the late medieval parish church of St Mary's Church, Truro, Cornwall, with which place the Vivians had been associated for generations. As Newman points out the best view of the Perpendicular-style church is from the east where 'the full splendour' of Woodyer's design is apparent in the massive seven- and six-light east windows of the chancel and south aisle with their rectilinear-style tracery in the heads. (Newman, 609)

ALL SAINTS' CHURCH, KILVEY, SWANSEA

1842–5: New church built on new site donated by Messrs Freeman & Co of White Rock Copper Works. Built as chapel of ease to Llansamlet Church to serve growing population of Kilvey, since parish church was some three miles away. Primarily intended for use of workmen and their families in copper works and collieries and also for inhabitants of hamlet of St Thomas in parish of Swansea. Foundation stone laid on 16 June 1842. (*The Cambrian*, 18 June 1842) Church consisted originally of nave only with projections at each end – that at east end containing Communion table etc. and that at west end being occupied by entrance and staircase to west gallery. Benefactor: Grenfell family, Maesteg House. Cost £800. ICBS grant £20. Opened for divine service on 22 May 1845. (*The Cambrian*, 31 May 1845)

1858–9: Enlargement of church by addition of south aisle, south porch, with extension of projection at east end to form chancel. Architect: Richard Kyrke Penson, Ferryside. (ICBS file no. 3158 (1840)) New vestry added and new gabled bellcote erected. External walls built of local Pennant sandstone with Bath stone dressings. Enlarged part of church built in Decorated Gothic style. New open seats with framed bench ends of Memel, wrought and stained. Roof over new aisle constructed with arch principals, purlins and rafters executed in Memel timber, wrought and stained, open to ridge piece and covered with Caer-

narfonshire slates. Passages paved with Stafford-shire tiles. Font moved from its improper position under gallery in nave and placed near entrance in south aisle. Seating accommodation for 424 worshippers, with 188 seats free and unappropriated. (*Bldr*, 4 June 1859, 379) Benefactor: Grenfell family, Maesteg House. Contractor: William Rayner, Swansea. Cost £900. ICBS grant £120. Reopened after enlargement on 26 May 1859. (*The Cambrian*, 27 May 1859)

1875: Consecrated on 4 November 1875. (*The Cambrian*, 5 November 1875)

1883: Restoration of church. Work consisted of new chancel, repair of fabric, new front to gallery and complete decoration of interior. Reredos added to chancel and church lighted by brass coronae. Contractor: D. Rees, Ystalyfera. Cost £1,000. Reconsecrated after restoration on 4 October, 1883. (*The Cambrian*, 5 October 1883)

Comments: All Saints' was not designed by a professional architect but was built under the superintendence of Pascoe Grenfell's agent, who was experienced in building matters. It was therefore originally a simple mission church with a large nave and projections at both ends. It had no claim to architectural merit whatsoever. In fact, the ICBS voiced serious criticisms about the plan of construction of the church roof. (ICBS file no. 3158 (1840)) Penson's enlargement of Kilvey Church in the years 1858–9 completely transformed the original plain and austere mission church into a typical Anglican Church of the High Victorian period with all its standard fittings and furnishings. Its present appearance is the result of further enlargement and embellishment of the chancel in 1883.

ST CYFELACH'S CHURCH, LLANGYFELACH, SWANSEA

1860: When Sir Stephen Glynne visited Llangyfelach Church in June 1860, he wrote that 'The nave has been rebuilt in very poor Gothic. The chancel, which is of unusual length, perhaps retains the original walls. The chancel arch is obtuse, of doubtful character: on the north is a flat arched doorway and opening to the north chapel from the church is a rude flat arch. This chapel is full of marble monuments; south of the chancel appear some ruined walls, probably of vestry or chancel . . . The tower is quite distinct from the church, on an elevated spot in the burying-ground. It is rude and characteristic of the country.' (Sir Stephen R. Glynne, 'Notes on the older churches in the four Welsh dioceses', *Arch. Camb.* (1897), 294)

1867–8: Refurbishment of church. Reading desk and pulpit remodelled and placed in far better position than formerly. Body of church reseated. New harmonium installed to accompany choir. (*The Cambrian*, 8 May 1868)

1891: From Glynne's description of 1860 and Dr Cowley's article in *Gower* it would appear that between 1830 and 1860 the tithe-barn had been rebuilt to form nave, chancel and north chapel. (F. G. Cowley, 'Llangyfelach Church', *Gower*, 31 (1980), 80) In 1891, when Canon D. Watcyn Morgan was vicar, existing chancel of this rebuilt church was in turn taken down to make room for new chancel, which was built by Ecclesiastical Commissioners at a cost of £500. Another £600 was spent by parishioners in carrying out many structural alterations of extensive nature in nave. Also old-fashioned square box pews replaced by open benches of pitch-pine and vestry provided at west end of church. Architect: E. M. Bruce Vaughan, Cardiff. Contractors: Thomas, Watkins & Jenkins, Swansea, and Messrs Bennett Bros, Swansea. Cost £1,100. Reopened after restoration on 12 March 1891. (*The Cambrian*, 20 March 1891)

Comments: In the absence of any firm documentary evidence, it is likely that the chancel was rebuilt by Ewan Christian, consulting architect to the Ecclesiastical Commissioners, and that E. M. Bruce Vaughan restored the nave as reported in *The Cambrian* newspaper at the time. It was most unusual for Bruce Vaughan to be engaged in church restoration, as hitherto he had been involved only in the building of new churches in Glamorgan. The rebuilding of the chancel and the restoration of the nave in 1891 was an attempt to improve St Cyfelach's from an architectural and structural point of view from its humble foundation, which originated in a tithe-barn.

The church did not assume its present appearance until a further restoration of the church in the years 1913–14 by William Douglas Caröe, who succeeded Christian as architect to the Ecclesiastical Commissioners in 1895. Porch was taken down and rebuilt, new windows erected in nave, floor of nave repaired, and new oak chancel screen erected. Other work included restoration of the detached tower situated some distance from the church and installation of new organ. Seating accommodation for 270 parishioners. Architect: William Douglas Caröe, London. Cost £1,635. ICBS grant £40. (ICBS file no. 11,194 (1913)) Reopened after restoration on 24 March 1914. (*The Cambrian*, 24 March 1914)

ST SAMLET'S CHURCH, LLANSAMLET, SWANSEA

1840: New gallery erected and general repairs made to fabric of church, thus providing 180 additional seats. Architect: John Roberts, Morriston. Cost £67. ICBS grant £20. (ICBS file no. 2602 (1840))

1878–9: New church built on new site to north of old church, donated by earl of Jersey. According to Revd Dr Thomas Walters, vicar of Llansamlet, existing church was 'small, ill-arranged and through decay devoid of all comforts. As a matter of fact it is in a tumbledown state of repair.' (ICBS file no. 7924 (1875)) At vestry meeting held on 23 July 1874, decision taken not to renovate old building but to build new church alongside old structure which would ultimately be demolished. (Brian H. Jones, *Llansamlet Parish Church: The First 100 Years* (Swansea, 1979), 4) Architect: Henry Francis Clarke, Briton Ferry. Foundation stone laid on 2 May 1878 by countess of Jersey. (*The Cambrian*, 3 May 1878) Built in Early English Gothic style consisting of large raised chancel, nave and north and south aisles with clerestory. Constructed of local Pennant sandstone with Bath stone dressings. Arcade of five bays supported on Bath stone pillars with square capitals decorated with large naturalistic foliage. Seating accommodation for 645 worshippers on modern pews of pitch-pine. Roof of nave, pitch-pine stained and varnished. Chancel roof barrel-shaped and covered with match boarding. Pulpit and chancel furniture of pitch-pine. Interior of nave 80ft by 24ft and 47ft to ridge. Chancel 35ft by 24ft and 42ft to ridge. (*Bldr*, 1 November 1879, 220) Immersion font installed towards west end of nave with black bitumen floor and white glazed brick sides. Contractor: David Joshua, Llansamlet. Heating apparatus supplied by William Porritt, Dixon Green, Lancs. Cost £4,556. ICBS grant £250; Ecclesiastical Commissioners £400 towards the chancel; earl of Jersey £500; several donations of £100 by various industrialists. (*Bldr*, 11 October 1879, 1139) Consecrated on 6 October 1879. (*The Cambrian*, 10 October 1879)

Comments: Because of the restricted funds Clarke included a poorly designed clerestory in his plan of the church. The most striking feature of the interior is the arcade of five pointed arches supported on square capitals with huge naturalistic leaf capitals on short round pillars.

In the years 1914–15 the tower, 80ft high, was erected at the south-east corner of the church. It was buttressed with a circular staircase and entrance on east side. Architect: Glendinning Moxham, Swansea. Contractor; David Rosser, Swansea. Cost £1,710. IBCS grant £15. (ICBS file no. 11, 247 (1914)) Tower dedicated on 15 July 1915. (*W. Mail*, 16 July 1915) Moxham built the tower in keeping with the character of the existing church and as such it forms a distinctive landmark in the surrounding countryside.

ST DAVID'S CHURCH, MORRISTON, SWANSEA

1890–1: New church built on new site. The correspondent in the *Church Builder* reported that 'The district for which the new church is intended has a population of over 10,000; but, including an adjoining district which at present is entirely unprovided with services in connection with the Church of England, there is a population of 18,000. For this population the only building available at present is a chapel-of-ease at Morriston, with accommodation for 340; the parish church is three miles distant. The bilingual difficulty is a great hindrance to the working of this district. The new church will hold 600 persons.' (*Ch. Bldr* (1888), 2) Foundation stone laid on 2 January 1890 by Lady Emma Llewelyn of Penllergare. (*The Cambrian*, 3 January 1890) Built in Early English Gothic style by E. M. Bruce Vaughan, consisting of chancel, nave, north and south aisles, organ chamber and vestry on north side, and north porch. (ICBS file no. 9201 (1887)) External walls faced with grey Pennant sandstone with Bath stone dressings under green slate roof. North and south aisles separated from nave by deeply chamfered stone arcade of five bays supported on solid round pillars with moulded caps and bases. Sedilia and credence of Bath stone. Reredos and altar of solid oak by Jones & Willis, Birmingham. Chancel roof barrel-shaped, of two bays, boarded with unpolished pitch-pine. Nave and aisle roofs also constructed of unpolished pitch-pine as are choir stalls and open benches of nave which seat 600 worshippers. Walls plastered internally. Passages in chancel, nave and aisles paved with Godwin's tiles. Oak pulpit executed by William Clarke, Llandaff. Church provided with immersion as well as ordinary font. Schoolroom constructed under chancel and part of nave. Heating apparatus by Messrs Killick & Cochran, Liverpool. Decorative sculpture by William Wormleighton, architectural sculptor, Cardiff. (*Bldr*, 14 November 1891, 374) Contractors: Messrs Jenkins Bros, Swansea and Joseph Gwyn, Sketty. Cost £4,000. ICBS grant £350. Consecrated on 15 October 1891. (*The Cambrian*, 16 October 1891)

Comments: Bruce Vaughan's design of St David's with its well-appointed sanctuary and chancel demonstrated that by the late Victorian period the influence of the High Church movement had affected church life with its demand for more ceremony and ritual in its services even in an industrial community such as Morriston in the parish of Llangyfelach.

ST JOHN'S CHURCH, MORRISTON, SWANSEA

1859–62: By 1854 it was reported that the original St John's, built in 1789, was in a dilapidated state and also that it was too small for increasing population of Morriston. Consequently, appeal launched for funds to replace old building. Original plan prepared by David Jones of Swansea rejected by the ICBS 'as incompetent and that the drawings could not be understood by any workmen, displaying a want of theoretic or practical knowledge'. In November 1854, Richard Kyrke Penson was asked to prepare plans, which were approved in December 1854. Rebuilding work started in October 1859 but delayed due to insufficient funds and not completed until early 1862. (ICBS file no. 4633 (1854)) Rebuilt in early Decorated Gothic style consisting of chancel, nave, south aisle and south porch. Constructed of local Welsh Pennant sandstone with Bath stone dressings and roof timbers constructed from Baltic Memel. East window of three trefoiled lights with Geometrical-style tracery in head. Chancel has a trussed-rafter, scissors-beam roof and nave has an open timbered, arch-braced roof whose principal rafters spring from plain stone corbels. Chancel arch pointed and springs from three pillarets with caps and pointed bases. Nave divided from south aisle by arcade of four pointed arches springing from alternate octagonal and circular capitals on similar columns. Nave lighted by west window of two trefoiled lights with quatrefoil in apex and by single lancet clerestory lights. Cost £2,000. Consecrated on 10 July 1862. (*The Cambrian*, 18 July 1862)

1872: Tower with octagonal stair turret built at east end of south aisle. North aisle never built and the bricked-up arches can be seen externally in the north wall. Benefactor: Messrs Vivian & Sons, Morriston. Cost £1,360. ICBS grant £151. (Beryl Thomas, *Eglwys Sant Ioan Treforys* (Morriston, 1989))

Comments: Before the tower and spirelet were erected in 1872 the church must have offered a poor appearance and was hardly a fitting memorial to those wealthy landowners and industrialists who responded to appeals for funds in 1859. Not only was the church unfinished, but there were obvious economies all around when it was built. The clerestory is so shallow that one might have expected paired lancets, particularly as some compensation was obviously needed for the lack of light at ground level on the north side. Internally, the chancel does not seem to have been designed at all beyond the necessary fittings and fixtures, and the only features of architectural merit are the double-chamfered chancel arch springing from triple-shafted corbels and the alternating round and octagonal pillars of the arcade of the south aisle. The trefoil-headed windows are small and plain, and the larger ones have only the minimal tracery with very basic geometrical shapes in the heads. The tower, obviously an essential addition to the church, quite inexplicably was given more detailed treatment than the main body of the church. The corbel table continues right around the tower and the belfry-stage lights have received rather more thought than one might have expected. The belfry is reached by an octagonal stair turret on the south side capped by a spirelet, which adds an attractive finish to the tower.

ST PAUL'S CHURCH, SKETTY, SWANSEA

1850: New church built on new site given by Henry Hussey Vivian of Singleton Abbey. Architect: Henry Woodyer, Guildford. Church built by the Vivian family as a memorial to Henry Hussey Vivian's first wife, Jessie, née Goddard (d. 1848), daughter of MP for Swindon. Built in Decorated Gothic style consisting of chancel,

58. St Paul's Church, Sketty, Swansea (Source: Photograph of south-west view of Singleton Church, Sketty) (By kind permission of Swansea Museum)

oak. Cost £5,630. (*SGH*, 2 October 1850) Consecrated on 27 September 1850. (*The Cambrian*, 4 October 1850)

1878: Stone reredos erected by Sarah Vivian in memory of her husband, J. H. Vivian, depicting The Last Supper. Executed by Thomas Nicholls, Lambeth. (SD/F/614. Reredos. Faculty dated 12 February 1878)

1888–9: Organ chamber and vestry added. Cost £300. Contractor: Joseph Gwyn, Sketty. (*The Cambrian*, 31 August 1888)

Comments: When an application was made to the ICBS in 1928 for grant aid to enlarge the chancel and to build new vestries, the plans for the work were drawn up by Glendinning Moxham, a Swansea architect. Revd H. J. Stewart, vicar of Sketty, decided to consult Sir Charles Nicholson, the architect in charge of Westminster Abbey, about the proposed exterior so as not to spoil the proportions of the church. Nicholson examined the church and agreed to Moxham's plans to extend the chancel and north aisle and rebuild the vestry. He wrote, 'I should like before offering any detailed observations on the proposed work to pay my tribute to the excellence of the work of the original architect of the church which appears to me to be one of the best works of its period (1850). Who the architect may have been I do not know, his work was evidently done under the influence of Pugin and the Ecclesiological Society and reproduces the feeling of an old village church with considerable success.' (ICBS file no. 10,749 (1926) Letter to Moxham dated April, 1928) Henry Woodyer of Guildford, Surrey was the architect chosen by Vivian instead of a local man to build his memorial church. Woodyer was influenced not only by his own locality, the Surrey countryside, but also by Pugin and the Ecclesiological Society, so that he did in fact re-create the atmosphere of a village church with notable success. He was the first pupil in 1844 of William Butterfield, the leader of the Gothic Revival and the favourite architect of the Ecclesiologists. Woodyer built St Paul's in the Middle Pointed or Decorated Gothic style, the favourite idiom of the Ecclesiologists. This is Victorian Middle Pointed at its best. John Hilling rightly regarded St Paul's as 'the best of Swansea's

south chapel to chancel, south aisle to nave, south porch and western tower with spire. (*Bldr*, 12 October 1850, 487) 100ft broach spire clad in oak shingles, and there is a good timber south porch. Constructed of Cornish sandstone from Vivian's quarries in Cornwall and with Bath stone and Painswick stone dressings. East window of three trefoiled lights with three cinquefoils in head. North side of chancel has two windows of two lights. On south side are two equal sedilia and to their west a door through which steps descend into sacristy abutting to south chapel. On north side of nave are one window of three and two windows of two lights. Nave divided from south aisle by five moulded pointed arches springing from octagonal Middle Pointed piers with two responds. Open timber roofs in chancel and nave, both of which are plastered between rafters. Passages in nave paved with black and red Staffordshire tiles. Woodwork of interior, pulpit, choir stalls and open benches in nave for 350 worshippers, is polished many churches'. (John B. Hilling, 'Architecture in Glamorgan', in Prys Morgan (ed.), *Glamorgan County History*, VI (Cardiff, 1989), 407) The reviewer in *The Ecclesiologist* said that 'we have to congratulate Mr Woodyer on a very successful village church: indeed for situation, character and detail taken conjointly, we could not easily point to a better example . . . we would call Mr Woodyer's attention to the local Nolton'. (*Eccl.*, 11 (1850), 145) It is curious why the Vivians went to the trouble of importing stone from their quarries in Cornwall when the Quarella sandstone at Nolton, Bridgend was so readily available only some thirty-five miles away. Clearly *The Ecclesiologist* thought that the architect might have considered using local stone in keeping with the principles of the Ecclesiological Society.

In 1908 the church was enlarged by the addition of a north aisle. Architect: Glendinning Moxham, Swansea. Cost £1,260. Donor of new aisle: Glynn Vivian. Furniture and fittings: £650, subscribed by local churchpeople. Additional accommodation for 148 worshippers. (SD/F/615. Aisle. Faculty dated 30 January 1908) New aisle dedicated on 16 September 1908. (*The Cambrian*, 18 September 1908) In the years 1928–9 the chancel was enlarged (almost doubled), north aisle extended and vestry rebuilt and organ loft erected. Architect: Glendinning Moxham, Swansea. Cost £5,936. ICBS grant £60. Work completed in July 1929. (ICBS file no. 10,749 (1928))

ST THOMAS' CHURCH, ST THOMAS, SWANSEA

1886–7: New church built on new site. Architect: Thomas Nicholson & Son, Hereford. When Nicholson's original plans submitted to ICBS he was asked to revise them and to design a larger building with seating for 512 worshippers. Revised plan approved by Society but, due to lack of funds, only nave, north and south aisles, west narthex and recess at east end of church for chancel built in years 1886–7. (ICBS file no. 1888 (1886)) Foundation stone laid on 17 June 1886 by General Sir F. W. Grenfell. (*The Cambrian*, 18 June 1886) Built in Early English Gothic style. Constructed of

local Pennant sandstone and internal walls faced with light-coloured stone ashlaring relieved with an intermixture of red Alveley stone in bands, pillars, voussoirs, corbels etc. Nave divided from aisles by arcade of five pointed arches springing from central clustered shafts. Wood-block floors throughout, oak in alley-ways and red deal under open benches of pitch-pine. Seating accommodation for 512 persons. Lofty triple lancet windows occupy west wall of nave with external buttresses. Scissors-beam roof of nave covered with Westmoreland slates. Contractor: John Wood, Malvern. Cost £4,792. Consecrated on 14 April 1887. (*The Cambrian*, 15 April 1887)

1890: Church completed by addition of chancel, transepts and tower with spire standing at north-west end of north aisle. Five-light group of lancet windows with moulded arches and polished Lizard serpentine pillars fills upper portion of east wall of chancel beneath which is arcade of nine compartments of trefoil-headed arches carried upon similar marble shafts. Double sedilia and piscina in south wall of sanctuary, which is floored with encaustic tiles. Semicircular ceiling over sanctuary. Chancel arch springs from clustered corbels having triple pillarets of polished Lizard serpentine marble. Additional 200 sittings provided. Benefactor: Grenfell family, Maesteg House, St Thomas. Contractors: Messrs Loveday, Evans & Co., Swansea; John Wood, Malvern. Cost £5,038. ICBS grant £225. Consecrated on 17 June 1890. (*The Cambrian*, 20 June 1890)

Comments: St Thomas' was the second church to be built by Revd Canon J. Allan Smith, vicar of Swansea, the '*Church Builder*' of Swansea, the first being St Matthew's in 1886. It was entirely due to the characteristic generosity of the Grenfell family of Maesteg House that the chancel, transepts and tower were completed as a tribute to the memory of their father, Pascoe St Leger Grenfell, who had always taken a deep interest in church extension in the district. Nicholson paid great attention to the chancel, which includes a five-light group of lancets with moulded arches and polished Lizard serpentine pillars filling the upper part of the east wall. The general impression of the chancel, traditionally the most sacred part of the church, is one of lavish ecclesiological decoration which appears incongruous in the working-class area of St Thomas. However, this was typical of church building in the Victorian era, where magnificent churches were erected by members of the gentry for the people who lived and worked on their land.

ST MARY'S CHURCH, SWANSEA

(Destroyed in blitz in 1941)

1895–9: The old church was so dilapidated that it was impossible to attempt any satisfactory work of restoration. However, in 1895 Revd Canon J. Allan Smith, vicar of Swansea, encountered strong opposition to plan to demolish old St Mary's Church, since plans for rebuilding involved building over some vaults and graves. Leading opponent was Colonel W. Llewellyn Morgan. Matter settled in Bishop's Consistory Court during summer of 1895 when vicar was finally granted faculty to rebuild his parish church. (SD/F/637. Misc. Corr. Restoration of church in two stages: Consistory Court Proceedings. Faculty dated 1892–7) Accordingly, whole structure of church rebuilt with exception of Herbert Chapel. Architect: Sir Arthur William Blomfield, London. (ICBS file no. 9822 (1894)) Work commenced in December 1895. Memorial stone laid by Lord Windsor on 19 May 1896. (*The Cambrian*, 22 May 1896) Rebuilt in Early English Gothic style consisting of chancel, nave, aisles, western porch and embattled tower on south-east corner, 85ft in height. Constructed of local Pennant sandstone in random courses with dressings of Bath stone. Interior lined with Bath stone. Roofs constructed of English oak, with some chestnut and covered with Westmoreland slates. (*Bldr*, 14 August 1897, 137) New chancel same length (58ft) as old one, but width (31ft) nine feet more than old one. East wall stood exactly on line of former one, but south wall and those of tower and vestries were new and broader lines. Height from floor to wallplate 40ft and to ridge of roof 62ft. Floor of Rust's vitreous mosaic. Seating accommodation on individual chairs increased by 300 to 1,500. Old monuments retained and refixed in or near old positions. (*BN*, 11 November 1898, 677) Principal carving done by Thomas Nicholls of Lambeth.

Heating installed by Haden's of Trowbridge. Contractor: Messrs Cornish & Gaymer, North Walsham, Norfolk. Cost £27,990. ICBS grant £350. New nave opened for divine worship on 5 August 1897. (*The Cambrian*, 6 August 1897) Reconsecrated on 20 October 1898. (*The Cambrian*, 21 October 1898)

Comments: Blomfield designed St Mary's in the Early English Gothic style, an idiom that he used frequently in the latter part of his career. He had originally intended to place a spire on top of the tower, but in the final design the spire disappeared. In the end, his design showed a square tower attached to the nave. This was obviously based on the former St Mary's Church and in keeping with the traditional type of embattled Glamorgan tower, but in this case with corner buttresses of great height and a stair turret stepped out in the Irish fashion as at Llanrhidian Church in Gower. The tower was 30ft higher than the former tower and it embodied the existing corbels below the parapet of the old one. After the church was completed many people remarked on its exceedingly plain appearance – indeed plain to the extent of coldness. Canon Smith replied to this criticism by stating that the object of the building committee had been to erect a church worthy of the town at the lowest possible cost. Had they decided upon a building designed in a late Gothic form with elaborate decoration and expensive window tracery the cost would have been enormous and the difficulties in carrying it out would have been insurmountable. As it stood, the church was a stately substantial structure, which had been erected as a result of great effort and perseverance. Blomfield's design was both impressive and dignified and represented the Early English Gothic style of church architecture at its best. For Revd Canon J. Allan Smith it was the crowning achievement of his vicariate at Swansea.

ST MATTHEW'S CHURCH, SWANSEA

1885–6: Restoration and enlargement of church. In June 1885 old St John's-juxta-Swansea Church,

Swansea stood derelict and unused and Revd Canon J. Allan Smith decided to restore and enlarge it as part of his programme of church extension in Swansea. The correspondent in the *Church Builder* reported that 'This is an exceptional and peculiar case, a new church having been erected in this parish (St John's-juxta-Swansea). With the consent of the bishop, patron, and incumbent, the old Church now to be enlarged has been handed over to the vicar of Swansea, to be a Church of a new district to be formed out of a population of 39,000 souls. The St David's Diocesan Building Board recommend that considering the urgent necessity for extended church accommodation in Swansea, this application should receive a liberal grant.' (*Ch. Bldr* (1886), 3) Existing walls of squared sandstone blocks and roof timbers retained from William Jernegan's church of 1823–5, but former lancets replaced in a subclassical style. General style of restored church was mixed Romanesque and Classical. Raised east gable with Celtic cross to apex and moulded cornice has a circular light over a stepped three-light round-arched east window with colonnettes, and fluted bands surmounted by volutes. Church extended westwards to accommodate a congregation of 531 worshippers. West window of five stepped lights, outer two being much smaller than inner ones. West gable surmounted by single bellcote with rounded arch. Polygonal south porch with hipped roof to round-headed doorway. Short chancel formed by triple-arch arrangement with high chancel arch and square piers flanking side arches. Nave has open-boarded roof and tie-beams with narrow Gothic braces. West gallery, built as concession to the Evangelical Low Church persuasion, supported on Corinthian cast-iron columns. Church intended for Welsh-speaking services. Architects: Alfred Bucknall & Edward William Jennings, Swansea. Benefactor: Swansea Corporation. Contractor: William Morgan, Camden Place, Swansea. Cost £3,000. ICBS grant £50. Consecrated on 22 July 1886. (*The Cambrian*, 23 July 1886)

Comments: The remodelling of old St John's-juxta-Swansea Church was considered to be a 'very unsatisfactory building' by the Committee of

Architects of the ICBS. However, despite their misgivings they voted a grant of £80 in November 1885. (ICBS file no. 9029 (1885)) It was most unusual for the Committee of Architects to allow the construction of a west gallery in a church remodelled in the 1880s. The correspondent in *The Cambrian* for 23 July 1886 stated that 'The style is Renaissance period', while John Newman refers to the windows as 'sub-classical'. (Newman, 585) The Low Church persuasion of St Matthew's is reflected in the Decalogue, Creed and Lord's Prayer which flank the altar. The peculiarities of this church, whose interior resembles a Welsh chapel, are displayed both in its structure and in its internal fittings. This unusual church building can only be attributed to the desperate need of the Anglican Church at that time in Swansea to find additional church accommodation at little expense.

ST BARNABAS' CHURCH, WAUNARLWYDD, SWANSEA

1887–8: New church built on new site. Much of groundwork which led to building of church laid in early 1880s by Mrs Illtud de Winton Thomas of Glanmor, Swansea. In 1882 she had built a mission church in Waunarlwydd and supported Mr Burrells, a lay reader, who did good work in establishing a Sunday School and preparing a congregation for the future Anglican Church there. (O. J. Lewis, *A Short History of St Barnabas Church, Waunarlwydd* (Swansea, 1948), *passim*) Foundation stone laid on 3 November 1887 by Miss Isabel de Winton Thomas of Glanmor, Swansea. (*CDL*, 4 November 1887) Built in Early English Gothic style consisting only of nave (57ftx25ft) with transept (15ftx11ft) at east end. Built of local Pennant sandstone with Bath stone dressings and facings. Roof of nave, furniture and fittings of pitch-pine, including open benches to seat 250 to 300 worshippers. Single-manual organ by John Squire, organ builder, Euston, London installed. Architect: Thomas Lawrence Lewis. Contractor: Messrs Gustavus Bros, Swansea. Cost £1,100. (*CDL*, 13 July 1888)

Comments: St Barnabas' was a simple structure built for the industrialized area of Waunarlwydd at a time when the population, numbering then some 2,000 inhabitants, was rapidly expanding. It provided much needed accommodation for 250–300 worshippers who wished to attend the Anglican Church in an area where Nonconformity had already established a firm foothold.

In the years 1902–3 the church was renovated and a chancel added. Chancel constructed of local Pennant sandstone with Bath stone quoins and covered with slate roof. Completed building measured 80ft in length, the nave being 53ft and chancel 27ft. Architect: Glendinning Moxham, Swansea. Contractor: Messrs Bennett Bros, Swansea. Reopened after renovation and enlargement on 6 January 1903. (*CDL*, 7 January 1903)

ST MARK'S CHURCH, WAUNWEN, SWANSEA

1887: New church built on new site donated by Swansea Corporation in 1873. Foundation stone laid on 26 May 1887 by Mrs E. T. M. Llewelyn of Penllergare. (*The Cambrian*, 27 May 1887) Built in Early English Gothic style consisting of chancel, nave, north and south aisles, vestry and western bellcote. Entrance by way of north porch or narthex with doors to east and west. Constructed of rubble work with Box Ground stone dressings. Length of church 91ft by 43ft width. External walls strengthened by solid single-stage buttresses. Main characteristic of church is its timber arcading by which nave and aisles are formed without usual stone and brick work and which gives more light and uninterrupted view of pulpit and Communion table. Chancel roof barrel-shaped with carved foliage bosses at intersection of purlins and rafters. Nave roof plastered between slender common rafters. Open benches of pitch-pine accommodate 500 persons and facility exists for hanging seats against walls, which would allow room for 100 more worshippers. Architects: Messrs William Gilbie Habershon & J. F. Fawckner, of London and Newport. Benefactor: Sir J. T. D. Llewelyn, Penllergare. Contractor: Messrs H. Hilton & Sons, Swansea, Birmingham and Oxford. Cost £2,000. (*W. Mail*, 2 December 1887) Consecrated on 1 December 1887. (*The Cambrian*, 2 December 1887)

Comments: The building of St Mark's marked a new departure in traditional ecclesiastical architecture in Swansea. Great efforts were made to build a church as cheaply as possible to meet the spiritual requirements of a district of the rapidly expanding town of Swansea, principally inhabited by the working classes. The building committee and the architects, W. G. Habershon & Fawckner of Newport, succeeded in achieving this objective, in that the church was constructed for little more than £3 per sitting. The church was constructed of rubble work (i.e. pieces of undressed Pennant sandstone) with Box Ground stone dressings. The main characteristic of the church is in its timber arcading by which the nave and aisles are formed without the traditional stone or brick work. This gives more light and an uninterrupted view of the pulpit and altar and greatly reduced the cost, whilst at the same time it could be expected to be as durable as traditional materials. The use of wood for arcading was not a new concept in Glamorgan churches. Prichard had used it at Michaelstone-super-Avon and St Clement's, Briton Ferry in the High Victorian period, and John Coates Carter used it at St Catherine's, Melincryddan and St Mary's Church, Briton Ferry with similar success in the late Victorian period. Nevertheless, its use at St Mark's enabled a large church seating 600 people to be built at a cost of £2,000.

ST ANNE'S CHURCH, TALYGARN

1887: New church built adjacent to old chapelry of St Anne, Talygarn. Designed and built by George T. Clark in memory of his wife Anne Price Clark (d. 1885), daughter of Henry Lewis of Greenmeadow, Tongwynlais, near Cardiff. Built in mixture of Decorated and Perpendicular styles consisting of chancel, nave, south porch and south tower. Constructed of Welsh Pennant sandstone with Bath stone dressings. (Dillwyn Lewis, *The History of Llantrisant* (Risca, 1975), 94) In absence of other documentary sources, following description of church taken from a structural examination of it. Although church mostly designed in a Neo-Perpendicular style, represented in large four-light windows of nave with square labels, the east

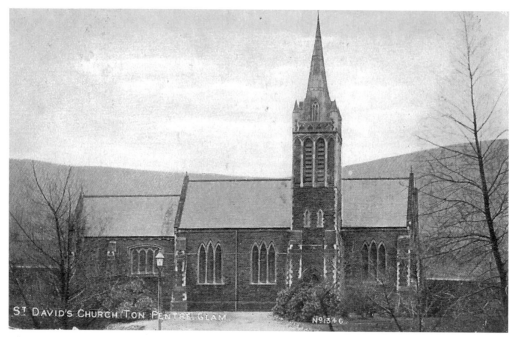

59. St David's Church, Ton Pentre (Source: Geoffrey R. Orrin: Postcard Collection of Glamorgan Churches)

window of chancel is in Decorated style as are windows on north and south sides of structure. South porch built with small trefoil-headed light in gable to give impression of two-storeyed fifteenth-century porch. Square tower on south side of east part of nave is a very plain structure with string-courses near base and just below belfry stage, lighted by paired trefoil-headed lights under square head. West window of nave of three trefoil lights with panel tracery in head. Nave has arch-braced roof with ogee-shaped arch braces springing from stone corbels. (Personal observation)

Comments: George Thomas Clark, who achieved fame as an antiquarian, was an engineer by profession, working on the Great Western Railway with Brunel. Therefore he was a practical man as well as a scholar, and he designed St Anne's in a mixture of Decorated and Perpendicular Gothic styles. He chose to build the chancel in the Decorated style, regarding it as an earlier part of the structure of a medieval church, and he built the rest of the church including the nave, tower and porch in a late Gothic form, Perpendicular Gothic, according to his own interpretation of that style. It

is noticeable that all the windows in the Perpendicular Gothic style have trefoil-headed lights as opposed to the usual cinquefoiled lights of the fifteenth century. Perhaps this was an attempt by Clark to interpret the style of the nave as of the early Perpendicular period following that of the Decorated style of the chancel.

ST DAVID'S CHURCH, TON PENTRE
(Demolished c.1980)

1880–1: New church built on new site given by Crawshay Bailey. Bailey built church for use of community occupying area of Ton Pentre in centre of parish in response to appeal by Archdeacon John Griffiths of Llandaff. Foundation stone laid on 17 June 1880 by Mrs Crawshay Bailey. (*W. Mail*, 18 June 1880) Built in Decorated Gothic style by John Bacon Fowler, Brecon. It consisted of chancel with organ chamber and vestry on south side, nave with south aisle of equal span and tower with spire. Principal entrance through porch beneath tower on north-west side of church. Total height of tower and spire 90ft. Constructed of local Pennant sandstone with Bath stone dressings and green Whitland slates. (*BN*, 23 December 1881, 862) East window of five trefoil-headed lights in a 2:1:2 arrangement; two principal centre mullions were arched and carried through head to admit cross patée within circle. Walls of nave and aisles, which were pierced by three-light lancet windows, heavily buttressed. Windows glazed with Cathedral glass. Floor of both chancel and nave covered with Godwin's encaustic tiles. Whole of building furnished with pitch-pine. Besides traditional font there was an immersion font in western corner of nave for adult baptism by total immersion. Open benches of pitch-pine. Seating accommodation for 560 persons. Building heated by hot water supplied by pipes from boilerhouse beneath church. (*Bldr*, 10 July 1880, 61) Contractor: Charles Shepherd, Cardiff. Cost £4,500. Opened for divine service on 27 October 1881. (*W. Mail*, 28 October 1881)

Comments: This prestigious church building with its extensive site, costing in total £8,000, was built at the sole expense of Crawshay Bailey, the younger, whose wealth was being considerably increased by the industrial development of the land in the area. He showed great concern for the parish of Ystradyfodwg because of extensive lands his father had shrewdly purchased there earlier in the century. With adequate funding, Fowler was able to build a church in a late Gothic form, Decorated Gothic, and to complete the building with a north-west tower and spire. It was one of the finest churches built in the Rhondda at that time. One unusual feature of this church was that the seats in the south aisle were arranged to face the nave and the pulpit and, another less unusual feature was that as well as the traditional font there was an immersion font for adult baptism.

ST JOHN'S CHURCH, TONDU

1868: New church built on new site given by dowager countess of Dunraven. In district of Aberkenfig and Tondu, development of iron works, collieries and railways quickly turned small rural community into thriving industrial area. At that time, church services provided by clergy of parish of Newcastle, Bridgend in small licensed room. This was unsatisfactory, so decision taken by diocesan authorities in 1866 to build permanent church at Tondu. (Margaret Robbins, *Parish of Newcastle, St John's Church, Tondu* (1968)) Built in early Decorated Gothic style by John Prichard, consisting of chancel, crossing, nave and south porch. Transepts and upper part of central tower never completed, although included in original design. (ICBS file no. 6517 (1867)) Length of nave (55ftx27ft), chancel including crux of tower (45ftx18ft), making total length of 100ft. Constructed of local Pennant sandstone with Bath stone dressings. Internal walls lined with grey bricks relieved by red ones in conjunction with greenish-grey Bridgend stone. Dressings of arches, quoins, jambs and windows of Bath stone. Chancel built at sole expense of Mrs Harriet Nicholl of Merthyr Mawr at cost of £800. East window of three trefoiled lights with Geometrical-style tracery in head. Choir stalls and chancel furniture of oak, and chancel floor covered with Godwin's encaustic tiles. Sanctuary steps of white marble with green lozenges and rectangles. Chancel has boarded ceiling over easternmost bay directly above sanctuary. Lower part of tower rests upon four pointed, moulded capitals. Pulpit and font of Bath stone. Roof of nave has carved braces to principal rafters which spring from stone corbels and are knit by moulded hoizontal beam and kingpost. Floor of nave laid out with slabs of stone, diamond-shaped in alternate colours of red and green. Open benches of pitch-pine. Seating accommodation for 285 worshippers. Contractor: Rees Roderick, Margam. Cost £2,000. (*CGG*, 22 September 1868) Consecrated on 26 September 1868. (*CMG*, 26 September 1868)

Comments: Prichard's original plan was to build a cruciform church with central tower, but the transepts and the upper stage of the tower were never built because of inadequate funding. The whole conception of the building is one of boldness conveying the idea of great solidity. The arches around the crossing, which convey a visual strength, spring for the most part straight out of the wall and make the most of the space available internally. The roof of the nave is remarkable for the intricate nature of its construction and the whole composition adds to the feeling of substantial strength. The interior is Prichard's first attempt in a Glamorgan church at Butterfieldian constructional polychromy. The internal walls are lined with grey bricks relieved by red bricks in bands in conjunction with the greenish-grey Quarella stone. The early Geometrical style predominates throughout the church particularly in the fenestration. The chancel is well appointed observing all the principles of the Ecclesiologists. A boarded roof over the easternmost part of the chancel distinguishes the sanctuary. Unfortunately this church is another example where Prichard's over-ambitious design was thwarted by the ever-present problem of lack of funds, leaving the church incomplete.

ST MICHAEL'S AND ALL ANGELS' CHURCH, TONGWYNLAIS

1875–7: New church built on new site given by Henry Lewis, Greenmeadow. Up to middle of nineteenth century, Tongwynlais was a mining district of some 2,000 people divided between parishes of Whitchurch and Eglwysilan. Rapid increase in population resulted from opening of Pentyrch and Melingriffith works and was noted by first vicar of Whitchurch, Revd Evan Price Thomas, who started mission services in the village in the early 1860s. Foundation stone laid on 10 June 1875 by Mabel Booker, eldest daughter of Thomas W. Booker of Velindre, and Henry Lewis Jnr. (*W. Mail*, 11 June 1875) Built in Early English Gothic style by John Prichard, consisting of chancel, nave, south porch and double bellcote above west gable. Constructed of local Welsh red sandstone (quarried on Greenmeadow estate and given by Henry Lewis) with dressings of Box Ground stone. Roof of open timber lined with polished wood and supported upon rafters with curvilinear braces, completed with a moulded rib extending along entire length of roof. It is covered with small green Penmoyle tiles. Stone pulpit decorated with sculptured foliage. Choir stalls of pitch-pine as are open benches which seat 300

parishioners. East window of four plain pointed lights and west window of three corresponding lights, both with Geometrical-style tracery in head with carved heads as label stops. Chancel arch supported on polished shafts springing from carved corbels with sculptured heads. Chancel lighted on south side by double lancet window and walls of nave pierced by six two-light lancet windows with plate tracery above. (Personal observation) Floor of chancel covered with tiles from Godwin's of Lugwardine, Herefordshire. Contractor: Thomas Williams, Canton, Cardiff. Cost £2,000. LDCES grant £100. (*W. Mail*, 23 February 1877) Opened for divine service on 22 February 1877. (*Cardiff Times*, 24 February 1877)

Comments: Tongwynlais Church was one of the few churches built by John Prichard in a mining district. Its architecture, particularly the tracery of the nave and west windows, is rather heavy and suggests that funds were restricted. The interior is very basic and the only attempt at flamboyance is the rather unkempt foliage on the capitals below the chancel arch and the leafy flourish to the terminations. The correspondent in the *Western Mail* for 23 February 1877 stated that 'the simplicity of the arrangements of the interior were in keeping with the humbleness of the locality'. The building was therefore typical of a village church erected for a poor mining community, a pattern that was to be repeated frequently during the late Victorian period in Glamorgan.

ST ANNE'S CHURCH, TONNA

1890–3: New church built on new site given by Griffiths family of Resolven. Built as memorial church to Mrs Anne Griffiths, wife of Revd Walter Griffiths of Dulais Fach. Foundation stone laid on 6 November 1890 by Miss Mary Griffiths, Resolven. (*The Cambrian*, 7 November 1890) Built in Early English Gothic style by E. H. Lingen Barker of Hereford. Cruciform in plan consisting of apsidal chancel, nave, transepts with lofty tower and spire on western side of north transept. (*Bldr*, 22 November 1890) Constructed of local Pennant sandstone raised on the estate of the donor with

Bath stone dressings. Entire length of building is 84ft (nave 50ft, chancel 34ft). Width of nave is 22ft and transepts 21ft. Above roof, tower assumes octagonal form, its angles being filled with bold octagonal pinnacles. Spire, which is substantially built, 90ft high. Main entrance to church by way of north porch beneath tower. Apsidal chancel lighted by three windows of two trefoiled lights with quatrefoil in head. Open benches of pitch-pine seat 300 worshippers. Heated by high-pressure steam apparatus. Contractor: Walter Dowland, Abergavenny. Cost £5,000, defrayed from estate of Revd David Griffiths. (*The Cambrian*, 24 February 1893) Consecrated on 20 February 1893. (*W. Mail*, 21 February 1893)

Comments: Although the church is a substantial structure, built of fine materials with a tower capped by a spire with bold octagonal pinnacles, its design in the Early English Gothic style is as John Newman says 'retardataire' for the late Victorian period. (Newman, 630) It would have been more appropriate for Lingen Barker to have built the church in a late Gothic form in keeping with the new trends in late Victorian church architecture.

ST MATTHIAS' CHURCH, TREHARRIS

1895–6: New church built on new site given by Colonel Lockwood as chapel of ease to St Tydfil's Church, Merthyr Tydfil. The correspondent in the *Church Builder* for 1896 stated that 'Treharris is a new colliery village with a population of about 5,000 and rapidly increasing; it will soon become a town of considerable size. It is seven and a half miles from the town and parish church of Merthyr Tydfil. Services have been held in the schoolroom hired from the School Board . . . A grant of £60 was made in May 1894 towards building the first portion of a new church for this district on more elaborate and costly plans. It is not intended to carry out the former plans and a grant is asked on the new designs now submitted.' (*Ch. Bldr* (1896), 65) Foundation stone laid by Frederick W. Harris, chairman of the Drapers' Company, London on 29 July 1895. (*W. Mail*, 30 July 1895) Built in Early

English Gothic style by John Loughborough Pearson, consisting of chancel, nave, north aisle, organ chamber, vestries with heating chamber beneath, north porch and western bellcote. (*Bldr*, 3 August 1895, 89) Constructed of Welsh Pennant sandstone laid in random courses with Bath stone dressings. Church entered from north by porch. This porch is fitted with open-framed roof and has a floor of stone laid in small diagonal squares. Chancel divided from nave by carved oak screen of three traceried arches. Nave separated from north aisle by three pointed arches springing from moulded capitals on octagonal and round pillars. East window of three pointed lancets with plate tracery in head. Nave and aisle lighted by single and double lancets. Chancel has semicircular arched panelled roof with moulded ribs. Nave and north aisle have open-framed roofs of New Zealand pine. Roofs covered with red tiles. Floor laid with plain red and black tiles and wood-block floors under seats. Doors of English oak with ornamental hinges. Seating accommodation on individual chairs for 365 worshippers. Contractor: Messrs William Cowlin & Sons Ltd, Bristol. Cost £4,500. ICBS grant £75; Bishop of Llandaff's Fund £400. (*Bldr*, 4 July 1896, 15) Opened for divine service on 29 June 1896. (*W. Mail*, 30 June 1896)

Comments: In 1895 it had become apparent that the original plans drawn up for the church by John Loughborough Pearson were too elaborate for the resources available. A new design, approved in April 1896, was for a more modest church excluding the south aisle. It is difficult to tell from a cursory glance at the exterior of St Matthias' that it is the work of an eminent Victorian architect, more accustomed to building great churches and cathedrals. However, the interior of the church has typical characteristics of Pearson's work. For instance, he had a penchant for Early English Gothic-style architecture and he has employed that idiom in a very marked style with the grouped triple lancets of the east window of the chancel, the Y-tracery of the west window of the nave and the choice of alternate round and octagonal capitals and pillars for the arcade between the nave and north aisle. Also the wagon roof of the chancel with its numerous square-ribbed vaults is evocative of Pearson's stone vaulting in his great churches, but executed here in timber instead of stone. The fittings and furnishings of oak, with ornamental hinges instead of the cheaper deal or pitch-pine, are also indicative of an architect of some discernment. Pearson must have been frustrated by the restriction of funds, which compelled him to place an ornamental oak screen between chancel and nave instead of the conventional stone arch and particularly by the omission of the south aisle after building had started. Consequently, this gives the structure an asymmetrical appearance, which was contrary to Pearson's architectural principles.

ST MARY'S CHURCH, TREHERBERT

(Church made redundant in 1967 and demolished in 1980s)

1867–8: New church built on new site given by marquess of Bute as chapel of ease to parish church of St John the Baptist, Ystradyfodwg. During 1860s Treherbert, which originally formed a hamlet of Ystrad, became a small town in its own right and consequently there was a pressing need for a permanent stone church. Built in Early English Gothic style by Charles Buckeridge of Oxford, consisting of chancel, nave, north and south aisles, north chancel aisle (acting as vestry and organ chamber) and saddleback tower. Principal entrance on south side through large porch capped with pyramidal roof and approached by flight of stone steps, church being far more elevated than adjacent ground from road level. Constructed of Newbridge stone with Bath stone dressings. Both aisles lighted by two large trefoil-headed windows, with clerestory lighted and relieved by introduction of six quatrefoil circular windows. Inside of church lined with red and white bricks in bands, and chancel floored with encaustic tiles. Pulpit constructed of Bath stone, richly carved and supported on short marble pillars. Font also of Bath stone but of plain appearance. Open timber roofs of deal left in its natural state. Open benches of stained deal. Seating accommodation for 350 parishioners.

Floor intersected along aisles by open iron grids, from which heat was made to rise to warm church when necessary. Architect: Charles Buckeridge, Oxford. Benefactor: marquess of Bute. Contractors: Workmen from the Bute Estate. Cost £4,000. (*BN*, 18 September 1868, 642) Opened for divine service on 8 September 1868. (*CMG*, 12 September 1868)

Comments: The fact that the proposed saddleback tower was never built over the south porch gave the church a rather bizarre appearance since the heavy full-height corner buttresses of the porch, which were evidently intended to transmit the considerable weight of the tower, remained *in situ*. Instead of being surmounted by a tower the porch was capped with a pyramidal roof. The gabled luffer-like openings of the small belfry with the pyramidal capping of the porch were presumably designed in accord with the gabled buttresses. Buckeridge's arrangement of a pair of double lights at the west end was unusual, since most churches of this plain style were often shown with a pair of single lancets at the west end.

ST MARY'S CHURCH, TRELEWIS

1886–7: New church built on new site. Built in Early English Gothic style by E. M. Bruce Vaughan, consisting of chancel, nave, south porch and western bellcote. Constructed of rock-faced Pennant sandstone with dressings of red moulded bricks. Nave and chancel under one continuous roof. Chancel arch and inner sanctuary arch. Church lighted by simple lancets. Entire woodwork of church of pitch-pine, including open benches, free and unappropriated. Seating accommodation for 250 worshippers. Cost £1,100. (*Kelly's Directory of South Wales*, 1926, 675)

Comments: Another cheap, 'lancet' church by Bruce Vaughan in the south Wales coalfield area. Inexplicably, Bruce Vaughan built two inner arches, the innermost being a sanctuary arch, which was a rare feature in a small church in a mining community. This design was rather unique in Glamorgan because he built the nave and chancel under one continuous roof and then constructed a lower sanctuary separated from the chancel by a sanctuary arch.

ST MATTHEW'S CHURCH, TREORCHY

1884: First recorded service at St Matthew's took place on Sunday, 20 April 1884. Building originally built in 1871 as St Matthew's National School. Outer walls constructed of local Pennant sandstone and inner walls lined with Tylacoch bricks. Architect: George Edward Robinson, Cardiff. Contractor: David Jenkins, Merthyr Tydfil. LDCES grant £40; Llandaff Education Board £10. **1887:** The correspondent in the *Church Builder* reported that 'In January 1879, £25 was voted towards building this mission church, but in consequence of the applicant not being able at that time to commence the work it was relinquished and was cancelled in November 1882. The present application is for enlarging and reseating the whole building, adding a chancel, a font, pulpit, reading desk and making it as church-like as possible. There are more than 5,000 inhabitants and the nearest church is two miles distant from any church.' (*Ch. Bldr* (1887), 108–9) Rebuilt in Early English Gothic style by E. M. Bruce Vaughan, consisting of chancel, nave and western bellcote. Enlarged by addition of apsidal chancel, reseating whole building and providing font, pulpit and reading desk to make it as 'church-like' as possible. Seating accommodation for 280 worshippers. Contractor: David Thomas, Treorchy. Cost £344. Bishop of Llandaff's Fund £50; LDCES grant £30. Reopened on 7 July 1887. (*Pontypridd Chr.*, 7 July 1887)

Comments: For about three years the townspeople of Treorchy worshipped in a building that still bore signs of its previous incarnation as a school. When funds became available in 1887, it was converted into a simple church by Bruce Vaughan, who was adept at building cheap churches in the Rhondda. He designed the apsidal chancel, because it was a cheap method of providing an east end to the church. At a later date,

1913, there was a plan to build an additional aisle with a new porch that would face Cardiff Street, but this project was not completed.

ST TYFODWG'S CHURCH, TREORCHY
(Demolished)

1895: New church built on new site for services in Welsh language. Prior to building of church, services conducted in English and Welsh at St Matthew's, Treorchy, but soon evident that church needed for worship in Welsh only to cater for large Welsh-speaking population of town. Site bought in Bute Street, opposite Noddfa Chapel, and in 1895 St Tyfodwg's was built. (Stephen J. Ryan (comp.), *St Matthew's Church, Treorchy, 1884–1984: centenary year programme and brief history of the Church and Parish* (Treorchy, 1984), 5) Built in Early English Gothic style by Jacob Rees, Pentre, consisting of chancel, nave, south porch and western bellcote. Constructed of local Welsh sandstone with red brick dressings. Its proportions were 80ft long by 32ft wide and its one span roof was of a massive type. Interior consisted of roof of red pine and stuccoed walls. Modern pews, which provided seating accommodation for 400 persons, of varnished red deal. Windows tinted with Cathedral glass and building heated by pair of Musgrave hot-air stoves. (*Glam. Free Pr.*, 26 October 1895) Contractor: Messrs Edward Davies & Sons, Treherbert. Cost £1,600. Bishop of Llandaff's Fund £300; Mrs M. G. Llewellyn £100. (*Bldr*, 26 October 1895, 298) Opened and dedicated on 21 October 1895. (*W. Mail*, 22 October 1895)

Comments: St Tyfodwg's was the second church to be built as part of Revd Canon William Lewis's 'Church Forward Movement' launched in August 1892. The building demonstrated that, faced with insufficient funds, William Lewis preferred to erect an inferior type of structure in the shortest possible time instead of biding his time and building a church with traditional features. Jacob Rees's design led the secretary of the ICBS to comment that 'a building without a chancel or central passage and seats so close together that kneeling would be impossible,

60. Interior of St John's Church, Troedyrhiw (Source: Geoffrey R. Orrin: Postcard Collection of Glamorgan Churches)

would hardly pass for a church'. (T. J. Prichard, *Representative Bodies* (Llandysul, 1988), 162) With its red brick dressings instead of the ubiquitous Bath stone and stuccoed walls it was clearly a simple and cheaply built structure. It was even inferior to the churches built by Bruce Vaughan in other mining communities in the south Wales coalfield.

ST JOHN THE BAPTIST'S CHURCH, PONT-Y-RHUN, TROEDYRHIW

1852–3: New church built on new site given by Hon. Robert H. Clive. The writer in *The Builder* stated that 'during the last two or three years a population has been rapidly springing up both at Troedyrhiw, where there had been previously a small village and at Pont-yr-un, on the other side of the Taff; and this population amounts to nearly 2,000, without any apparent diminution of the rate of building'. (*Bldr*, 8 January 1853, 23) Built in Early English Gothic style by John Prichard. (ICBS file no. 4378 (1851)) It consists of chancel (30ftx21ft), nave (64ftx26ft), sacristy (14ftx8ft), south porch and western bellcote. At this time provision was made for a considerable enlarge-ment of the church which had been so constructed as to admit of north and south transepts each 26ft long by 21ft wide. Constructed of Welsh Pennant sandstone with dressings of Bath stone. Western elevation is extremely unusual comprising west gable flanked with buttresses and surmounted by light and elegant bellcote, the buttresses of which are supported by long and slender shafts springing from boldly projecting stringcourse over west doorway. These are ingeniously contrived to form a portion of a west window of six lights, the centre portion consisting of two lights higher than the rest, surmounted by a circle, with label flanked on either side by two single lancets of unequal heights. East wall of chancel pierced by large window of five lights under a comprising label, the centre light the highest with others diminishing in gradation. Side walls of nave lighted with simple two-light, trefoil-headed windows while those of chancel have three separate lancets. Fine open timber roof plastered between rafters. Open benches of pitch-pine for 305 persons. Benefactor: Anthony Hill, Cyfarthfa. Contractor: Messrs Thomas & Norris, Merthyr Tydfil. Cost £1,355. ICBS grant £130; Church Commissioners' grant £100; LCBS grant £50; LDCES grant £100. Consecrated on 6 January 1853 (*CMG*, 8 January 1853)

Comments: The most striking feature of St John the Baptist's, which was one of the eleven Commissioners' churches erected in Glamorgan, is the west gable flanked by buttresses and surmounted by an elegant bellcote, the buttresses of which are supported by long and slender shafts springing from a boldly projecting stringcourse over the west doorway. These shafts, which one would normally associate with the inside of windows, have the effect of dividing the gable into bays. Although they provide an unusual termination to the bellcote, which is more interesting than the ubiquitous corbelling out, they also have the detrimental effect of separating the windows. As John Newman says, the west elevation is a development of the west end of Merthyr Mawr Church, designed by Ferrey and executed under Prichard's supervision. (Newman, 640) The buttresses appear to be large by comparison with other churches of similar size, and the rest of the exterior is very simple and dull. Thereafter, Prichard developed a penchant for designing unusually fine bellcotes and west gables for his churches in Glamorgan. Another unusual feature of Prichard's design is that the chancel and nave are built under a continuous ridge contrary to the principles of the Ecclesiologists, which Prichard embraced. However, the fine arch-braced roof of both chancel and nave is plastered between the many numerous dark brown common rafters giving a magpie effect. Provision was made by Prichard for transepts but only the south one was ever built.

HOLY TRINITY CHURCH, TYLORSTOWN

1882–3: New church built on new site given by Revd Thomas Edmondes, vicar of Cowbridge. The correspondent in the *Church Builder* reported: 'This parish is in the Rhondda Valley, and of great extent. There are several villages belonging to it, and all-bilingual; to four of these districts the Society has voted grants. The present application is for aid towards building a Church at a place where there are 3,000 inhabitants and which is rapidly increasing. A colliery company has given most

liberally.' (*Ch. Bldr* (1883), 3) Built in Early English Gothic style by E. M. Bruce Vaughan (ICBS file no. 8763 (1882)) consisting of apsidal chancel, nave, vestry and south porch. Western gable surmounted by bellcote. Constructed of hammer-dressed Welsh Pennant sandstone with Bath stone dressings. Roof is open timbered with arched braces and with principal rafters supported on stone corbels. Roof covered with green slates and red tile cresting ridge. Nave walls supported by two-stage buttresses. Moulded chancel arch springs from square capitals on corbels of two pillarets. Chancel lighted by three broad trefoil-headed lancets. West window of five trefoil lights with plate tracery above. Octagonal stone font. Seating accommodation for 305 parishioners on plain open benches of pitch-pine. Contractors: Messrs Jenkins & Sons, Treherbert. Cost £1,352. ICBS grant £150. (*BN*, 26 October 1883, 665) Consecrated on 18 October 1883. (*W. Mail*, 19 October 1883)

Comments: The initiative for the building of Holy Trinity in Tylorstown in the Rhondda Fach came, not from the vicar of Ystradyfodwg, Revd Canon William Lewis, but from Revd Thomas Edmondes, vicar of Cowbridge, who was the owner of the tenement of Cynllwyndy, the land over which the mining village of Tylorstown was being extended. William Lewis, still mindful of his disappointment with the half-completed church of St Andrew's, Llwynypia, insisted on a stone-built structure, but Thomas Edmondes thought that a less expensive iron church was more suited to the fluctuating population of the coal-mining district. Canon William Lewis finally triumphed and the stone church that was eventually built at Tylorstown was considered a model church for the upland communities of the diocese. Holy Trinity was more or less a copy of Bruce Vaughan's first church, St Mary Magdalene's at Cwmbach. The church met all the requirements of the Ecclesiastical Commissioners for stability and economy. Bruce Vaughan chose to design an apsidal chancel as it was a cheap method of building a chancel. It was a pattern to be repeated throughout the valleys of the diocese by Bruce Vaughan, who became the most prolific church builder in the county.

ST ALBAN'S CHURCH, TYNEWYDD

(Made redundant 1999)

1890–1: New church built on new site given by earl of Dunraven. The correspondent in the *Church Builder* reported that 'This church is intended for the three villages of Tynewydd, Blaen-y-cum (*sic*) and Blaen Rhondda and the site is a very eligible one and very accessible to the three villages. The population, which numbers 4,000, is much poorer than lower down the valley.' (*Ch. Bldr* (1890), 71) Foundation stone laid by countess of Dunraven on 27 November 1890. (*W. Mail*, 28 November 1890) Built in Early English Gothic style by E. M. Bruce Vaughan. (ICBS file no. 9446 (1890)) It consists of chancel (26ftx25ft), organ chamber and vestry on south side of chancel (23ftx10ft), nave (63ftx25ft), south porch and western bellcote. Constructed of grey Pennant sandstone with jambs and arches of doors and windows of Bath stone. Nave roof open to apex and constructed of unvarnished pitch-pine. Chancel roof emphasized by coloured rafters and divided from the nave by double principals with moulded curved knees; space between knees filled with trefoil perforations, and supported by carved stone corbels. Chancel is continuation of nave and of same width. Long roof covered with green slates and red tile ridge cresting. Chancel has a three-light trefoil-headed window and two small traceried lights in north wall. On south side of the chancel are sedilia and credence. Nave lighted from west by large five-light trefoil-headed window, and nave walls pierced with single and double trefoil windows set alternately in bays between buttresses. Open benches of pitch-pine for 350 persons. Contractor: John Haines, Cardiff. (*BN*, 12 December 1890, 841) Cost £1,400. ICBS grant £80. Consecrated on 9 November 1891. (*W. Mail*, 10 November 1890)

Comments: St Alban's in the parish of Ystradyfodwg was another church built by the indefatigable efforts of Revd Canon William Lewis, vicar of the parish and 'church builder extraordinaire'. Bruce Vaughan designed the nave and chancel practically of the same width. The advantage of this plan was that every worshipper in the church would have a clear view of the altar and pulpit. The chancel is distinguished from the nave by a double-coloured principal carried on carved stone pillar corbels, instead of the more expensive interposing chancel arch. Although the church was a cheap building with very few features of architectural merit, it was suitable in every respect for the district it had to serve as an Anglican Church with traditional fittings and furnishings.

ST TYDDWG'S CHURCH, TYTHEGSTON

(Now redundant)

1864: Church repaired and reseated in 1864 at expense of parish. (*CGG*, 18 August 1876)
1872–6: Restoration of church. When Sir Stephen Glynne visited the church on 24 September 1847, he described it thus: 'A small church – chancel, nave, south porch and western bell-gable. The whole apparently late. Several of the windows are bad insertions; but the eastern, a two-light Third Pointed one. The chancel arch is depressed of Tudor form and low with continuous mouldings. Over it is a great expanse of bare wall. On the north side of the chancel is a single narrow slit, walled. The south-east window is closed. The porch is rude. The font has a circular bowl, the base like a reversed cup.' (Sir Stephen R. Glynne, 'Notes on the older churches in the four Welsh dioceses', *Arch. Camb.* (1901), 274) Committee of Architects of ICBS remarked that 'The scantlings of the timber are not given in the drawings as required by the rules. The construction of the main roof seems scarcely interpreting the height of the collar. The absence of bolts and wall plates are points of much concern. The stone corbels being placed in front of the principal rafters have no hold of the walls and therefore cannot bear any weight. The architect's attention is called to these points.' (ICBS file no. 7371 (1872)) Passage of time had destroyed the original fabric of the church, which was built in the fifteenth century. John Prichard, under whose supervision restoration was carried out, was careful to preserve ancient features of church so that as nearly as possible it was facsimile of original. Work commenced in March 1875, and owing to failure of local contractor some

time afterwards the local clergy took work in hand with restoration completed under supervision of Griffith David of Bridgend, who acted as foreman of workforce. Stone used for rebuilding work obtained from Pyle and Bridgend. Walls almost completely rebuilt and new windows of Perpendicular Gothic style inserted. Roof also entirely new, of red pine and covered with Welsh slates. Floor of church completely relaid and old-fashioned square box pews replaced by open benches of pitch-pine providing accommodation for ninety-eight persons, an increase of fifty-four seats. New pulpit of Bath stone installed and new chancel furniture provided. South porch thoroughly renovated and west end of church embellished with small bellcote of Bath stone surmounted by cross. Font, a rare old specimen of its kind, allowed to remain *in situ*. Chancel restored at expense of patron of living, C. R. M. Talbot of Margam Abbey. Contractor: Griffith David, Bridgend. Cost £850. ICBS grant £25. Reopened after restoration on 15 August 1876. (*W. Mail*, 16 August 1876)

Comments: In terms of Professor Edward Freeman's principles, the restoration of St Tyddwg's in the years 1875–6 was certainly neither destructive nor eclectic, but this was clearly Prichard in a more conservative mood. Although he was compelled to rebuild most of the decayed walling, he preserved what was there including the chancel arch, the window rere-arches, the rood-stair projection on the south side of the church and the fifteenth-century font. However, he did replace the 'bad insertions' described by Glynne with a window designed in the Perpendicular Gothic style in keeping with the architectural style of the building.

ST DONAT'S CHURCH, WELSH ST DONAT'S

1890–1: Restoration of church by Kempson & Fowler, Llandaff. The correspondent in *The Builder* reported that 'The church of Welsh St Donats, near Cowbridge, is now to undergo substantial restoration. It is reported to be quite unfit for use at present.' (*Bldr*, 6 December 1890, 449) Work included restoration of fifteenth-century roof with new oak scantlings, replastering of walls, tower repointed and rebuilt where necessary, and new wood floors and ceiling placed in tower. Chancel floored with Godwin's encaustic tiles and nave concreted and covered with wood-block flooring. New oak pulpit, lectern and font-cover provided and priest's door opened out in chancel. Windows reglazed throughout church with fret lead. New seats placed in chancel and two new windows inserted in walls of church, one in south-west wall and other, a small lancet, in south wall at base of the tower. Nave furnished with individual chairs in place of old-fashioned high-backed pews. New heating apparatus and hanging coronas fitted with veritas lamps for lighting church provided. Contractor: W. A. James, Cardiff. Cost £700. (*BN*, 23 October 1891, 597) Reopened after restoration on 14 October 1891. (*W. Mail*, 15 October 1891)

Comments: Apart from the rebuilding of decayed parts of the tower, the restoration of Welsh St Donats was undertaken without any structural alterations being made to the medieval fabric of the church. Kempson & Fowler's restoration was a conservative affair and, like so many restorations carried out at this time, was more concerned with reparation than restoration. As was customary in the final decade of the nineteenth century, there was more provision for 'creature comforts' in the church by the installation of a heating apparatus. The old high-backed pews were replaced by individual seats, which gave the nave an atmosphere of space after the clutter of the pews. The survival of the old box pews late into the final decade of the century gives us an indication of the slowness of the Anglican Church in the Vale of Glamorgan to react and to adopt the new liturgical arrangements. The restoration was a complete refurbishment of the church with standardized Victorian fittings and furnishings, which brought it into line with the new concept of the Anglican Church in the late Victorian period.

ST MARY'S CHURCH, WENVOE

1866: When Sir Stephen Glynne visited Wenvoe in September 1866, he wrote 'This church has a nave and chancel, south porch, and west tower; the body much modernised, and in great measure rebuilt. The chancel arch is plain Pointed, possibly original.' (Sir Stephen R. Glynne, 'Notes on the older churches in the four Welsh dioceses', *Arch. Camb.* (1901), 278)

1876–7: Restoration of church. Petition for restoration stated that 'the parish church has for some years past been in a state of decay and requires considerable restoration, alteration and reseating in order to afford convenient accommodation for the inhabitants of the parish'. (LL/F/737P. Petition for restoration. Dated 6 December 1876) Consequently, faculty issued and following work carried out. Gallery at west end of nave removed, flagstones in porch replaced by encaustic tiles, and wood-block floors laid down in nave. New open benches of pitch-pine replaced old-fashioned square box pews and new octagonal font of Bath stone with red marble stem erected. Queen Anne windows in nave replaced by present trefoiled lancets in Bath stone, and doorways to porch and tower reconstructed in Bath stone. New quoins and dressings of Bath stone put to exterior angles of church. New window of three trefoiled lights with Decorated-style tracery placed in east wall of chancel and new trefoiled lancets inserted in south wall. New chancel arch constructed springing from elaborately carved corbels of nondescript architecture. Seating accommodation increased by forty places to 120 sittings. Cost £700. (LL/F/837. Restoration, alteration and reseating. Faculty dated 2 July 1877)

Comments: The fact that the petition for restoration stated that the parish church was in a state of decay and required considerable restoration is surprising in the light of Glynne's remarks, made ten years earlier, that the body of the church had in great measure been rebuilt. Presumably Glynne was referring to work which had been carried out much earlier, probably in the eighteenth century, when a west gallery was erected in the nave. The restoration of St Mary's in 1877 was a thorough Victorian remodelling and reordering of the eighteenth-century church with its west gallery, square box pews and Queen Anne windows. This 'destructive' restoration transformed the church with its refenestration and reconstruction of the chancel arch into a typical early Decorated Gothic structure. This took place at the time of the founding of the Society for the Protection of Ancient Buildings, which was a protest against the type of 'destructive' church restoration witnessed here.

ST MARY'S CHURCH, WHITCHURCH

1864–5: Reseating of church with additional sixty-three seats. Architect: John Prichard, Llandaff. Cost. £200. ICBS grant £10. (ICBS file no. 6326 (1864))

1882–5: New church built on new site adjacent to old church which was later demolished. Foundation stone laid by Mrs T. W. Booker on 29 March 1882. (*W. Mail*, 30 March 1882) Building of new church first mooted when Revd J. T. Clarke appointed as vicar of parish in October 1875. Not only was old parish church too small for increasing population of parish, which numbered more than 2,000 inhabitants, but it had been in a dilapidated state and unfit for divine worship for some time. On 3 August 1875, Ecclesiastical Commissioners granted two acres of land for erection of church and burial ground. (*Cardiff Times*, 30 May 1885) Built in early Decorated Gothic style by John Prichard, consisting of chancel (37ftx25ft), nave (60ftx33ft) and south-western tower with south porch. Tower 66ft high with turret on east side leading to all levels. (ICBS file no. 8466 (1879)) Constructed of Pontypridd Pennant sandstone all laid in regular courses and lined internally with yellow Ruabon bricks occasionally coursed with red bricks. Roof covered with red machine-made tiles and floor is covered with encaustic tiles. Improving biblical texts on each side of chancel arch. East window of three trefoiled lights with early Geometrical-style tracery in head, west window of four lights with similar style tracery and nave windows of two lights with Y-tracery in head. Chancel has wagon roof formed by series of closely set arch braces; portion over sanctuary panelled. Chancel fitted with oak choir stalls and pulpit and font taken from old church. Nave has arch-braced roof with curved braces between traceried wallplate and purlins, and principal rafters are supported by moulded stone corbels. Open benches of pitch-pine, stained and varnished for 334 parishioners. Contractor: D. C. Jones, Gloucester. Cost £3,559. ICBS grant £200. (*W. Mail*, 30 March 1882)

Comments: John Prichard constructed the church of dark and pinkish Pontypridd sandstone all laid in thin regular courses as was his custom. However, he chose to line the inside of the church with yellow Ruabon bricks banded occasionally with red bricks with strident constructional polychromatic patterns. As a result the stridency of the church's interior decoration detracted from the graceful sensitivity apparent in the architect's design of the exterior of this traditional Glamorgan country church with unbuttressed tower. Although it was an idiom used particularly in the High Victorian period, 1850–70, and to some extent later as part of the Gothic Revival, the harsh polychromy of the interior was obviously regarded as overbearing by the parish authorities in a country church, since it was completely rendered over at a later date.

ST JAMES' CHURCH, WICK

1869–70: Rebuilding and restoration by John Prichard during incumbency of Revd Thomas Jones. Church underwent such thorough restoration that present structure has aspect of new building. In his letter of 20 January 1869 to ICBS requesting grant aid to restore church, Revd Jones stated: 'The poor church for which help is asked is extremely decayed and dilapidated so much as that its wet and uncomfortable state prevent many from attending services. The parish is small and poor. It consists of small farmers and labourers, who however willing, can afford to contribute but little towards such a large outlay.' (ICBS file no. 6911 (1869)) Most of walls rebuilt, new roofs raised and modern windows inserted. New porch

and vestry added. Tower also partially rebuilt at this time. Church restored in Early English Gothic style of architecture. Nave lighted by five nineteenth-century windows, all of same design: two on north wall are probably insertions and three on south wall are most likely replacements. Each window consists of two broad trefoil-headed lights with obtusely pointed arch over embrasure of internal splay. Restored nave has arch-braced roof with crenellated purlin. Laudian east window, Norman chancel arch and two large squints or hagioscopes on each side of arch preserved by architect, but all traces of rood-loft arrangements have disappeared. Stone altar surmounted by its pre-Reformation altar slab and Early English niche set in east wall both preserved in chancel. Accommodation on open benches of pitch-pine increased by an additional thirty-one sittings to total of 127 seats. Cost £900. ICBS grant £25. (*MCVG*, 417–20)

Comments: Prichard preserved the original oak principals and provided new rafters and purlins of deal. He chose to construct arch-braced roofs in the chancel and nave; the latter with a crenellated purlin. The north wall of the nave was in such a bad state that he was forced to rebuild it entirely and to repair the masonry of the rest of the structure. He inserted three new windows matching those which he had restored in the north wall. These windows were modelled in the Early English style, based on the niche with Early English-style head in the sanctuary. He left his personal impression on these windows by introducing polychromatic stonework in the outer relieving arches, an idiom that he also used in St Mary's Church, Aberavon (1859). Prichard was of the opinion that the slender tower had been 'tampered' with at some stage in its history and he therefore decided to heighten it by some four or five feet, capping it with a saddleback roof so characteristic of the Vale of Glamorgan churches. The restoration of St James' Church was typical of the High Victorian period for it resolved the two problems confronting incumbents at that time, namely the dilapidation of the fabric of the church and the need for additional church accommodation.

ST ILLTYD'S CHURCH, WILLIAMSTOWN

1891–4: New church built on new site given by Revd John Edmondes, father of Revd Canon Frederick W. Edmondes, rector of Coity. Prior to building of church, Anglican services in English first held in Williamstown Board School in 1884. Followed by services held at Graigddu School in the year after. Not until 1891 was building fund for new church inaugurated. (Muriel Howells, *History of the Church of St Illtyd, Williamstown, 1894–1944* (Cardiff, 1944), 3) Petition for consecration of church stated that 'In consequence of the great increase of the population in the district of Dinas Isaf in the said parish and of the inadequacy of the Church accommodation provided for the purpose of divine service in the said district and the need for the provision for the inhabitants of further accommodation, a new church or chapel of ease has been erected so as to meet the requirements of the said district.' (LL/C/91. Sentence of consecration. Dated 30 April 1894) Foundation stone laid on 6 August 1891 by Mrs Archibald Hood, wife of Dr Archibald Hood of Bridgend and granddaughter of Revd Canon Edmondes. (*W. Mail*, 7 August 1891) Built in Perpendicular Gothic style by E. M. Bruce Vaughan, consisting of chancel with organ chamber and vestry on north side, nave and north porch. Gable above chancel arch surmounted by bell-turret. (ICBS file no. 9542 (1891)) Constructed of local Pennant sandstone in hammer-coursed work while dressings of windows are of Box ground stone from the Bath quarries. Chancel has barrel-shaped roof, panelled with moulded ribs and gilded bosses at intersections of purlins and main braces. East window of three trefoiled lights with early Perpendicular-style tracery in head. Nave lighted by west window of five trefoiled lights beneath four-centred arch between two-stage buttresses and by four two-light trefoiled windows beneath square head. Chancel floor as well as that of aisles paved with Godwin's encaustic tiles. Nave has arch-braced roof of unpolished pitch-pine. Pulpit also of unpolished pitch-pine but lectern of oak and designed by architect. Open benches of pitch-pine accommodate 310 worshippers. Contractor: W. A. James,

Cowbridge. Cost £1,700. ICBS grant £75; LDCES grant £50; Bishop of Llandaff's Fund £250. Consecrated on 30 April 1894. (*W. Mail*, 1 May 1894)

Comments: Bruce Vaughan's design of St Illtyd's in a late Gothic form, Perpendicular Gothic, was a considerable improvement on previous churches which he had built in the Early English Gothic or 'lancet' style in the south Wales coalfield.

ALL SAINTS' CHURCH, YNYSFEIO
(Demolished in late 1970s)

1893–4: New church built on new site given by Mrs Madelina Llewellyn of Baglan Hall. The correspondent in the *Church Builder* reported that 'The parish of Treherbert, in which the proposed new Church is to be built, has been recently formed out of the parish of Ystradyfodwg, and comprises an area of 5,800 acres. The population, consisting entirely of miners and labourers, numbers over 9,000, is bi-lingual, and services are now held in English and Welsh in the school-room at Ynysfeio. The new Church is to be built for the Welsh people of the new parish; there are 4,000 people in the district.' (*Ch. Bldr* (1893), 82) Foundation stone laid on 4 September 1893 by Mrs Llewellyn. (*W. Mail*, 5 September 1893) Built in Early English Gothic style by E. M. Bruce Vaughan, consisting of chancel, nave with south aisle, transepts, vestry and south porch. Western gable surmounted by bellcote. (ICBS file no. 9743 (1893)) Constructed of local Welsh Pennant sandstone with Bath stone dressings and covered with slate roof. Chancel arch constructed of timber. External buttresses on north and south side of church supported nave walls. Open timber roof, seats and choir stalls of pitch-pine, left free from stain and varnish. Seating accommodation for 350 worshippers on open benches. Contractor: John Edwards, Ton Ystrad. Cost £2,380. ICBS grant £150; Bishop of Llandaff's Fund £350; LDCES grant £60; Mrs Madelina Llewellyn, Baglan Hall £1,450. Consecrated on 24 September 1894. (*W. Mail*, 25 September 1894)

Comments: All Saints' Church, Ynysfeio was the first church to be built under Revd William Lewis' church-building programme, 'The Church Forward Movement', a title borrowed from Nonconformity. Lewis launched his appeal for the building of five churches in 1892, and within little over four years these five churches had been erected if only after considerable difficulties. Had it not been for the patronage of Mrs Madelina Llewellyn the project might well have foundered. Lewis chose his favourite architect, E. M. Bruce Vaughan to build his church at Ynysfeio. As was his custom, he built All Saints' in the cheap 'lancet' style. He had originally intended to build a north aisle, but lack of funds prevented this and the pillars and arches were left *in situ* in readiness for an extension at a later date. Vaughan was used to using timber in place of stone in his churches, usually in the arcades, but at Ynysfeio he also designed the chancel arch of wood.

ST ANNE'S CHURCH, YNYSHIR

1885–6: New church built on new site donated by Charles Whitting of Glandore, Weston-super-Mare. The correspondent in the *Church Builder* reported that 'This district is one that has sprung up rapidly within the last three years; there is no Church Accommodation in the place, except the use that is made of the Board schools. An adjoining village with a large mining population is to be annexed to this district, the inhabitants will then number 10,000. The tower is not now to be built.' (*Ch. Bldr* (1885), 69) Built in Early English Gothic style by E. M. Bruce Vaughan, consisting of chancel with organ chamber and vestry, nave with north and south sides, north porch and western bellcote. (ICBS file no. 8997 (1885)) Constructed with hammer-dressed Pennant sandstone with Bath stone dressings. East window of four trefoiled lights forming two separate pointed arches within head, in apex of which are quatrefoils. Head of window filled with large sexfoil. West front of church is obviously architect's personal statement; west window is exact replica of that in east wall. Above it is a double bellcote, whose inner arch is pierced with small quatrefoil

springing from slender shaft on moulded base, separating the bell arches. At ground level, a gabled and pinnacled west doorway with three orders of mouldings spring from nook shafts with bell caps. It is flanked by single trefoiled light with hood mould. West front strongly buttressed at corners, and western extremities of aisles reveal solid wall pierced with two single trefoiled lights with hood moulds below moulded cornice displaying quatrefoil ornamentation. Nave divided from aisles by five chamfered pointed arches springing from short round pillars. Bays of aisles have transverse gables, the timbers of which are supported on stone corbels. Aisles have two-light pointed windows with circle in plate tracery above. Chancel has trussed-rafter roof with scissors-beam arrangement, while nave has arch-braced type. Buttressed north porch. (Personal observation) Seating accommodation for 500 worshippers. Cost £2,500. ICBS grant £200; LDCES grant £100; Bishop of Llandaff's Fund £400. (*Pontypridd Chr.*, 21 August 1886) Consecrated on 19 August 1886. (*W. Mail*, 20 August 1886)

Comments: St Anne's was one of the churches not built under William Lewis's direct supervision. The most striking feature of the church is its west front, whose breadth is enhanced by the transverse gables of the aisles and the solid west walls of the aisles with a moulded cornice of quatrefoil decoration. This was one of Bruce Vaughan's finer churches in the Rhondda, because he was provided with improved funding.

CHRIST CHURCH, YNYSYBWL

1886–7: New church built on new site. The correspondent in the *Church Builder* reported that 'The extent of this district is four miles in length, and one in breadth, in the hitherto secluded valley of Clydach, which is likely to become at an early date a busy centre of mineral traffic. A large mining populuation will then be gathered in the course of a few months. It is hoped this Church now to be built will be welcomed by Church-going families who will settle there, who otherwise would be attracted to Nonconformist chapels.' (*Ch. Bldr*

(1884), 6) Built in Early English Gothic style by E. M. Bruce Vaughan, consisting of apsidal chancel with vestry on south side, nave and western bellcote. (ICBS file no. 8858 (1883)) Constructed of rock-faced Pennant sandstone with Bath stone dressings. Five-sided apsidal chancel lighted by three single trefoil-headed windows with hood moulds. Nave lighted with identical trefoil-headed windows between two-stage buttresses. West window of two trefoiled lights. Corner buttresses to west gable surmounted by single bellcote with hood mould over bell arch. High-pitched, gabled south porch with doorway displaying mouldings springing from bell caps and nook shafts. Interior perfectly plain and simple in its arrangement with open timber roof to nave covered with Welsh slates. (Personal observation) Seating accommodation for 302 worshippers. Cost £1,600. ICBS grant £105; LDCES grant £60; Bishop of Llandaff's Fund £200. Consecrated on 10 October 1887. (*W. Mail*, 11 October 1887)

Comments: This was yet another cheap church by Bruce Vaughan. It was built with a five-sided apsidal chancel to keep down costs and the windows are all plain lancets without mullions except at the west end. The only concession to embellishment on the exterior is the moulded doorway of the south porch with a pair of engaged shafts with bell caps and rounded bases on each side.

ST DAVID'S CHURCH, YSTALYFERA

1890–1: New church built on new site given by Fleming Gough of Yniscedwyn. The correspondent in the *Church Builder* reported that 'Ystalyfera was until four years ago a most flourishing and prosperous place, large iron and tin works having been carried on for many years successfully by a Mr Budd. A great depression in the iron trade overtook the country and this place suffered in a pre-eminent degree so that Mr Budd was unable to carry out the good object he had in view of erecting a new church for the benefit of his numerous employees. Divine service has been carried on in an

unconsecrated building and a licensed schoolroom most unsuitable as places of worship and especially inconvenient. The St David's Diocesan Building Board strongly recommend this case to the committee of the Society. The new church will hold 350, all seats free. Estimated cost £2,000. Applicant Rev. D. Jones . . . £200 voted.' (*Ch. Bldr* (1889), 74–5) Built in early Decorated Gothic style by James Buckley Wilson of Wilson & Moxham, Swansea, consisting of chancel, nave, south transept, north porch and circular eastern tower running into an octagon and terminating in a sharply pitched roof. (ICBS file no. 9262 (1889)) Constructed of local Pennant sandstone with Bath stone dressings and Bath stone windows, and roofs covered with Caernarvonshire slates. Inside of St David's Church, Ystalyfera presents a remarkable appearance, the plaster having been entirely dispensed with, and the pulpit, like the walls, is of hammer-dressed stone. Chancel with choir stalls 23ft wide, with transept on south side and vestry and organ chamber on north side. On chancel's south side are sedilia with richly carved credence niche and opposite an aumbry, all in Bath stone. Chancel has arch-braced roof, but part of roof over sanctuary is barrel-shaped and boarded with unpolished pitch-pine. East window of five lights with Geometrical-style tracery in head. Nave 60ftx30ft. West end of nave lighted by pair of two-light trefoil-headed windows beneath Rose window. Nave has arch-braced roof with principal rafters supported on moulded stone corbels. Seating accommodation for 350 persons on individual chairs of pine wood. Decorative sculpture by Mr Wall, sculptor, Newport. Contractor: David Rees, Ystalyfera. Cost £2,100. ICBS grant £200. (*The Cambrian*, 26 June 1891) Consecrated on 25 June 1891. (*W. Mail*, 26 June 1891)

Comments: The Committee of Architects of the ICBS reacted unfavourably to the plans submitted by Wilson and his then partner, Maurice Adams, in June 1888. 'The design for this church is so eccentric and objectionable that it cannot be recommended.' The plans were sent back for amendment several times and were finally approved in February 1889. (ICBS file no. 9262

(1888)) However, in March 1889 the architectural partnership of Wilson & Adams was dissolved and Wilson formed a new partnership with Glendinning Moxham. In March 1889, they submitted a new design for the church in the early Decorated style and this was approved. This new design was a great improvement on the former plans. However, it is strange that James Buckley Wilson, whose chancel at St David's, Penllergaer in 1886 was highly commended and illustrated in the *Building News* at that time, should have had so much difficulty with the design of the church at Ystalyfera. The correspondent in *The Cambrian* had the following to say about it: 'The architects have taken into consideration the surrounding rugged mountainous scenery and have been most successful in designing a church which is of a simple and at the same time artistic character. It is one of the most handsome and massive in district and the general effect inside and out, is extremely good.' (*The Cambrian*, 26 June 1891) John Newman, on the other hand, regarded it as 'an awkward cruciform design'. (Newman, 647) Despite the remarks in *The Cambrian* it appears that the promise shown by Wilson at Penllergaer in 1886 was not fulfilled in the design of St David's, Ystalyfera a few years later.

HOLY TRINITY CHURCH, YSTRAD MYNACH

1855–7: New church built on new site. In 1854, Revd George Thomas of Ystrad Fawr House in parish of Llanfabon decided to build new church at Ystrad Mynach at own expense. Though a clergyman, he held no preferment in the Church, but was deeply sensitive to everything that concerned its interest and welfare; at Ystrad Fawr House there was a private chapel where family, staff and servants of estate worshipped. When population of Ystrad Mynach increased considerably in 1850s a church was much needed since parish church of Llanfabon was some four miles distant in what was a widely scattered and extensive parish. (Edgar Lawrence, *Parish of Ystrad Mynach, Holy Trinity Church: Centenary, 1857–1957* (1957), 7 and 23–4) Foundation stone laid on 10 August

1855 by George William Griffiths Thomas of Ystrad Fawr House. (*CMG*, 18 August 1855) Built in Early English Gothic style by John Norton, London, consisting of chancel with organ chamber and vestry, nave, tower with spire on north side of nave and south porch. Crypt of family vault of Thomas Family of Ystrad Mynach beneath church. Constructed of blue Pennant sandstone with ashlar dressings of Doulting stone. Chancel (28ftx13ft 6ins), nave (45ftx21ft). Windows of nave are lancets, alternately single and in couplets with equal triplet at west end and three-light window at the east end. Chancel with priest's door in middle of south side and door opposite it into vestry. Chancel has five stalls on each side and altar approached by rise of several steps. Passage from south-west corner of vestry leads into pulpit with similar passage from nave to tower at corresponding corner of west end. North tower of two stages, lower one recessed with corner buttresses and a low belfry stage of three equal broad lancets on each side below a corbelled parapet within which is low pyramidal capping. Chancel has wagon roof and nave has trussed-rafter arrangement. Seating accommodation for 124 worshippers. Contractor: workmen from Ystrad Fawr estate. Cost £3,700. Church completed in 1857. Consecrated on 1 June 1889. (*W. Mail*, 3 June 1889)

Comments: John Newman says that 'Norton introduced a more advanced, more muscular style at Ystrad Mynach.' (Newman, 94) It is certainly true that Holy Trinity is more 'muscular' from a constructional point of view, in that the asymmetrically placed north tower is a bold, massive structure. Ruskin believed that a tower and most other buildings as well should be 'one bold square mass of brickwork'. (John Ruskin, *The Stones of Venice* (London, 1851) Vol. I, XIX, 11–14) In this particular case the tower is constructed of blue Pennant sandstone, but the principle was the same. Its large lower stage, recessed within unobtrusive corner buttresses at the base, rises sheer and uninterrupted but for a slit lancet at mid-point to the height of the belfry stage, below a heavy medieval-style parapet. Old photographs of the church in 1857 show the tower surmounted by a broach spire, and local tradition has it that it was struck by lightning at some time in the past and that the resulting fire destroyed the structure, so that it had to be removed. The absence of buttresses and the small lancets accentuate the simple massiveness of the walling of the church. The sheer west wall, only broken by a triplet of elongated lancets and five smaller similar lancets lighting the nave and crypt below respectively, is characteristic of this simple massiveness, which typified the change from delicate and pretty early Victorian Gothic churches towards bold, masculine, massive buildings in the High Victorian period. The reviewer in *The Ecclesiologist* in 1857 described Norton's design as 'rather fantastical'. (*Eccl.*, 16 (1855), 257–8) This was a reference to the various passages of the interior of the church which was indeed a singular arrangement. We can perhaps assume that this eccentric plan was carried out by Norton on the instructions of his client, Revd George Thomas. Hywel Davies, the church historian, suggests that the passageway in question could have been used by the clergy to process to the altar by way of the chancel steps and also by the choir as access to their seats near the organ. Furthermore, he writes that this passageway was subsequently removed and the location of the pulpit was changed from the right to the left of the chancel steps. (Hywel Davies, *A History of Holy Trinity Church, Ystrad Mynach, 1857–1957* (Hengoed, 1996), 6–10)

In 1906 the church was enlarged by extending the nave westwards by 30ft and by adding a transept on the south side, corresponding to that already built on the north side, and constructing a south chancel aisle. The existing south porch was taken down and rebuilt further to the west. Additional accommodation for 182 worshippers increased the capacity to 306 sittings. Cost £2,050. Miss Clara Thomas £500. Architect: E. M. Bruce Vaughan, Cardiff. (LL/F/854. Ystrad Mynach. Extension of church. Faculty dated 19 May 1906)

ST STEPHEN'S CHURCH, YSTRAD RHONDDA

1895–6: New church built on new site given by Mrs Madelina Llewellyn of Baglan Hall and beneficiaries of Bailey estate. The *Church Builder* reported that 'Ystrad Rhondda is a large colliery village and contains a population of 4,500 which is increasing. The population is composed almost entirely of coal miners and their families. The proposed church is intended to replace a small mission building which has been in existence for years, but is totally inadequate for its purpose. A church with all the necessary accessories of divine worship is sorely needed, the nearest church being two miles away.' (*Ch. Bldr* (1896), 28) Foundation stone laid on 5 September 1895 by Mrs Emily Curre. (*W. Mail*, 6 September 1895) Built in Early English Gothic style by E. M. Bruce Vaughan, consisting of chancel, nave, north aisle and west porch with north and south doors. West gable surmounted by double bellcote. (ICBS file no. 9876 (1895)) Constructed of Welsh Pennant sandstone with Bath stone dressings. East window of three pointed lights with Geometrical tracery in head and internal hood mould with carved heads as label stops. Chancel has semicircular arched, panelled roof with moulded ribs and gilded bosses at intersections. Stone sedilia and credence table, and altar table and choir stalls of pitch-pine installed in chancel. Floor paved with Godwin's encaustic tiles. Chancel arch, which is pointed and moulded, springs from capitals decorated with stiff-leaf foliage above sculptured heads. Nave roof of open timber construction and open benches for 406 worshippers of pitch-pine, stained and varnished. North aisle divided from nave by arcade of six pointed, moulded arches springing from circular capitals on round pillars. Nave and aisle lighted by two-light windows with plate tracery in apex. West window of four trefoiled lights with three quatrefoils placed within circles in head. Contractor: A. J. Howell, Cardiff. Cost £3,487. ICBS grant £180; LDCES grant £50; LCBS grant £20; Bishop of Llandaff's Fund £250; Mrs Madelina Llewellyn £2,200. (*Bldr*, 14 September 1895) Consecrated on 28 July 1896. (*Glam. Free Pr.*, 1 August 1896)

Comments: Bruce Vaughan's design of St Stephen's was a vast improvement on the churches he had previously built in the parish of Ystradyfodwg. This is exemplified by the well-appointed chancel with east window of three grouped lancets with Geometrical-style tracery in the head with internal hood mould and carved heads as label stops, the finely carved sedilia and credence table under three trefoiled arches and the semicircular panelled chancel roof with moulded ribs and gilded bosses. Furthermore the chancel is furnished with traditional choir stalls, the floor is paved with Godwin's encaustic tiles and the chancel arch springs from capitals decorated with Early English-style stiff-leaf foliage above sculptured heads. Bruce Vaughan was able to design such a well-appointed chancel only as the result of Mrs Llewellyn's generosity, for out of the total cost of £3,487 she donated £2,200 – £1,000 in 1895 and two sums of £500 and £700 respectively in 1896, the later sum settling the outstanding debt on the church.

ST OWAIN'S CHURCH, YSTRADOWEN

1853: Repairs carried out to chancel of church under direction of Ewan Christian, architect to Ecclesiastical Commissioners who were acting as lay rectors. His survey of chancel revealed fractures in walls, rotten lintels and jambs, damaged coping stones and uneven flooring. Water had been allowed to penetrate walls due to absence of rainwater pipes. Cost £34. (RBCW: (Cardiff) Eccl. Comm. file no. 7932)

1867–8: Rebuilt on same site, old structure having been in a dilapidated condition for many years. By 1859, fabric of church had deteriorated to such an extent that it was decided to demolish entire building. Architect: John Prichard, Llandaff. Foundation stone laid on 7 March 1867 by Mrs Daniel Owen, Ash Hall. (ICBS file no. 6405 (1865)) Old materials used from former church. Work of rebuilding ancient church started in spring of 1867 and was completed by summer of following year. Built in Early English Gothic style consisting of chancel, nave, vestry on north side, south porch and western tower. Constructed externally of Forest of Dean stone and Bath stone; the rougher part of structure built of blue lias limestone. Inner walls composed of courses of white stone relieved by courses of red brick. Whole of building floored with tessellated pavement. Arch-braced roofs of chancel and nave covered with small Welsh slates, but saddleback tower capped with Forest of Dean stone tiles. Open benches of pitch-pine. Seating accommodation for 116 worshippers, seventy of which were additional and free. Communion table is of polished wood inlaid. Railings in front of medieval pattern and gilded. On south side of chancel is sedilium in Bath stone and credence table on north side is carved of same stone. Font of Forest of Dean stone. Stone pulpit erected. Rebuilt partly by subscription, partly by church rate and donations by local gentry. Contractor: Rees Roderick, Margam. Cost £800. (*CMG*, 1 August 1868) Reopened after rebuilding on 23 July 1868. (*CGG*, 24 July 1868) Consecrated on 22 December 1868. (*CMG*, 26 December 1868)

Comments: Although the constructional poly-chromy of the interior was uncharacteristic of a thirteenth-century Glamorgan church, which the new building was supposed to replicate, it was nevertheless typical of the Victorian architecture of the period and was intended to represent the colourful decoration of the archetypal medieval church interior. However, the plate tracery of the general fabric and the single trefoil-headed and lancet lights without hood moulding anchor the rest of the building firmly to the thirteenth century. So too does the predominant Vale of Glamorgan type saddleback roof of the tower, which Prichard copied faithfully from the old church with its gables running east to west. Prichard wisely retained the quirks of the old building and resisted the temptation to replace the tower stairs in such a way as would have enabled him to improve visually the north west part of the church. Although the external appearance of the church bore a close resemblance to the former structure, internally the church had been altered substantially. The old high narrow chancel gave way to a much wider entrance to the chancel providing an unrestricted view of the altar as the new form of liturgy dictated. Gone were the old-fashioned square box pews, which were replaced by the low open benches. The old rood-loft stairway in the north wall of the nave and the staircase leading from the back of the tower to the gallery had all been swept way. Larger and more numerous windows were inserted in the walls, banishing forever the dimly lit interior of the old church. Instead of the flagstones and tombstones which once covered the floor of the old church, Victorian encaustic patterned tiles formed the new pavement. Prichard's church at Ystradowen is clearly intended as an idealization of the typical medieval Border Vale of Glamorgan church with its characteristic saddleback roof on the tower. As at St Mary's in Whitchurch, the polychromy of the interior of the church was rendered over later in the following century. (Hilary M. Thomas, *Ystradowen: A Tale of Princes, Priests and People* (Ystradowen, 1993), 54–64)

ST JOHN THE BAPTIST'S CHURCH, YSTRADYFODWG
(Demolished in 1980s)

1843–6: Rebuilding of church. Old church collapsed in 1842 from a lightning strike. Application made to ICBS for grant-aid for rebuilding. Rebuilt on same site to similar dimensions but 5ft higher and 2ft wider incorporating surviving vestry. Rebuilding completed in April 1846 with thirty-five additional seats. Architect: John Williams, Cardiff. ICBS grant £50. (ICBS file no. 3102 (1843))

1866–7: Restoration of church by Charles Buckeridge of Oxford. Exterior underwent little alteration except for raising of windows. East and west windows both considerably altered. Building entered by north porch. Lath and plaster ceiling taken down and roof thrown open to ridge. Chancel separated from nave by Gothic arch springing from pillarets with foliated caps and bases. Chancel paved with coloured encaustic tiles by Harding of Hereford. Interior walls of church not defaced with plaster or stucco but showed open brickwork. Circular pulpit of white sandstone. Church also repewed. Contractor: James Price, Cardiff. Cost £550. LDCES grant £50. (*Bldr*, 23 February 1876, 136) Reopened after restoration on 22 January 1867. (*CMG*, 25 January 1867)

1892–4: Rebuilding of church by E. M. Bruce Vaughan. Architect's plan showed new nave to north separated by arcade from old nave. Chapel to east of new nave and north of chancel. Vestry to south of chancel. Architect's sketch shows fenestration of new parts similar to old. Height of new nave and chapel same as that of old nave. (ICBS file no. 9164 (1887)) The correspondent in the *Church Builder* reported that 'In consequence of houses having been built around the church and the public roads raised, it is now in a hollow and in wet weather is occasionally flooded. It is therefore proposed to raise the floor and ceiling at least four feet. The Church also needs enlargement, as it cannot contain one-half the persons who wish to worship in it. All the services held in the Church are in the Welsh language, and the congregation is entirely composed of working men and their families. In 1801 the population of the parish was 542; it is now upwards of 33,000. 253 seats will be added, and the estimated cost is £1,575.' (*Ch. Bldr* (1887), 86) North and west porch built, new pulpit erected and new bellcote constructed. Floor and ceiling of new building raised by 5ft to prevent flooding. Contractor: Alban Richards, Pentre. Cost £2,000. ICBS grant £80; Bishop of Llandaff's Fund £300; LDCES £50; Mrs Madelina G. Llewellyn £825; Miss Olive Talbot £240. (*Bldr*, 23 June 1894, 485) Opened for divine worship on 18 June 1894. (*W. Mail*, 19 June 1894)

Comments: The original church building was not only an austere building with little internal decoration and uncomfortable seating for the congregation but it was also poorly designed by the architect, who was probably not used to building churches and who constructed it of low-grade materials on account of the lack of adequate funds. Buckeridge's restoration of 1866 completely transformed the whole character and appearance of the building, especially the interior. The embellishment of the chancel, now separated from the rest of the church by a Gothic chancel arch, reflected particularly in this remote part of Glamorgan the new liturgical arrangements of the Anglican Church and also made it a more comfortable and aesthetically pleasing building in which to worship. In 1892, the poor state of the building led to a decision to rebuild the church completely. This provided much better accommodation for the parishioners. Bruce Vaughan rebuilt the church in the Early English Gothic style in keeping with that of the former building. An analysis of the figures, taken from the Ystradyfodwg Parish Church Building Fund Account of 10 October 1894, shows how heavily Revd Canon William Lewis relied on church building societies and donations from landowners and wealthy individuals, such as Mrs Madelina Llewellyn and Miss Olive Talbot, to finance the rebuilding of the church in 1894.

SELECT BIBLIOGRAPHY

A full list of sources is given in my thesis 'Church Building and Restoration in Victorian Glamorgan, 1837–1901', University of Wales, Lampeter, 1999. Below is a select bibliography of the main sources for this volume together with some recent important publications.

MANUSCRIPTS

Aberystwyth: National Library of Wales

1. Schedules of the Church in Wales records. Diocese of Llandaff. Vol. III. Faculties. LL/F/1–893.
2. Schedules of the Church in Wales records. Diocese of St David's. Vol. II. Faculties. SD/F/1–691.
3. Schedules of the Church in Wales records. Diocese of Llandaff. Vol. III. Consecrations. LL/C/1–287.
4. Schedules of the Church in Wales records. Diocese of St David's. Vol. II. Consecrations. SD/C/1–276.
5. Bishop's Visitation Returns for the Archdeaconry of Carmarthen: queries and answers, 1804–1900. SD/QA/63–114.
6. Bishop's Visitation Returns for Llandaff Diocese: queries and answers, 1802–1900. LL/QA/19–42.
7. Bishop of Llandaff's Fund. Printed reports, Minute Book. Registers of applications for grants, etc.

Bridgend: Mid Glamorgan County Council: Reference Library

1. Aeron Price Papers.
2. Roderick G. Williams's manuscript notes on the Vale of Glamorgan and its churches.

Cardiff: Cardiff Central Library

1. Evans, T. C. (Cadrawd), A history of the parish of Llandough. 1902. (MS. 4.304)
2. Jones, David (of Wallington), Notes on some Glamorgan churches, 1881–82. (MS.1.187)
3. Jones, David (of Wallington), Outline of the history of Llysworney, Llanmihangel, Llanmaes with extra-parochial places of Nash and Stembridge. (MS. 2.355)
4. Thompson, Herbert M., Manuscript notes on the old churches of Glamorgan. 1935. 2 vols. (MS. 3.535)

Cardiff: Glamorgan Record Office (Archive Service)

1. Schedules of ecclesiastical parish records in Glamorgan. 2 vols. (P/1/CW)
2. Merthyr Mawr MSS. E/187/1–50. Correspondence, design and building of new church at Merthyr Mawr (Benjamin Ferrey and John Prichard, Architects). 1845–51, 1853.
3. Plymouth Estate Collection: Correspondence in reference to Glamorgan churches in the nineteenth century. DD/Pl/1–11.
4. Aubrey family of Llantrithyd records. Llantrithyd parish church (D/D/AU303/1–9)

Cardiff: Representative Body of the Church in Wales

Records of the Ecclesiastical Commissioners relating to Glamorgan Churches. Files EC. 7932 (Ystradowen), 10771 (Llanblethian), 66494 (Pendoylan).

Gloucester: Gloucestershire County Record Office

Fulljames and Waller Collection (D2593)
Records from the collection of Frederick William Waller, (1846–1933) Diocesan Architect, Gloucester.
1. GLRO/D2593/2/3Y/R4. Restoration of Oxwich Church, Glamorgan, 1891–92.
2. GLRO/D2593/2/VK/S37. Restoration of Penrice Church, Glamorgan, 1893–94.

London: British Newspaper Library (Colindale)
Various issues of Glamorgan newspapers unavailable in Wales, e.g. *Barry Dock News*, *Bridgend Chronicle*, *Cardiff & Merthyr Guardian*, *Central Glamorgan Gazette*, and *Penarth Chronicle*.

London: Church of England Record Centre
Church Building Commissioners' Records: Surveyor's Reports relating to: St Fagan's, Aberdare; St Elvan's, Aberdare; St David's, Maesteg; St John's, Skewen; St Peter's, Cockett; Rhondda Valley; Newbridge (Glam.); St David's, Merthyr Tydfil; Pontyrhun; and St Mary's, Cardiff.

London: General Synod of the Church of England: Council for the Care of Churches
Manuscripts of the late Canon B. F. L. Clarke on the churches in Glamorgan. (1976).

London: Lambeth Palace Library
Incorporated Church Building Society Archive: Glamorgan.

London: Royal Institute of British Architects: British Architectural Library
H. S. Goodhart-Rendel's card-index of nineteenth-century churches and architects in the RIBA Library.

London: Society for the Protection of Ancient Buildings (SPAB)
Manuscripts relating to the restoration of St Donat's Church, St Donat's, Glamorgan by George Eley Halliday in 1892.

Oxford: Bodleian Library
Church Builder, 1862–1915.
The Ecclesiologist, 1841–68.

Pen-y-fai (Bridgend): All Saints' Church, Pen-y-fai: Parish Archives
Transcript of a manuscript made by Colonel Llewellyn, the son of the builder of the church. Deposited with church deeds at the Vicarage, Pen-y-fai, Bridgend.

Pontypridd: St Catherine's Church, Pontypridd Parish Archives
Historical notes and associated notes collected by Mrs Gertrude Hughes-Williams, relating to the church in Pontypridd and in the custody of the incumbent of the parish church.

Swansea: West Glamorgan Archive Service
1. Report of a Commission to enquire into the spiritual wants of the parishes of the Deanery of Gower East in the Archdeaconry of Carmarthen. 1883. (P/123/CW/473)
2. Agreement for restoring St. Michael's Church, Loughor. 1885. (P/112/CW/29)

PRINTED BOOKS AND ARTICLES

ADDLESHAW, G. W. O., and ETCHELLS, Frederick, *The Architectural Setting of Anglican Worship: An Inquiry into the Arrangements for Public Worship in the Church of England from the Reformation to the Present Day* (London, 1948).
ALLEN, Lyn, 'Some notes on the architectural work of John Prichard (1817–86) and John Pollard Seddon, 1827–1906', *The Victorian Society South Wales Group Aberystwyth Weekend*, 9–11 April 1976, 1–2.
BOYNS, Trevor, and BABER, Colin, 'The supply of labour, 1750–1914', in Arthur H. John and Glanmor Williams (eds), *Glamorgan County History, Vol. V. Industrial Glamorgan from 1700 to 1970* (Cardiff, 1980), 311–62.
BROOKS, Chris and SAINT, Andrew (eds), *The Victorian Church: Architecture and Society* (Manchester, 1995).

BROOKS, Michael W., *John Ruskin and Victorian Architecture* (New Brunswick and London, 1987).

BROWN, Roger L., *Reclaiming the Wilderness: Some Aspects of the Parochial Life and Achievements of the Diocese of Llandaff during the Nineteenth Century* (Welshpool, 2001).

CLARKE, B. F. L., *Church Builders of the Nineteenth Century: A Study of the Gothic Revival in England* (Newton Abbot, 1869).

COWLEY, F. G., 'Religion and education', in Glanmor Williams (ed.), *Swansea: An Illustrated History* (Swansea, 1990), 145–76.

CURL, James Stevens, *Victorian Architecture* (Newton Abbot, 1990).

DAUNTON, M. J., *Coal Metropolis, Cardiff, 1870–1914* (Leicester, 1977).

DAVIES, E. T., *Religion and Society in the Nineteenth Century* (Llandybïe, 1981)

DAVIES, E. T., *Religion in the Industrial Revolution in South Wales* (Cardiff, 1965).

DAVIES, E. T., *The Story of the Church in Glamorgan, 560–1960* (London, 1962).

DAVIES, J. B., 'The parish of Penllin', in Stewart Williams (ed.), *Saints and Sailing Ships* (Cowbridge, 1962), 97.

DAVIES, John, *Cardiff and the Marquesses of Bute* (Cardiff, 1981).

DAVIES, T. G., *Howel Gwyn of Dyffryn and Neath, (1806–1888)* (Neath, 1992).

FRANCIS, David, *The Border Vale of Glamorgan* (Barry, 1976).

GUY, John R., *The Church in Cardiff* (Cardiff, 1974 , 2 vols.) (The Cardiff Book, Vols.1–2).

HILLING, John B., 'Architecture in Glamorgan', in Prys Morgan (ed.), *Glamorgan County History*, VI (Cardiff, 1989), 407–17.

HILLING, John B., *Cardiff and the Valleys: Architecture and Townscape* (London, 1973).

HILLING, John B., *Plans and Prospects – Architecture in Wales, 1780–1914*: catalogue of Welsh Arts Council Exhibition, 1975 (Cardiff, 1975).

HODGES, T. M., 'The peopling of the hinterland and port of Cardiff (1801–1914)', in W. E. Minchinton (ed.), *Industrial South Wales, 1750–1914: Essays in Welsh Economic History* (London, 1969), 10–11.

HOPKINS, T. J., 'The village and parish of Pendoylan', in Stewart Williams (ed), *History on my Doorstep* (Cowbridge, 1959), 80.

HOWELL, Peter, and SUTTON, Ian, *The Faber Guide to Victorian Churches* (London, 1989).

JONES, Ieuan G., *Communities: Essays in the Social History of Victorian Wales* (Llandysul, 1987).

JONES, Ieuan G., 'Ecclesiastical economy: aspects of church building in Victorian Wales', in R. R. Davies et al. (eds), *Welsh Society and Nationhood: Historical Essays Presented to Glanmor Williams* (Cardiff, 1984), 216–31.

JONES, Owain W., and FENN, R. W. D., 'Church building in the nineteenth century', in Owain W. Jones and David Walker (eds), *Links with the Past: Swansea and Brecon Historical Essays* (Llandybïe, 1974).

Kelly's Directory of South Wales 1926.

NEWMAN, John, *The Buildings of Wales: Glamorgan* (London, 1995).

ORBACH, Julian, *Victorian Architecture in Britain* (London, 1987) (Blue Guide).

ORRIN, Geoffrey R., *The Gower Churches* (Penmaen, 1979).

ORRIN, Geoffrey R., *Medieval Churches of the Vale of Glamorgan* (Cowbridge, 1988).

PRICHARD, Thomas J., *Representative Bodies: Glimpses of Periods in the History of the Church in Upland Glamorgan with the aid of Contemporary Personalities* (Llandysul, 1988).

READ, John C., *The Church in our City* (Cardiff, 1954).

WALKER, David G. (ed.), *A History of the Church in Wales* (Penarth, 1976).

WALKER, Margaret S., *Inventory of Parish Records of Swansea Churches, compiled by Margaret S. Walker, 1965–67* (Swansea, 1967).

WEBSTER, Christopher and ELLIOTT, John (eds), *'A Church as it should be': The Cambridge Camden Society and its Influence* (Stamford, 2000).

WHITE, James F., *The Cambridge Movement: The Ecclesiologists and the Gothic Revival* (Cambridge, 1962).

WILLIAMS, Thomas, *A Letter to the Lord Bishop of Llandaff on the Peculiar Conditions and Wants of his Diocese* (London, 1850).

WILSON, J. M., *Imperial Gazetteer of England and Wales Embracing Recent Changes in Counties, Dioceses and Parishes* (London, 1865–9).

YATES, W. N., *Buildings, Faith and Worship: The Liturgical Arrangement of Anglican Churches, 1600–1900* (Oxford, 1991).

CHURCH AND PARISH HISTORIES: A SELECTION

ALDEN, Jeff, *Holy Cross Church, Cowbridge* (Cowbridge, 1985).

ARNOLD, John T., *The Story of St Cynon's Church* (Pontypridd, 1963).

BELCHAM, Elizabeth, *About Aberpergwm: The Home of the Williams Family in the Vale of Glamorgan* (1992).

BELCHAM, Elizabeth, *About Aberpergwm Church: A History of St Cattwg's in the Vale of Neath* (Glynneath, 1994).

BEVAN, F. L. G., *History of Christ Church, Cyfarthfa, Merthyr Tydfil* (1957).

BEVAN, S. W., *St Bride's Major, Southerndown and Ogmore-by-sea: A Chronicle of a Parish in the Vale of Glamorgan* (Cowbridge, 1978).

BROWN, Roger L., *The Churches in the Parish of Tongwynlais* (Tongwynlais, 1982).

BROWN, Roger L., *Through Cloud and Sunshine: A History of the Church in the Upper Afan Valley* (Port Talbot, 1982).

BROWN, Roger L., *The Tribulations of a Mountain Parish, Glyncorrwg: Queen Anne's Bounty and the Ecclesiastical Commission* (Cardiff, 1988).

CAERPHILLY PCC, *Centenary of the Present St Martin's Church, Caerphilly, 1879–1979* (Caerphilly, 1979).

COWLEY, F. G., *A History of St Paul's Church, Sketty, Swansea* (Swansea, 2001).

COWLEY, F. G., *Llanmadoc and Cheriton: Two North Gower Churches and their Parishes* (Llanmadoc and Cheriton, 1993).

DAVID, Colin, *A Short History of the Parish of Saint Dyfan and Saint Teilo (Merthyr Dyfan), Barry, Glamorgan* (Barry, 1968).

DAVID, Colin, *Some Notes on the Church of St David, Laleston, Bridgend, Glamorgan* (Bridgend, 1958).

DAVIES, Alan, *St John the Baptist Church, Glyncorrwg: Souvenir 1957: Observations on the History of the Church* (1957).

DAVIES, Charles D., *The History of the Church situate at Newton, Porthcawl in the Parish of Newton Nottage* (Cowbridge, 1938).

DAVIES, Hywel, *A History of Holy Trinity Church, Ystrad Mynach, 1857–1957* (Hengoed, 1996).

DAVIES, J. D., *Historical Notices of the Parishes of Llangenydd and Rhosili in the Rural Deanery of West Gower* (Swansea, 1885).

DAVIES, J. D., *A History of West Gower*, Vol. IV (Swansea, 1894).

DAVIES, J. Gwyn, *A Brief Account of the Church of St. Gwynno* (Llanwonno, 1967).

DAVIES, John H., *History of Pontardawe and District from Earliest to Modern Times* (Llandybïe, 1967).

DAVIES, M. M., *The Young Valley: A History of the Church in the Garw Valley* (Blaengarw, 1969).

EVANS, Geoffrey, *An Account of the History of the Ancient Chapelry of St John Baptist and Parish Church of Aberdare and its Memorials* (Aberdare, 1982).

EVANS, Geoffrey, *St Elvan's Church, Aberdare* (Aberdare, 1989).

EVANS, Leslie, *Margam Abbey* (Port Talbot, 1958).

EVANS, Leslie, *The Story of Taibach and District* (Port Talbot, 1963).

EVANS, Muriel, *The Story of the Parish of St David, Ton Pentre* (Pentre, 1960).

EVANS, Thomas, *The Story of Abercynon* (3rd edn, Abercynon, 1976).

FRENCH, Colin, *St Barnabas Church, Waunarlwydd, 1888–1988: Centenary* (Swansea, 1988).

FRY, Christopher, *All Saints' Church, Llandaff North: Centenary Year, 1991* (Cardiff, 1991).

GAINER, Jeffrey, *A Short History of St Mary Magdalene's Parish Church, Cwmbach* (Aberdare, 1982).

GRIFFITH, J. D., *St George's Church, Cwmparc, Golden Jubilee Book, 1896–1946* (Treorchy, 1946).

GRIFFITHS, Jeffrey L., *St Matthew's Church, Dyffryn: A Short History, 1871–1971* (Neath, 1971).

GRIFFITHS, Royston, *The History of the Church of St Mary, Coity in the Diocese of Llandaf* (Cardiff, 1976).

GUY, John R., *A History of Rudry* (Risca, 1976).

GUY, John R., *'The P'she Church called Saynete Maris': A History and Description of the Mother Church of Cardiff* (Brampton (Cumberland), 1971).

GWYNN, D. R., *A Guide to St Andrew's Church, Penrice* (Swansea, 1975).

HAINES, Jean (ed.), *St Peter's Church, Newton: History and Guide* (Swansea, 1984).

HOWELLS, Muriel, *History of the Church of St Illtyd, Williamstown, 1894–1944* (Cardiff, 1944).

JAMES, Brian Ll., and FRANCIS, David, *Cowbridge and Llanblethian: Past and Present* (Cowbridge, 1979).

JONES, Brian H., *Llansamlet Parish Church* (Swansea, 1979).

JONES, Brian H., *St Paul's Church, Glais, 1881–1981* (Clydach, 1981).

JONES, Florence, *St Mary's Church, Glyntaff, 1839–1989* (Pontypridd, 1990).

JONES, D. Huw, *The Story of St David's Church, Neath: The First Hundred Years, 1866–1966* (Neath, 1966).

JONES, D. R. L., *The Restoration of Llangynwyd Church, 1891–93* (Maesteg, 1993).

JONES, D. R. L., *Richard and Mary Pendrill Llewelyn: A Victorian Vicar and his Wife* (Maesteg, 1991).

JONES, Glyn M., and SCOURFIELD, Elfyn, *Sully: A Village and Parish in the Vale of Glamorgan* (Caerphilly, 1986).

JONES, Les, *A Backward Glance . . . A Centennial History of Saint Mary the Virgin, Parish of Troedyrhiw Garth, Maesteg, 1892–1992* (Bridgend, 1992).

KELLY, Vivian, *St Illtyd's Church, Llantwit Major* (Cowbridge, 1993).

LAWRENCE, Edgar, *Parish of Ystrad Mynach, Holy Trinity Church: Centenary, 1857–1957* (1957).

LEE, Rebecca, *A History of St David's Church, Merthyr Tydfil* (Merthyr Tydfil, 1980).

LEECH, Peter, *The Parish of Roath* (Cardiff, 1970).

LEWIS, D. Islwyn, *St Catharine's Church, Baglan, 1882–1982* (Port Talbot, 1982).

LEWIS, Dillwyn, *The History of Llantrisant* (Risca, 1975).

LEWIS, O. J., *A Short History of St Barnabas Church, Waunarlwydd, Swansea* (Swansea, 1948).

LOUGHER, John L., *Guide to St John's Church, Radyr* (Cardiff, 1992).

LUCAS, R. L. T., *A History of Reynoldston Church* (Reynoldston, 1978).

LUCAS, R. L. T., *Reynoldston* (Swansea, 1998).

LUCAS, R. L. T., *Rhosili Parish Church and the Old Church in the Warren* (Swansea, 1982).

LUXTON, Brian C., *St Cadoc's: A History of the Old Village Church, Cadoxton-juxta-Barry* (Barry, 1980).

MAINWARING, M. J., *The Church of St Michael and All Angels', Maesteg: 75th anniversary* (Maesteg, 1973).

MEAR, John, *The Story of Cwmdare* (Aberdare, 1991).

MOORE, Donald (ed.), *Barry: The Centenary Book* (2nd rev. edn, Barry, 1985).

MORGAN, C.D., *Wanderings in Gower* (Swansea, 1862).

MORGAN, W Ll., *Antiquarian Survey of East Gower* (London, 1899).

ORRIN, Geoffrey R., *A Guide to the Parish Church of St Teilo, Bishopston* (rev. edn, Bishopston, 1983).

ORRIN, Geoffrey R., *A History of Bishopston* (Llandysul, 1982).

ORRIN, Geoffrey R., and COWLEY, F. G., *A History of All Saints' Church, Oystermouth* (Llandysul, 1990).

PARRY, John, *The Church of St Isan Llanishen Handbook* (Cardiff, 1991).

PENTRE PCC, *St Peter's Church, Pentre, 1890–1990: Centenary Celebrations* (Pentre, 1990).

PENTYRCH PCC, *Guide to the Parish Church of St Cattwg, Pentyrch* (Pentyrch, 1988).

PHILLIPS, D. Rhys, *The History of the Vale of Neath* (Swansea, 1925).

PORTH PCC, *The Parish of St Paul: Centenary, 1887–1987* (Porth, 1987).

PRITCHARD, Ken, *St John's Church, Birchgrove, 1891–1991* (Swansea, 1991).

RANDALL, Henry J., *Bridgend: The Story of a Market Town* (Newport, 1955).

REDPATH, John, *The Church of St John the Evangelist, Canton, Cardiff: 1854–1979* (Cardiff, 1979).

READ, J. C., *St John's Church, Cardiff and the Churches of the Parish* (Bridgend, 1995).

REES, Hywel, *St John's Church, Gowerton* (Swansea, 1996).

REYNOLDS, P. R., *St Gabriel's: 1889–1989* (Swansea, 1989).

ROBBINS, Margaret, *Parish of Newcastle, St John's Church, Tondu* (1968).

RYAN, Stephen J., *St Matthew's Church, Treorchy, 1884–1984: Centenary Year Programme and Brief History of the Church and Parish* (Treorchy, 1984).

SHEPHERD, Charles F., *Annals of St Fagans with Llanilterne: An Ancient Glamorgan Parish* (Cardiff, 1938).

SHEPHERD, Charles F., *A Short History of St. George-super-Ely* (Cardiff, 1933).

SHEPHERD, Charles F., *St Nicholas: A Historical Survey of a Glamorganshire Parish* (Cardiff, 1934).

SMITH, Clive, *St Peter's Church, Nantyffyllon, Parish of Caerau, 1887–1987: Centenary Souvenir* (Caerau, 1987).

SPENCER, Marianne, *Annals of South Glamorgan* (Carmarthen, 1913).

THOMAS, Beryl, *Eglwys Sant Ioan, Treforys* (Morriston, 1989).

THOMAS, Beryl, *St David's Church, Morriston: Centenary* 1891–1991 (Morriston, 1991).

THOMAS, D. Gethin, *The Parish church of St Catwg, Gelligaer: A Short History of an Ancient Church and Parish* (Gelligaer, 1977).

THOMAS, David, *Eglwys Dewi Sant, Maesteg: Dathliad Canmlwyddiant yr Eglwys, 1852–1952* (1952).

THOMAS, Dewi-Prys, *The History and Architecture of Lisvane Parish Church* (Cardiff, 1964).

THOMAS, Glyn, *The Church of St John the Evangelist, Cymmer: Centenary,1889–1989* (Porth, 1989).

THOMAS, Handel, *Llanbradach and its Church: A Short History of All Saints' Church* (Cardiff, 1947).

THOMAS, Hilary M., *The Parish Church of Llandough (near Cowbridge)* (Cowbridge, 1985).

THOMAS, Hilary M., *Ystradowen: A Tale of Princes, Priests and People* (Ystradowen, 1993).

THOMAS, J. E., *St Fagan, Aberdare, 1854–1954: Centenary Souvenir* (Aberdare, 1954).

THOMPSON, H. M., *Old Churches in the Vale of Glamorgan* (Cardiff, 1935).

THORNE, Roy, *Penarth: A History*, Vol. 1 (Risca, 1975).

TILNEY, Chrystal, *A History of the Parish of Penarth with Lavernock* (rev. edn, Penarth, 1988).

TILNEY, Chrystal, *A History of the Parishes of St Andrew Major and Michaelston-le-Pit* (Penarth, 1960).

TREW, W. H., *Christ Church, Swansea, 1872–1972: Centenary Brochure* (1972).

TUCKER, Keith, *A History of St Catwg's Church, Cadoxton* (Neath, 1990).

VILE, Walter B., *A Brief History of St Mary's (Church, St Fagans)* (Cardiff, 1978).

VILE, Walter B., *A History and Description of the Parish Church of St Michael, Michaelston-super-Ely* (rev. edn, Cardiff, 1981).

WALKER, David G., *Saint James' Church, Swansea, 1867–1992* (3rd edn, Swansea, 1992).

WALKER, David G., *St Mary's Church, Swansea* (Morriston, 1959).

WALTERS, T. M., *St Luke's Church, Cwmbwrla, Swansea: Some Highlights of the First Eighty Years* (Swansea, 1970).

WARNER, Marmaduke and HOOPER, A. C. (eds), *The History of Roath St German's* (Cardiff, 1934).

WILLIAMS, E. Iris, *St Peter's Church, Parish of Llangiwg, Pontardawe* (Pontardawe, 1996).

WILLIAMS, Huw, *A History of the Church in Dowlais on the 150th Anniversary of St John's Church, Dowlais, 1827–1977* (Mountain Ash, 1977).

WILLIAMS, Margaret, *St David's Church, Penllergaer, 1838–1988* (Swansea, 1988).

WILLIAMS, R. J., *St John's Church, Swansea: Centenary, 1880–1980* (Swansea, 1980).

WOOLS, R. M., and GUY, John R., *Souvenir of the History and Re-opening of St Mary's Parish Church, Caerau* (Cardiff, 1960).

YEOMAN, David, *The Parish of Mountain Ash: An Illustrated Guide* (2nd edn, Mountain Ash, 1990).

PERIODICAL ARTICLES

ADAMS, D. J., 'The restoration of Margam Abbey Church in the nineteenth century', *Transactions of the Port Talbot Historical Society*, III (3) (1984), 60–7.

ALLEN, J. Romilly, 'Notes on Porthkerry Church, Glamorganshire, with special reference to the churchyard cross', *Arch. Camb.* (1876), 45–8.

CLARK, George T., 'Some account of the parishes of St Nicholas and St Lythan, Co. Glamorgan', *Arch. Camb.* (1862), 92–116 and 176–201.

CLARK, George T. and JONES, Robert O., 'Some account of the parish of Penmark', *Arch. Camb.* (1861), 1–29.

COWLEY, F. G., 'Llangyfelach Church', *Gower*, 31 (1980), 80.

COWLEY, F. G., 'Reverend John David Davies: Anglo-Catholic pioneer, woodcarver and local antiquary', *Morgannwg*, 38 (1994), 9–41.

FOWLER, Charles B., 'Discoveries at Llanblethian Church, Glamorganshire', *Arch. Camb.* (1898), 121–31.

FREEMAN, Edward A., 'Notes on the architectural antiquities of Gower', *Arch. Camb.* (1850), 41–61.

GIBBS, Michael, 'Yesterday and the day before yesterday', *Gower Journal*, Vol. 22 (1971), 54–7.

GLYNNE, Sir Stephen R., 'Notes on the older churches in the four Welsh dioceses: Llandaff', *Arch. Camb.* (1901), 245–78.

GLYNNE, Sir Stephen R., 'Notes on the older churches in the four Welsh dioceses: St David's Diocese. Archdeaconry of Carmarthen', *Arch. Camb.* (1897), 293–303.

GROSS, Joseph, 'St John's Church, Penydarren', *Merthyr Historian*, 3 (1980), 23–32.

GUY, John R., 'Churches of Cardiff: 27 articles', *South Wales Echo*, 3 April–2 October 1964.

GUY, John R., 'The churches of the Vale of Glamorgan: 27 articles', *South Wales Echo*, 22 March–11 October 1963.

HILLING, John B., 'The buildings of Cardiff', *Glamorgan Historian*, 6 (1969), 41–7.

HILLING, John B., 'The buildings of Llandaff, Penarth and outer Cardiff: an historical survey', *Glamorgan Historian*, 7 (1971), 102–47.

HILLING, John B., 'The buildings of Merthyr Tydfil: a historical survey', *Glamorgan Historian*, 8 (1972), 167–93.

HUGHES, Sioned Wyn, 'St. Teilo's Church, Llandeilo Tal-y-bont: interpreting a late medieval church,' *Amgueddfa*, 2 (1998–9), 8–11.

JONES, Ieuan G., 'The building of St Elvan's Church, Aberdare', *Glamorgan Historian*, 11 (1975), 71–81.

JONES, Owain W., 'Church building in the nineteenth century', *Merthyr Historian*, 3 (1980), 17–22.

O'BRIEN, J., 'Cwmavon and St Michael's Church', *Transactions of the Aberfan and Margam District Historical Society* (1929), 50.

ORRIN, Geoffrey R., 'Church restoration at St Teilo's Church, Bishopston, during the nineteenth and twentieth centuries', *Gower*, 52 (2001), 6–17.

ORRIN, Geoffrey R., 'The contribution of the Talbot family to church building and restoration in Victorian Glamorgan', *Morgannwg*, XLVI (2002), 57–70.

SAINT, Andrew, 'Charles Buckeridge and his family', *Oxoniensis*, 38 (1973), 357–72.

SEDDING, John D., 'Architecture of the Perpendicular period', *Transactions of the St Paul's Ecclesiological Society*, I (1881), 31–44.

WALKER, Diane, 'The Bute Mausoleum at St Margaret's Church Roath', *Archaeological Journal*, 150 (1993), 482–97.

UNPUBLISHED DISSERTATIONS

BRANDWOOD, Geoffrey K., 'Church building and restoration in Leicestershire, 1800–1914' (Ph.D. thesis, University of Leicester, 1984, 2 vols).

DAVIES, Michael, 'The restoration of St Hilary's Church' (thesis for the Diploma of Building Conservation presented to the Architectural Association, London, 1990).

DREWERY, Graeme R., 'Victorian church building and restoration in the Diocese of York' (Ph.D. thesis, University of Cambridge, 1993, 2 vols).

FREEMAN, David P., 'Influence of the Oxford Movement on Welsh Anglicanism and Welsh Nonconformity in the 1840s and 1850s' (Ph.D. thesis, University of Wales, Swansea, 1999).

JENKINS, Olwen, 'Illustrative examples of the effect on medieval and later parish church fabric in the post-1844 Archdeaconry of Llandaff of restoration work by John Prichard and John Pollard Seddon' (thesis for the Diploma of Building Conservation presented to the Architectural Association, London, June 1985).

LODWICK, Brian Martin, 'The Oxford Movement and the Diocese of Llandaff during the nineteenth century' (M.Phil. thesis, University of Leeds, 1976).

ORRIN, Geoffrey R., 'Church building and restoration in Victorian Glamorgan, 1837–1901' (Ph.D. thesis, University of Wales, Lampeter, 1999, 2 vols).

PRICHARD, Thomas J., 'The Anglican Church in the Rhondda from the Industrial Revolution to Disestablishment' (Ph.D. thesis, University of Keele, 1981).

WILLS, Wilton D., 'Ecclesiastical reorganisation and church extension in the Diocese of Llandaff, 1830–1870' (MA thesis, University of Wales, Swansea, 1965).

INDEX

Briton Ferry, St Clement's 22–3, 31, 53, 111, 179; St Mary's, Llansawel 23
Brockett family 39
Brown, N., Cardiff 134
Brown, William, Swansea 96
Browne, J. C. 51
Bruce, Tyndall 28
Bruce family, of Dyffryn, Aberdare: Henry Austin, 1st Baron Aberdare 51, 109; Nora, baroness, Aberdare 8, 51, 109, 131
Bruce, Revd W. C., St Lythans 159, 163
Brunel, Isambard Kingdom 180
Bruton, Edward Henry 134
Bruton & Williams 17, 48, 88, 95, 126, 141, 143–4
Brynaman, Carms. 116
Bryncethin, St Theodore's 23–4
Buckeridge, Charles 27, 55, 58, 74–5, 139–40, 184, 198
Bucknall & Jennings 178
Bucknall, Alfred 178
Budd family, of Alltygrug 11
Budd, Mr, Ystalyfera 194
Burgundian-Romanesque style 105
Burnett, E. W. 14
Burrells, Mr 178
Burry estuary 62
Burton & Co. 35
Bury, Thomas Talbot, London, 5
Bute estate 27, 47, 62, 68, 184; trustees of, 4, 29, 77, 87
Butterfield, William xviii, 29, 75–6, 124–5, 175, 182

Cadoxton-juxta-Barry, St Cadoc's 24–5
Cadoxton-juxta-Neath, St Cadoc's 25–6
Cadw 74
Cadwalladr, W. 43
Cae Nanty-gwennith, Merthyr Tydfil 103
Caerau, St Mary's 26
Caerau-with-Ely, St David's 26–7
Caerphilly, St Martin's 27
Campbell, Revd J. C. 103
Cambrian Archaeological Association 153
Cambridge Camden Society xvi, xviii, 65
Cambridge University, Trinity College 25
Capel Dewi Sant Mission Church 32
Cardiff xvii, 31, 36, 39, 41–2; All Saints' 27, 63; Cathays District 42; Eglwys Dewi Sant 32; St Agnes' 28; St Andrew's 13, 29, 42; St Anne's 29–30; St Andrew's and St Teilo's 42; St Catherine's 22, 30–1; St Dyfrig's 31; St Dyfrig's and St Samson's 32; St Dyfrig's Mission 31; St German's xviii, 32–4, 40–2; St James 34–5, 122; St John the Baptist's 29, 34, 35–6; St John the Evangelist's 31, 36–7; St Margaret's 28, 37–9; St Mark's 38–9; St Martin's 39–40; St Martin's Iron Church 39; St Mary's, Butetown 31, 32, 40–1; St

Paul's, Grangetown xviii, 41–2, 123–4; St Saviour's 42; St Teilo's 42–3
Caröe & Passmore 30
Caröe, W. D. 17, 93, 130, 172
Carter, J. Coates xviii, 23, 38, 41–2, 111, 123–4, 179
Carters of Poole 32
Caswell (Oystermouth) 121
Cathedral of the Rhondda 133
Cefn Bryn 117, 149
Cheriton, St Cadoc's 43
Christian, Ewan 62, 69, 126, 150, 172, 197
church building and restoration xv
Church Building Commission xvii, 40, 45
Church Commissioners 4, 40–1, 44–5, 61, 73, 96, 103–4, 168, 186–7
church extension xv–xvi, xviii
Church Forward Movement 185, 193
Church of England xiv, 173
Church reform xiv
churchwardenized repairs xv
Cilybebyll, parish of 10; St John the Evangelist's 44–5
Clark family, of Talygarn: Anne Price 139, 179; George Thomas 85, 89, 106, 129, 151, 159, 162–3, 179–80
Clark, J .W. 165
Clarke & Son, Llandaff 38
Clarke, Edward 19, 50
Clarke, Henry F. 23, 60, 172–3
Clarke, Revd J .T. 190
Clarke, Revd Thomas 74
Clarke, Thomas Guy 49
Clarke, William 1, 15, 20–1, 26, 35–6, 69–70, 76, 82, 85, 89–90, 92–3, 100–1, 109, 118, 130, 134–5, 137, 155, 173
Classical style xvi
Clydach, St John's xviii, 44, 137
Clydach Vale, 193; St Thomas's 45
Cockett, parish of 169
Coe, Hector Allan 32
Coedrhydglyn Collection see National Museums & Galleries of Wales
Cogan, Holy Nativity 45–6; Pill, 45–6; St Peter's 46–7
Coity, St Mary's 20, 47
Cole, Lady Mary 102
Collins, Revd John 64, 72
Collins, Thomas 133
Collins, Revd William Lucas 43, 64
Colwinston 48; St Michael's 48
Company of Copper Miners in England 51
Coneybeare, Revd W. D. 164
Consett Ironworks, Durham 123
Constantinople Quarry 144
constructional polychromy xviii
Cook & Edwards 67
Cooksley, Charles 90

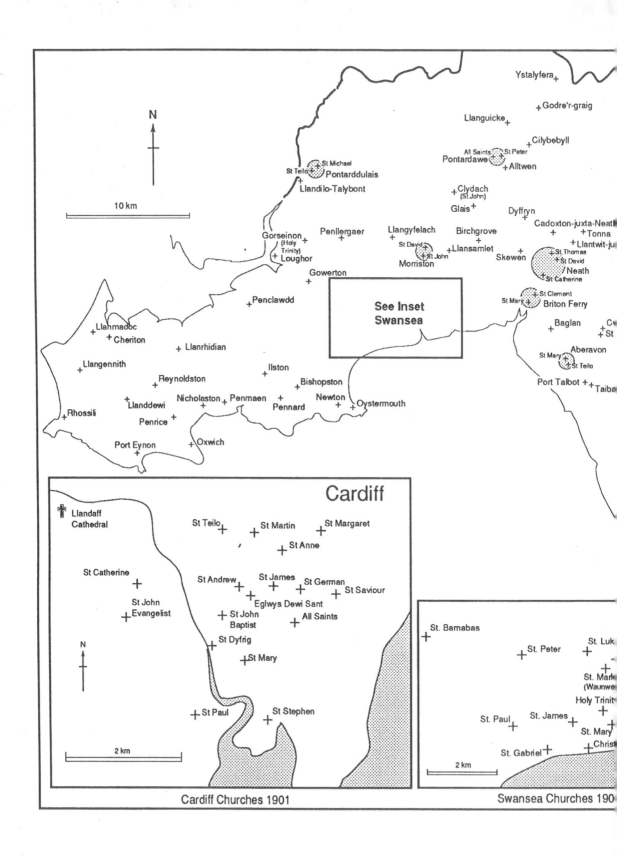

N

10 km

Ystalyfera
Godre'r-graig
Llanguicke
Cilybebyll
All Saints St Peter
Pontardawe
Alltwen
St Michael
St Teilo Pontarddulais
Llandilo-Talybont
Clydach
(St John)
Glais
Dyffryn
Gorseinon
(Holy
Trinity)
Loughor
Penllergaer
Llangyfelach
Birchgrove
Cadoxton-juxta-Neath
Tonna
St David
Llansamlet
Llantwit-ju
St John
Skewen
St Thomas
Gowerton
Morriston
St David
Neath
St Catherine
See Inset
Swansea
St Clement
St Mary
Briton Ferry
Penclawdd
Baglan
C
St
Llanmadoc
Aberavon
Cheriton
Llanrhidian
St Mary
St Teilo
Llangennith
Ilston
Port Talbot
Taiba
Reynoldston
Bishopston
Newton
Nicholaston Penmaen
Oystermouth
Llanddewi
Pennard
Penrice
Rhossili
Oxwich
Port Eynon

Cardiff

Llandaff
Cathedral

St Teilo St Martin St Margaret

St Anne

St Catherine

St Andrew St James St German
St Saviour
Eglwys Dewi Sant
St John St John All Saints
Evangelist Baptist
N St Dyfrig

St Mary

St Barnabas
St. Peter St. Luk

St. Marl
(Waunwe

Holy Trinit

St Paul St Stephen
St. Paul St. James
St. Mary
2 km
St. Gabriel Christ
2 km

Cardiff Churches 1901 Swansea Churches 190